In Redeeming the Post Affair Divorce, Linda MacDonald offers a deeply compassionate and much-needed resource for anyone navigating the devastation of betrayal and the unwanted reality of divorce. Drawing from her own personal journey, her professional training as a clinician, and her unwavering commitment to biblical truth, Linda invites readers into a process of holistic healing—one that embraces the emotional, psychological, physical, and spiritual dimensions of our lives. She writes with both tenderness and strength, offering not only practical wisdom but also the assurance that redemption and restoration are possible even in the wake of profound loss. Moving forward alone after divorce is never part of the dream, but for many, it becomes the necessary next step. Linda's focus on hope, healing, and wholeness creates a blueprint for rebuilding a life marked not by shame or despair, but by courage, resilience, and a renewed sense of God's presence on the journey.

~Brandi Wilson, coach, speaker, and author of
Better than Okay: Finding Hope and Healing After Your Marriage Ends

This is the book I wish I'd had during my own divorce. With wisdom and clarity, Linda speaks to those who've walked through betrayal, offering biblical insight and practical care. Though my divorce was many years ago, I felt seen and understood as I recognized my own story in hers. *Redeeming the Post-Affair Divorce* will help readers bring their pain to the Lord and walk with him through it. Highly recommended!

~Vaneetha Rendall Risner, author
Walking through Fire: A Memoir of Loss and Redemption

Within these pages, you will discover solidarity, practical tools, and invitations to deepen your understanding of your own journey and God's healing. The wisdom and honesty shared here are keys to your freedom. Get ready to experience validation, challenge, and encouragement from Linda's rich store of knowledge and experience.

~Ruth Erickson, author
(UN)FAITHFUL: Finding Healing After Your Husband's Affair

This is a book of hope. If you have experienced the dual trauma of betrayal and loss of your marriage, Linda provides the path out of victimization to wholeness. Many practical chapters walk hurting women through shame, abandonment, rejection, fear, and anger to the next steps in healing. MacDonald shares the spiritual journey that can deepen from the woundedness of 'betrandonment', leading women to seek God and all that he provides for their future purpose, peace, and joy.

Debbie Laaser, MA, LMFT, author
Shattered Vows and *From Trauma to Transformation*

As a betrayed and abandoned trauma survivor myself, I can greatly appreciate the gifts Linda brings to us: comforting reassurance that we're not alone, deep wisdom and insights for growth and strength, and the hope of unexpected blessings. And the best part for me is knowing that the source and power of these beautiful gifts comes from God Himself, our hope!

~**Welby O'Brien, M.S.**, author
Formerly a Wife: A Survival Guide for Women Facing the Pain and Disruption of Divorce

Linda has crafted a beautiful blend of personal story and practical wisdom. With honesty and grace, she weaves her journey of betrayal and divorce together with clear, accessible insights that make the book both relatable and informative. Her thoughtful incorporation of faith and scripture adds depth and comfort, offering readers spiritual grounding alongside practical understanding. This book is a powerful companion for anyone navigating the devastation of marital betrayal—both a heartfelt story and a source of knowledge for the healing journey.

~**Kim Hansen Petroni**, MA, APSATS, author
NOT a Casserole Widow: Navigating Betrayal Trauma and Divorce with Strength & Strategy

REDEEMING
THE
POST-AFFAIR DIVORCE

REDEEMING
THE
POST-AFFAIR DIVORCE

Heal Your Life, Restore Your Faith
After Infidelity Breaks Up Your Marriage

Linda J. MacDonald, M.S.

H+ HEALING COUNSEL PRESS

H✚ HEALING COUNSEL PRESS

Copyright © 2025 by Linda J. MacDonald, M.S.
Published by Healing Counsel Press, Gig Harbor, WA
Inquiries and permissions: info@lindajmacdonald.com

ISBN: 979-8-9864143-1-7 (paperback)
ISBN: 979-8-9864143-3-1 (hardcover)
ISBN: 979-8-9864143-4-8 (eBook)

All rights reserved. No part of this publication may be reproduced, stored in a retrieval system, or transmitted in any form by any means, electronic, mechanical, photocopy, recording or otherwise, without the prior permission of the publisher, except as provided by USA copyright law.

Unless otherwise indicated, Scripture quotations are taken from:

The Holy Bible, Berean Study Bible, BSB Copyright © 2016, 2020 by Bible Hub. Used by Permission. All Rights Reserved Worldwide. Biblehub.com

Scriptures marked (NIV) taken from the Holy Bible, New International Version®, NIV®. Copyright © 1973, 1978, 1984, 2011 by Biblica, Inc.™ Used by permission of Zondervan. All rights reserved worldwide. www.zondervan.com The "NIV" and "New International Version" are trademarks registered in the United States Patent and Trademark Office by Biblica, Inc.™

Scripture quotations marked (NLT) are taken from the *Holy Bible*, New Living Translation, copyright ©1996, 2004, 2015 by Tyndale House Foundation. Used by permission of Tyndale House Publishers, Carol Stream, Illinois 60188. All rights reserved.

Scripture quotations marked (AMP) are taken from the Amplified Bible, Copyright © 2015 by The Lockman Foundation. Used by permission.

Scripture quotations marked (ISV) are taken from The Holy Bible: International Standard Version® Release 2.1, Copyright © 1996-2012, The ISV Foundation. All Rights Reserved Internationally. Used by permission.

Scripture quotations marked (CEV) are from the Contemporary English Version Copyright © 1991, 1992, 1995 by American Bible Society, Used by Permission.

Scripture quotations marked (ESV) are from The ESV® Bible (The Holy Bible, English Standard Version®), © 2001 by Crossway, a publishing ministry of Good News Publishers. Used by permission.

Text dividers, designed by FreePik
Chapter and Section Titles: RonySiswadi Architect 3, by Rony Setya Siswadi
Cover Photo: ©Said Erdogan
Author Photo: Connie Riggio Photography
Cover Design: 100 Covers

The events described in this book reflect the author's recollection and may differ from others' recollections. Most names have been changed (as introduced in quotes), and minor details have been omitted or altered to protect the identities of the people involved.

"And after you have suffered for a little while, the God of all grace, who has called you to His eternal glory in Christ, will Himself restore you, secure you, strengthen you, and establish you."

~1 Peter 5:10

Foreword

The book you are about to read is a gift to everyone who has walked through the storm of infidelity and divorce. Linda MacDonald's professional expertise and her personal experience weave together to create a strong, trustworthy, balanced and steady anchor in the midst of the storm. Whether you find yourself in the middle of divorce, or you are discovering this resource years after the dust has settled, Linda's perspective and application of God's truth will be a great resource in your healing.

Twelve years ago, I read Linda's previous book, *How to Help Your Spouse Heal From Your Affair: A Compact Manual for the Unfaithful*. My life had been upturned by the shock and devastation of my ex-husband's infidelity, and a friend recommended this book to help me decipher if my husband was truly repentant or not. I took myself on a retreat to a nearby lake and cried out for God to speak to me.

Beside the beautiful, still waters, the Lord used Linda's words, her wisdom and the clarity in her book to confirm what I already knew deep down; my husband's efforts to save our marriage were inadequate. He was only adding to the manipulation to save face and keep me available, rather than doing the honest work of repair that Linda unpacked in her book. I believe that Linda's candid wisdom saved me from years of unfruitful wrestling and exposure to more harm. By the end of my retreat, I felt God's peace and strength equip me to accept that my marriage was over, grieve the loss, and walk through the divorce and healing that was ahead of me.

Years later, when I wrote my own book on healing from infidelity, I was humbled and delighted that Linda had heard of my work. She reached out and has been a source of encouragement to me in my ministry. It is a great honor to have had the privilege to read *Redeeming the Post-Affair Divorce* and offer my highest endorsement. Linda has once again crafted a book that will bring clarity and healing to countless people like you and me.

Having coached many women through infidelity recovery and having walked that road myself, I am so grateful for the labor of love that this book represents. Even though I am over a decade beyond my own divorce and have experienced many layers of healing, I found myself deeply touched by Linda's words. I saw my own story reflected in every chapter and experienced a fortification of my healing that I am grateful for.

Within these pages, you will discover solidarity, practical tools, and invitations to deepen your understanding of your own journey and God's healing. The wisdom and honesty shared here are keys to your freedom. Get ready to experience validation, challenge, and encouragement from Linda's rich store of knowledge and experience.

I pray that as you read, you will know that you are not alone, there is hope for your future, and that God's love and grace are able to heal and restore every part of your life.

~Ruth Erickson
author of *(UN)FAITHFUL: Finding Healing After Your Husband's Affair*
(Whether Your Marriage Survives Or Not)

Preface

As a Marriage and Family Therapist and infidelity specialist for over 33 years, I've walked with countless couples through the storm of intimate betrayal. I've read hundreds of books, attended dozens of trainings, and enjoyed helping couples do the hard work of repair. I found it deeply rewarding to witness reconciliation and watch families stay intact.

But all my professional experience couldn't prepare me for the personal devastation of spousal infidelity and abandonment in my own life.

When I discovered my beloved husband was romantically involved with a colleague at work, my world imploded. As he emotionally detached and eventually gave up on our marriage, I unraveled. I lost not only my husband, I lost my identity, sense of worth, and feared I'd lost my credibility as an infidelity specialist.

At the time, there were few resources for someone like me—someone facing the *double trauma* of betrayal and unwanted divorce. Back then, most books on affairs focused on how to save your marriage. Those that addressed divorce glossed over any role infidelity may have played in the breakdown of the marriage. A few spoke to spouses of sex addicts, most of whom were still married. But few addressed what it means to be left by a spouse due to the influence of an affair—grieving both the unfaithfulness and the abandonment, one right after the other.

Each of these alone is devastating enough. But together, they inflict a compounded grief that few understand and even fewer address. In my case, talk therapy helped only so much. Medication dulled my emotions but didn't bring healing. I was left to navigate my nightmares, spiritual disillusionment, and profound emotional pain on my own.

And yet, out of that suffering came new purpose.

After watching many unfaithful spouses unintentionally sabotage their chances of reconciliation, I wrote my first book, *How to Help Your Spouse Heal from Your Affair*. It was one of the first resources written specifically for straying partners who wanted to save their marriages. I continue to be humbled by its impact on couples worldwide.

But every time a pair left my office hand-in-hand, rekindled and hopeful, I'd quietly grieve. *Why didn't my husband choose to fight for us?* My own pain fueled a deeper desire to help others avoid the losses I endured.

This book, *Redeeming the Post-Affair Divorce*, is written for those whose marriages didn't survive. Unlike my first book, which I wrote for the general public, this one speaks directly to people of faith. That's because my most significant turning points in recovery were spiritual in nature.

True healing must engage every dimension of who we are—emotional, psychological, physical, and spiritual. For Christians, infidelity doesn't just wound the heart; it often shakes the soul.

I make no apology for addressing sin, morality, and betrayal through a biblical lens. Not to shame, but to bring clarity and justice to a culture increasingly afraid to call harmful behavior what it is. Naming infidelity as immoral isn't about condemnation—it's about discernment.

This does not mean I don't appreciate the many deep reasons a person might be vulnerable to temptation at a particular time in their life. All sinful behavior arises from one's brokenness, and we are each susceptible to differing weaknesses. And while I firmly believe both partners usually have areas to grow in, no one deserves intimate betrayal. I continue to support unfaithful spouses in their growth and healing, but I refuse to minimize the deep wrong done to betrayed spouses, their children, and their legacy.

This is the book I wish I'd had in the aftermath of my own crisis—a guide that validates the depth of this double wound and offers a roadmap for recovery.

Many books are too general, upbeat, or detached to resonate with a newly betrayed and abandoned spouse. This book is different. It addresses the *combined devastation* of infidelity and divorce. It's more raw. More personal. And more tailored to those who feel completely unmoored.

I've woven my own story (organized thematically, not chronologically), along with real stories of others who've walked this painful road. I've tried to balance clinical insight with spiritual wisdom—without overwhelming those who are still shell-shocked or insulting those who are already therapy-savvy.

This is my offering to the community that I now understand from the inside:

- To help you feel less alone.
- To assure you you're not crazy or beyond help.
- And to give you lifelines of hope, truth, and healing.

If you're struggling to believe there's life after this kind of loss, I want you to know: **God isn't done with your story.** His healing love offers you hope, purpose, and a future worth rebuilding.

Author's Note

A Few Qualifiers for You to Know

If you have experienced divorce or spousal betrayal, you may have picked up this book out of curiosity. But unless you have experienced the combined devastation of infidelity and unwanted divorce, you will likely think much of what I describe in this book is overstated. The Post-Affair Divorce poses unique aspects of suffering and recovery that the average reader may not relate to. The following chapters are intended for the eyes and ears of those who have suffered both tragedies in succession, against their wills.

From personal and professional experience, I believe the dual calamities of infidelity and spousal rejection deserve their own category. That is why, for simplicity's sake, I've coined the term "Betrandoned," a conjugated word for "betrayed" and "abandoned," to capture the specific heartbreak faced by millions of people who were left behind after an affair ended their marriage. I use this term throughout the book to give language to a pain that's often misunderstood or ignored.

Since I've primarily conducted workshops and groups for betrayed Christian women, many of my illustrations are about women. However, I wanted to address the plight and healing journey for both men and women who've gone through this experience. Statistically, married men engage in affairs at a higher rate than married women, and women tend to file for divorce more often than men. Sadly, both sexes suffer similar harm from a post-affair breakup.

To keep the language flowing smoothly and inclusively, I've chosen to use neutral pronouns like "they," "them," and "their," and sometimes mix singular and plural pronouns to avoid clunky phrasing like "he/she" and "him/her."

I've chosen to place all Bible verses in quotation marks—regardless of length—to clearly distinguish them from other content. And because I refer to God so often throughout the book, I've used the more current grammatical convention of "he" rather than "He" (unless quoting others or a particular translation), with no disrespect intended.

The stories shared in this book are all true, though names and identifying details have been changed for privacy. My ex-husband's name has also been changed, and though I now have a new last name, I've done my best to present our story as honestly as I remember it. Naturally, if you asked him, he might offer a different perspective.

While I wrote this primarily as a self-help book, parts of it will read like a memoir. My purpose in sharing many examples from my life is that there are not enough personal narratives in print for Betrandoned folks of faith to relate to. My hope is for you to find encouragement, knowing that even an infidelity specialist like me was fooled, missed Red Flags, experienced post-traumatic stress, and struggled hard to find her bearings, restore her faith, and rebuild her life.

Too many Betrandoned people experience their distress in isolation. I've found that recovery thrives in community. That's why I created the companion resource: ***Redeeming the Post-Affair Divorce Workbook***—a biblical and psychological guide designed for small groups of spiritually hungry, broken-hearted spouses who want to process their healing journey *together*.

If you'd like to order the Workbook or to be notified when new publications and offers are available, please sign up on my website for my occasional newsletters:

https://www.lindajmacdonald.com

Wishing you all the best on your path to wholeness.

Linda

CONTENTS

Foreword i
Preface iii
Author's Note: v
Introduction 1

SECTION I: Reviewing the Damage 13
Chapter 1: My Battle 15
Chapter 2: Betrandonment Grief 19
Chapter 3: The Trauma from the Drama 35
Chapter 4: Healing The Trauma 50
Chapter 5: Betrayal As Abuse 64

SECTION II: Refuting the Shame 81
Chapter 6: The Double Humiliation 83
Chapter 7: The Shame Of Divorce 93
Chapter 8: The Shame Of Rejection 104
Chapter 9: Shame For Leaving 111
Chapter 10: Missing The Red Flags 122
Chapter 11: Shame For The Rage 136

SECTION III: Revealing the Source 145
Chapter 12: The Iceberg Below 147
Chapter 13: Underlying Disorders 159
Chapter 14: Footholds 172

SECTION IV: Rejecting the Lies 183
Chapter 15: Emotional Distortion: 185
Chapter 16: Cognitive Dissonance 199
Chapter 17: Rewriting The Marital History 208
Chapter 18: The Alien Syndrome 222

SECTION V: Restoring Your Faith 237
    Chapter 19: Religious Excuses 239
    Chapter 20: Shattered Beliefs 256
    Chapter 21: When Helpers Harm 273

SECTION VI: Removing the Angst 289
    Chapter 22: Is It Charm Or Contrition? 291
    Chapter 23: Misconceptions About Forgiving 307
    Chapter 24: Forgiving Your Betrayer Without Betraying Yourself 318
    Chapter 25: Letting Go of Regrets 336

SECTION VII: Recovering With Grace 353
    Chapter 26: Your Story is Not Over 355

Endnotes 367
Appendix A 381
Appendix B 384
Appendix C 385
Appendix D 388
Acknowledgments 391
About the Author 393

INTRODUCTION

My Story

Mingling in a sea of media professionals, clutching a drink, I felt like a fish out of water. I cast a nervous glance at my date, "Spencer," a well-known radio personality. He was engrossed in a lively conversation with several television cameramen across the room. A swatch of blond hair playfully curled over his brow, adding to his charm. He seemed so at home amongst his peers. Meanwhile, I wanted to crawl out of my skin.

Aside from the usual discomfort of socializing with strangers, I felt like a malfunctioning robot—with dangling, disconnected wires. My brain had blown a few circuits, and the intended networks in my chest failed to respond. I chided myself for expecting anything else. For the past three years, ever since learning about my husband's affair—detachment and numbness had been my constant companions.

Spencer was my first foray into the dating world after my unwanted divorce. I hoped his deep, resonant voice would push a button to reconnect my wires and erase my sense of female inadequacy. So I stepped into Spencer's world for an evening to mingle with a room full of strangers. Yet, I felt as out of place at the Media Bistro's annual party as a street sweeper at a black-tie gala.

I forced myself to engage in small talk when I wanted to scream, "I don't care about your high-sounding superficial interests. I lost my husband's heart three years ago and can hardly think about anything else. Everywhere I go, I feel out of place. I may look okay on the outside, but I'd rather hide in the bathroom!"

Ever since my ex-husband's affair and rejection, I had lost my self-confidence. Other than grief and hate, my emotions were as flat as carbonless Coke. I enjoyed fantasies of finding justice, thriving on movies like *The First Wives Club* and *Double Jeopardy*. Who was I kidding? I wasn't ready to date, let alone attend parties with remarkably happy and talented people.

Focus on something positive, I coached myself. *You are still alive.* After all, I had suffered through five "D-Days"—Discovery of Attraction Day, Discovery of Affair Day, Divorce Threat Day, Divorce Informed Day, and Divorce is Final

Day—each of which was a decision against my will and beyond my control. I told myself, *You survived those. You can survive a gathering of unfamiliar faces pretending you are partnered again.*

Summoning my courage, I approached two female journalists: one, a magazine editor with a sleek, dark bob, and the other, a striking freelance writer with long, sun-kissed hair. I hoped that simply being a woman would offer me some common ground with them.

After a few minutes of surface chit-chat, the sun-kissed writer asked me, "So, what do you do?"

Desperate to fit in and sound important, I said, "Oh, I am a Marriage and Family Therapist, and I'm writing a book."

I winced. Announcing I was a therapist didn't segue into writing a book as fluidly as I had hoped. And the "book" was only an idea in my head with scrappy notes on file for a few chapters.

"Oh? What is your book about?"

"Well, I'm writing about how to recover from infidelity... alone."

Cocking her head, she raised her eyebrows. "Oh?"

Hmm. Somehow, my topic piqued her interest, which gave me a boost of encouragement.

"Yeah. Most books only focus on repairing a marriage after an affair or recovering from a divorce. I aim to tackle the unique challenge of recovering from both—a spouse's affair and when the unfaithful one abandons the marriage." (Not that I had made much progress in my own recovery, mind you.)

She nodded in understanding. "My mom went through that. My dad left her for another woman."

I sensed instant camaraderie with this person's anonymous mother.

"Oh, wow. That's too bad. How's she doing now?"

"Well, she's bitter and depressed. She's a hopeless alcoholic, keeps her drapes perpetually closed, and rarely leaves her house except to replenish her liquor supply." Looking down, the writer shook her head. "I don't think she'll ever get over it."

"Gosh, how long ago did he leave?" I asked, expecting to hear "four or five years ago."

"Twenty years ago," she replied.

My eyes widened in shock. "Twenty years ago?" I was stunned. And scared. The writer's portrayal of her mother was my greatest nightmare—that I would remain a pitiful mess twenty years after my husband's affair and unwanted divorce.

I politely conversed with the women for a few more minutes, barely able to concentrate. "Twenty years" kept flickering in my mind like a neon sign. Could I end up just like her mother two decades later? I shuddered at the thought.

Wandering over to Spencer, I touched his hand, seeking security. Her ominous words echoed in my mind like an endless loop.

Twenty years. Twenty years of low self-esteem. Twenty years of agonizing over my loss. Twenty years of unending sadness. Twenty years of doubting my own perceptions. Twenty years of feeling disconnected from others. Twenty years of unresolved anger. Twenty years of feeling like an outcast. Twenty years of shame. Twenty years of feeling sexless. Twenty years of yearning for justice. Twenty years of negative self-talk. Twenty years of feeling let down by God.

Scrunching my eyes shut, I tried to extinguish the neon sign without success. It blinked intermittently, flashing its intrusive light in my mind the rest of the evening. When Spencer hugged me goodnight, I clutched him close. *Please make my deadness go away. Please.*

Overcoming Inertia

Until my encounter at the Media Bistro party, I had lulled myself into believing that one day, my second prince would come, snap me out of my malaise, and I'd be okay. But when I heard about the writer's mother, my illusion shattered. I realized I had to heal first or risk pushing everyone away—including a potential suitor.

The writer's mother became my new inspiration for how *not* to live. I did not want to sabotage my chances of re-engaging with life. I understood how the mother ended up in her emotional prison. Yet, like the shabby ghost of Jacob Marley when he visited Ebenezer Scrooge, the mother's imagined gloomy face and glassy eyes served as a chilling cautionary tale of where I could end up if I didn't act. Soon.

Before I attended the Media Bistro party, I had scoured books, websites, and blogs to explain my crazed condition with limited success.

At first, I despaired. Then, I got mad.

Someone needed to connect the dots between infidelity and unwanted divorce. After all, affairs blow apart thousands of marriages yearly, leaving suffering spouses and children in their wake. The opportunities for unfaithfulness have surged over the last few decades, negatively impacting everyone involved.

Numerous studies have identified several factors behind what I refer to as the "Infidelity-Virus" in America: increased contact with members of the opposite sex in the workplace[1], the ability to reconnect with past loves and pursue new flirtations through social media, the prevalence of internet pornography[2], the diminishing inhibition regarding sex outside of marriage, the normalization of casual sex in television and films, and the shift away from traditional Judeo-Christian values. These elements have contributed to a concerning moral decline in Western society.

The Many Faces of Infidelity

So, what constitutes an affair? Affair expert Dr. Shirley Glass says it this way: "Infidelity is any emotional or sexual intimacy that violates trust."[3] Therapist Rob Baker elaborates on this definition, stating that an affair involves "any activity that takes your sexual expression outside your marriage."[4]

In my view, any intimate act that breaks trust and the romantic or sexual integrity of a committed relationship constitutes affair behavior. This includes emotional affairs, sexually explicit texts, varied depths of pornography, massage parlors with "happy endings," kissing and fondling, oral sex, intercourse, visiting strip clubs, soliciting sex from prostitutes, extra-marital gay sex, and polyamory.[5]

> Any intimate act that breaks the trust and romantic or sexual integrity of a committed relationship constitutes affair behavior.

Affairs Create Emotional Distance

Secret sexual betrayal, in any manifestation, causes emotional distance to creep into a marriage, anguishing unwitting spouses.

But when the cheating involves a live, new heartthrob, the strayer often detaches from their original partner and forms a tight (but often temporary) bond with the new paramour. Once this change of heart occurs, the unfaithful find it difficult to reverse course, which devastates the loyal spouse.

In my situation, once my husband attached to *her*, he lost his feelings for me. I no longer mattered. Like trying to turn on a light switch after a storm blew out the transformer, I lost my power as a wife. Reeling from my reduced status, I determined to understand what happened and how to recover.

The Statistics

One study led researchers to estimate that an affair precedes divorce in 60–88% of marital breakups[6]. Combining these statistics with the latest numbers of divorces in America reported by the National Center for Health Statistics suggests that a range between 1200 to 1800 affair-influenced divorces occur *every day* in America (not including the five states that no longer report divorce statistics).⁷

Another interesting study reported by the American Psychological Association found that people who'd been secretly unfaithful, without disclosing it to their spouses, had a divorce rate of 80%, whereas folks who admitted their infidelity divorced at half the rate (43%). This reveals the increased corrosive effect of infidelity on marriages when critical secrets are kept from the non-offending partner. The lies and erected barriers remain hidden without a means to address them. Which only worsens matters.⁸

Another social trend has to do with the "grey divorce." Among adults aged 50+, the national divorce rate has roughly doubled since 1990 and tripled among folks aged 65 and older.⁹ Since most partners in seasoned marriages seldom leave without a soft-landing place, I reasonably assume that some form of infidelity also preceded a high percentage of these later-life breakups.

This idea is reinforced by an intriguing study that revealed,

> "People born between 1940 and 1959 report the highest rates of extramarital sex. These are the first generations to come of age during the sexual revolution, so it's understandable they are more likely to have sex with someone without their spouses. They may have firsthand experience with 1970s-era experiments with nonmonogamy."¹⁰

What is an Unwanted Divorce?

No matter who files first, an unwanted divorce is when one partner feels forced into a divorce against his or her will. While Christians, Jews, and people of faith think of marriage as a covenant, in the secular world, marriage was at least legally considered both a status and a contract by the state until 1972.

However, the landscape of marriage changed significantly when California passed its no-fault divorce law. All but two other states followed in kind, removing the marital agreement's contractual power. This changed how the courts handled non-mutual divorces and ramped up the divorce-industry money machine.

With these changes, it suddenly didn't matter if one partner breached the previous legal standards of guilt due to adultery, abandonment, mental cruelty, insanity, or alcohol addiction. The unwilling spouse lost all rights to any advantage in the negotiations.¹¹

The excuse lawmakers gave was that no-fault laws would lead to less acrimonious divorces. While it streamlined divorce for judges and guilty spouses, unilateral non-mutual divorce eliminated the effort required of petitioners—an effort that might have allowed more time for possible reconciliation.

I've heard it said, "It takes two to get married, but only one to get divorced,"—an aggravating fact for protesting partners who often have no vote in the decisions that lead to their marriages' breakup.

Like infidelity, unwanted divorce goes against the will of the betrayed spouse. Marital rejection violates the couple's vows of lifelong commitment to each other in marriage. It robs a wounded partner of their rights as a wife or husband. When an unfaithful deserter fails to protect the marriage's legal, relational, and emotional integrity, they unilaterally inflict deep, personal harm on their partner. The negative ripple effects are legendary.

Those who stray and detach from their original spouses are often the ones to file for divorce. In other cases, betrayed spouses feel backed into a corner and feel forced to petition for divorce by default. When an uncooperative, disengaged spouse refuses to change, an injured spouse may be pressed to formalize the obvious—the marriage is irretrievably broken. Even this doesn't prove they wanted the divorce—only that they saw no other way to stop the hemorrhaging.

The Dilemma

In the aftermath of my marital crisis, one friend suggested that I would like myself better because of what I'd been through. I scoffed. I could not imagine ever liking myself again, let alone liking who I became because of my painful, affair-instigated divorce. I felt like a permanent train wreck.

I remember one betrayed client, "Roger," who fell sobbing on my office floor. "Now I understand Uncle Gerald! Now I understand Uncle Gerald!" His uncle, "Gerald," was a highly respected professor at a major university. Gerald's world crumbled when his wife left him for another man. He lost his purpose in life, relinquished his professorship, gave up his home, and lived on the streets. Twenty years later, he was still homeless, with only rare contact with his relatives.

Roger used to think Uncle Gerald overreacted to his misfortune. Now that he had experienced his own trauma of infidelity and spousal abandonment, he was beside himself. He completely understood Uncle Gerald's prolonged disengagement from life.[12] And so did I.

In my search for answers for myself and others, I considered such questions as:

- How do you recover from betrayal when the betrayer is not sorry?
- How do you silence the memories of learning about the affair or shed the shame of being the last to know?

- How do you stop the nightmares, flashbacks, and other symptoms of trauma-induced distress?
- How do you let go of the natural rage that stems from romantic betrayal when the betrayer justifies his or her actions by blaming you?
- How do you recover from infidelity and desertion by the one you most trusted to love and protect you?
- How do you untwist the lies and rationalizations of an unfaithful spouse when he or she refuses to accept responsibility for his/her hurtful behavior?
- How do you rid your mind of the awful things the betrayer said and did before he or she abandoned the marriage?
- How do you stop feeling unloved and thereby unlovable?
- How do you overcome the embarrassment of behaving in desperate ways when trying to save your marriage?
- How do you restore your faith in God when you worry that he, too, has forsaken you or let you down?

A Plan of Action

I decided to document my progress and turn it into a book to encourage fellow travelers on the rough road from betrayal and abandonment to a new and brighter normal.

If you are stuck somewhere in your recovery process, I hope that sharing my journey and professional insights with you will provide a template for your own healing. Uprighting your life won't occur by happenstance. You will need to set goals for yourself.

Here are some goals I established for myself and included in this book:

1. Honest

Firstly, I resolved that my recovery process had to be honest. If I scratched and clawed for health, I wanted to do this authentically without disrespecting myself. No more phony niceties, no more religious masks. I was done with acting nobler than I felt.

Besides, being too nice had gotten me nowhere in my marriage. In hindsight, I realized I had permitted my husband to neglect and belittle me far more than I deserved. And when our crisis began, I lacked the nerve to draw stronger boundaries at the first hint of betrayal. Without reality checks to slow him down, I unintentionally enabled his spiral into a full-blown midlife meltdown—one he had yet to recover from.

2. Intentional

I realized that my goals would never happen by accident. I needed to be *proactive* and *intentional* about my recovery.

I wrote furiously in my journals and participated in two women's small groups, even though I felt out of place and hated small talk.

While I avoided weddings, I continued to attend church, sitting in the back so no one would see my tears. I pursued counseling for myself, even when it didn't seem like we were getting anywhere. And when we reached a stalemate, I kept looking for and eventually found the type of therapy I needed for the next step.

Self-care rose to the top of my priorities. I reduced my work hours to the degree that I could afford. Since I was easily triggered, I refrained from accepting new clients who suffered from spousal infidelity for a while. I allowed myself a lot of room to grieve, stopped trying to please others, and moved my counseling practice closer to where I lived.

3. With Grace

I aimed to survive with grace. I'd seen plenty of embittered, divorced people make foolish decisions that cost them a happy future. Some bashed members of the opposite gender, bolstering their cynicism and undermining their appeal to potential mates. Others acted out their pain through a string of one-night stands, desperate romances, and partying their brains out. Still others squandered their money on senseless toys, gave up on life, and ended up financially broke. I wanted none of it.

To reclaim my dignity and self-respect, I had to overcome the deadness inside—without making reckless choices. I needed to re-enter the land of the living. No more hiding out in my pajamas on the weekends, burying my nose in a mystery novel. No more indulging in a bowl (or two) of Pralines n' Cream ice cream to dull the constant ache within. No more avoiding social situations with happy, well-adjusted people. I was determined to emerge from my season of shame with my head held high and renewed self-assurance.

> To reclaim my dignity and self-respect, I had to get over this deadness inside—without making reckless choices.

4. With God

I knew I would not fully heal without the help of God. As much as I appreciated the support of friends and family, I realized I needed the Lord's help to bring health to my battered heart, mind, and spirit. Only he has the power to redeem what was intended for evil, both directly and indirectly. Any therapy, book, or wisdom that did not incorporate the spiritual dimension of life would not sufficiently compensate for my injuries of injustice, loss, and betrayal. Despite feeling let down by God, I believed his love, truth, and power were central to recovering my sense of meaning, purpose, and wholeness.

I love what Becky, a betrayal-trauma therapist and podcast host of *Rise Up Restored,* says:

> One of the biggest keys to my healing journey was mending my broken relationship with the Lord and letting Him FULLY restore me to even more than I was before. I have come to know that God is the only one who I can fully trust to never hurt me or let me down. I had never had a relationship like that and didn't know it was even possible.
>
> As I found healing for my trauma and I offered my shattered heart to the Lord, I found that my relationship with Him deepened and He filled in the broken parts of me with the healing salve of His love.[13]

Jesus warned us that in this fallen world, we will have tribulation. But we can have peace in Christ because he has overcome the world.

As you read on, I hope to share ways for you to access God's peace and healing, helping you overcome the wounds caused by the world's immoral influence on your spouse.

The Process

I have broken this book into seven sections, each exploring the progressive stages of insights necessary to move you forward on the road to recovery.

SECTION I explores the types of damage you've suffered: the despair, the unique grief, the trauma, and the abuse. Once you've identified "What just happened??" you'll be prepared to read **SECTION II** to identify common sources of shame that Betrandoned folks experience, especially in the Christian community, and how to refute them. The purpose of these first two sections is to validate the devastation you've been through.

SECTION III goes over the many factors *within* an unfaithful person that make them susceptible to infidelity: family history, mental and personality issues, and footholds that the enemy uses to gain access to otherwise decent people. This understanding will help you dismiss undue blame for your spouse's treasonous actions. After all, as psychiatrist and author Frank Pittman III states, "It is very difficult to force someone to have an affair if they don't want to."[14]

These truths lay the groundwork for **SECTION IV**, which covers the neurobiology of affairs and how this distorts a wayward person's reality. You need to understand how your former spouse invented rationalizations to make sense of the unsensible and, if they never pulled out of their delirium, how it changed their character for the worse. Once you understand these phenomena, you'll be empowered to reject the lies that pummeled your self-worth during and after your crisis.

SECTION V contains chapters to help you, as a follower of Christ, regain your spiritual equilibrium after so much has been shaken: your trust in your partner, yourself, pastors, counselors, and even in the Lord. These insights will help you feel less alone, enhance your discernment, counter the enemy's lies, and develop a more mature view of God, yourself, and others.

Once you have gathered the previous insights, you are ready to deal with the understandable angst you feel over the life-altering offenses and injustices you have suffered. **SECTION VI** will help you recognize the difference between a strayer's true and false repentance, discover ways to channel your anger in a healthy manner, and understand the harm that comes from premature forgiveness. This will put you on the path to gradually let go of specific wrongs without dishonoring your pain or absolving your betrayer.

Finally, **SECTION VII** contains a hope-filled chapter for reclaiming your confidence and worth, restoring your lovability, re-imagining your future, and allowing God to redeem your sorrows and transform them into new purpose and your ultimate good.

After much emotional processing, writing, soul-searching, therapy, and truth-seeking, I eventually emerged from my hellhole of sorrow and found a life full of love and personal satisfaction. The book you are currently reading reflects the many lessons I've learned from my journey—lessons I trust will bring you hope and encouragement.

Pulling out of my season of despair wasn't easy. But I am glad I did the hard work of recovery. At twenty-four years out, I am thankful that I did not end up like the writer's mother.

I have wrestled with relational stressors of the worst kind, from without and from within. Battle scars remain. But rather than view these scars as proof of my unworthiness, I wear them with dignity, grateful they are no longer open sores. I consider them badges of courage—evidence of a war I've fought and survived with renewed purpose and joy.

What About You?

Experiencing the loss of a life partner due to the impact of an affair is a devastating blow, leaving you feeling as if someone has ripped the ground out from beneath your feet.

Why should you navigate this emotional tempest alone, hoping your wounds will spontaneously heal over time? There is no guarantee that your self-esteem will fully recover even two decades from now without your conscious and targeted efforts.

Are you ready to embark on the journey of healing presented in this book? Join me as I accompany you on the arduous path of crawling out from under the lies, false blame, shame, injuries, and misconceptions that have held you down. Together, we can explore ways for you to come to terms with your past and embark on a new phase of spiritual strength, purpose, and a fulfilling life.

If you engage deeply with the lessons, stories, and insights within these pages, I believe it will enhance your healing and rejuvenate your spirit.

Whether your marital rejection happened yesterday or years ago, you can gain life-affirming insights and resolution from reading this book—the book I wish I could have found over two decades ago.

SECTION I

Reviewing the Damage

> "So I went out at night through the Valley Gate toward the Well of the Serpent and the Dung Gate, and I inspected the walls of Jerusalem that had been broken down and the gates that had been destroyed by fire."
> ~ Nehemiah 2:13

Before Nehemiah rebuilt Jerusalem's walls, he first walked through the wreckage—examining what had been torn down and burned. He didn't rush to restore. He stopped to assess the damage.

In the same way, when betrayal shatters our lives, we must begin by facing what's been lost. Infidelity and spousal abandonment reduce the structure of our marital "home" to rubble. The devastation is real. It's personal. It's sacred ground scorched by sin.

In this first section, we walk through the ruins. We name the losses—not to wallow, but to grieve what mattered. We validate the trauma—not to stay stuck, but to honor what our hearts have endured. And we begin to expose the abuse so healing can take root with clarity and strength.

You may have pleaded with God to redeem your marriage. But even if your spouse refused to cooperate, God hasn't stopped writing your redemption story.

The rebuilding will come. But first, we must survey the brokenness—piece by piece—so the ruins can be cleared, and a new, stronger foundation can be laid.

VOICELESS

By Linda J. (MacDonald)

I pound
Your steel heart
To no avail.
I reach out ... to air.
I whisper warmly ... to the wind.
I call out. Deafness.
I weep from my toes. No response.
I plead with heaven. Silence.
You remain a stone.
Cold. Unreachable. Immovable.

Nothing
I do, say, or feel
touches you.
So I yell inside myself.
My rage
turns inward.
My grief...inconsolable.
I wail.
Comfortless. Alone. Disposed.
From Valued to Discarded.

I am
bereft of love.
Voiceless. Powerless. Abandoned.
As good as dead
to you
And wishing
I were
To me.

Chapter 1

My Battle

No Final Solution

> Therefore now, O Lord, please take my life from me,
> for death is better to me than life.
> ~Jonah 4:3

As the garage door closed behind me with a clunk, I sat in my car, engine idling, final divorce papers in my lap. A familiar moan rose from deep inside—a gut-wrenching sound that erupted into a wail I couldn't contain.

Why not just let the engine run? Let the carbon monoxide take me out of this misery. I already feel dead inside. Why not finish the job?

I heaved as memories flooded in—our sweet beginning, our tragic end. I had passed up many suitors waiting for a strong, ministry-minded man I could love for a lifetime. His charm, pursuit, and big personality swept me off my feet. After years of waiting, dozens of weddings attended, and graduate school completed, I was finally getting married.

Our wedding was a joy-filled celebration with 700 guests. I was in love and full of hope—cherished, chosen, and ready for a lifetime of shared ministry.

Now, holding the divorce papers, I felt wrecked. Miserable. Utterly unloved.

Not long after our wedding, we moved to a new town. My counseling practice flourished, especially with couples recovering from infidelity. I loved helping them fight their way back to connection.

Years earlier, before entering the Marriage and Family Therapy program, the Lord had whispered to me during a worship service: "I will give you a ministry in reconciliation." That promise had been fulfilled in my counseling practice.

Ironically, I had helped countless marriages heal from the ravages of betrayal. But I couldn't save my own.

I remembered a solo session with our couple's counselor, when I told Dr. Tim, "I adore him." He raised an eyebrow. "Adore?" he repeated. "That's a word I usually associate with God." His gentle correction planted a seed. Maybe I had elevated my husband too high.

James had confessed to a one-way crush on a coworker. I took his story at face value. What I didn't know—but Dr. Tim did—was that he was already emotionally and physically involved with her. Despite my training, I had missed the signs.

Now, sitting in my car, shame burned through me. How could I have been so blind? I felt foolish, duped, and discarded.

From the beginning of our courtship, I had felt secure in James's affection. He hugged me daily, told me he loved me often, and seemed emotionally invested. The idea that he could fall in love with someone else felt absurd—until I looked back and recognized the red flags I had ignored.

The final blow wasn't just that he left—it was how he left. With disdain. As if I didn't matter. I traced his emotional withdrawal back to the first time they kissed. That was the moment I lost him. The moment he attached to her, he detached from me.

I pounded the steering wheel, sobbing. Our relationship was over. The love of my life was gone. Our family was broken. My professional credibility—especially as an infidelity specialist—felt ruined. My past had been stolen; my future dreams were gone. I feared I would never feel normal again.

Maybe I've already done all I was meant to do. I had written a play that pointed many to Jesus, discipled young women, helped save countless marriages, and raised two sons to adulthood. *Was there anything left for me?*

Talk therapy, fervent prayers, and even spiritual warfare hadn't stopped the nightmares, flashbacks, and trembling. I felt hollow. Despairing.

Friends tried to help. I knew they cared. But I could sense their weariness. Still, as I sat there with the engine running, longing to end my pain, a quiet interruption stirred within me: *What about my mom?* She had already lost my father and both parents in under three years. *Would she survive this?*

Then came another question: *What about my sons? What kind of legacy would my suicide leave them?*

I cringed.

Then I wondered, *What about my clients—including many I had talked out of suicide? How would my self-imposed demise undermine all I had ever taught? And, how would it affect the reputation of Christ, whom I claimed to serve?*

Suddenly, I saw the ripple effect. And I knew: I couldn't go through with it. I turned off the engine. I chose to live—but barely. I fought the urge to end my life for another six months. Nevertheless, that day, something shifted. I realized suicide was a lose-lose proposition. I couldn't inflict that pain on those I loved. I would have to somehow find the strength to keep going.

Reflections

Not every betrayed and abandoned spouse becomes suicidal. The risk depends on many factors: past trauma, depression, coping skills, support systems, and the depth of emotional investment in the lost relationship.

But make no mistake—Betrandonment is one of the most demoralizing experiences a person can endure. Being supplanted by another person, fantasy, or addiction sends a message: *You are replaceable.* And when that betrayal is followed by rejection, the pain magnifies exponentially.

We were created for love and connection. When someone who vowed to love us in sickness and health suddenly detaches, it's not just grief—it's psychological disintegration. The loss isn't just physical; it's emotional and spiritual.

For some of us, earlier wounds deepen the crisis. For example, my father was emotionally unavailable due to alcoholism. His addiction sent me an unspoken message: *You're not worth it.*

When he died from a heart attack at 54, I grieved not only the man but the father I never had. Unconsciously, I carried a deep-rooted fear into adulthood: *I must be unlovable.* So, when James fell for someone else and decided to end our marriage, it felt like confirmation of an old lie.

Years later, I came across a model of suicidality taught by Dr. M. David Runn.[1] He identified three core beliefs common among those at risk for suicide:

- *I am unlovable.*
- *This pain is unbearable.*
- *My situation is unsolvable.*

If you've had suicidal thoughts after betrayal, you are not alone. The pain can distort your thinking. But these beliefs are not truths—they are trauma-induced lies. With time, support, and spiritual healing, they can be dismantled.

I wince now when I remember how close I came to ending my life. I would have missed so much—my children's graduations, weddings, grandchildren, new friendships, and the unexpected gift of a second, beautiful marriage.

More than all of that, I would have missed the quiet joys of a restored inner world: strengthened faith, emotional resilience, and a deeper walk with God.

The Hope of Redemption

The word "redeem" first took hold of me at a women's retreat one month before I married James. The speaker, Myrna Larson, declared: "There isn't anything beyond God's ability to *redeem*. He can *redeem* anything!"

Years later, when the hurricane of Betrandonment tore my world apart, her words returned like an anchor in the storm: *God can redeem anything!* I clung to them for dear life.

Today, four decades after Myrna's preparative message, like Job, I can say, "My ears had heard of You, but now my eyes have seen You" (Job 42:5). I've progressed beyond mental assent to experientially knowing there isn't anything beyond God's ability to redeem in our lives.

Are there scattered remnants of carnage still lying around? Yes, here and there. But not in my soul.

If God can redeem and give new meaning to the worst of my losses, he can redeem yours, too. My hope for this book is to accompany you through the rubble of Betrandonment and into your own redemptive, healing story.

The next chapter explores Betrandonment Grief—how it differs from the grief of widowhood and how to find comfort, clarity, and companionship as you begin to heal.

> "The Lord is near to the broken-hearted and saves those who are crushed in spirit" (Ps. 34:18).

Chapter 2

Betrandonment Grief

When You'd Rather Be a Widow!

Grief is the price we pay for Love.
~ Queen Elizabeth II

Grief may be the price we pay for love,
but traumatic grief is the price we pay when our
spouse abandons us for another person or lifestyle.
~Linda MacDonald

On the morning of September 11, 2001, just three weeks after my divorce was final, I lounged in my robe, idly watching the morning news. My quiet morning was shattered as footage of a plane crashing into one of the Twin Towers filled the screen. Like many, I assumed it was an isolated, tragic accident—until a second plane struck the other tower in a fiery explosion. In that instant, the sickening reality hit me—our nation was under attack.

Glued to the television, I watched in horror as desperate souls, trapped in the burning towers, hung from windows before plunging hundreds of feet to their deaths. The live footage felt surreal, like a nightmare unfolding in real-time. My heart ached, and tears streamed down my face as I listened to haunting voicemails—final pleas for help and heartbreaking goodbyes to loved ones.

As I grieved with the nation, I felt a strange connection to that day's terror. While terrorists had inflicted death from the outside, my husband had detonated a different kind of destruction from within. He had conspired with another woman—not to take lives, but to assassinate our marriage.

James was still alive in body, but emotionally and spiritually, he was gone. Detached. Indifferent. Severed from me in every way that mattered.

In the days following 9/11, I found myself identifying with the ambiguous loss[1] experienced by the families left behind—many of them had no "body" to bury as evidence of their deaths. All had been incinerated under the rubble. The ruins of the Twin Towers felt like a metaphor for my current reality. My beloved spouse was gone forever, our family permanently altered, and my life seemed like a rubble of smoldering ash and contorted metal, with no visible remains to acknowledge and bury.

While I could strangely relate to this national tragedy, I felt alone. I didn't have a country collectively sharing my grief. I heard no parting, "I love you," as my husband brutally cut me out of his life. No outcries by others against the injustice of my loss. No public displays of sympathy. No rallying the troops on my behalf. For the most part, I suffered my humiliating loss in isolation.

Please don't misunderstand me—the horrors the 9/11 families endured were unimaginable. And for the sake of his parents, himself, and our children, I never wished my husband dead. Yet, in some ways, his death would have been easier to bear than his desertion. At least then, I would have known I was loved and been met with respect and condolences, rather than discomfort and isolation.

> Yet it in some ways, his death would have been easier to bear than his desertion. At least then, I would have known I was loved and been met with respect and condolences.

Instead, dejected, I had to unravel a messy ball of scorn. I felt shame for not keeping my husband faithful. And I winced when I noticed the averted eyes of others who struggled with how or whether to acknowledge my loss. A romantic delusion had ripped his heart away from me, leaving a gaping, jagged hole behind. Since he was still alive in their eyes, they couldn't comprehend that for me, he was worse than dead.

The losses from an affair-sparked divorce paint a different picture than loss through death. Both are life-altering. One is met with reverence, the other with disgrace.

The wreckage I saw on television on September 11th gave me a visual aid for my personal devastation. My husband's affair and change of heart blew my dreams and hopes for the future to bits. The ugliness of our split overshadowed my once-happy memories of our life together. The toxic fumes of mistrust and betrayal, once absent, now tainted what was once beautiful. Our friends, ministry, and community lay in ruins, never to be rebuilt. Losing my husband's love, devotion, and presence—against my will—was the most agonizing experience of my life.

It never occurred to me that James would fall in love with someone else, let alone forsake our marriage. Before our divorce was final, I had cried out to God for months, begging him to save our marriage. But no restoration ever came. So here I was—forsaken, traumatized, and alone. Heaven felt silent, and a suffocating cloud of desolation hung over me.

That is, until I saw President Bush with his megaphone, standing on top of the heap of destruction that used to be the Twin Towers. He aimed his megaphone upward for the cameras and the terrorists to see: "I can hear you. We can all hear you. And soon, you will be hearing from us!" I burst into tears.

As I sobbed, I heard more than just the president's voice. I sensed God saying, "I hear you, too." It felt as if the Lord himself was assuring me—he had heard my cries, seen the wreckage, and would summon heaven's armies to stand by my side. That moment has never left me. God was with me in the rubble.

The Retreat

A month later, I attended a women's retreat at my church. Just two months divorced, I felt awkward and out of place. My husband had once been a respected elder there. Now, he was gone, and I was the discarded spouse sitting among mostly married women.

Few knew what to say. I was still raw, longing for someone to acknowledge my pain.

Eventually, I found two women I could relate to—one a recent widow, the other suspecting her husband of same-sex infidelity. We gravitated toward each other, skipping the usual activities to avoid pretending we were having fun.

During one of the worship times, I saw our pastor's wife slip her arm around my widowed friend to comfort her. I rejoiced for my friend, but I envied the outpouring of sympathy everyone showed her. She was showered with hugs and expressions of support. Yet, I don't remember anyone even touching me over that weekend. No one said a word of condolence for my loss.

> I don't remember anyone even touching me over that weekend. No one said a word of condolence for my loss.

I wondered if the ladies thought I deserved my unwanted divorce. Or that my broken marriage was somehow contagious. I felt like a leper.

During a break, my widowed friend invited a small group to visit her cabin near the retreat center. I stayed back, sad that I had lost everything we owned together. It struck me how different our losses were. While she had lost her husband, she never lost his love or their marital assets. While I felt compassion for her, I also felt awkward about my own devastation. I, too, had lost a beloved spouse. Only two people out of a hundred women at the retreat seemed to notice.

Widowhood vs. Betrandonhood

Author Miriam Neff became a widow after 41 years of loving marriage to her husband, Bob. On her blog, "7 Tips to Help a Widow," she wrote advice for friends of widows. When I reached the fourth point on her blog, I stopped short. Miriam advised friends of widows to continue referring to the deceased partner in fond ways. She states,

> Do refer to our husband's acts or words—serious or humorous. We are so comforted by knowing our husband has not been forgotten. Do not leave our husbands out of the conversation.[2]

Oh, how I wished that were true for me! Instead of fond remembrances from my friends, my ex-husband remained a hushed subject as though he never existed. And if he did come up, it was not about his finer qualities or our happy moments together. It was about his betrayal.

Yet, from the moment he proposed and throughout our marriage, I was convinced he loved me. In all my years of dating, I'd never had a man pursue me so vigorously. He charmed the socks off me. We embraced and kissed throughout our marriage, expressing our love multiple times a day.

But when he fell in love with *her* and told me, "I'm not sure I ever loved you," that vanished. His blunt declaration cast a shadow over our past, darkening every good memory of our life together. Whoosh! Gone! Smashed!

Rather than bringing comfort, memories of our life together mocked me. I questioned my perceptions. Had I been delusional about his love for me? Had he been faking it all those years? The love, security, and connection I always felt when he wrapped his arms around me evaporated. I took James's disloyalty and desertion very personally, as if he had marked my worth as a wife with a big, fat "F."

Unlike a widow, I had no comforting memories to cling to—nothing to remind me I was once loved. The love I once believed in now seemed suspect. His betrayal turned every treasured moment into a mockery.

If he had died, at least the goodness we once shared could've remained intact. Instead, I had to bury my marriage without the dignity of a memorial or Celebration of Life.

After all, he was still alive—just not in my home.

In my discussions with others, I have noticed some unique ways Betrandonment Grief differs from other kinds of losses. One woman, "Alice," who had experienced both the sudden death of a spouse and later intimate betrayal by a second husband, explained,

> My shock over my first husband's sudden, premature death was devastating in the beginning. He was only 45. It helped that I had lots of good support from friends and family. My second husband's betrayal and upcoming divorce seemed less horrible in the early days. But as I thawed over time, the devastation from his unfaithfulness and our pending divorce became even bigger than the death of my first husband. This time, I had to suffer alone. I felt unloved. It was more personal.[3]

Complex Grief

One widowed client came to see me a year after her husband died from a heart attack. She'd been through the phase of receiving sympathy cards, meals delivered to her home, and the support of friends and family. With her adult children grown and gone, she sold their home and purchased a smaller house. As she prepared for the move, she rifled through a box in the attic, only to discover love letters exchanged between her now-deceased husband and another woman.

Instantly, her internal status switched from Woeful Widow to Scorned Wife. She questioned her entire marriage. Was he unhappy with her? Who was this woman? Did she sneak into the memorial service unbeknownst to her? How long were they involved? How did he manage to deceive her?

Oh, the rage! The insult! How dare he!? Who knew? Who didn't know? She wondered if she should keep this terrible secret to preserve his image and their reputation as a couple. Or should she tell her closest friends the truth so she could receive additional support?

My heart went out to her. She had been robbed of a normal grief process and thrust into Complex Grief, which forced her to navigate a confusing labyrinth of unexpected trauma and prolonged agony.

A year after my divorce, I briefly dated a pastor I'd met on a Christian dating site. I learned that "John" had lost two wives. His first wife was an alcoholic who eventually went to treatment. Excited to welcome home a sober wife, his happiness turned to dread when she arrived and announced she had fallen in love with a man in the program and planned to leave and file for divorce. She then went on to live with and marry the other man. John's world came crashing down.

A few years later, he met and married a woman he fondly called his "soulmate." After they'd been happily married for four years, she was diagnosed with a virulent form of breast cancer and died.

I once asked him, "Which was worse for you? Losing your spouse to another man or the death of your second wife?"

John didn't hesitate. "Oh, the first loss was more painful than the death of my wife." He meant no disrespect to his second spouse. He still missed her horribly. But the rejection, shame, and pain of being replaced by another man was a crushing blow beyond the sorrow of losing his newer wife to death. At least this time, he found comfort in knowing he was loved. I appreciated hearing this.

I met with a grief specialist, Suzanne Kirsch, who, with six children to raise, lost her first husband in an airplane crash. I wanted to know the similarities and differences between what she experienced as a widow and what I went through in losing my spouse through betrayal and unwanted divorce. With her input, I created a chart (included in the Workbook) that I will partially discuss here.

I recognize that many factors can deepen the pain of losing a spouse through death, such as trauma, stigma from murder or suicide, medical mistakes, drug overdoses, a loved one missing in action, or other complexities.

However, in the list below, I aim to distinguish the experience of losing a spouse to an uncomplicated death versus the pain of betrayal and unwanted divorce.

1. Loss of Self-esteem. While a widow's loss is heartbreaking, the death of their partner is not personal. Typically, no rejection was involved. On the other hand, a Betrandoned person feels intentionally abandoned. Often, the departing spouse shifts blame onto the rejected partner, disregarding the affair's influence on their decision to leave. Betrandoned partners lose not only their spouse's commitment and presence but also their love, leading to a deep sense of rejection and diminished self-worth. They question their lovability and value as a man or woman and may even mistakenly blame themselves for their partner's affair and choice to leave. As Dr. James Dobson says, "Rejection by the one you love, particularly, is the most powerful destroyer of self-esteem in the entire realm of human experience."[4]

2. Shattered Trust. While a widow(er) may lose trust in the world for a season, Betrandoned spouses lose trust in their partners and themselves as well. The deceit, lies, and secrecy shake their previous assumptions of loyalty and commitment to the marriage. They often second-guess their own judgment and doubt their perceptions. Many avoid socializing because they fear risking another experience of betrayal.

3. A Stigmatized Loss. When a spouse dies by accident or disease, widows/widowers receive the deserved honor, respect, awe, and empathy of friends and family. While the widow may feel alone once the furor dies down, there is typically no shame associated with the death. Society accords them an elevated status for their grief. In contrast, the Betrandoned experience a stigmatized loss akin to suicide, murder, or a drug overdose.

Friends and acquaintances often feel awkward or avoid the forsaken spouse, as if spousal desertion were contagious. Others silently judge, assuming fault. Despite divorce's prevalence, those abandoned against their will often face disapproval—especially in the church. The shame of being replaced and discarded by a mutinous spouse is a heavy burden to bear.

4. No Rituals. We perform rituals around death that we do not perform around divorce: We write affirming obituaries, organize memorial services, deliver glowing eulogies, conduct reverential burial rites, send kind cards, offer flowers, give hugs, bring meals to the bereaved, and allow time for the widowed to grieve (although often not enough time is allowed). The support is open and involves no dishonor.

However, the Betrandoned have little public acknowledgment of their losses: no services, cards, few hugs, and no meals brought to the aggrieved. Their rituals consist of sequestered courtrooms, legal papers confirming their failure, and discreet glances from others. Deserted, unwanted spouses suffer in isolation. Well-meaning friends encourage divorced people to re-enter the dating scene and "move on" much sooner than they might the recently widowed.

5. Loyalty Conflicts. When a partner dies, no one needs to "choose sides" between the living and the deceased. Everyone is safe to care for and support the surviving spouse. Yet, divorce tends to divide certain parties. In-laws no longer show equal concern for the discarded spouse. They usually side with the spouse who is biologically related, despite knowing about the affair. Some friends may struggle to maintain equal closeness with both partners, while others may only hear and believe the infidel's side of the story, further deepening the betrayed spouse's wounds.

6. The Loss of an Intact Family. When a spouse dies, children experience profound loss but typically feel secure staying close to the surviving parent, maintaining a sense of home. Widows find comfort in this stability. In contrast, divorce—especially after infidelity—fractures the family unit. The abandoned spouse must navigate shared time, resources, and holidays with the rejecting ex and, at times, their new partner. Losing both a spouse and an intact family magnifies grief by stripping away the comfort and cohesive family unit they once knew.

7. No Closure. A tangible death brings a sense of finality that divorce does not. When a partner dies, family members identify the body, which is then laid to rest in a casket, preserved in an urn, or scattered in a meaningful place. Reminders for the deceased remain, but the person is no longer on earth. However, the death of a marriage offers no body to bury, leaving the grief process suspended. The one who left is still alive, walking around—yet as good as dead to the rejected partner.

The Betrandoned endure the loss of their spouse's love and presence without the solace of closure. Wounds are reopened through ongoing contact—such as during exchanges with children, milestone events, or painful updates from the kids and well-meaning friends. Unlike death, the deserting spouse remains alive, often becoming a prolonged source of torment. When legal battles over custody and finances resurface, it feels as though the agony will never end.

My Zoom group friend, "Melanie," expresses this well:

> Grief from betrayal is fierce and merciless and misunderstood by those who have not experienced it. The "unfinished story" chosen by someone else without my consent has left my heart exquisitely tender with a yearning for a goodbye that will never be understood. Finding closure alone in the deafening silence of betrayal has been the hardest road I've ever traveled.[5]

8. Painful Mementos. Widows have a mix of sad and fond memories associated with mementos like pictures and photo albums. Yet, down the road, these serve as treasured reminders of love and affection shared with the deceased. Widows keep cherished photos on the walls. Mementos are proof of having been loved by the deceased spouse, even if imperfectly.

For those who are divorced, this is not the case. Pictures tend to mock the deserted spouse. Photos are ripped up or concealed in a box, closet, or attic. If still displayed, the betrayer gets snipped from family photos. Such mementos only remind the one who is deserted that they were unwanted. The painful behaviors of the betrayer have tarnished the sheen of past vacations and family gatherings.

9. Divided Assets. Widows and widowers may experience a loss of funds due to the death of their spouses. If they are retired, they lose their partner's Social Security income. Yet, whatever assets they possessed (other retirement plans, cars, houses, furniture, etc.) remain with the family. Even if they need to be sold for financial or aging reasons, the survivor has the option to choose what to keep, give to the children, or sell at their discretion.

This is not the case with divorce. Almost no one comes out of a divorce feeling like the property division was fair. Women often experience a significant decline in their standard of living. For both men and women, everything once shared as a couple is divided, sold, or lost. Mothers who home-schooled their children—some of whom may have disabilities or social anxiety—are forced to place them in public schools they find inadequate or objectionable. Stay-at-home moms entering the workforce may have to settle for low-wage jobs (or even multiple jobs) just to make ends meet.

10. A Stolen Past and Future. Widows/widowers mourn the loss of future dreams shared with their deceased spouse, often cherishing the good memories while filtering out the bad. Meanwhile, Betrandoned spouses lose both past and future dreams—their history rewritten through the lens of rejection and their futures stolen by the same spouses they planned them with. While widows find comfort in the bond they once had, the Betrandoned suffer an irreparable attachment wound. Their loss feels intensely personal—intentional, even malicious.

My new mother-in-law, Hope, was married to her cherished husband one month short of 70 years. They had a sweet marriage and shared a love for family and ministry over their decades together. Harry always fondly referred to Hope as his "bride."

Hope and Harry's lovely home of 27 years was the center of all the family gatherings. My brother-in-law, Tom, referred to their former home as "The Mother Ship." As they aged, Harry wanted to ensure his wife was cared for, so they moved into a local retirement center. He passed away several years later.

Hope kept pictures of her deceased husband stationed all over her condo. She placed the photo of Harry smiling in his doctoral robe on a low cabinet near her entry, where she talked to his picture daily as if he were still alive. Her cozy place still felt like home. While she greatly missed Harry, she bore no shame over their relationship. His memorial was a beautiful event that still brings tears to my eyes whenever we watch the DVD.

What a contrast to my divorce. No ceremonies. No public support. No couple or family photos on the walls as a testament to my former life. My kids have no intact home to come back to for holidays and special events. While I know they enjoy my current husband, Dan, it is still not the same as the original family they grew up in.

I recently scanned the wedding pictures from my first marriage into my computer for the sake of the kids and then tossed the album in the trash. Sadly, I felt no desire to display them or share the memory of my first wedding with anyone. I doubt a widow or widower would similarly dispose of their precious wedding album in the same way.

One former client, a schoolteacher, put it this way:

When I was in the midst of my gut-wrenching divorce, the husband of a co-worker died suddenly and unexpectedly. Knowing of my predicament, she said to me, "Well, at least your husband is still alive." While I know she was in shock and probably later regretted what she said, her words and the actions of our staff magnified the disparity of how our society treats the victims of divorce and widowhood. I was expected to continue to work and compartmentalize my emotions; she was given weeks off to mourn and recover. I was left in financial shambles with half of an estate but full-sized bills; she was left with an entire estate, death benefits, meal trains, and a monetary gift from our staff (to which I, ironically, contributed). I was pitied; she received love and empathy.[6]

The Value of Tears

Part of healing from Betrandonment Grief is allowing yourself to feel your sorrow and cry out to the Lord. Tears are a gift from God, given to help us express pain and process loss. Yet, sometimes we resist them, fearing that once we start, we won't be able to stop—afraid we will be consumed by our grief, unable to function. However, unexpressed emotions don't disappear; they stay bottled up, often surfacing in unhealthy ways.

Have you been afraid to express your sorrow? To allow yourself to weep and cry over your many losses? While the reminders of your losses may hit you out of nowhere, and tears may surface at inopportune times, such as in front of your kids or at work, it is possible to "take note" and set aside later, private time to weep over whatever painful reminder arises.

Each crying session will only last so long. Your body will automatically stop. You may experience moments like this over the course of several years. But eventually, each bout will lessen in frequency and intensity.

Productive Grief

I've found there's a difference between general grief and productive grief. *General Grief* is a broad, overarching sadness. It involves crying without being able to pinpoint the aspect of sorrow you are sobbing about. You are just plain sad.

Productive Grief is specific. It involves identifying the particular losses you are grieving over. Such as,

"I've lost my best friend!"

"I feel so ripped off!"

"Where are you, God? I feel so alone!"

"I feel ruined!"
"My kids have lost their security!"
"I'm scared about my lack of finances."
"I'll never feel normal again!"

I remember lamenting, over and over again, to the Lord, "I'm *so* disappointed!"

Effective grieving will encompass both broad and explicit sorrow over our losses. However, I encourage you to put the most energy into productive, specific grief. List as many losses as possible and vent your sorrow to the Lord in prayer. And, if you have a close confidante or therapist, allow them to join you as you grieve. This creates a validating space for you to express your feelings of sorrow. When an empathetic person joins you as a witness to your grief, your heart receives a message: "I am with you. Yes, these losses are real. It's OK to let them out. You will live."

Therapist, workshop leader, and author Lorie Dwinell described how she allows emotional space for wounded clients to grieve by sitting beside them as they cry. She made a statement I never forgot: "Grief is the pain that heals itself."[7]

So many people bury their pain, fearing that if they allow themselves to feel it, it will consume them. But true healing requires us to acknowledge our sorrow, to give it a voice through both words and tears. God, in his wisdom, designed tears as a release, a way to process grief so it doesn't remain trapped inside us, festering.

> "Grief is the pain that heals itself."
> ~Lorie Dwinell

Unexpressed tears keep our losses frozen in time, preventing them from fading into the past. However, when we allow them to flow, sorrow is gradually wrung out, and the raw wound of lost love begins to mend. Over time, grief shifts from an overwhelming flood to a gentle ebb. Slowly, the sorrow subsides, and we begin to reclaim our strength.

Losing a life partner via infidelity is cataclysmic. Like a mud-flow that moves and destroys cars and homes, it negatively shifts major aspects of our lives—our identity, attachments, family life, self-esteem, faith, finances, and security. Each of these arenas is shaken to the core. This can lead to prolonged and convoluted grief, more recently known as Prolonged Grief Disorder. While all major losses are gut-wrenching, complicated grief traps us in certain phases, making it difficult to move forward. This is especially true when the loss is intertwined with personal trauma.

I wish more researchers would broaden their study of complicated grief beyond widowhood or the death of a family member. As noted in my Introduction, at least 1200 affair-sparked divorces occur every day in the United

States. I believe Betrandoned spouses are especially vulnerable to Prolonged Grief Disorder, which can keep them stuck, ruminating over their losses for years. Their pain consumes their thoughts, making it difficult to move through the natural stages of grief. Like the depressed writer's mother, whose twenty years of misery inspired me to pursue healing, they risk remaining trapped in sorrow unless they actively work toward recovery.

The Comfort of Shared Grief

Most suffering people find it refreshing to connect with others who have experienced similar heartbreak. We feel understood and less isolated. And, in the case of Post-Affair Divorce grief, sharing our grief reduces our feelings of shame. We all know the difference between someone who tries to comfort us who has not experienced a similar loss and the comforting presence of those who've "been there."

I attended two weekly women's groups during my marital crisis. I had been with one group for ten years and the other for two. The members of my long-term group were all lovely women, but they struggled to understand the depth of my pain. As they talked about their family vacations and home renovations, I felt sad that I could no longer join in with them. Yet, I found it grounding to be around mature, healthy people with whom I shared a history and who cared about me. While they had faced life disappointments, their marriages and families remained intact.

The other group, "The Glory Girls," enjoyed delving into Bible studies such as Kay Arthur's *Lord Heal My Hurts* and Beth Moore's *Getting Free*. Each member had encountered some form of interpersonal trauma in their lives. They allowed me the space to be where I was and to cry without attempting to distract or "fix" me. Two years later, they gently teased me about the first day I walked in, looking like "death warmed over," assuring me that I had come a long way since then.

I benefited from both groups, each in its own way.

Still, I was eager to find people who could relate to the experience of intimate betrayal. So, when my friend "Elizabeth" invited me to attend a weekend retreat for partners of sex addicts, I jumped at it, even though it wasn't an exact match for my situation. Most of the women were still married and living with spouses who struggled with sexual compulsivity. Yet, despite a few differences, each one had been injured by infidelity. It turned out to be a wonderful experience for me. We bonded over our shared pain and the various levels of brokenness in our lives and marriages. I felt safe, understood, and free to show my grief.

In times of loss, it's common to feel the urge to isolate ourselves. While allowing time for healing is vital, it's equally important to occasionally step cherish and protect us would jeopardize our safety and security in such a terrible way.

The combined losses from intimate betrayal and rejection run deep and often lead to protracted grief, long past when your friends think you ought to be over this. It is essential for you to give yourself the space to grieve as productively as possible.

Grieving such multitudinous personal losses takes time. Yet, the more specific you are when expressing your losses, the more effective your grief will be.

In my case, my grief lingered long and deep, even into my second marriage. After seeing me tear up over my broken family, some friends approached me and suggested that perhaps I was suffering from a "spirit of heaviness," as described in Isaiah 61. They kindly prayed for me, which I greatly appreciated. However, that hole in my heart still felt like a lead weight. I worried I would never feel fully alive again. I didn't understand how I could be so happy in my new marriage, yet simultaneously numb. But I was. Happy with Dan—yet living with a dead zone in my heart that I couldn't shake.

Fortunately, when my Presbyterian pastor husband was on a trip to Israel, I stayed home and visited First Love Church two Sundays in a row. This local fellowship believed in the active work of the Holy Spirit. After each service, I went forward for prayer. On the second Sunday, the sermon focused on the Lord setting us free. After receiving prayer, I sensed God's spirit come over me. When the service ended, I lingered in my car to savor his presence.

As I prayed, the familiar moan-turned-wail began in the depths of my abdomen, traveling upward to the surface. But this time, it didn't end with me still agonizing and wrung out. Instead, after a final despairing wail, poof! The heaviness was gone. In its place, I could feel a joy-filled spiritual release—a lightness I hadn't experienced in years. I was free!! I can honestly say that I haven't felt that same deadness in my heart since that day. And that was fifteen years ago.

Everyone comes to terms with the pain of grief in their own unique way and time. As followers of Christ, we have the advantage of the Holy Spirit's guidance and assistance. Author, worship leader, and life coach Ruth Erickson puts the value of processing Betrandonment Grief with Jesus this way:

> A strength and resilience was forged inside of me as I labored through my grief ... If we are brave enough to turn to God in the process, grief can introduce us to new aspects of who God is. I never knew God as my strong tower, my refuge, until I needed a place to hide. I never knew God as my rescuer, my deliverer, until I was placed in a terrible battle. I never knew God as my healer until I was deeply wounded. He is my comforter, my redeemer, my rock, the lifter of my head—and

my grief was the painful pathway to meeting these beautiful parts of Him.⁹

Whether you are experiencing normal grief or complex grief, I am confident the Lord wants to heal you. Grieving *with* him will take you to new depths of *knowing* him. I encourage you to pray as authentically and specifically as possible. Invite the Lord into your season of sorrow alongside another safe person or two. I believe that in time, God will set you free.

I'm not saying you will never feel moments of loss again. Every holiday, wedding, and a child's or grandchild's birthday or graduation will remind you of the brokenness of your once-intact family. However, these brushes with grief won't have the same enduring heaviness you experienced in the early years of your loss.

If any remnant of loss lingers, it will likely retreat to a small corner of your heart, overshadowed by the abundance of goodness now present in your life. The pain that once engulfed you will no longer dominate your every moment. When memories or events occasionally stir echoes of your past, let them serve as gentle reminders of the meaningful ways you were comforted during your earlier stages of grief, the insights you've gained, and how far you've come.

The topic of Betrayal Trauma has gained significant attention in recent literature, podcasts, and social media—particularly in the context of partner sex addiction. However, there is a notable lack of material that acknowledges the *cumulative impact* when a faithful spouse endures the double traumas of spousal betrayal and rejection in succession. That is what we explore in the next chapter.

Chapter 3

The Trauma from the Drama

> Trauma is perhaps the most avoided, ignored, belittled, denied, misunderstood, and untreated cause of human suffering.
> ~ Peter A. Levine

King David was on the run. Absalom, his son, and Ahithophel, his trusted friend and confidante, conspired to overthrow his throne and take his life. During this harrowing time, David wrote Psalm 55, pouring out his anguish. The betrayal cut deeply—he had never suspected that his closest friend would collude with his own son against him. Fear gripped him, and his words reveal symptoms of profound distress akin to what we now recognize as Post-Traumatic Stress.

> "My heart is in anguish. The terror of death overpowers me. Fear and trembling overwhelm me. I can't stop shaking. O how I wish I had wings like a dove; then I would fly away and rest!" (Psalm 55:4–7)

Do you identify with some of David's feelings? Were you as frightened as I was when your spouse joined up with another person to deceive, betray, and threaten your marriage?

None of us gets married expecting our beloved spouses to betray us with an outside affair partner. We assume they meant their vow to "forsake all others" and stay faithful to us alone.

And when they promised, "Till death do us part," we never imagined that one day they would drag us through a heartbreaking, involuntary divorce. It's all rather shocking, like a double betrayal. Rarely do we anticipate that the person we love, form families with, and intertwine our lives with would turn against us, crush our self-esteem, poison our past, and threaten our future.

I appreciate how Dr. Shirley Glass describes it:

> Following the discovery of a betrayal, there will never again be the blind trust that existed before. In just a few seconds, the safest haven in the world is turned into the source of the greatest treachery.[1]

My Symptoms

When James mentioned his secret one-way crush on Judy, I was convinced our love could weather this temporary midlife storm. I naively figured this admission would burst his fantasy about her. Although he swore me to secrecy and refused to seek support from his Christian friends, I blindly shoved further suspicions aside and didn't ask him any more questions.

Six weeks later, when he was supposedly taking a nap, I walked in on him under the covers, talking with *her* in hushed tones on our phone. This rattled me. He made up an excuse about their discussion being related to work. My gut told me otherwise.

Once I composed myself, I let him have it. I told him he had three options: to discuss the matter with our pastor, his weekly small group, or a therapist. I could no longer bear the burden of his struggle alone. He chose the confidentiality of a counselor. I relaxed again, figuring therapy would make a difference and set his heart straight.

The next month, I noticed something different when he left for a ministry trip abroad. Instead of his usual warm hug and kiss goodbye, he set his suitcase on the porch to adjust his collar, averted his eyes, and slightly turned his back toward me before he left. My heart froze. Something was wrong. Our marriage was in deeper trouble than I thought. This snapped me out of denial mode and into panic mode. I went from a confident wife to a terrified girl in an instant.

That was the day my trauma symptoms began to manifest.

After I closed the door, my body began to tremble. My hands shook so badly that it was difficult for me to hold a glass or pen. I couldn't concentrate. I had little appetite and couldn't find a way to calm myself down. My mind raced, reviewing the hints I had missed over the past few months. *Maybe there is more to the story.*

That night, I lay awake, quaking for hours. I couldn't shut my mind off as a thousand questions pelted me from every angle. With only an hour and a half of sleep, I beelined it for my doctor the next day. I knew I needed sleep medication if I was going to get any rest at all.

I couldn't shake the ominous feeling that my survival as a wife, woman, mother, and therapist were all at risk. I was on the brink of losing everything I cared about—especially him.

Nine days later, after James arrived home, he met with his counselor, Dr. Tim, who suggested he tell me "the truth." That night, we sat stiffly across the kitchen table from one another, both on edge. Rather than tell me the *real* truth—that he and the other woman had been cavorting behind my back for several months—he told me a cleverly concocted tale of why he'd been popping Tums and occasionally sleeping on the couch.

He said, "The reason I've been acting so strange is because I've been worried about the performance pressure of what everyone would think of me if I got a divorce." *Oh, no!* The dreaded "D-word," something that had never been uttered between us before. I was stunned.

He continued, "I've always tried to plan out my life ahead of time. I no longer believe that God brought us together. I love you, but I'm not in love with you. In fact, I'm not sure I ever loved you." Another shocker. He might as well have told me he had secretly murdered his best friend.

"Besides, I think you are boring. I don't even like hanging out with you in the kitchen." There it was. In two minutes, he had dismantled our entire marital story.

I said, "This is really about *her*. Isn't it? You think you are in love with *her*, which has ruined your feelings for me!"

"No, that isn't true. This isn't about Judy. It's about our *marriage*." He repeated this over and over with vehemence. He denied any link between his attraction to the other woman and his shift in feelings toward me. I felt dizzy, invalidated, and helpless.

As the evening wore on, he continued to whack away at my reality. By the night's end, his twisted reasoning had my head spinning—I doubted myself and almost believed his distorted version of reality. *Perhaps his feelings for her have not hijacked his feelings for me. Maybe he's right. I'm boring. No wonder he finds her more appealing.*

Then, as soon as I got away from him, I shook my head and came to my senses, knowing that his perspective was skewed. I was not the root of his problem. A strange and powerful undertow had gripped his heart, dragging him out to sea, with the potential to pull me and our marriage out with it. I felt stymied as to what to do.

Over the following months, I felt so physically weak that I could barely function. Wherever I went, it seemed like I was losing something—my keys, my purse, my credit cards, or even where I parked my car. Despite taking nightly medication, my sleep was restless and typically lasted only three hours. Additionally, my doctor prescribed a mild antidepressant to help alleviate my heightened anxiety.

In the meantime, I developed what I later learned was a symptom of "hypervigilance." As soon as James walked in the door, my brain shifted to high alert. My eyes would involuntarily lock onto him, like a heat-seeking missile, following his every move, facial expression, and body language, trying to gauge his mood: *Is his heart leaning toward or against me today?* I knew it unnerved him, but I couldn't help it.

Frozen and numb inside, I had to coach myself. *You will make dinner tonight. Just put one foot in front of the other. Walk over to the refrigerator and pull out something to fix. And do not burst into tears in front of your teenage son, no matter how grief-stricken you feel.*

My brain was scrambled, and my movements felt mechanical. All I wanted was to stay in bed, curl up in a ball, and cry my eyes out.

One month later, well-meaning friends gave us tickets to a Seahawks game with our sons. I remember my petrified state as I walked into the stadium, afraid that I might collapse at any moment. Legs numb, and my brain disconnected from my body, I toddled down the stairs to our seats. Having to fake being a secure family seemed surreal. I watched the game with my mind suspended above my body despite sitting next to my kids, who seemed clueless about my condition. *Don't they realize our family life is hanging by a thread, about to be blown to smithereens?* I wanted to scream.

Over the following months, I tried everything I could think of to save our marriage: being overly kind, acting distant, intercessory prayer, moving out, arranging for a friend to do an "intervention," confronting the other woman, and moving back home. Nothing seemed to make a difference.

After we separated and I learned he planned to divorce me, I stopped taking the antidepressant medication I had been on for the past twelve months. *After all, what was the use? It's over.* I had no idea that, as traumatizing as his betrayal and ambivalence were, his choice to abandon and divorce me against my wishes pushed me over the edge.

And that's when my nightmares shifted from occasional to every night without fail. I woke up sobbing hysterically, usually around 2 a.m., my heart pounding after enduring some horrid dream about "them"—his disdainful looks at me, the sweet tone in his voice when I overheard him talking to her, imagining them saying, "I love you" to one another, and laughing about me behind my back. I even dreamed of him trying to kill me.

Most of the time, I was so distraught that I couldn't go back to sleep. Instead, I typically sobbed into my pillow for hours until daylight, called my clients in the morning, and canceled my workday. The stress aged me ten years.

As bad as my nights were, the days bore their own torment. For example, I remember a new client, a pastor's wife, who shared her secret fear that her husband was involved with someone else. Triggered, I started trembling. Her story was too close to home. Her face fell when I returned her money and referred her to someone else. I felt terrible that I couldn't fully explain why I couldn't take her case.

I remember driving when a sudden flashback startled me out of nowhere. The vision was usually a composite of some unbidden, painful memories: his cold facial expressions toward me, the glow on his face when he placed bets with her over the World Series by phone, her soft voice and sexy laugh, and him brooding over the piano, wistfully playing romantic music, wishing he were with her. Such images flashed across the screen of my mind with a fair amount of frequency for nearly three years.

I had to deal with "triggers"—physical reactions to reminders of him, her, their affair, our lovely waterfront home, shared friends, and information through my kids—all painful associations of my former life. I steered clear of specific places and people who reminded me of him or their affair. I avoided driving by her house or going to Fred Meyer, knowing that was where she shopped for groceries. I turned down wedding invites and changed the television channel whenever certain scenes hit too close to home.

These reminders mocked me: "You weren't lovable enough." "That attractive NFL sports announcer looks and sounds just like her. No wonder he preferred her over you!" "See that devoted couple sitting closely together at church? That used to be the two of you." I noticed disparaging messages everywhere: *You are a discarded, undesirable relic, likely to die a lonely old lady.*

And oh, the obsessing. I had missed so many signs of their involvement. Perhaps if I had figured it out earlier, I might have been able to stop the affair before it gained so much traction. I kept replaying the details, examining them from every angle, desperately trying to piece together the clues I had somehow overlooked.

My blood boiled at the memory of his sneaking around, the alibis that didn't add up, and the shame I felt over some of my reactions. I replayed our past conversations endlessly, searching for missed signs and questioning how I had allowed myself to be so deceived. What could I have done differently? What might have changed the outcome? I filled thousands of journal pages, desperately trying to piece together the puzzle.

Although I started meeting alone with the clinical psychologist, Dr. Tim, neither of us realized that my rumination, nightmares, fear, rage, tormented mind, hypervigilance, flashbacks, and avoidance were not merely symptoms of Generalized Anxiety. In fact, I was experiencing classic signs of Post-Traumatic Stress Disorder.

As a marriage therapist in 1999, I was unaware of the emerging literature supporting a PTSD diagnosis for betrayed spouses and those suffering from abandonment trauma. I understood that post-war veterans, rape victims, and individuals involved in sudden car accidents could develop PTSD. But Betrandoned spouses?

A Brief History of PTSD

During and immediately after the Civil War, experts labeled the disorder in post-war soldiers as "Hysterical Neurosis." After World War I, it was referred to as "Shell Shock." Following World War II, the psychiatric condition was named "Acute Situational Maladjustment." In 1952, when the first DSM manual for mental health professionals was published, it was termed "Gross Stress Reaction," attributed to combat or civilian catastrophes—all with negative and shaming descriptions.

After the Vietnam War, a new label appeared: Post-Vietnam Syndrome. Eventually, psychologists settled on the term Post-Traumatic Stress Disorder.

I remember a friend from the 1980s whose extended family vacationed in Hawaii. She reported that her son-in-law hid in their condo the entire time. He refused to go outside and join them at the pool or the beach with everyone else. The reason? The tropical foliage triggered panic, reminding him of his deployment to Vietnam during the war.

Beyond the fallout of combat, experts began to recognize similar maladaptive reactions in those who had endured other types of trauma, such as abuse. This led to the introduction of terms like "Abused Child Syndrome" and "Battered Women Syndrome."[2]

Intimate betrayal can be profoundly shattering, leading many to experience dysregulating symptoms similar to those of war veterans, rape survivors, and other crime victims. Over time, the psychiatric community has recognized intimate betrayal as a legitimate cause of PTSD.

What is PTSD?

Post-Traumatic Stress Disorder can arise when we are overwhelmed by a shocking or unbearable event that threatens our sense of safety, leaving us feeling helpless to act. The trauma intensifies when the threat originates from someone we depend on and trust.

We are wired for self-protection. When unexpected danger arises, our brains release stress hormones like cortisol and adrenaline, fueling our "fight or flight" response. If neither option is feasible, we may freeze—our body's way of playing dead, hoping that the threat will pass.

However, when the danger persists without relief, these stress hormones continue firing, keeping our systems in overdrive. This prolonged survival mode diminishes our ability to engage our rational minds, making it increasingly difficult to process emotions, make decisions, and cope effectively.

Dr. Jill Manning, a betrayal trauma specialist, distinguishes betrayal trauma from other kinds of fear-based traumas:

> Betrayal trauma occurs when someone we depend on for survival, or are significantly attached to, violates our trust in a critical way. Although betrayal trauma shares many of the same psychological, physiological, and neurological symptoms associated with fear-based traumas, it is distinct in two important ways:
>
> (1) The perpetrator is in close relationship with the victim:
>
> Perpetrators of betrayal traumas are in close relationship with the victim, and therefore the violation of trust is experienced as a deeply personalized (versus random) offense. Due to the personalized nature of the betrayal, betrayal trauma can be more destabilizing to one's social schema than a strictly fear-based trauma. Research has also shown betrayal trauma to be associated with more physical illness, anxiety, dissociation, and depression than traumas low in betrayal [also validated by Jennifer Freyd's research].
>
> (2) High risk of reoccurrence:
>
> Due to the close and interconnected relationship between the perpetrator and the victim, it can be difficult to confront or sever ties with the perpetrator. As a result, victims may feel trapped and remain in the relationship out of necessity, thereby making the risk of future reoccurrence of betrayal trauma higher than with random or accidental traumas.

Thus, she concludes,

> A betrayed spouse ... typically shares a life, home, children, extended family, and finances with the perpetrator. These life ties make extrication infinitely more complex and prolonged—even if the victim chooses to divorce the perpetrator.[3]

Betrandonment: A Life-Altering Experience

We marry those we love and who we believe love us. We begin our new lives together with a foundation of trust. Initially, as we connect, our brains are flooded with endorphins, which draw us together. As we settle into married life, these neurohormones are then reduced by an increase in oxytocin, often called the "cuddle hormone"—the same bonding hormone released when a mother nurses her baby. We form what we believe to be a safe, private attachment with our spouses and expect to remain married for life.

So, when the first Discovery Day occurs (also known as "D-Day," which is not usually the entire story), our minds are blown to discover our beloved has violated our agreed-upon romantic or sexual exclusivity. Our secure attachment has been breached. It seems surreal.

I've known spouses so shocked by their partner's unfaithfulness that their bodies immediately reacted in extreme ways. Some began vomiting, while others lost their hair—either in chunks or entirely—within a short period. One woman shared the deep discouragement she felt watching strands of her hair disappear down the shower drain. Many lost their appetite and shed weight involuntarily.

Some hurled their phones across the room or smashed their wedding photos in a fit of rage. Others collapsed onto the floor, screaming in anguish. Still, others—like me—began to shake uncontrollably, overtaken by the relentless symptoms of post-traumatic distress.

Author Vaneetha Risner describes her first response to discovering her husband's betrayal,

> I grabbed the counter to stop myself from falling onto the hardwood floor. The ground beneath me seemed to be swaying uncontrollably. I lurched to a barstool and sat, waiting for my racing heart to calm down.[4]

> When you learn that his or her heart has turned away from you enough to leave, it can feel as if your entire world has caved in.

The initial discovery of unfaithfulness by your beloved spouse is traumatic enough. However, when you learn that his or her heart has turned away from you enough to leave, it can feel as if your entire world has caved in. Such emotional upheaval can seem life-threatening and lead to high-stress reactions.

Romantic betrayal ruptures our marriages, erodes our attachments, and threatens our stability on many levels: emotionally, physically, financially, and psychologically. It shatters our closest family and social connections, leaving us exposed and vulnerable. The sense of safety and stability we once relied on crumbles. Intimate betrayal not only wounds the heart—it undermines our ability to trust our own judgment and perceptions. In some cases, it even shakes the very foundation of our faith, making us question God's presence and care amid our pain.

Betrayal Trauma

Separated and in the lead-up to my unwanted divorce, I scoured the internet for books and blogs to see if anyone else suffered the way I did. I found a few online articles and some books that provided helpful information on trauma. Yet, in the late 1990s, materials linking PTSD with intimate betrayal were just beginning to emerge, primarily due to the explosion of internet pornography and its devastating effect on marriages. Several organizations that sought to help the sexually addicted began providing materials and support groups for their betrayed spouses.

However, in the early days, support and treatment for betrayed spouses adhered to the "addiction" model used for families of alcoholics. Instead of recognizing the true impact of betrayal trauma on the innocent spouse, professionals burdened the recovering faithful partner with labels such as "co-dependent" and "co-addict," which led to the formation of "COSA" (Codependents of Sex Addicts) groups across the United States. This inadequate labeling portrayed the spouse as enabling their unfaithful partners, similar to the dynamics observed among family members in an alcoholic household.

The difference? Most betrayed spouses are unaware of what is happening behind their backs. Unlike alcohol addiction, which is obvious to sober family members, much of the thrill of an affair or sexual compulsion for the strayer lies in its secrecy. The wayward become experts at concealing the truth from their trusting partners. This raises the question, "How could their partners co-dependently enable secret behaviors outside their awareness?"

In 2003, Dr. Shirley Glass noted the shocked responses of the betrayed upon discovery:

> The reactions of the betrayed spouse resemble the post-traumatic stress symptoms of the victims of catastrophic events. Common reactions to the loss of innocence and shattered assumptions include obsessively pondering the details of the affair; continuously watching for further signs of betrayal; and physiological hyperarousal, flashbacks, and intrusive images.[5]

Fortunately, the counseling community is now recognizing the assaultive impact of partner betrayal and gradually correcting the "co-dependent" misnomer for partners. Similar to the shift from "Hysterical Neurosis" in the Civil War era to "Post-Traumatic Stress Disorder" after the Vietnam War, professionals have developed more accurate terms than "co-dependent" to explain the desperate reactions, flashbacks, hyper-anxiety, nightmares, and other symptoms exhibited by wounded spouses.

Recent authors and researchers have recognized that romantic betrayal can have profound psychological effects, often mirroring the symptoms of PTSD. While some experts fully support the PTSD diagnosis, others prefer more nuanced terms like Betrayal Trauma, Relationship PTSD, Betrayal Violence, Post-Infidelity Stress Disorder, or Post-Betrayal Trauma to capture the unique emotional and psychological fallout of intimate deception. Regardless of the terminology, the consensus remains: the impact is deep, disruptive, and deserves serious attention.

Trauma Bonds

During our Post-Affair Divorce, when I still hadn't recognized my symptoms as signs of PTSD, I searched bookstores for answers. As awful as James's romantic betrayal was, I could not comprehend how my husband could fall out of love with me and change his values to the point that he would choose to walk away. His decision to divorce me against my will felt even more calamitous to me than his unfaithfulness. Being torn away from my husband *by* my husband leveled me. I needed more information to explain how fractured I felt. Consequently, I continued my research.

I found initial help when I discovered Patrick Carnes' book, *The Betrayal Bond*. It helped explain why I was still so traumatically attached to someone who no longer loved me. He describes how humans can sometimes develop inappropriate bonds with those who threaten or abuse them. People may form trauma bonds with a hostage taker, an abuser, or a remorseless, rejecting spouse. Dr. Carnes defines this condition: "Trauma bonds are the dysfunctional attachments that occur in the presence of danger, shame, or exploitation."[6]

Danger? Shame? Exploitation? Do these feelings sound familiar to you? During our marital crisis, I felt as though my very life was in danger, as if my husband was dangling me over the side of a ship at sea while he debated whether to let go. As a woman scorned, I felt shame for my inability to recapture his love. It seemed he exploited my trust by secretly engaging in an affair, tormenting me with his ambivalence, assuming that if he changed his mind, I would accept him back. In my frozen state, I was at his unjust mercy.

I believe the abusive impact of unfaithful rejection can make us grip our spouses (or our memory of them) for dear life. Like a hand locked onto a live wire, we feel powerless to let go, even as currents of pain pulse through us. In my case, the fear of losing him magnified my attachment to him, which elevated his importance to me beyond the norm. My feelings of rejection-shame fooled me into thinking I was nothing without him.

Are you holding onto an untrustworthy, straying spouse? Are you hoping for reconciliation despite multiple red flags, your gut instincts, common sense, and the advice of friends and family? Do you still yearn for your partner to wake up and come running back to you, even though he or she has left, moved in with another lover, or treated you with contempt? Dr. Carnes' book provides inventories for betrayal-bond sufferers to assess how many signs of PTSD they are exhibiting. Untangling this kind of unhealthy attachment requires a form of deprogramming, much like that needed for those who escape a cult.

Abandonment Trauma

Not only does intimate betrayal sometimes trigger signs of PTSD, I also learned that spousal abandonment can cause similar symptoms. When a beloved spouse changes from loving to heartless, it's a shockwave to the system. For me, the jolt from the sudden loss of my husband's affection was an agonizing source of traumatic grief. Even though neither my two therapists nor I had yet identified my full-blown PTSD, I kept searching for resources to make sense of my bizarre emotions and physical symptoms. In the process, I discovered two invaluable sources that confirmed the deeply traumatic nature of partner heartbreak.

In one book, *The Love Trauma Syndrome*, psychiatrist Dr. Richard Rosse discusses a variety of relationship ruptures that can cause trauma symptoms in the brokenhearted:

> A love trauma occurs when there is a perceived threat to a desired romantic relationship. The stronger the desire for the relationship to last, the more severe the love trauma may be. Additionally, the more "in love" someone feels, the greater the risk of developing Love Trauma Syndrome if the relationship ends.[7]

Dr. Rosse describes the signs of what he calls "The Love Trauma Syndrome."[8] My heart raced as I noticed these "signs" mirrored the symptoms I was experiencing. Furthermore, they aligned with the symptoms of PTSD. Wow. Perhaps this was my problem. I wasn't overreacting after all.

I found Susan Anderson's book, *The Journey from Abandonment to Healing*, a validating source of insight for me in my recovery process. I highlighted nearly every page. Here, she describes what she calls the "Post-Traumatic Stress Disorder of Abandonment":

> During the shattering stage, abandonment survivors experience many of the same symptoms as victims of other types of trauma, such as rape or physical attack. The problem is that abandonment survivors are not often recognized as such.[9]

I heard one simple definition of PTSD at a conference: "A natural reaction to an unnatural experience." We were designed for secure attachment, not for life-altering ruptures to our primary bond.

Evolutionary biologists believe that fundamental attachments have a preservation role in nature and developed among humans to ensure the survival of our species. When a spouse or parent abandons us, it evokes visceral terror within us. In the natural world, danger lurks when we are left alone to fend for ourselves.

God designed us to bond with a parent and, later, with a life partner as a protective mechanism. Human beings are hard-wired for a safe primary connection—a linked teammate with whom to fend off the potential perils of life in a fallen world. We feel grounded when our spouse provides a safe home base from which to function. It's all about survival and creating a protective family unit for raising the next generation.

When our closest attachment is threatened, our bodies release stress hormones that trigger the fight, flight, or freeze response. In those moments, our logical thinking shuts down—explaining why people often react in desperate or irrational ways when they first discover a partner's betrayal. Because betrayal feels shocking and threatens the loss of what is most important to us, our nervous system automatically goes into self-protection mode. If those stress hormones keep firing—through triggers, flashbacks, or nightmares—the body begins to act as if the danger never ended, and the symptoms can become long-lasting.

Once I understood this dynamic, that it was normal to feel greatly threatened by spousal abandonment, it helped me feel less crazy for the way it jolted me off my foundations.

Overt and Covert Abandonment

Traumatic partner rejection can manifest in both overt and covert ways. Overt desertion occurs when a spouse openly leaves the marriage and files for divorce. In contrast, covert abandonment can be equally painful. This situation arises when a disaffected partner withdraws emotionally, disengages from the relationship during or after infidelity, remains physically present in the home, or lives separately without initiating a legal divorce.

Why would a disengaged partner choose to stay married? Sometimes, they worry about what others might think of them if they left. Alternatively, they may want to avoid appearing as the "bad guy" by filing for divorce. Some people fear the financial fallout of dividing hard-earned assets. Others want to continue their sex addictions or affairs, selfishly expecting their partners to tolerate their shenanigans. Or they believe they can continue to lie and hide these offensive activities.

Spouses with narcissistic tendencies may resist losing control over their vulnerable partners; therefore, they employ mind games, mixed messages, and other manipulative tactics to maintain their dominance despite lacking exclusive commitment to the marriage.

Still, other wayward spouses refuse to do the hard work of repair, expect their hurt partners to "get over it," show no interest in getting outside help, and make little effort to make amends with their devastated family members. They may be physically present, but emotionally, they are absent.

That is often because the affair or addiction has changed them. They have detached from their life partners and lack the motivation to seek the emotional, relational, and spiritual renewal necessary to recapture their first love and reverse the effects of their destructive ways. Their bodies may be in the home, but their hearts are not. They have insidiously abandoned their faithful spouses.

Living with unfaithful neglect often compels the injured spouse to file for divorce by default, as someone must break the destructive stalemate—forcing the spouse who most wants to salvage the marriage to face the reality that the relationship is irretrievably broken. Filing for divorce does not necessarily mean the betrayed spouse wants to end the marriage; it simply means they recognize that they can't save it alone.

Most of us feel doubly traumatized when our spouses betray us romantically and then either overtly or covertly reject us by not fighting for our marriages. We feel ashamed and humiliated when they discard us as if we meant nothing to them.

Identifying our injuries, recognizing our symptoms, and understanding their corresponding diagnoses are essential for recovery. For those of us who develop PTSD symptoms after betrayal and abandonment, healing begins with having our experiences accurately named and validated. It's important to know that interpersonal trauma is a real and expected response to such profound relational wounds. There is comfort in realizing that PTSD symptoms in these cases are not unusual—they align with established research on betrayal trauma, trauma bonding, attachment wounds, and abandonment trauma.

While not everyone experiences full-blown Post-Traumatic Stress Disorder after the calamity of partner betrayal and rejection, I've met and spoken with many who do. There wasn't much information available 25 years ago when I went through my own experience. Thankfully, today, numerous articles, books, and videos explore interpersonal trauma in greater depth than I can cover in two chapters. [10]

In **Appendix A**, I've included a list of the symptoms of Post-Traumatic Stress Disorder, adapted from the DSM-5, for Betrandoned spouses. Review this list and check the boxes next to the symptoms you can relate to. The more boxes you check, the more significant your current or recent degree of Post-Traumatic Stress. If your symptoms are current, I encourage you to consult a trauma-informed therapist to confirm your diagnosis and seek help. More information about this will be provided in the next chapter.

Have you been traumatized by the reverberations of betrayal? Did he or she further compound the affront of unfaithfulness by walking away, literally or figuratively? Are you wondering what to do?

David, fleeing for his life from his betraying friend and rebellious son, suffering many PTSD-like symptoms, ends Psalm 55 with,

> "Give your burdens to the Lord, and he will take care of you. He will not permit the godly to slip and fall" (Psalm 55:22).

The fact that you are reading this book tells me something important: You're hoping—perhaps even aching—for God to come through for you. The Lord uses many avenues to bring healing to our hearts: the truth of his Word, the support of safe and caring friends, the guidance of skilled professionals, and, above all, his steadfast love.

As overwhelming as our circumstances may be, it is often the *meaning* we attach to the betrayal and rejection that causes the deepest harm. The losses themselves are shattering—but when the one we loved and trusted wounds us so profoundly, it fractures our sense of worth, identity, purpose, and safety. We begin to question everything: our value, our judgment, even our place in the world.

Who but the Lord can transform the devastating messages of betrayal and abandonment into something redemptive? Only he can speak healing truth into our shattered places and remind us of who we are in Christ. In the next chapter, we'll explore tools to begin healing the trauma—body, mind, and soul.

Chapter 4

Healing The Trauma

*Don't be afraid, for I am with you. Do not be dismayed, for I am your God.
I will strengthen you. I will help you. I will uphold you
with my victorious right hand.
~Isaiah 41:10*

My father picked me up after school from my junior high musical practice. The longer he drove, the more I could tell that he was drunk ... again. As he sped past our usual freeway exit, I realized he didn't remember the way home. I had to direct him to an exit in the next town and help him navigate a detour back toward our house. Cars honked at us as he swerved and knocked over a sign. He somehow managed to reach the long descent on the Bellevue-Redmond Road. About halfway down the hill, one eye twitching, he began to veer off the road. Now I was really scared. When the car hit the graveled shoulder, I couldn't help but notice the steep drop-off to our right and the telephone pole in front of us. Terrified, I reflexively grabbed the steering wheel, jerked left, and put our wheels back on asphalt again.

Rather than being grateful for my intervention, he sneered, "Oh, you think you're so smart? YOU drive!" and took his hands off the wheel. Shaking, aged thirteen and having never driven before, I held the steering wheel from the passenger's side the rest of the way down the hill.

When we arrived home, I asked my mother, "Why did you send him to get me!?" and headed straight to my bedroom. I threw myself onto my bed, trembling for the next hour. *My dad, who is supposed to protect me, could have killed me!*

For years, I had nightmares of our car careening off a cliff, rolling endlessly before crashing at the bottom. Trapped in the wreckage, I'd see emergency lights flashing above and wonder if I was dying—only to wake up with my heart pounding, relieved to be alive.

These were the roots of my post-traumatic stress that fully bloomed when I lost the heart of my husband. James disappeared emotionally under the influence of a forbidden affair, and just like with my father, I felt powerless to stop it. My husband was careening our family down a steep road, on the verge of going over a cliff. When I made various efforts to put us back on track, he shamed me for scrambling to save our marriage.

What Increases Our Chances of Developing PTSD?

During our marriage crisis, my unnamed PTSD symptoms were more intense and enduring than those I experienced as a child—yet they felt eerily familiar. Researchers have found that while any severe trauma can trigger PTSD, certain factors, such as a history of early trauma, can increase susceptibility. When a new trauma crashes into our lives, it often reawakens past wounds, compounding the distress. To truly heal from the devastation of my marriage, I had to address not only my present pain but also the unresolved injuries of my childhood.

Trauma specialist Joyce E. Smith puts it this way:

> If you've had any prior traumatic experiences, (i.e. been raped, been physically or sexually abused, a car accident, have grown up in an alcoholic household, etc.) each one of those events has its own collection of individual triggers. If there's anything in common with your experience of being betrayed, ALL of those neuro-networks light up together, like one giant nuclear explosion.[1]

In addition to a history of trauma, Dr. Glass and others report that the higher the expectation of trust and commitment, the greater the shock when that trust is broken. I believe people of faith are particularly vulnerable to this, as most of us hold the belief that God established marriage as a sacred, exclusive, lifelong commitment. Strong assumptions about monogamy are significant predictors that an unsuspecting spouse may exhibit symptoms of traumatic stress upon discovering their partner has been unfaithful. In such situations, the impact of betrayal is profound.

As Dr. Glass often says,

> "It's like being married to a four-star general and finding out that he's really a Russian spy."[2]

Another factor contributing to a person's vulnerability to PTSD is simply being female. Statistically, women are more likely than men to develop PTSD due to trauma.

Trauma cuts deepest when inflicted by someone we trust. When an unfaithful spouse not only betrays but also abandons their mate, the devastation is twofold. It's as if they jumped into their Chevy truck, deliberately swerved to hit their partner, and left them bleeding in a ditch. But the worst pain isn't just from the impact—it's from looking through the blood streaming over their eyes and recognizing the driver. This wasn't an accident. The real wound comes from knowing the person who once vowed to protect them chose to strike and leave them broken, with little remorse.

Author Dr. Glenn R. Schiraldi states:

> Of the three categories of stressors...Intentional Human traumas are usually the worst. PTSD symptoms resulting from such stressors are usually more complex, are of longer duration, and are more difficult to treat...Such traumas are typically the most degrading and cause the most shame. They often involve feelings of being stigmatized, marked, or different...Man-made traumas also are most likely to cause people to lose faith and trust in humanity, in love, and in themselves.[3]

The identity and intent of the offender are important. The closer the bond, the deeper the wound, as the victim assigns greater significance to the betrayal. His point is that when the source of the trauma is intentionally inflicted by a trusted family member, such as a parent or spouse, you are more likely to develop PTSD symptoms than if such events arise from an act of nature, an accident, or a stranger. If these experiences are repeated and prolonged, the chances of developing complex or chronic trauma increase. (See the chart in **Appendix B** to visualize the progressive effects of various traumas.)

If you are like me, you need to have your traumas validated and know that your symptoms are understandable, given the source and degree of devastation you have endured. We all need assurance that our anxiety, jumpiness, and rage don't mean there is something defective about us. Rather than being an overreaction, our responses reveal that what happened to us profoundly jolted our system and threatened our emotional, physical, or mental survival.

It helps to know we aren't alone—that others have endured similar experiences and that our nervous system's overdrive has a name and an explanation.

To heal, we must not only acknowledge that we have experienced trauma but also recognize that earlier painful experiences in our lives may have intensified our reactions. Making these connections helps us better understand our present triggers.

FACE, TRACE, REPLACE, ERASE

There is a saying I picked up from therapist and author Jan Frank: to heal, we need to **Face, Trace, Replace,** and **Erase** the painful experiences that plague us.[4]

While we can't literally erase our memories of traumatic events, we can connect recent betrayals with earlier traumas and overlay dreadful memories with loving truths. Then, with the added help of connecting these truths with our logical brains, the memory gains proper perspective and fades into the past, stripped of its power to haunt us in real time.

Facing the Trauma

My goal in Chapter 3 was to help you identify your trauma symptoms, validate your experience, and find a name that aligns with your symptoms, whether that is Betrayal Trauma or PTSD. *Facing* your trauma involves identifying the events, feeling your emotions, and naming them accurately.

As Dr. Kathy Nickerson says,

> Betrayal doesn't just "hurt your feelings." It shatters your nervous system, hijacks your sense of reality, and rewires your brain for fear and hypervigilance.[5]

She notes that betrayal activates the brain's threat system. It causes our rational thinking to go offline and activates the same neural pathways as physical pain. Trauma interferes with our brain's ability to properly store memories, so we are fooled into thinking the traumatic event is happening now. This causes our brain to become stuck, replaying these events in repetitive loops, as it tries to restore our worldview.

Facing what you've been through means no more minimizing your feelings or putting yourself down for being overwhelmed by the agony of your spouse's betrayal. No more pretending it was no big deal or that you shouldn't feel so upset. No more feeling foolish for your panicked reactions. No more blaming yourself for your partner's betrayal and rejection. No more guilting yourself into forgiving prematurely.

You aren't crazy. As my friend "Elizabeth" always says, "It *is* as bad as it feels!" Writing about how your partner's betrayals, lies, and ultimate rejection impacted you can be helpful. Name the insults, the wrongs, and the true nature of the offenses. Then, feel the agony, the shame, and the rage. Let it out. Weep, scream, and stomp your feet.

Recognize the destructive effect these had on your self-esteem, your trembling body, your difficulty functioning, your low mood, your compromised health, and your insecurity. Once you acknowledge your feelings to yourself, express them to God, write them down furiously in your journal, and share them aloud with a trusted friend or therapist.

Tracing Recent Traumas to Earlier Ones

After admitting how betrayal and rejection have harmed us and expressing our feelings about these unfortunate events, the next step in healing is to *trace* our reactions to earlier, similar feelings back to their roots. Recent wounds from spousal mistreatment often awaken old, hidden injuries. Ed Smith of Transformation Ministries refers to these derisive messages as "echoes" from our past. He explains that our pain stems from "lie-based beliefs" associated with past hurts—beliefs that must be replaced with God's truth for proper healing.

In sharing my story of growing up in an alcoholic home, I hope you see how prior trauma in our lives contributes to our vulnerability to PTSD. My husband's betrayal and abandonment seemed to confirm similar mistaken beliefs, such as "I'm unlovable" and "I'm not worthy of protection," that I took away from my unsafe, drunken father. These submerged beliefs surfaced when my marriage was threatened. *Tracing* our recent wounds to earlier ones helps us recalibrate our faulty thinking and gives us more grace for ourselves.

Replacing the Lies

My nightmares and heightened reactivity began the moment I sensed my husband was seriously contemplating leaving me. I lived in constant terror that his infatuation with the other woman had already stolen his heart—permanently. After our third "tough love" separation, I was emotionally unraveling but still clinging to the hope that he might come to his senses. Then, through a friend, I learned he was planning to file for divorce. In that moment, all remaining hope drained from me. My fight to save our marriage was over.

As I mentioned before, I stopped taking my antidepressant medication, which only caused my PTSD symptoms to worsen. Nightmares awakened me every night without fail. I sobbed uncontrollably for hours, unable to fall back asleep. I had to reduce my work hours, which affected my financial situation. Even after our two-year ordeal and the finalization of our divorce, I still shook constantly, suffered from nightmares and flashbacks, and frequently misplaced items like my keys, wallet, and car.

I worried that I was wearing out my friends, so I tried "talk therapy" for a couple of years. Paying a professional provided me with a much-needed outlet for processing my pain without feeling the need to edit what I was saying. While I found this therapy emotionally supportive, it had little impact on alleviating my distressing symptoms.

What I didn't realize was that trauma resides in a part of the brain isolated from our capacity to reach it through talking about it alone. Dr. van der Kolk says, "Traumatized people suffer speechless terror."[6] That is, a sensation that defies words.

And, as Dr. Florence Williams learned through her experience,

> "Healing trauma is complicated. Emotions reside in parts of the brain not related to linear thinking. Simply talking about traumatic memories [by itself] doesn't work" (brackets mine).[7]

My Christian friends encouraged me to engage in spiritual warfare and rebuke Satan for the way I felt harassed by my frequent, terrifying nightmares. I was willing to do so and prayed against Satan's attacks. I pleaded with God for deliverance from my disturbing flashbacks and frightening dreams, but nothing changed at that time.

In the meantime, I found my greatest comfort in Scripture. While I had studied the Bible for many years, during my crisis, the words of God became like diamonds to me. I needed to know that even if my husband didn't love me anymore, the Lord still did. Several verses, although familiar, brought me a fresh degree of solace:

"I will never leave you or forsake you" (Hebrews 13:5).

"Nothing can separate us from the love of God" (Romans 8:38–39).

I desperately needed the assurance that although my husband had left me, God never would. While the lure of forbidden fruit pulled my husband's heart away, I found comfort in knowing that no power, no creature, and no force on earth—including a faithless spouse—could separate me from God's love.

Despite the intellectual consolation these promises provided, I still needed God's truth to penetrate me on a deeper level, to replace the lies I believed about my worth, lovability, and identity.

For a long time, I believed the only solution to my torment was for my distant husband to do an about-face and return to the genuinely remorseful and empathetic person I had known in years past. I yearned for him to lovingly take me back into his arms, weep with me, whisper words of comfort, and recommit to our marriage. I longed to matter to him again. I had seen this occur in the couples I had worked with. Sadly, although I was effective in helping others reconcile after infidelity, that did not happen in my case.

Even though God wasn't answering my pleas to redeem my *marriage*, I needed evidence the Lord still planned to redeem my *life*. Unbeknownst to me, help was on the way.

One Way to *Replace* the Lies: Healing Prayer Therapy

More than a year after our divorce was finalized, I sought the help of a therapist, Terry Bell, who had been using a new kind of prayer therapy in his work with clients called "Theophostic Prayer."[8] He encouraged me to invite a girlfriend to join me for support during our extended 90-minute sessions.

During our initial meeting, he asked me to close my eyes and allow my mind to float back to a particularly painful experience. The first one that came to mind was the night my husband sat across from me at our kitchen table, saying he didn't love me anymore, claiming his change of heart wasn't about *her*—it was about our marriage.

I briefly described the scene to Terry. Then he asked if I could "see" where Jesus was during that moment. He assured me it would be okay if I couldn't. With my eyes closed, he encouraged me to open myself to the Holy Spirit to reveal anything—the Lord's thoughts, voice, or presence.

Instantly, I could "see" Jesus sitting at the end of the table between us. Then Terry asked, "Do you see Jesus doing anything?" I had raised two boys who always left their bundled socks lying around-on the floor, on the couch, or anywhere they found convenient. Only the Lord would have known that about me. So, when I saw Jesus pick up a wadded sock and stick it in my husband's mouth, I couldn't help but laugh. In fact, I kept laughing, and a sense of relief washed over me. It was as if Jesus was saying, "Put a sock in it, James!"

This picture comforted me. I had held James in such high regard that I worried his rejection-filled words might also reflect God's sentiments. Yet this revelation showed me that Jesus saw the truth and didn't endorse his rationalizations for his affair. In one powerful act, God countered James's distorted statements with a vision of Christ's truth, dispelling the "embedded lies" (as Ed Smith calls them) tied to that dreaded night. James's damaging excuses no longer held credibility with me. They lost their power.

I only needed three more 90-minute sessions with Terry. He helped me trace my recent traumas back to earlier ones I'd experienced growing up. My experiences with my addicted father bore similarities to the terror, shame, and powerlessness I'd felt over my husband's affair and abandonment. Terry helped me connect the dots between how I felt about my husband's threatening romantic compulsion and the message I took away from my father's out-of-control alcoholism. He gently supported me as I mentally revisited several traumatic incidents and invited Jesus into pivotal traumatic incidents.

By revisiting key traumatic memories, both past and present, with Jesus' comforting presence, my distorted interpretations melted away. As a result, my nightmares vanished for good. I stopped shaking and began sleeping through the night. No more flashbacks. No more hypervigilance. No more need for me to turn clients away who were suffering from spousal unfaithfulness because they innocently triggered my symptoms. I was amazed.

What the Lord accomplished in four 90-minute sessions of envisioning prayer surpassed the benefits of two-plus years of talk therapy. When I allowed the Holy Spirit access to the wordless part of my brain, he instilled new perspectives from God's vantage point, which changed the *meaning* I attached to certain painful events. The Lord's perspective and comfort became more real to me than the terror and shame I associated with the traumas I experienced both as a kid and as an adult.

When the Lord *Replaced* my painful memories with a visual representation of Christ's perspective, the lies faded into the background as his loving presence took center stage. Knowing the truth intellectually wasn't enough—I needed him to overlay my anguish with reflections of his heart and metaphors of his truth for real healing to take place.

What about you? Did you have terrifying, threatening, or abusive experiences growing up? Did some of the tumultuous emotions and recriminations during your marital crisis feel familiar to you? Could they be related to previously unhealed echoes from your past?

I realize that my experience of only needing four extended sessions to ameliorate my symptoms of PTSD is rare. Looking back, I suspect that the talk therapy, while not effective in relieving my PTSD symptoms, provided the emotional support I needed to help me *Face* and identify the depth of my pain.

I also think my efforts to grieve loudly, journal with fervor, wrestle with God in prayer, and steep myself in Scripture tilled the ground of my beat-up heart and set the stage for me to allow Jesus to join me in my traumatic experiences and plant healing truths in their place.

When Jesus tells us to "seek," "ask," and "knock," the literal meaning in Greek is for us to "keep on seeking," "keep on asking," and "keep on knocking."

Similarly, I encourage you not to give up. Pray like crazy and write down your feelings with abandon. Keep seeking the Lord for answers and for the resources you need.

If your first counselor isn't as effective as you'd like, keep searching until you find a Christian, trauma-informed therapist, spiritual director, or Betrayal-Trauma counselor or coach grounded in the Word of God—someone you can trust and who feels like a good fit. I hope that sharing my story of how the Lord healed me from my daunting symptoms encourages you to seek creative therapy for your own healing journey.

When we've suffered trauma, we must engage the right side of our brains—where fragmented, painful memories are stored—through non-verbal means such as imagery, visualization, music, sensory input, or targeted body movements. These exercises open the way for healing truths to replace distorted, negative beliefs.

With therapeutic guidance, new neural pathways form, linking traumatic memories to the rational, sequential part of the brain where wisdom, perspective, and self-control reside. As this integration occurs, the body begins to relax, recognizing that the danger is no longer present. The *sting* of the memory has been **Erased.**

Summarizing Face, Trace, Replace, and Erase:

The best healing occurs when we first **Face** the events that injured us, which includes naming the feelings we felt at the time. Then, we need to **Trace** these trauma-induced feelings to earlier, similar experiences when we felt comparable emotions and adopted mistaken beliefs to make our original wounds seem tolerable at the time.

A well-trained therapist can help us **Replace** the negative beliefs we adopted as children that seeped into our current injuries. This is best achieved by having a "corrective emotional experience," such as envisioning a nurturing parent, our adult selves, or Jesus entering and disrupting the shameful meaning of an early traumatic event. When we sense this person's love, acceptance, or empathy toward us, our unfortunate situation no longer holds the harmful power it once did.

Everything transforms when we allow the Holy Spirit to use our sanctified imaginations to replace the lies we believe about ourselves with what is true, good, and right.

When the Lord reveals spiritual realities to us and implants them visually or auditorily in the memory centers of our brains, the meaning of distressing events is recalibrated. We understand:

- "I didn't deserve this."
- "It wasn't my fault."
- "I am loved."

- "God was with me."
- "The Lord was my witness."
- "I am in a safe place now."

When this happens, the barrage of stress hormones subsides, and the "high alert" button, which kept our nervous systems on overdrive, stops flashing. Once we absorb these assurances, our minds and bodies calm down, knowing we are not in mortal danger. Satan's power is broken, and the negative hit to our self-esteem is removed.

Once a beautiful image, lovely words, or peaceful sensations overlay a particular trauma, we no longer need to defend ourselves against its haunting memory or the ugly meaning we once associated with it. The lies are declawed. The terror is banished. And God's love and peace take center stage. Our minds are renewed to align with what is wholesome and accurate about ourselves. The power of its shameful meaning, is, in essence, **Erased.**

The Scriptural Basis

Have you noticed how often the Lord used stories, metaphors, parables, and symbols in the Bible to convey profound wisdom? He gave people "visions" and spoke to them in various ways. Our master designer knows how our brains and nervous systems work—that we learn best through stories and metaphors that engage our senses.

We need sensory-awakening tools to envision, hear, and sense God's heart concerning our emotional wounds, allowing us to absorb transformative truths that will renew our minds and set us free.

As Christians, we have the unique privilege of knowing the One who "heals the brokenhearted and binds up their wounds" (Psalm 147:3, TAB).

If you carefully read Isaiah 61:1–3, you will see that the coming Messiah was predicted to heal us physically, spiritually, and emotionally. His mission, along with the Good News of the Gospel, was to bind up the brokenhearted, proclaim liberty to the captives, comfort those who mourn, give us beauty instead of ashes (of grief), and provide a garment of praise instead of a spirit of despair. The Lord wants to free us from fear and heal our grief, sorrow, and hopelessness. So, how do we allow him to do that?

Remember, God is With You

The predicted Messiah was to be called "Emmanuel," meaning "God with us" (Isaiah 7:14, Matthew 1:23). Jesus promised his disciples, "I will be with you always" (Matthew 28:20). Since Jesus Christ is "the same yesterday and today and forever" (Hebrews 13:8) and the great "I AM" (Exodus 3:14, John

8:58), we know that God's presence is not limited by time and space. God is what theologians refer to as "omnipresent" (everywhere at once). Thus, we can confidently affirm "he was there" when our shaming or terrifying experiences occurred.

Remember when a fierce army surrounded Elisha and his servant? The servant was terrified. Here is what Elisha said,

> "'Do not be afraid,' Elisha answered, 'for those who are with us are more than those who are with them.' Then Elisha prayed, 'O LORD, please open his eyes that he may see.' And the LORD opened the eyes of the young man, and he saw that the hills were full of horses and chariots of fire all around Elisha" (2 Kings 6:16–17).

When we are tormented or afraid, we need the Lord to "open our eyes" as he opened the eyes of Elisha's servant, to "see" the spiritual realities that stand between us and our enemies. This transcendent truth has the power to change everything. Do you need the Lord to open your eyes to see where he was during your frightening experiences? Here is another example of how the Lord can accomplish this.

The Missionary

I remember praying with a missionary named "Susan," who had endured numerous instances of shame while growing up. One particular experience severely impacted her self-esteem. As a toddler, she played outside with her friends, fully engrossed in the fun, and ignored the urge to pee until she accidentally wet her pants. When she went inside to change, her mother was furious. She strapped a portable potty to Susan and sent her back outside to "teach her a lesson." Susan felt so mortified and ashamed that she hid in the bushes to avoid being seen by her friends.

I suggested that she close her eyes and revisit that painful scene in her mind. Then, I encouraged her to picture her surroundings and allow Jesus to reveal where he was during her humiliating experience. After a minute, I asked her if she could sense where Jesus was. First, she paused. Then, the tears flowed. She whispered, "He's hiding with me in the bushes."

I found myself moved to tears alongside her. This picture comforted her, replaced the isolating stigma with the Lord's comforting presence, and erased the shame she felt during that painful childhood moment.

Isn't that just like the Jesus you know? The One who joins us in our suffering, assuring us that we are not alone—that he is with us in our traumas, cares about our pain, dispels the lies, and removes our shame.

When I work with shame-filled clients who are open to prayer therapy, I have them breathe deeply, close their eyes, and drift back in their minds to a specific, frightening event. Then, I encourage them to allow Jesus to enter their painful memory to show them where he was in that scene.

This gives the Lord room to demonstrate his caring heart toward them. I never know how the Lord will reveal himself, but he always shows up in some gentle, loving way that counters and replaces the shaming message of the threatening incident. This new experience recalibrates the *meaning* of the trauma and nullifies the disgrace caused by an abuser's actions.

I've heard clients report "seeing" Jesus enter the scene of the maltreatment to comfort them. Sometimes, victims sense him sitting beside them in their pain. Other times, he wraps a comforting arm around them. Or he holds them on his lap like a loving parent comforts an injured child. Still, others picture themselves curled up in the palm of his immense, caring hand. Or they see him weep or furrow his brow with a disapproving look toward the offender.

Having a visual experience like this removes the worry that we somehow caused the abuse and dispels the belief that we made a big deal out of nothing. With Christ as our validating witness, he confirms the wrongness of what occurred. It wasn't our fault. He preserved our lives. Knowing Christ "was there" lets us know he cares deeply about our sorrow and wants to console us. God's loving presence causes the condemning, shame-filled message of the painful event to melt away.

Betrayed spouses who feel tainted by their partner's sexual sins benefit from envisioning Christ discreetly washing them in a shower of his tears and wrapping them in a pure white robe. In other instances, layers of shame dissolve when the disgraced spouse "sees" Jesus washing their feet of the grime from their partner's immoral behaviors, just as Christ washed the feet of the disciples of the world's filth.

Such images serve to change the *meaning* that a betrayed person associates with the devaluing mistreatment they received from an unkind parent, caregiver, or spouse. And who better to correct our mistaken interpretations of traumatic incidents than God?

While the Lord wants to heal our wounds from the past, the triggers from Betrandonment often reverberate into future events.

Another Personal Example

Eight years after my divorce, when my youngest son married, I wrote a poem to share at their wedding reception to honor their union. Someone snapped a picture of me reading the poem. When I later saw the photo, I noticed my ex-husband in the background, head down, with a familiar, disdainful smirk on his face. My face flushed at his obvious disapproval.

I cried out to the Lord, "Why does he still look down on me?" In prayer, I "saw" the Lord slip between James and me, a big grin on his face, completely blocking the view of my disaffected former spouse. My tears turned from sorrow to joy when Christ's comforting approval replaced the shame I felt after noticing my ex-husband's look of contempt. Now, when that photo comes to mind, all I see is Jesus.

Such non-condemning, spiritual, and purifying images can replace the degrading imprints left by our offenders. For Christians, one of the most effective ways to eliminate the terrible shame from abuse is to replace the untrue narratives about our worth with truthful images that reflect the beauty of Christ's loving and affirming care.

What About You?

Do you need a similar breakthrough? Are Satan's lies—that you somehow deserved your partner's affair—still haunting you? Do you struggle with feelings of unworthiness, as though your spouse's rejection means you're unlovable and unworthy to be loved by anyone else?

Perhaps you wonder if your feelings of desolation are a sign that God has forsaken you. Or maybe you've begun to distrust yourself, feeling deceived by someone you once trusted. Does your future seem grim, as if it's no longer worth living? After all, does it seem like your torment will never end?

> Just because the Lord didn't prevent your divorce doesn't mean he was indifferent to the harm that came to you and your children.

I understand. I once felt that way, too. Help is truly available, so please don't give up. Just because the Lord didn't prevent your divorce doesn't mean he was indifferent to the harm that came to you and your children. He witnessed everything and desires to bring you the comfort and healing you need.

God is not finished crafting your story to fulfill his purposes. I encourage you to keep asking God to guide you to the right sources of assistance so you can recover and walk more deeply into his calling for your life.

Next Steps

I encourage believers to seek a Christian trauma-informed therapist, spiritual director, or skilled life coach who allows space for the Holy Spirit to reveal Jesus' presence and heart. After all, he is the Wonderful Counselor and Great

Physician who can powerfully "heal the brokenhearted and bind up their wounds" (Psalm 147:3).

I am confident the Lord wants to heal your heart, soul, mind, and body from the damaging impact of Betrayal and Abandonment Trauma. At times, you can pray on your own or with a friend to envision Jesus in the situation where a particular trauma occurred. Other times, we benefit from exercises led by a trained Christian professional who integrates healing prayer with other trauma therapies.

Ask a potential counselor if he or she has special training in some form of Betrayal Trauma. Many more therapies have been developed to treat interpersonal trauma than I knew about two decades ago. (See **Appendix C.**)

Have you ever wondered why your partner's actions hurt you so deeply and made your grief and trauma so intense? Once you examine the engine of the vehicle that nearly killed you, you'll never let yourself—or anyone else—minimize your devastating experience again.

This is exactly what we'll explore in the next chapter.

Chapter 5

Betrayal As Abuse

Deliver my soul, O LORD, from lying lips and a deceitful tongue.
~Psalm 120:2

When I met "Stacy,"[1] she was as emotionally defeated as any client I've ever worked with. With her eyes down, she fidgeted and kept putting her hand to her mouth whenever she said something she thought I'd disbelieve. I wondered where this beautiful, intelligent woman's lack of confidence came from. I understood some of it once I learned more about her family background. But her disconnected, sexually addicted husband, whose invalidation picked up where her family of origin left off, inflicted the worst damage to her self-esteem.

She'd been married for over twenty-six years to a man who had immersed himself in pornography for decades, starting before their marriage. Throughout their life together, he spent hours in front of the computer late into the night, indulging in his habit. She had also caught him lusting after other women at church, flirting with them in front of her, and staring at them with "glistening eyes." His longing gaze toward other women unsettled her, haunted her dreams, and even made her daughter's friends uncomfortable as they could sense his inappropriate interest.

His addiction had so thoroughly hijacked his brain that he was neither mentally nor emotionally present with Stacy or their children. After the youngest one's birth, he showed no sexual interest in her and expressed no affirmation. She lived in excruciating marital isolation. Whenever she gathered enough courage to broach the subject, he lied about his preoccupation with porn, denied his obsession with other women, and dismissed any reason she might feel unloved or rejected.

She tried dragging him to a weekend marriage intensive with a famous Christian sex addiction therapist, but her husband managed to charm him into minimizing his issues. He was an expert at touting religious platitudes.

Stacy's husband quoted lengthy Scripture passages and expounded spiritual-sounding wisdom as a buffer to avoid genuine interaction or emotional intimacy with his wife, children, and friends. He knew how to use biblical language to impress church friends and extended family members, relishing the praise and admiration of others. She recounted several painful instances of how her husband convinced church leaders that she was the one bringing them down as a couple, not the other way around.

This was one of the largest constellations of invalidating people around a betrayed client I had ever witnessed. No one—from the family she grew up in, nor her pastors, friends, and church family—took her reports of her husband's betrayals and gross negligence seriously. They assumed her depression, fatigue, stomach issues, sleeplessness, and anxiety were due to her personal issues. After all, she had no "proof" he had been physically unfaithful with an outside live human being. They told her that she should be more content, loving, and appreciative of him.

The one bright spot for her was that her children knew better. They had lived with him and experienced their father's inattention first-hand—from his bursts of anger to his neglect of family activities due to his secret preoccupation. They had also witnessed his maltreatment of their mother for years on end.

Now that they were young adults, her children watched in horror as Stacy's health deteriorated. She shed weight she couldn't afford to lose and developed a dangerous heart condition. She lost her ability to fend for herself and nearly lost her will to live. Finally, the children got together, kidnapped their demoralized mother, and helped her return to her hometown for respite. They did for her what she lacked the strength to do for herself at the time.

That was when I met Stacy—demeaned, downcast, and broken. Her spouse and social network had so thoroughly dismissed her intuitions that she doubted her own perceptions and constantly second-guessed herself.

Together, we collaborated to uncover the truth and restore her confidence. After attending several groups and conferences for betrayed Christian women, Stacy gradually recognized that she was not crazy. She wasn't overreacting to something trivial. His sexual compulsions and severe emotional neglect were real, damaging, and not mere figments of her imagination.

Over time, we pieced together the mental, emotional, and spiritual abuse she had endured, as well as the resulting trauma. Gradually, she found the courage to file for divorce despite her non-pursuing husband's objections and her church's lack of support. Her journey to psychological health was not linear, but she developed self-compassion and assertiveness. Ultimately, she ceased seeking validation from her lifelong, legalistic friends and discovered a biblically sound yet less stern church.

Thankfully, she still receives the emotional support of her wounded adult children. Considering the environment in which they grew up, I was amazed by their common sense and their ability to see through the religious rigidity they, too, faced. While Stacy has remained steadfast in her faith, all three adult children, disillusioned by their father's religious facade and the church leaders' failure to recognize their mother's abuse, have deconstructed their former Christian beliefs. Yet, fortunately, these young adults remain clear-eyed about the extent of the abuse they and their mother endured during their upbringing—a saving grace for Stacy.

People often think domestic abuse only involves physical harm or rape, but other forms can also inflict severe emotional damage. The worst impact of abuse often comes from the victim's interpretation of the abuse, which can lead to feelings of worthlessness and self-loathing, especially when the abuser is someone they trust and love. This emotional trauma can be deeply scarring, and the victim requires informed support, understanding, and guidance to overcome it.

Interpersonal abuse has many faces besides physical violence. Betrandoned spouses experience partner abuse on many levels: relational, emotional, spiritual, sexual, physical, and psychological. Intimate betrayal is abusive, as is partner desertion. We can't break free of the effects of such abuse until we first name it for what it is.

Once we stop discounting our pain, the maltreatment begins to lose its power over us, and we don't need to replay wounding incidents over and over, trying to figure out why they made us feel so awful. We know why we felt so bad: because it *was* bad.

Partner infidelity and rejection are not like a mere high school breakup (an unfortunate assumption by inexperienced individuals who urge you to "move on"). Marriage is a big deal, hopefully for the positive. And when that bond is broken, the harm is life-altering for the negative.

We enter our marriages believing our partners want the best for us. We assume that we've found our safe haven, the "one" whom we can count on, raise children with, entwine our finances with, and who will stand by us through life's storms. When we are securely attached, at least on our side, we assume that our partner's marital commitment says, "I'm here for you," "You can count on me," and "You matter to me."

But when those assumptions are brutally shattered by infidelity and spousal rejection, the betrayal cuts deep. We lose our safety net, forsaken by the one we believed we could depend on. Intimate betrayal shakes our very foundation, leaving us frightened, shivering, and alone in freezing waters.

I remember writing the following in my journal:

> It is so painful to be violated, wounded, and betrayed by the person I love most in the whole world. It is aggravating to be helpless to stop something that feels so destructive to me. I have no recourse. No advocate. It bears some similarity to date rape—being overpowered, violated, and treated like an object by a person I know and trust—all against my will. My will had no bearing on the outcome. My feelings carried no weight. My worth was smashed without conscience—by the person who knew me best and whom I esteemed above all other people in my life.

When our partners betray us in a deeply intimate way, they harm our trust, security, emotional well-being, and psychological safety. Our assumptions about our marital pasts and future dreams are shattered, leaving us without a secure anchor. I hear Betrandoned spouses use words like "wrecked," "ruined," "devastated," and "discarded" to describe how they feel after spousal infidelity and rejection.

Stephen Stosny, an expert at treating both perpetrators and victims of abuse, defines domestic abuse as "a betrayal of the attachment bond."[2] Stosny explains:

> Attachment bonding first emerged in humans as a survival necessity to ward off predatory threats but evolved over time to provide emotional security, support, value, meaning, and purpose.[3]

From birth to adulthood, humans function best when they have a primary secure attachment for physical and emotional protection. Parents and spouses hold the greatest power to uplift or crush our sense of worth and threaten our safety. When that attachment is threatened, it causes us tremendous distress. Dr. Stosny says,

> Attachment power is unique—only someone you love can make you unlovable. All forms of betrayal result from misuse of the unique power inherent in attachment bonds.

Stosny frames any form of personal abuse, including infidelity, as an act of betrayal, [in that it betrays] "the implicit promise...that the person you *love and trust will care about your wellbeing and never intentionally hurt you* (italics, his)."[4]

As you can see from Stacy's story, her husband violated that implicit promise. His secret sexual betrayals and emotional withdrawal threatened her security, robbed her of support, and stole her sense of value as a beloved partner. And when so few people acknowledged that abuse, her mental, emotional, and physical health deteriorated. The only thing worse than being abused is when no one believes you or validates your pain.

> The only thing worse than being abused is when no one believes you or validates your pain.

If your life partner engaged in infidelity, they violated your rights as a spouse and concealed their actions from you—at least for a time. Sexual betrayal is exactly that: a deceptive, hidden involvement—whether with a habit or a person—that broke their promises of fidelity, carrying grave consequences.

No wonder you emerged from your crisis mentally wounded and emotionally bleeding. It felt like abuse because it *was* abuse. Your partner's betrayal shattered your trust and inflicted deep harm on your psyche.

Here are a few examples of the damaging messages we may receive from unfaithful desertion:

- You are unworthy of protection.
- Your need for personal safety doesn't count.
- Don't resist or complain, or you'll pay for it.
- Ignore your gut instincts.
- My needs are all that matter.
- I'm not attracted to you.
- You don't matter to me.
- You're making a mountain out of a molehill.
- You deserve what I've done.
- In fact, you're at fault.

To be so unloved by our primary attachment person is a penetrating form of domestic abuse. While the bruises may remain invisible to others, the strayer's interpersonal violence injures other parts of a trusting partner's being.

One member of an online betrayed women's group I help moderate responded to another member questioning whether infidelity is abuse:

It's abuse.

Yes. It's literally the very definition: "Abuse is the improper usage or treatment of a thing, often to unfairly or improperly gain benefit." [https://en.wikipedia.org/wiki/Abuse.]

He misused your relationship, your trust, and your body. You did not consent to share your marriage with another woman (be it in person or in heart). He lied to reap the benefits of a marital relationship for himself while secretly gaining from his sexual deviance. He did not get your permission. He treated you unfairly and improperly. He abused you.

My husband had a big problem swallowing that word. He believed that at least he hadn't abused me. He had. When our therapist referred to his behavior as abuse during one of our counseling sessions, my husband was very upset. What put it into perspective for him was this:

I was sexually abused for years. He knew that. He was appalled by that. He had no problem attributing the title of "abuser" to my perpetrator. I told him, "Truthfully, I'd rather relive those years a hundred times than to relive the night of discovery even once."

It's abuse.[5]

As you can see, her husband didn't grasp the abusive nature of his betrayal-injuries to her until she compared the trauma of discovering his affair to earlier sexual abuse in her life, which he *knew* was abusive.

Let's explore the damage in more detail:

Emotionally Abusive

Spousal Betrayal is a direct *assault on our worth* as husbands and wives. When a beloved spouse sneaks around to cavort with a love object (person, habit, or activity), we are violated without fully realizing it. Our unfaithful spouse has manipulated us into believing that any distress in the relationship is our fault, while it is their secret sexual or romantic activities that have decreased their emotional investment in the marriage.

Once discovered, we interpret their infidelity as a sign that our beloved no longer values us—implying that we are unworthy, unattractive, or unlovable in their eyes. We feel personally deceived, demeaned, and insulted. Such unloving actions wound us on a profound emotional level.

And when our spouse follows their unfaithfulness by abandoning us, it's as if they've demoted us from "cherished spouse" to "disdained non-person."

"Love Withdrawal" and "Affection Deprivation" are considered abusive and harmful forms of punishment in parenting. Therefore, it stands to reason that in a marriage, when one partner withdraws their love from the other, the rejected partner perceives this withdrawal as a form of abuse, resulting in significant mental and emotional distress, especially if they are still in love with the partner who abandoned them.

Sexually Abusive

A partner's waywardness harms the couple's sexual relationship in many ways. Infidelity violates our rights to sexual exclusivity with our spouses. Whether we consciously acknowledge it or not, our sexual privacy has been breached. Once discovered, these sexual activities feel like a brutal attack on the innocence of our marriages. It's as if our once-trusted spouse has invited a mortal enemy into the inner sanctum of our bedrooms.

Besides injuring our privacy, sexual betrayal *harms our sexual esteem*. Sometimes, this abuse shows up in the form of sexual neglect. When unfaithful partners put their sexual energies into an outside habit or relationship, they often have little to no interest in sexually connecting with their spouses. Consequently, betrayed spouses feel intense sexual rejection by the involuntary celibacy they didn't sign up for when they got married. This makes the betrayed feel unacceptable, undesirable, and unappealing—a terrible disgrace to their value and identity as sexual beings.

> Besides injuring our privacy, sexual betrayal *harms our sexual esteem*.

On the other hand, a secretly straying spouse may pursue excessive sex with their partner to avoid suspicion or to ease a guilty conscience. Some unfaithful partners escalate their sexual pursuit of the spouse due to a spiraling compulsion, where nothing ever feels like "enough" to soothe their internal conflicts. In other cases, wayward spouses use sex with their mate as an attempt to physically bridge the emotional disconnect caused by their outside involvement, usually to no avail.

At the other end of the spectrum, an innocent spouse may be the one who avoids sex for a couple of reasons. One reason is that they feel "used" when an addict tries to imitate the impersonal, twisted, demanding sex they saw online or experienced with a prostitute. No one wants to feel like an object during vulnerable moments of intimacy.

Another difficulty with enjoying marital sex sometimes occurs in the aftermath of discovery. A betrayed spouse may be so traumatized that they can't participate in sex without envisioning sickening images of the illicit lover in bed with them. Their confidence as an adequate lover may be diminished by comparing themselves to a real or imagined heartthrob. Difficulties with arousal may ensue. This kind of torment requires the help of a trauma-informed therapist and, ideally, a supportive, empathetic spouse.

For all these reasons, betrayed spouses often sense the insincerity behind their unfaithful partners' advances (or lack thereof), which makes them feel undesirable, eroding their sexual self-esteem.

Comparing ourselves to our partner's outside lover or fantasies can foster insecurities about our appearance and sex appeal. Even though we may intellectually understand that outward appearances do not define the deeper chemistry behind affairs, these comparisons are often a source of torment for us after a betrayal.

Relationally Abusive

Infidelity ruptures our marital bond and destroys our previous "safe haven." Sexual betrayal shatters our trust in our partner's loyalty and damages our bond. We can no longer rely on our partners to support and nurture us. Instead, the person who was supposed to shield us from the storms of life has become dangerous to our emotional and mental well-being. And if an impenitent partner trades us in for someone else or an ideal we cannot fulfill, the damage to our relationship is irreparable.

Physically Abusive

Unfaithfulness harms us physically by *overstressing* our body's systems. We become more vulnerable to depression, post-traumatic stress, and/or anxiety. As our bodies suffer from sleeplessness, trembling, racing hearts, and low energy, we may struggle to accomplish our daily tasks. The distress from betrayal wears us down and often makes us susceptible to such illnesses as fibromyalgia, chronic fatigue, irritable bowel syndrome, and even cancer.

Certainly, another way infidelity is physically abusive is that it can expose the faithful spouse to various sexually transmitted infections or even HIV, without their knowledge. In this regard, partners have been "deprived of their right to consent regarding their own physical bodies."[6]

Spiritually Abusive

As in Stacy's case, some straying spouses use spiritual-sounding language, "God-words," and Scripture taken out of context to conceal their illicit sexual activities.[7] This is an *abuse of power* of the highest order. After all, who wants to challenge "God" and the Bible? Spiritual manipulation causes great confusion for spouses who wish to please God and trust their seemingly religious partners. Betrayed believers often become disillusioned about their faith when "God" is used by the wayward as a pretext to justify their betrayals, minimize their wrongs, or assert their innocence.

As seen in Stacy's case, betrayers may use a spiritual façade to deceive those around their innocent spouses, which robs victims of the social validation and spiritual support they need. (I go into further depth about religious excuses and abuse in Chapter 19.)

Psychologically Abusive

The psychological harm of intimate partner sexual betrayal has been well-documented by various researchers, with mental impacts such as suicidal ideation, compulsive self-comparisons with others, "morbid pre-occupation," "mental contamination," lowered self-esteem, anxiety disorders, obsessive-compulsive disorders, post-traumatic stress, panic attacks, and ruptured trust in self, others, and God.[8]

Some betrayed partners even describe a form of "psychological death" resulting from their loss of identity, illustrating a clear division in their lives between the time "before" the discovery and "after" the discovery.[9]

Triggers and flashbacks are common psychological effects post-discovery. Most betrayed spouses are haunted by visions of their partner with someone else. The resulting nightmares and intrusive thoughts often persist for months or even years, especially when the strayer refuses to participate in the healing process.

A strayer's duplicity gives them an unfair advantage over the unsuspecting spouse. Dr. Omar Minwalla refers to this as "integrity abuse."

Let's dive more deeply into the tactics betrayers use to protect themselves in ways that inflict mental injuries on innocent spouses:

Lying (Covert And Overt)

Covert lying involves lying by omission. Initially, most unfaithful people lie by sneakily leaving out important information. They fail to inform their spouses of their whereabouts, who they were with, and what happened. They wrongly believe in the old myth, "What you don't know can't hurt you," while they indulge in practices that harm their marriages.

Reflecting on past events, many of you found that your unfaithful partner conveniently omitted crucial details, such as who they sat next to on a flight to a business conference, or stated that their colleagues left the bar at

10 p.m. without mentioning a specific person who remained. Some of you might have thought your spouse was just playing computer games when, in fact, they were watching pornography or sending love notes to their affair partner. Alternatively, you believed they were having coffee with a business associate, only to later discover they stopped at a hotel for a quick romp on the way home.

Overt lying is a more direct form of deceit. They may insist "nothing" is going on with this other person. As illicit activities progress, the deceiver uses increasingly elaborate and outright lies, such as claiming to have attended a late business meeting while they were actually at their lover's house for the evening. Another example might be stating that a company conference was held in New York when, in fact, they flew to their lover's hometown in Nashville.

Gaslighting (Insidious Deception)

Gaslighting is a psychological weapon that exploits the mental state of the one being deceived.

The term "gaslighting" has become a common part of our modern vernacular. This phenomenon represents a particularly sinister deception that disorients the betrayed. It's a type of lying that deserves its own category. Entire books have been written about the damaging effects of gaslighting. However, I will briefly discuss its relevance to intimate betrayal.

Counselors adopted the term "gaslighting" from the movie "Gaslight." In the 1944 version of the film, actress Ingrid Bergman plays the role of Paula, a niece who inherits the house of her wealthy aunt, murdered ten years earlier. Paula and her new husband, Gregory, return to London in 1880 and move into her deceased aunt's house. The cunning Gregory is up to no good; he wants to find the family jewels. However, to obtain them, he needs to convince his wife that she's losing her mind so he can involuntarily commit her to a mental institution.

He systematically undermines Paula's perceptions by denying her observations. He rearranges objects and pictures from their original locations and accuses her of moving them. In some instances, he claims the items never existed. He accuses her of lying, stealing, and forgetting things, which makes her feel crazy. When he sneaks into the attic and turns on the lights to enhance his search for the jewels, the gas available to feed the lamps in the living space below is reduced.

When Paula hears the noises above and notices the dimming, flickering lights, Gregory dismisses her observations as figments of her imagination. He does this to convince her that she is losing her sanity. He even enlists the maid's cooperation, publicly shames Paula, and spreads rumors to convince others that she is "not well." His goal is to undermine her sanity and have her committed to an asylum so he can hoard the valuable jewels for himself.

Today, when psychologists and authors use the term "gaslighting," they refer to a deceitful person's efforts to undermine their partner's perception of reality to conceal nefarious activities, such as an affair.

GASLIGHTING, AS A VERB, INCLUDES:

a. **Partial disclosures and half-truths** (such as, "Everyone went to Olive Garden after work to grab a bite" when your partner went to Hooters with his or her lover.)

b. **Denying the other person's perceptions** (Such as, "I never said I'd be home by 6:00!" when they actually did say that but want you to question your memory.)

c. **Angry reactions** ("I told you I was at the company Christmas party!! Geez! What's your problem?") A fuming spouse can intimidate you from asking follow-up questions—questions you need to know and have every right to ask.

d. **Counter-blaming** ("If you weren't so controlling," (or) "If you'd dress more nicely, I wouldn't look at her twice!") Such comments may cause a betrayed spouse to blame themselves for the strayer's wrong behaviors.

e. **False accusations** ("You're just jealous!" or "You are so *boring*!"). These are said to make you feel inadequate or like the "bad guy" when the strayer is either projecting his/her motives onto you or trying to reverse the blame to alleviate your suspicions.

f. **Minimizing** ("You're just making a big deal out of nothing," or "Everyone is doing it. What's your problem?" or "He's only a *friend*" when they've already crossed forbidden boundaries, or "We *only* kissed (or fondled or had oral sex). It's not like we committed adultery or anything.") Such dismissals can make your head spin as if your alarm is unfounded.

g. **Deflecting** ("How could you doubt me?" "You're just being paranoid!" or "How do you expect me to come home on time when you *never* clean up the house when you say you're going to?") They do this to get you off-track, so you don't ask further questions.

h. **Attacking** ("You're just being vindictive!") A classic attempt at character assassination to take the heat off the betrayer's activities. It is easier for them to accuse you of being vindictive than to acknowledge your right to object to their wrong behaviors.

i. **Projecting** (Accusing you of doing the very things he or she is doing, such as, "I saw the way that _____ looked at you. I just *know* you're having an affair with our neighbor!") Sometimes this is merely a decoy to distract from their own betrayals. At other times, since strayers are aware of their own untrustworthiness and rationalize that "everyone is unfaithful," they may wrongly accuse you of doing the very things they are doing.

j. **Self-pity** ("I'm such a louse!" or when looking sad, "I keep beating myself up" or "How could you be so mean to me?" when you're only asking for the truth.) The unrepentant are often so self-absorbed that they feel sorrier for themselves, as if they are the victims, rather than for those they are hurting. This robs the betrayed of the empathy they deserve.

k. **Victim-blaming** ("If you weren't so _____, I would never have done this" or "This isn't about my friend at work, it's about our *marriage* [i.e., you]") is an abusive maneuver commonly used by unfaithful people. It can make you wonder if you caused or deserved their violations.

A betrayer's use of gaslighting is a deceptive strategy to protect themselves from exposure and suppress their innocent spouse's legitimate suspicions. By tricking their partners into disregarding any signs of betrayal, strayers can prolong their illicit sexual pursuits without detection or accountability.

Once the faithful spouse learns of the infidelity, a duplicitous betrayer may continue to distort the truth to downplay the seriousness of their offenses or to cast aspersion on their wounded spouses. Explanations like "We only had sex one time" rarely convey the whole story. It usually means many times.

The Harm from Gaslighting

Gaslighting is a cruel attempt at brainwashing and causes psychological and emotional harm to betrayed spouses. This form of abuse interferes with a betrayed partner's God-given, self-protective instincts.

Humans are endowed with what some call our "second brain," commonly known as our gut instincts or intuition. Neuroscientists have discovered that we have 100 million "brain" cells lining our abdomen, known as our enteric nervous system. These cells can quickly sense danger and send warning signals to our upper brains for instant action before our logical minds can make sense of them. This gut-brain system serves as a survival mechanism to alert us to unsafe situations, improve our decision-making speed, and avert threats.[10]

When unfaithful spouses engage in secretive, damaging behaviors, our intuition often senses that something is "off." However, as Dr. Omar Minwalla explains, a strayer's secrecy, gaslighting, and invalidation disrupt the connection between our instincts and logic, making it more challenging to trust ourselves and seek immediate safety.

Security expert and author Gavin de Becker, who grew up in a violent home, studied the signs of danger and how people can protect themselves. His research emphasizes the importance of trusting our intuition—what he calls the "sixth sense"—which serves as our best defense against crime and abuse.[11]

A strayer's deceit causes us to doubt ourselves to the point that we may discount the alarm bells going off inside us. When a defensive betrayer downplays their behavior or turns our questions back on us, we may begin to second-guess our perceptions and withdraw, rather than attend to our gut instincts trying to tell us that something is amiss.

A spouse's denials and lies, combined with their negative reactions, can distort our ability to trust our internal warnings. The fear of retribution or losing approval can suppress our God-given intuition, making it harder to act in our best interests.

Over time, when a spouse is subjected to lying, gaslighting, or defensive reactions, this protective mechanism becomes increasingly ineffective. A betrayer's deception chips away at our ability to distinguish between healthy skepticism and paranoid suspicion while also impairing our capacity to differentiate between legitimate fear and irrational panic.

When an unfaithful partner's fraudulent push-back overrides our body's survival instincts, our mental health deteriorates, leading to emotional, physical, and spiritual suffering, as illustrated in Stacy's story.

If you're like me, you may look back and realize your body was picking up on signals long before you had tangible proof. Your unconscious mind, gut feelings, and even the Holy Spirit may have warned you of an invisible threat. Maybe you had disturbing dreams, unsettling premonitions, or noticed subtle inconsistencies that didn't quite add up. But without solid evidence—or a shred of honesty from your spouse—you likely dismissed those inner nudges as unfounded fear.

Now that you have greater clarity, you likely recognize that your past gut hunches were telling you the truth.

Information Control

Most forms of abuse involve misusing power within the relationship. In cases of infidelity, the primary advantage the betrayer has over the betrayed, apart from the power of their primal bond, is the amount of critical information they are concealing. And information is power.

Deceitful partners hold an unfair advantage by knowing the full extent of their betrayal while keeping their spouse in the dark. This dynamic allows them to control the narrative and evade accountability. The knowledge imbalance deepens the betrayal, leaving the faithful spouse vulnerable to unseen consequences while the unfaithful partner maintains control.

When wayward spouses hide their fidelity-violating sexual activities, they act as though they are entitled to secret sexual privileges that supersede the rights of their spouses. The faithless one's deceit blocks the spouse's rightful "vote" in the equation. There is no "informed consent" in these situations. This abuse of power keeps betrayed spouses off-balance, operating in the dark.

Unless you were manipulated, I doubt you agreed to your spouse's affair or other forbidden sexual activities. Thus, you didn't have enough information to effectively protest, protect yourself, get outside help, or draw firmer boundaries about what you would and wouldn't put up with.

Dr. Omar Minwalla labels a betrayer who intentionally withholds critical information as engaging in the "deceptive management of the spouse." Information control is a misleading tactic strayers use to manage outcomes, at least temporarily. They reserve "the right to know" for themselves, as though the impact on the abused partner is irrelevant. When betrayers control the flow of information by hiding and lying about their sexually subversive worlds, they reduce their spouses from equal partners to disadvantaged victims. This withholding of crucial information prevents legitimate partners from detecting the marital jeopardy that lurks in the shadows.

Information deprivation resembles being forced to wear a blindfold, rendering you unable to see who's striking you or where the blows originate. You might sense that something is amiss. However, without a clear vision, you become confused, disoriented, and unable to defend yourself.

Dr. Hope Ray describes this deprivation of information and lack of consent as a form of "Betrayal Violence." She explores this concept through her private podcasts and website, where she explains why secret romantic and sexual betrayals constitute a damaging form of domestic abuse. For deeper insight, I highly recommend signing up for access to her content.[12]

Your Need for Validation

I share this material on domestic abuse as it relates to infidelity and desertion, not to discourage you, but to *validate* how awful Betrandonment feels. You were not delusional. You felt abused because both infidelity and abandonment are abusive. You felt injured because you truly were—both emotionally and psychologically. Intimate betrayal and spousal rejection are fierce one-two punches against your self-worth. You entered into matrimony in good faith. Evidently, or eventually, your partner did not.

These combined insults serve as below-the-belt attacks on your worth as a human being, regardless of whether you are a man, a woman, a husband, or a wife. Your partner's behind-the-back, stolen vows have ripped the rug of security out from under you—a rug you believed you could count on.

Now that you have another term for your painful experience—domestic abuse—hopefully, you feel some relief. Your spouse's lies, gaslighting, and information control placed you in a disadvantaged position that you did not deserve. You may have stumbled in the dark, encountering rocks of deceit, unable to identify them for what they were. But now the lights are on. You can see your way out of the cave of betrayal. The more enlightened you become, the better you can navigate around the sharp stalactites that made your head bleed and the stalagmites that blocked your way to freedom.

Learn to Trust Your Intuitions

Another takeaway is that, upon reflection, you can hopefully see that your original intuitions were accurate and trustworthy after all. Rather than beating yourself up over what you missed, see this as a valuable lesson—one that will come in handy to protect you in the future.

Part of your recovery from betrayal involves learning to notice your body's foreboding feelings, giving them credence, and acting on them before your logical mind (or a deceitful spouse) interferes. Dr. Minwalla trains betrayed spouses how to listen to their bodies and validate their gut hunches regarding their partners' secret sexual activities. Once they learn to trust their bodies' signals, betrayed spouses can better detect what is going on behind their backs, piece together the missing puzzle pieces of the past, and reclaim their personal power in the future.

I remember working with a young adult named "Amy," who was paranoid that her fiancé would cheat on her. When they were dating and discussing the prospect of marriage, he unexpectedly broke up with her to pursue other relationships. She was shocked by this. He later realized the new relationships weren't worth losing his former fiancée. So, hat in hand, he returned to Amy to ask her to reconsider dating him and to resume their marriage plans.

> Upon reflection, you can hopefully see that your original intuitions were accurate and trustworthy after all.

Even though she said "Yes" to reconciling, the first betrayal loomed large for her. Unable to calm herself down, she was suspicious of everything: his whereabouts, his friendships, his texts, his long hours at work, and his devotion to her. A nervous wreck, Amy was easily triggered, causing her fiancé to feel over-controlled and unable to appease her.

My best help for her was to retrace their history and the unexpected breakup through a trauma lens. She recalled noticing when he turned away from her, sensing his interest in other girls. Before he informed her, she had a certain "knowing" in her gut that something threatening was afoot.

Yet, after they reconciled, her brain worked overtime as if the former threat was an ever-present reality. Amy suffered from hypervigilance—a poor substitute for her protective, natural intuitions.

We reviewed several instances for her to practice distinguishing between her overactive upper brain and her deeper gut sensations. As she tested each with reality checks, she found that her "second brain" was more reliable than her overactive mind. This, combined with learning to trust the promptings of the Holy Spirit, helped her calm down and believe her fiancé's current words and actions, confident that if something were indeed "off," she would know. They are happily married today and have several children in tow.

With practice and feedback from safe, validating people, you, too, can reconnect with your "second brain" again. This new self-trust can free you from the hypervigilance you developed during your trauma. In future relationships, you'll be able to relax enough to notice your gut instincts, validate your feelings, and listen to the Holy Spirit. This will be a relief compared to all the second-guessing you were conditioned to do when your reality was under assault.

Once you learn to believe your intuitions and attend to their signals, you can make wise, self-protective decisions more swiftly and accurately.

God Understands And Longs To Comfort Us

In conclusion, I'd like to leave you with some encouraging spiritual thoughts to consider. Thankfully, as Christians, we belong to a God who understands and cares about abuse. He suffered the agony of immense betrayal and rejection by his people in both the Old and New Testaments. And he suffers the same in our world today.

> "We despised him and rejected him—a man of sorrows, acquainted with bitterest grief. We turned our backs on him and looked the other way when he went by. He was despised, and we didn't care" (Isaiah 53:3, TLB).

Even when it seems like no one understands, the Lord does.

In addition to empathizing with our pain, he sent us the Holy Spirit, referred to as "The Comforter," to support us. No external lover or substance can replicate the lasting peace of the Holy Spirit. Although the shock of trauma and grief may temporarily obscure our perception of his presence, he assures us that he will never leave us or forsake us.

In fact, it is during times of great distress that we learn to walk by faith and not just by sight. We may feel emotionally numb or sad, but when we turn to God's Word, we can find comfort in his promises. Here are three that I found incredibly reassuring:

> "The LORD Himself goes before you; He will be with you. He will never leave you nor forsake you. Do not be afraid or discouraged" (Deuteronomy 31:8).

This promise is repeated almost verbatim 13 times in Scripture and is similarly promised in many more. I think God wants us to get this.

We also need to know that God is not abusive and does not endorse abuse:

> "A bruised reed He will not break and a smoldering wick He will not extinguish; He will faithfully bring forth justice" (Isaiah 42:3).

Instead of the harshness you experienced from your rejecting partner's treatment, the Lord is gentle and compassionate.

> "He will feed his flock like a shepherd. He will carry the lambs in his arms, holding them close to his heart. He will gently lead the mother sheep with their young" (Isaiah 40:11, NLT).

This is how God leads. He desires to hold us, his injured lambs, close to his heart and gently guide us, not with an iron fist, but to places of refreshment and safety. I hope these verses bring you as much comfort as they have for me.

In **Section I** of this book, "Reviewing the Damage," we explored the devastating despair, grief, trauma, and abuse of the Betrandoned experience. To heal, you first need to grasp the severity of what you've been through. Reminding you:

- You are not crazy.
- It is as bad as it feels.
- You are not alone.
- Trust your God-given intuitions.
- God is not like your former spouse.

In **Section II**, "Refuting the Shame," we will identify the many layers of SHAME we suffer when our partner betrays and abandons us and explore ways to overcome their undermining effect on our self-esteem.

SECTION II

Refuting The Shame

"Instead of shame, My people will have a double portion, and instead of humiliation, they will rejoice in their share; and so they will inherit a double portion in their land, and everlasting joy will be theirs."
~Isaiah 61:7

Shame stalks the Betrandoned, whispering, *"You deserved this. You were the reason for the betrayal. You weren't enough."* It echoes in the rejection of a spouse, the silence of the church, and the sting of our own self-reproach.

But shame is a lie. It's a burden we were never meant to carry.

Before we can heal, we must acknowledge, expose, and reject the shame. Jesus—the One who bore public rejection and disgrace—knows our sorrow and has come to cleanse us from its stain.

This section invites you to release false guilt, receive God's truth, and reclaim your worth. He promises beauty instead of the ashes of disgrace, honor in place of humiliation, and a future marked not by shame—but by joy.

IRONY

~Linda J. (MacDonald), 2001

He detached.
I shattered.

He had all the power and information.
I had no view, no voice, no vote.

He made decisions ... with her.
I bore their consequences ... alone.

He felt entitled.
I felt deprived.

He found relief.
I suffered trauma.

He felt guilt for disappointing others.
I felt shame for being unloved.

He has moved on.
I
am
buried
in
sorrow.

Chapter 6

The Double Humiliation

> See, I lay in Zion a chosen and precious cornerstone;
> and the one who believes in Him will never be put to shame.
> ~ 1 Peter 2:6

One of my favorite movies is *"Ghost Town"* (2008). Much of the story surrounds a widow named Gwen, who learns of her husband's affair after he is dead. This fact complicates her grief and causes her to doubt her worth as a woman and wife.

The most poignant scene for me is when Gwen, distraught with questions, wants answers from a dentist named Bertram, who, after a near-death experience, can see the ghost of her unfaithful husband. Exasperated, pacing, Gwen furrows her brow, throws up her hands, and demands answers to the three questions that most trouble her:

1. "What was the matter with me?"
2. "Why didn't he love me?"
3. "Why wasn't I enough?"

The first time I saw the movie, I thought to myself, "These are the three most haunting questions spouses ask themselves in the aftermath of infidelity."[1]

Those of us who have experienced romantic betrayal find it difficult not to take our spouses' unfaithfulness personally. Since intimate disloyalty cuts us deeply, we assume our partner must not love us. We spend hours agonizing, trying to understand what was so wrong with us that our spouses felt compelled to look elsewhere.

Betrayed spouses often blame themselves for failing to keep their partners satisfied and faithful. We question our worth, lovability, and adequacy as companions. Like Gwen in "*Ghost Town*," we see romantic betrayal as evidence that we were not enough for our partners. We feel belittled, disgraced, and devalued.

Truth be told, their unfaithfulness reveals more about them than about us. It signifies a fundamental character flaw in the betrayer. We may not have even crossed their minds when they committed infidelity; they were likely only focused on themselves.

Unfaithfulness is bad enough. However, when our straying partners further insult us by completely abandoning our marriages after being unfaithful, they impose a double dose of shame for being considered unworthy of their loyalty and long-term commitment.

Double Humiliation

I refer to this as The Double Humiliation of Betrandonment. The First Humiliation occurs when your spouse breaks their promise "to forsake all others" and "to keep myself only unto you." The air-sucking assault of unfaithfulness knocks the wind out of your emotional sails, leaving you stumbling and gasping for air. Then, when your spouse refuses to re-commit to your marriage or its repair, the Second Humiliation occurs. Still gasping for breath from the initial betrayal, you cry out as your spouse forsakes you and forces you to face a host of devastating losses all by yourself.

Your loved one shamed you twice, first by abandoning you romantically and then by abandoning you altogether.

Perhaps you can relate to the following metaphor of your marital crises:

It's as if your partner's poor steering skills cause the ship of your relationship to lurch left, throwing you down portside into the chilling waters. You can't believe your spouse would do this on purpose. Still determined, you keep trying. Shivering, you crawl back onto the deck, hopeful it was just a mistake—certain they will improve next time.

However, each new betrayal pushes you overboard again. The lies, the subtle hints of favoritism towards someone else, and every new discovery chips away at your self-worth, leaving you feeling cast aside and inconsequential. Your confidence plummets to an all-time low as the First Humiliation exacts its toll.

Then, dark clouds gather on the horizon. The wind picks up. With great effort, you and your unsteady crewmate steer the boat toward the harbor, battling the waves along the way. As you sail into calmer waters, you believe the worst is behind you. You've already endured the violent seas of infidelity. Now, safely docked, you brace yourself for what you anticipate will be a milder storm—one you are finally prepared to face.

But this is no ordinary bluster.

Unbeknownst to you, the Second Humiliation is closing in.

You reach for your shipmate—only to discover they've disappeared. The realization tightens in your chest. The storm is gaining strength, and you're alone.

Winds howl through the marina, more forceful than anything you've ever experienced. Pipes, deck pieces, ropes, and torn sails whip through the air. Looking outside, you see that all other boaters have fled. A terrifying truth dawns: what seemed like a passing squall has morphed into a full-throttle hurricane.

Your ship smashes against the pier. Boards splinter. Water floods in. You scramble to the ship's deck, gripping anything to stay upright. Your breath catches. Your hands shake. You leap onto what's left of the pier, stumble, and run for the shore.

Drenched, breathless, you look back at the wreckage—the mast broken, your boat submerged, the shoreline littered with debris. And as you collapse onto solid ground, you whisper in anguish: "What happened to 'in sickness and in health'? And 'as long as we both shall live'?"

This is the Second Humiliation: unwanted divorce. The final, soul-wrecking wave that destroys what little was left.

In this chapter, we will explore how the combined storms of infidelity and spousal rejection instill deep feelings of shame in Betrandoned spouses. As we uncover the many layers of shame, I will offer nuggets of truth for you to hold onto as you emerge from the humiliating waves of betrayal and abandonment onto the safety of solid, dry land.

I appreciate how author Vaneetha Risner explains her own experience:

> Dave's leaving brought an unshakable sense of worthlessness and shame. Shame that my Christian marriage had fallen apart. Shame that my husband had left me for someone else. Shame that I had proclaimed how good our marriage was, only to have my words turn against me.[2]

Guilt vs. Shame

Have you ever wondered what the difference is between guilt and shame? Guilt is about the wrongs we do or don't do. Most of the time, guilt pricks our consciences to prevent or stop destructive behaviors. Healthy guilt tells us we've done something wrong and motivates us to correct and repair the damage to ourselves and others. Human guilt prevents us from lying, speeding, stealing, or cheating on our employers, taxes, or spouses.

When we violate our consciences, healthy guilt helps us correct our course, seek forgiveness, and make amends when possible. When we acknowledge and address legitimate feelings of guilt, we lead more productive lives and strengthen our relationships.

But when we disobey what we know to be right, guilt piles up. Cumulative guilt leads to self-condemnation—an unpleasant burden to bear. No wonder some folks seek to quiet their consciences with numbing substances, a dopamine high, or rationalizations.

While guilt makes us feel bad about the wrongs we *do*, personal shame makes us feel bad about who we *are*. We tend to experience others' disapproval, shunning, or criticism as a blot on our personhood—like a stain everyone can see and that we can't erase. Shame makes us feel unworthy of love, deficient as partners, and uniquely flawed. Such shame can bury us with feelings of insecurity and failure.

When shame shouts, our self-esteem shrinks.

Betrandonment magnifies whatever shame we dragged forward from our childhood. Thus, we may interpret our partner's betrayal as evidence of our inadequacy as mates. Even without a history of abuse or neglect, most people feel ashamed or embarrassed when a life partner betrays and exchanges them for a new lover, lifestyle, or habit.

Tainted by Betrayal

Among all the painful experiences life hands us, few evoke the kind of inner shame that comes with sexual or romantic betrayal. We feel tainted by our partner's sexual misconduct, as if their repulsive actions are a direct reflection of our worth—a feeling that worsens when our emotional need for reassurance from the unfaithful partner remains unfulfilled and undermines our self-respect.

Betrayed spouses feel sullied by the actions of their offenders, even when they bear no guilt themselves. As the Scripture states, extramarital sex defiles the marriage bed (Hebrews 13:4). To "defile" means to contaminate or pollute something that was once pure. When we learn our spouse has engaged in secret sexual sin, we often feel tainted by their misconduct.

It's like discovering we've been affectionately embracing Bert the chimney sweep from Mary Poppins—only to find ourselves covered in soot. We realize that every hug, every kiss, every intimate moment with our spouse was shared with someone else. It makes us recoil, as if the grime of their shameful behavior has rubbed off on us.

This may seem irrational to an outsider since the guilt belongs to the unfaithful. Yet victims of intimate betrayal often carry a weight of shame that isn't theirs. To heal, we must release the burden of undue shame and recognize it as misplaced.

The Shame of Rejection

Intimate betrayal sends a message of disgrace—that we weren't valued enough for our spouse to remain faithful. Yet, when followed by rejection, it adds another layer of shame to the spurn of betrayal—the shame of being discarded.

In the lead-up to our divorce, I lived on "The Eve of Destruction" (Barry McGuire's hit song from the sixties). Terror stalked me in my dreams at night, and with each new slight by my husband during the day, it hissed, "See? You're worthless and undesirable." Even worse, I could tell James viewed my elevated anxiety as further evidence that he needed to get away from me.

Whether you suffered the threat of rejection for days, weeks, months, or years beforehand, when the second Humiliation arrived in the form of an unwanted divorce, it hit hard. The brutal winds ripped away your human bulwark—the one you counted on to face life's storms together.

The shame of spousal rejection, whether by their refusal to try or walking away, leaves a betrayed spouse humiliated beyond measure—as though we weren't worth our partner's protection, loyalty, and commitment.

The Shame of Discovering Your Spouse is LGBTQ+

Another humiliating form of betrayal is to have your spouse come out as gay, lesbian, trans, bisexual, queer, a cross-dresser, or polyamorous. This isn't what you signed up for when you married them. It is painful to learn your mate isn't "into you" and wonder if they used you to cover up their same-sex attractions or gender identity issues. You may even question if your spouse ever found you appealing.

While some same-sex attracted and gender-confused people know their inclinations before they marry, others develop non-traditional sexual proclivities later on. Either way, straight spouses experience feelings of betrayal and shame over learning their partners are attracted to people of a different gender or orientation. Here is one example by journalist, Juliet Jeske:

> Our entire wedding haunts me now, as one big farce. I had an absolutely beautiful ceremony, perfect weather, supportive families, and

a wonderful, gorgeous celebration. I look back at it now and want to erase it from my brain.

I still feel a deep sadness that will flare up from time to time at times completely unexpectedly. I will find myself staring off thinking about one aspect of it, and others around me will comment that I look sad or lost. I don't realize I'm doing this, it is as if my mind just takes over for a few minutes and I sink back into the sorrow if only for a moment. My trust issues are tantamount; I can't fathom being married again, it is just so foreign a concept after what I went through.[3]

In an article featured in OUT.com[4], Chadwick Moore interviews several women, two of whom had this experience in their personal lives and lead a support group for straight women whose spouses come out of the closet.

"When a man represses his sexuality and he starts to come out, it's like he was stuck in adolescence and now it's a newfound freedom," Barbetta says. "He feels joyful and happy, but for the straight wives, our lives have been lost. Our hopes and dreams are shattered." ~Therapist, Francine Barbetta

The article goes on to say,

The revelation that a spouse is gay is so incredibly traumatic for many women that they are often in counseling for years or decades to come. Society tends to view them as either naive (how could you not have known?) or deficient (if you'd been a better wife, he wouldn't have turned gay), while their husbands are lauded for having the courage to be their authentic selves.

As husbands embrace their non-traditional sexuality, some marriages reportedly experience manipulation and abuse. "I call it gay-lighting," Group leader Bonnie Kaye says. "Like gaslighting, they make you feel like you're crazy when you start to have suspicions. You question your ability to have clear judgment. They make you feel like you're imagining it."[5]

Chadwick notes, "And an overwhelming number of Kaye and Barbetta's support network are devout Christians." I was not surprised. I've talked with many Christian spouses who wished to salvage their marriages despite the LGBTQ+ leanings of a spouse and were devastated when their efforts were spurned or unsuccessful.

I've also known men whose wives came out as lesbians and were shattered by the revelation. Many people feel embarrassed that their life partner prefers a person of the same sex over themselves. It can feel like an added insult.

After the divorce, a straight parent may feel helpless when their same-sex attracted spouse hauls their children to "Gay Rights Parades," "Drag Queen Story Time," or other confusing and age-inappropriate exposures. This is especially true when this goes against the values they want to instill in their children. Sadly, the law tends not to support objecting parents.

While LGBTQ+ folks in the Christian community have their own shame battles to fight, the disgrace experienced by the straight spouses who married them is often overlooked. In today's society, many onlookers expect spouses to affirm or even celebrate their partner's "coming out," forgetting there is a grieving spouse left behind.

I try to help such sufferers not take their spouses' orientation or fetishes personally. These preferences have nothing to do with them and everything to do with whatever is going on within the non-straight partner.

As friends, we should remember that losing a spouse's affection to someone of a different gender carries its own unique shame and complications.

If you've lost your spouse to the LGBTQ+ community or identity, you could benefit from connecting with others who've been through a similar experience. You might appreciate Bonnie Kay's podcast.[6] I've also listed some online resources, both Christian and secular, affirming and non-affirming, in the endnotes to this chapter.[7]

Only 7% of couples stay together long-term after learning their partner has same-sex attractions. But a few find a way to stay in a "mixed-orientation" marriage, such as Laurie and Matt Krieg, authors of the book *An Impossible Marriage*.[8] They are believers and have handled this issue well. Yet, keep in mind they are among the exceptions.

SHAME FOR THE BLAME

Self-blame

Upon discovering a partner's affair, we often blame ourselves for our spouse's wayward actions and ultimate rejection. Blaming ourselves gives us an illusion of control. We may not be able to change our offenders, but if we hold ourselves responsible for their behaviors, we mistakenly believe we at least have *some* control over the situation. Yet, rather than help us, self-blame only complicates our lives.

Firstly, we might contort ourselves into pretzels to satisfy someone who is unsatisfiable—ultimately losing our own identity in the process. Self-blame erodes our self-esteem, projecting an image of weakness and desperation that further alienates our spouses. Attempting to resolve marital discord by striving for unattainable perfection is futile, especially when the root causes of the conflict lie within the betrayer and are magnified by the affair itself.

A few years after my unwanted divorce, I remember giving a keynote talk at a conference for betrayed Christian women, aptly titled, "Betrayal Redeemed." When I finished telling my story, including some of my hard-earned lessons, the organizer, psychologist Sandy Wilson, came to the podium. She summarized my fifty-minute talk in four simple words:

"It's not your fault."

If there was ever a message that betrayed spouses need to hear, that's it.

This does not mean you were a perfect partner or had no role in setting the stage for your spouse to do something stupid. But you didn't hold a gun to their head and threaten, "Go have sex with your secretary, or I'll shoot!"

Part of your recovery is learning how to separate your own growth areas—such as your unhealed wounds of the past, hypercriticism, lack of assertiveness, misuse of alcohol, or mental health issues—from your spouse's personal responsibility for stepping outside your marriage. In this case, A + B does NOT equal U (Unfaithfulness). Rather, A + B = C (Counseling) or A + B = G (Get Help). And, many times, your own weaknesses didn't even surface until your spouse shook your security by their treachery.

Blame by Your Spouse

With our self-confidence shaken, we may accept outsized blame from our unfaithful partners and recoil from the finger-pointing of others.

It's easy to doubt ourselves when we hear such things as,

- "If you hadn't _____, I wouldn't have gotten involved with _____."
- "If you weren't so _____, this never would have happened."
- "I just wanted my needs to be met, and you weren't doing that."
- "It's not about the other person; it's about our *marriage* (i.e., you)."

Whatever their excuses, like Adam and Eve in the garden, when in trouble, the guilty try to pass the buck for their deeds onto someone else. Even if your marriage was less than perfect (like everyone else's), that isn't an excuse to stray.

Your Spouse Had Other Options

No matter the stressors, griefs, or situations that preceded your partner's faithless actions, he/she had many other options to cope with their distress. I don't care if you are a carjacker or an addict. It didn't give your spouse permission to leap into the arms of another lover. Two wrongs don't make a right.

Here are just a few alternatives he or she could have chosen instead:

- Sit you down and have a "big talk."
- Drag you into couples' counseling.
- Seek therapy for themselves.
- Ask you to read a book that addresses their concerns.
- Write down their complaints in a letter and read it to you.
- Invite you to read their journal entries.
- Insist you enter an addiction treatment program.
- Eat a lot of chocolate.
- Take an antidepressant.
- Sleep in the other bedroom to get your attention.
- Arrange for an intervention.
- File for separation or divorce.

If the marriage was indeed "the problem," your spouse could have enacted any of the above strategies *before* seeking the mood-lifter of a fresh dalliance or sexual compulsion.

Remember that your spouse's complaints about you or your marriage were worsened by their choice to go astray. Infidelity has a toxic effect on a couple's relationship and skews the perspective of both parties. Legitimate marital issues are far more challenging to sort through once infidelity enters the picture.

Undeserved Shame

My desire is for you to recognize that your feelings of shame are normal but undeserved. Like Gwen in the movie "*Ghost Town*," your experience of spousal betrayal may have led you to question your perceptions, worth, and role in the failure of your marriage. Instead, I hope you can let the shame go—all of it. Don't hold onto what God himself doesn't hold against you. Accept this time as an opportunity to shed undeserved shame from your life.

Most of all, I pray you press into Christ rather than distance yourself from him in your ashes of sorrow. He wants to be with you amid your pain, like he was with Shadrach, Meshach, and Abednego in the fiery furnace. He desires to bring you out of your flaming crucible more faith-filled, loving, and compassionate than you were before.

> "It is just as the Scripture says: 'Anyone who believes in Him will never be put to shame.'" (Rom. 10:11).

God does not aim to shame us. His purpose isn't to condemn but to save us and lift us from our shame (John 3:17).

The best antidote to The Double Humiliation is receiving a double portion of the Lord's provision for us as believers.

> "Instead of shame, My people will have a double portion, and instead of humiliation, they will rejoice in their share" (Isaiah 61:7).

That means *twice* the spiritual empowerment and wisdom you had before your two-fold shame. There is no other way to increase your spiritual maturity, credibility, and effectiveness in ministering to injured people than to come through such life-changing storms as infidelity and unwanted divorce. At such times, we must cling to the Lord and allow our roots to go deep. Claim the above promise for a double portion of Spirit-infused healing, anointing, and blessings to counter your double shame.

I hope that this chapter helped you feel less alone and better able to identify some of the reasons why Betrandoned spouses experience feelings of degradation after partner betrayal and rejection. In the next chapter, we'll explore the ways the stigma of divorce adds to that shame, especially in the church, and how you can combat divorce shame with general and biblical truths that have the potential to set you free.

Chapter 7

The Shame Of Divorce

*Do not be afraid, for you will not be put to shame;
do not be intimidated, for you will not be humiliated.
For you will forget the shame of your youth
and will remember no more the reproach of your widowhood.
~Isaiah 54:4*

Someone once told me the verses in the Bible that exhort us to care for widows in need also apply to today's divorcees. A widow's experience in biblical times resembles the reproach, the grief, the aloneness, and the financial strains of divorced people, particularly women, in this day and age.

The phrase "the reproach of your widowhood" refers to the shame widows experienced in ancient Semitic culture. You could replace the word "reproach" with shame, blame, discredit, or disapproval. Widows in biblical times and divorced individuals today often experience shame due to their lowered financial, familial, and social status.

As forsaken spouses, this verse helps us know that the Lord understands the earthly reproach we feel and longs to gather us under his wings for his spiritual comfort and protection. And he wants the body of Christ to care for us as well.

After my divorce, I sought advice from a local Christian doctor about a shared counseling case. Although I knew he had also experienced a divorce, I was concerned that my recent divorce might affect his perception of me as a marriage therapist. Wanting to tell him before he learned it from someone else, I mentioned my divorce during our conversation.

His response? "Oh, the shame!" My shoulders instantly relaxed at his validation. His words made me feel heard and understood. I cried after I hung up, as he so aptly named the shame I had been feeling.

In today's world, divorce doesn't carry the same stigma as it used to. Yet, it is still an unpleasant label that can make us feel out of place in a society or church full of couples. Most pastors, being married, often emphasize God's design for marriage in their sermons, unintentionally overlooking the many single, re-singled, and widowed adults who didn't choose their current status or who would prefer to be married.

And while pockets of our permissive society have adapted to the commonness of divorce, many people, perhaps especially Christians, still struggle with excessive shame over the status of divorce. They feel self-conscious, as if they walk around with a "Scarlet D" on their chests. Divorced believers often feel like second-class citizens, the outliers in groups, and disqualified from certain kinds of ministry.

People of faith may worry they've disappointed God by getting divorced, even when they didn't want their marriages to end or had to leave for their own or their children's well-being. Regardless of our personal values, divorce sometimes happens—whether we like it or not. The humiliation of an unwanted divorce, especially after multiple broken marriages, can be particularly painful for those striving to honor God, especially in faith communities where intact families are the norm.

One Betrandoned woman, "Julie," wrote to me,

> I think one of the biggest sources of shame for me was being raised in a family that "didn't believe" in divorce. I've had to overcome ideas like: it is my job to make it work, going to enough counseling can fix anything, and that setting expectations or limits in a relationship is ungodly because it is God's job to meet our needs, not our husband's.[1]

Such notions from well-meaning but unsympathetic fellow believers add shame to our already shame-filled experience and can discourage us in our walk with the Lord. As Julie laments, other people may pressure devoted partners to stay married to an unrepentant spouse even though they see no progress. They may even criticize them for establishing healthy boundaries as if a betrayed spouse has no right to do so.

While marriage counseling can help, it can't make up for an unmotivated, disloyal, misbehaving spouse. Christians can be overly rigid in their efforts to discourage divorce. Yet, suffering spouses end up carrying a load of shame as a result.

If you're like me, you resent it when people say the well-worn phrase, "After all, it takes two to tango," hinting that if the marriage broke up, the speaker assumes both people contributed equally to the breakdown.

I don't claim to have been the perfect spouse. I had my own areas for growth. Still, I was willing to do whatever it took to address any legitimate concerns—if only he had met my efforts with the same commitment and sincerity. I was even willing to forgive James for his affair, but only if he had done the deep, introspective work to confront his issues rather than shift the blame onto me. I couldn't force him to take responsibility, change, or re-commit to our marriage.

Today, I *know* I didn't deserve his betrayal. But back then, his blame and rejection of me magnified my insecurities. I worried my inadequacies had somehow chased him away. I feared other people might assume the same thing—that there was something insidiously horrible about me that pressed him into the arms of another woman and made him leave our marriage.

In later years, I found comfort in the phrase: "While it takes two to get married, it only takes one to get divorced." I hope you, too, can take this to heart. No matter how badly you wanted to save your marriage, you couldn't do it alone, especially in light of today's no-fault divorce laws.

Even if you were the one who was forced to file, be assured that this doesn't mean you broke the marriage. Without actual heart change on the part of the one who strayed or abused you, staying just to avoid the appearance of fault would have only prolonged the agony. God knows the truth. Trust him in this. He witnessed your spouse's broken vows long before you knew of the breach.

The Myth of Affair-Proofing

Another source of divorce shame is the many books that claim to help you "Affair-proof Your Marriage." Dr. Glass refers to this as "the Prevention Myth." One well-known book that implies you can prevent partner betrayal is *His Needs, Her Needs: Building an Affair-proof Marriage* by Willard Harley. (To be fair, in 2022, he re-titled his book *His Needs, Her Needs: Making Romantic Love Last*.) While I generally appreciate Dr. Harley's books and blogs, I came across an old journal entry of mine on this topic.

> What if his book was titled *His Needs, Her Needs: How to Keep Your Spouse from Becoming a Drug Addict*? Or, *an Alcoholic*? Or, *an Anorexic*? Or, *a Tax Evader*? I doubt such books would sell very well, at least to the non-co-dependent types. Yet this is what such titles and subtitles imply: "You are responsible for your spouse's lousy moral

choices. If you don't meet their needs, they are likely or entitled to be unfaithful."

Try as we might, no one has that much power. Even God doesn't assume that much control. The gift of free will means we are free moral agents responsible for our own decisions and moral development.

> The gift of free will means we are free moral agents responsible for our own decisions and moral development.

For example, if you are a parent, you may have taken pride in how one of your children turned out, only to be embarrassed when the other child rebelled or became a drug addict. Same parents. Same home. Same values. Different personalities and wills.

Ask yourself the following questions:

Was it God's fault that Eve fell for Satan's lies and ate the forbidden fruit?

He had given Adam and Eve access to every tree in the garden except one. Had he failed to provide "enough" for them? No, he hadn't. They were the ones who failed.

Did God deserve Israel's unfaithfulness—their worship of empty idols and rejection of him? Was he to blame for their betrayal? No, the Lord had not let them down. Their own desires led them astray. They let themselves down.

We live in a fallen, broken world. A place where children and spouses sometimes make terrible choices over which we have no control. If our perfect Lord can't keep all his children faithful, how can we, mere humans, expect to have that much influence over the behaviors and decisions of those we love?

Accept the humbling not as a sign that there is something horrible about you, but as a chance to identify with God's experience of rejection and betrayal.

Not Judging Divorced People

When I was securely married to James, I am sorry to admit, I was as smug as many married people are, believing my relationship was a cut "above" those that end in divorce. I firmly believed our marriage was invincible, not subject to the foibles of others. Unless I knew them personally and understood their stories, I assumed most divorced people had failed. I believed they must have had some fatal flaw; otherwise, their marriages wouldn't have fallen apart.

I've since been humbled.

During our separation, someone asked a friend of mine, "What's wrong with Linda?" I flinched. I interpreted this as her wondering, "Why would Linda's husband betray her and leave unless something was wrong with her?"

Had I thought further, she may have meant her question as a compliment—that she couldn't understand why my husband would leave such a wonderful person like me. (Smile.)

I'll never forget the moment I stood to speak at a large, mature group at a local church known as "Positive Christian Singles." No one knew about the marital crisis I was in. I was worried that if they knew my marriage was on the brink of divorce, they might discredit me as a therapist, discount the workshops I'd taught in the past, and dismiss what I was about to teach. Even so, despite my hope that my husband might have a last-minute change of heart, I felt like I needed to brace them, as the news of my pending divorce was about to become public.

Before I began my talk, I said, "I know some of you have heard me speak on healthy dating and finding the right person to marry. That was when my marriage was the *least* stressful part of my life. Today, it has become the *most* stressful part of my life."

You could have heard a pin drop. Stunned by the unspoken swell of empathy from the audience, I gripped the podium and ruffled my notes to keep from crying. I felt blanketed in an invisible wave of acceptance and understanding by these single, mostly divorced, adults. Tears still come to my eyes when I recall that moment of awe and compassion from this group of divorced strangers. They knew. They understood. I was not alone.

I felt accepted with compassion.

Never again will I look down on a divorced person as inferior. As someone who failed. As someone who should have been able to save their marriage if they had only tried harder. These are myths that we unfairly assign to the painfully divorced.

Does God hate all divorce?

One of the greatest sources of shame I see among believers is from the oft-quoted phrase: "God hates divorce," based on Malachi 2:16, "'For I hate divorce,' says the LORD, the God of Israel."

Well-meaning Christians tremble at such a thought, no matter their situations. Their deeper worry is, "If God hates divorce and I get divorced, God will hate *me*." Some people remain in destructive marriages for fear that they will incur God's wrath or be disobedient to the Lord if they accept or initiate a divorce from their spouses.

I've watched a few women use this verse as their basis for tolerating gross disrespect by their philandering or addicted husbands. They clung to the fear of God's disapproval despite knowing the universally accepted "exception clause" in Matthew 5:32 for permission to divorce because of immorality.

As a Christian with a high view of Scripture, I can appreciate their concerns. Yet, when I study the Bible, I always ask myself, "What is the *context* of this verse?" I consider the cultural setting, the nearby verses, and other related passages throughout the Bible.

Here is the context of the phrase "God hates divorce" in Malachi Chapter 2: The priests of Israel were living immorally; despite knowing they were forbidden to commit adultery or marry non-Jewish women—unions that often led to idol worship. Yet, they engaged in these very sins, even divorcing their Jewish wives to justify their extramarital affairs and marry foreign women.

> "And this is another thing you do: You cover the altar of the LORD with tears, with weeping and groaning, because He no longer regards your offerings or receives them gladly from your hands" (Malachi 2:13).

These leaders were upset with God for not responding to their prayers. Life was not going well for them, so they wept at God's altar. They were indignant when their requests went unanswered—evidence of their unrepentance. Then God makes it clear why he is upset with them.

> "Yet you ask, 'Why?' It is because the LORD has been a witness between you and the wife of your youth, against whom you have *broken faith*, though she is your companion and your wife by covenant" (Malachi 2:14, emphasis added).

God witnessed their marriage vows, which he considers a covenant. The same goes for you. The Lord was there and witnessed your vows. He views your marriage as established by a covenant before God. When your spouse intimately betrayed you, they "broke faith" with you and ruptured their vows to you, just like these priests had done to their spouses.

> "Has not the LORD made them one, having a portion of the Spirit? And why one? Because He seeks godly offspring. So guard yourselves in your spirit and do not break faith with the wife of your youth" (Malachi 2:15).

The oneness he is referring to is the sexual union. Staying faithfully married protects your children and gives them the best chance to choose to follow the Lord. Infidelity and divorce have deleterious effects on kids and our society. God is concerned about this.

> "'For I hate divorce,' says the LORD, the God of Israel. 'He who divorces his wife covers his garment with violence,' says the LORD of Hosts. So guard yourselves in your spirit and do not break faith" (Malachi 2:16).

Note that in verse 16, he instructs them to guard their spirit—similar to other verses where we are encouraged to guard our hearts. Staying faithful and true is a spiritual discipline, a matter of the heart.

Scholars have long debated what was meant by "covers his garment with violence." Most seem to think the "garment" refers to the wife herself. Others view it as the husband's own garment splattered in blood from emotionally beating up the wife.

Some newer Bible translations seek to clarify this mysterious phrase:

> "The man who hates and divorces his wife," says the LORD, the God of Israel, "does violence to the one he should protect" (Malachi 2:16, NIV, 2011).

Besides the most recent NIV, a few other new translations associate the word "hate" with the one who desires to divorce his spouse unjustly, rather than God hating divorce. Indeed, a loyal spouse experiences divorce as an act of hate on the part of the rejector.

While I appreciate this view, I prefer the traditional translations that quote God as saying *he* is the one who hates divorce. In my opinion, the earlier version of The New Living Translation captures the nuanced meaning best:

> "For I hate divorce!" says the Lord, the God of Israel. "It is as cruel as putting on a victim's bloodstained coat," says the Lord Almighty. "So guard yourself; always remain loyal to your wife" (Malachi 2:16, TNLT, 1996).

This was the version I read during my unwanted divorce, and its vivid imagery resonated deeply. The prophet, speaking for God, paints a striking picture: A husband's unfaithfulness leaves his wife a battered, emotionally bloody mess. Then, when he heartlessly divorces her against her will, it's as if he snatches her coat—perhaps symbolizing her assets or protection—and drapes her bloodstained cloak over his shoulders, wearing it without remorse.

This is how many Betrandoned spouses feel—as if they've been abused by a partner's faithlessness and robbed of any protection by their conscienceless partners.

What do we learn about the Lord from this graphic description of unfaithful divorce in Malachi 2?

1. He *understands* the ripping violence of infidelity and unwanted divorce.
2. He *hates* rationalized divorce because of how it injures the victims (the spouse and children).
3. He views the vow-breaker's infidelity and divorce as a reflection of a person's spiritual condition, influencing their heart attitude toward family members and God.
4. He sees the pure *cruelty* of a post-affair divorce and the *collateral damage* it causes spouses and their children (vs. 15).
5. He considers marriage a *covenant* (vs. 14), not a mere contract, as we treat it in modern times.

In summary, here is the kind of divorce that God hates: The unfaithful, cruel rejection of a devoted spouse.

Although men had more rights in that culture, and women are the victims here, I'm confident God exhibits the same compassion for men who are similarly betrayed and forsaken.

Knowing the Lord's sentiments about your wrenching experience should help you love him all the more. I hope you find comfort knowing he understands. That he values marriage as much as you do. God recognizes the collateral damage of infidelity and unwanted divorce. And he *hates* how it has harmed you and your children.

> What he [God] abhors is the DAMAGE caused by an unjustly betrayed and severed marriage.

So, please let go of the mistaken notion that God hates all divorce. What he abhors is the DAMAGE caused by an unjustly betrayed and severed marriage.

I trust this helps you to let go of the false condemnation you may feel for having gone through an unwanted divorce. No matter who filed, the one who broke the marriage vows through infidelity (or other abuse) is the one who bears the responsibility for breaking up the marriage.

What About Divorce And Remarriage?

Another passage that some folks misinterpret in ways that add to a divorced person's shame is Matthew 19:8–9. In this passage, the Pharisees are trying to trap Jesus into either agreeing with Hillel, a liberal Jewish rabbi, or Shammai, the more conservative rabbi, regarding the grounds for divorce. Hillel had reinterpreted Deuteronomy 24:1, arguing that Moses *commanded* divorce for two reasons: immorality and "any cause," the latter allowing Jewish men to divorce their wives for even minor offenses. In contrast, Shammai taught that Moses *permitted* divorce for sexual immorality, not for trivial reasons.

While Jesus appears to agree with Shammai's traditional interpretation of Deuteronomy 24:1, after studying the passage further and reading several theologians' research, it appears to me that Jesus made several interesting points:

- God's original design for marriage was life-long.
- A man should only leave his parents, not his wife.
- God ordained marriage between one man and one woman at a time (not polygamy or polyamory as noted when Jesus quoted Genesis 2:24 and referred to Genesis 1:27).[2]
- Moses allowed for divorce as *protection* for the victimized spouse from an immoral, hard-hearted partner. (This sets an uncherished partner free to escape a callous, unfaithful partner so they can move on with their life and remarry if desired.)
- Some believe that just because Jesus didn't mention other, traditionally accepted grounds for divorce from Old Testament times (such as abandonment, neglect, abuse, and unloving treatment), it didn't mean these were excluded. Yet these reasons would have been *assumed* by the questioners in Jesus' day.[3]
- Regarding remarriage, Jesus considered it adulterous for someone to divorce a spouse for "any (minor) cause" as an excuse to marry someone else, as indicated in the following translation,

> "I say if your wife has not committed some terrible sexual sin, you must not divorce her to marry someone else. If you do, you are unfaithful" (Matthew 19:9, CEV).

I hope this discussion brings you some relief. That, like you, God intended marriage to be lifelong. However, God allows divorce for serious offenses. As the victim of such offenses, you are free to remarry. He allowed for divorce as a protection from a hard-hearted and/or unfaithful spouse.

There's nothing like a heart-involved affair to turn a loving spouse into a cold-hearted rejecter. And the Lord knows that.

What about "Standers"?

Some of you may have heard of or taken part in one of the national groups that promote the idea of "standing for your marriage," even after an unwanted divorce. The premise these groups promote is that even if one person broke the marriage covenant, you didn't. Therefore, you must stand your ground as a believer and remain true to your vows, trusting the Lord to change the heart of your wandering, rejecting partner.

Occasionally, I read stories of people reconciling after divorce. This is a special, grace-filled calling for a few waiting spouses. Once in a while, this works out. A rejected spouse waits and prays, and the unfaithful one does a U-turn and desires to reconcile. Two examples that stand out to me are Roanne and Eva Hunter, authors of the book *Sex, God, Chaos,* and Jeff and Cheryl Scruggs, authors of *I Do Again*. Their stories are uplifting and worth reading if you sense such a call in your life.

Although they weren't fully divorced, *Surprised by Love: One Couple's Journey from Infidelity to True Love* by Jay and Julie Kent-Ferraro is another good story about an estranged couple who reconciled after infidelity and separation.[4]

For others, waiting for years for the return of an errant spouse can become a wrenching form of denial. Deserted spouses may self-righteously declare that since they didn't break their marriage vows, God still expects them to honor them, even though the other person has walked away. This can lead to a lopsided stance, as if you are holding onto a rope that has been cut, acting as though you are still tied to the other person.

In such a case, the rejected spouse may have adopted unrealistic expectations. They might assume they're following God's will by hoping for the ex-partner to return when, actually, they are merely stuck in the denial phase of grief over their loss. It may not be God requiring them to uphold their end of a broken agreement; rather, it could be their refusal to accept reality, preventing them from moving through the stages of grief that lie ahead.

As I said, you may feel inspired to stand for your marriage because of a special dispensation of grace. But that is the exception. Most of the time, such fantasies don't work out. You've probably heard the saying, "Hope for the best, but plan for the worst." It is better to accept the actuality of your situation and move forward with your life than cling to an unrealistic hope that puts your life on hold.

You risk nothing by letting go.

To vigorously fight against your completed divorce is not necessarily noble. It may prolong the emotional bleeding and cause more damage to you and your children in the long run.

What About Abandonment?

In cases of spousal abandonment, Paul suggests, "But if the unbeliever leaves, let him go. The believing brother or sister is not bound in such cases. God has called you to live in peace" (1 Corinthians 7:15). Some argue that if your spouse is a so-called Christian, this doesn't pertain to you. Yet, if your partner is engaged in affairs or other abusive behavior and doesn't want to abide by his/her marital vows, your partner is *behaving* like an unbeliever, which leaves room for this verse to apply to your situation.

Most theologians interpret the phrase "not bound in such cases" as free to divorce and remarry. And "God has called you to live in peace" suggests the Lord's desire for a generally peaceful atmosphere in your home instead of warring, abusive factions.

When a disobedient spouse chooses to leave, it's best to let the marriage "die" and allow yourself to grieve your many losses. After all, we serve a resurrection God. The Lord can resurrect the marriage with his supernatural power, assuming that would be best for everyone concerned. But apart from a miracle, wishful thinking will not bring your partner back once they've hardened their heart toward you.

Best to let the dream go.

There is no shame in accepting what "is" and seeking to create a new life without your former partner. That way, you'll be ready for whatever and whoever else God has in store for you next. God has other ways to redeem your situation.

I hope you can extend grace to yourself and accept your divorce status without shame. God does not hate you. He hates the *damage* you suffered from your unwanted or undeserved divorce. Let him come alongside you to be your advocate and comforter.

I recognize that unloading a heavy cloak of shame is easier said than done. There are many layers of shame for you to identify and shed, much like a moldy old coat that no longer belongs to you. In addition to the general shame of divorce, the Shame of Rejection adds another layer to the shame we already feel. That is what we will explore next.

Chapter 8

The Shame Of Rejection

For God has said:
"Never will I leave you, never will I forsake you."
~Hebrews 13:5

The wife of a popular pastor in a nearby town, "Carol," stumbled into my office, dragging her feet like a zombie. Once she sat, she dissolved into tears, burying her head in her hands. Between gasps for air, her tragic story tumbled out. I learned that her husband of twenty years had disappeared, and no one knew where he was.

She reported faint premonitions that something was amiss. For example, she had noticed her husband, "Michael," often sat beside a certain elder's wife in staff meetings, and his face brightened when interacting with her. Carol even had a nightmare that their beautiful church caught fire and burned to the ground. Yet, she never made the connection between the nightmare and her husband, who later ran away with the elder's wife, which devastated the church as well.

Her husband had left envelopes in the church office with notes for the elders, the children, and her. Then he picked up his lover and left town.

The next day, Carol's parents invited her and the kids to their home to read the notes her husband had left for them. Her mind scrambled after reading his note informing Carol he was leaving her and the pastorate. Numb, she headed downstairs to have a moment for all this to sink in. On her way back upstairs, her knees buckled, and she collapsed on the stairs, heaving.

Her parents suggested that she and the kids stay with them for a while until Michael was located and they sorted out some matters. The next few nights, unable to sleep, Carol drove from motel to motel, looking for her husband's car. Between inconsolable sobs, she cried out, "Michael, where are you? I'll find you! I'll find you! Please come home! Come home!"

No one knew the illicit couple's whereabouts for several weeks. "Dennis," the other woman's husband, finally hired a private detective to track them down. Ultimately, they were found in a cheap rental fifty miles away.

In the meantime, both affected families and the entire church were in shock. The tremors of their pastor's behavior reverberated throughout their community. In the following months, several couples from that church sought my help, as many marriages were crumbling due to the disillusionment caused by their former pastor's dramatic fall. The ripple effect went on for many years.

The Shame of Being Left

It is difficult enough to endure the shame of betrayal when a marriage unravels over time. But when a spouse leaves without warning, the shock and trauma are magnified. Stripped of any chance to prepare or respond, the forsaken one is left hemorrhaging from the catastrophic loss, adding an extra layer of harshness to the abandonment.

From Carol's story, we see that a unique sense of humiliation occurs when what you thought was a stable marriage is abruptly shattered by your spouse's sudden abandonment.

You may have sensed a subtle distance creeping into your relationship, but the actual loss leaves you reeling. When you later realize that this estrangement was no accident, a wave of embarrassment washes over you. Your partner surrendered to temptation without resistance—whether with another person or an addiction—and then compounded the betrayal by willfully leaving you.

The shock, trauma, and unpreparedness for what author Madeline Bennett calls "Wife Rejection Syndrome" leave an unsuspecting partner, male or female, hemorrhaging over their spouse's hasty departure. She says,

> In my eyes, our marriage was solidified by exceptional compatibility and dedication to family. I could no more imagine my husband walking out on me than I could imagine deserting him. Yet that is exactly what happened. My husband not only exited without warning but eliminated me from his life as if I were a parasite strangling his vital organs.[1]

I've heard similar horror stories from people who came home from work or a brief trip only to find their house emptied of its contents by a straying, deserting partner. Other confounded mates stop for gas and discover their credit cards don't work. After calling the bank and gathering other data, spouses' mouths drop open when they realize their dishonest partner left town with some new paramour after maxing out their credit cards and emptying their bank accounts—pure cruelty.

Nearly twenty years after Bennett's book came out, therapist and author Vikki Stark elaborated on the phenomenon of sudden endings. In *Runaway Husbands*, Stark addressed what she calls "Wife Abandonment Syndrome"—the phenomenon of a husband suddenly leaving his wife out of the blue, usually with another lover in the wings.[2] The same can occur with the unexpected departure of a wife. No warning. No discussion. Just poof! Gone.

When the traitor abruptly absconds with a partner in crime, the trusting spouse is thrust into a state of emotional toxic shock. While all forms of abandonment are injurious, the shame of sudden desertion cuts deeper and lingers longer, leaving the betrayed partner spinning with unanswered questions and no time to process the loss. The swift and stealthy departure of a once-beloved partner magnifies the disgrace—as if the strayer was fleeing a deadly threat.

Calculated escapism requires incredible deceit on the part of the leaver, as it involves cunning planning. For the one left behind, the abrupt loss feels more like the premeditated murder of the marriage than an awkward exit. In reality, sudden abandoners are chicken-hearted. They tend to be conflict-avoiders who would rather run away than face their disheartened, offended spouses or grapple with their own issues.

> If your partner left you in this underhanded way... you've been spared greater heartache down the road.

If your partner left you in such an underhanded way, consider it a painful but necessary mercy—you've been spared even greater heartache down the road. Chances are, they hadn't been honest with you for a long time. I'd question whether they were ever truly capable of genuine intimacy. Like a duck gliding smoothly across the water while paddling furiously beneath the surface, their hidden hostility was likely simmering long before their departure.

And beyond the ruthlessness of sudden abandonment, the buried antagonism often resurfaces in drawn-out battles over custody and settlement issues. Believe it or not, living with such a privately hostile person would have been worse for you long-term, surfacing in other distressing ways.

Shame For Re-Trusting

If you stayed in your marriage post-discovery and offered your unfaithful spouse an olive branch, only to have it swatted away, no doubt you felt horribly rejected. Or, if your spouse accepted your offer to forgive him/her and appeared motivated to reconcile but later refused to link arms with you toward healing, you may feel let down.

Perhaps your spouse was too far gone to re-engage in the marriage or lacked the desire to do the hard work of repair. Or maybe overcoming his/her love or sex addiction required more profound changes than they were willing to make.

If so, you may feel tremendous shame for staying with your unfaithful partner as long as you did. Shame for re-trusting again. Shame for forgiving too soon. Shame for putting up with so much heartache, only to feel humiliated that your love wasn't enough for both of you.

We feel shame if we tried to salvage our marriages, invested in counseling, recovery groups, and online videos, and spent hours in long conversations, only to discover our efforts were one-sided. It's embarrassing to finally notice you're the one doing all the work, and your partner is doing little to none.

Moreover, if your partner pretended to reconcile only for you to learn he or she was still engaged in dishonest activities, you may feel humiliated for giving your spouse a second chance, only to be fooled again.

For example, one of my clients, "Marsha," agreed to allow her husband to continue to live in their house with her and their daughter after he agreed to end his affair and attend personal counseling sessions. She moved into the guest room but continued working full-time, cooking, cleaning, doing his laundry, and praying for his progress. After five months, she pressed him for answers, and he admitted, without any remorse, that he had continued his affair and only met with his counselor sporadically. Needless to say, she was mortified to learn that he had taken advantage of her goodwill to continue his affair.

You didn't choose the affair, and you didn't choose to forsake the marriage. Having your will violated twice—by infidelity and the refusal to try—can knock your feet out from under you. You may feel like you wasted precious time and energy to no avail.

Shame If We Stayed

Betrayed spouses often wrestle with shame—whether from unexpected abandonment, trusting an unfaithful partner again, or staying in the marriage longer than they later thought was reasonable.

Many injured spouses feel embarrassed about giving their unfaithful partners a second (or third, or fourth) chance. In retrospect, they worry that they lacked the dignity to leave or to quickly expel the one who betrayed them.

This consternation is especially strong in those who previously vowed to leave immediately if their partner ever cheated on them. However, upon discovering the affair, many find themselves unexpectedly longing to reconnect with their unfaithful spouse, seeking comfort and reassurance from the very person who hurt them.

Despite a prior determination to leave, injured partners often reverse course when faced with the gravity of losing their marriages and depriving their children of a two-parent household. The prospect of a permanently broken bond and the ensuing financial strain can feel overwhelming. And if a strayer shows a degree of remorse, a person's longing for repair and closeness may override the urge to send the faithless one packing.

For some, the desire to repair the relationship outweighs the urge to divorce, especially when they believe the cost of separation is too high and their partner seems willing to work on rebuilding.

While emotions can be turbulent after discovering infidelity, they can spark a crisis that forces the couple to confront unresolved issues and rebuild their connection. These are the couples I spent most of my career helping and who inspired me to write my first book, *How to Help Your Spouse Heal from Your Affair: A Compact Manual for the Unfaithful*.

I never disrespect a betrayed spouse who chooses to stay. Or at least give the marriage enough time to stop quaking and see if the relationship can be repaired. It takes a certain humility to give an indiscreet spouse the opportunity for a do-over.

If you gave your marriage a second chance after betrayal, there is no shame in that. Every option post-affair is fraught with its unique journey of shame and recovery, including the choice to stay. After all, it might have worked out.

On the other hand, if you are reading this book, and your decision to stay didn't result in a repaired marriage, you may feel more foolish than ever.

All is Not Lost

Regardless of your original goal for staying, you likely grew significantly in the meantime. You may have learned to set clearer boundaries, formed deep friendships with others who've experienced relational trauma, or gained a better understanding of your partner's family-of-origin dysfunctions. Perhaps you have grown more assertive or better at validating others' feelings.

Along with these lessons, hopefully, you also strengthened your trust and dependence on the Lord, despite wrestling with God over this outcome, moving forward with a limp like Jacob.

No one should feel ashamed for giving the Lord time to heal an ailing marriage, no matter the result. God gives us many chances to repent and turn around. And sometimes we do, and sometimes we don't. But there comes a moment when enough is enough. As the Preacher says:

> "To everything there is a season, and a time for every purpose under heaven...a time to search and a time to count as lost, a time to keep and a time to discard" (Ecclesiastes. 3:1, 6).

Most of the people I know who tried hard to make their battered marriages work after infidelity look back with satisfaction for at least giving it a solid shot. Some receive a long-term, mended marriage for their willingness to take a chance, and some do not.

Among those who tried and still lost out, many are grateful they stayed long enough to recognize the snags that would have ultimately doomed the marriage. They realize they were spared further heartache with an entitled, unregretful, unsympathetic, addicted, unmotivated, or self-absorbed spouse. These insights may prove valuable when considering future relationships.

Overall, I hope you can let go of any lingering shame for giving your spouse the time and space to turn their life around and their heart toward God, even if that never happened.

The Comfort of God

One of the greatest comforts we can find after being rejected by an unfaithful spouse, sudden or prolonged, is to be assured that your spouse does not reflect God's heart toward you. God's character is not like that of your betraying, abandoning partner.

Even if others, such as society, the church, fellow believers, friends, or family members, look askance at you for being divorced, know that the Lord does not view you this way. He understands betrayal and abandonment like no other. After all, the Lord knows firsthand what it's like to be "despised and rejected." He sees your heart and knows you didn't want to lose your marriage, no matter who filed first. God allows for divorce when a spouse is unfaithful, abusive, addicted, abandons you, or is hard-hearted.

Even though it may feel like it now, your spouse is not the only one who gets to determine your worth. Don't let one callous partner's distorted perspective rule out others' potential positive votes.

The most important vote you have is from God. He's on your team and values you immensely, enough to die for you. Look for ways to absorb the Lord's love, accept his design of you, and share that love with others.

As Pastor Lee used to say to folks in crisis or depression, "Put yourself in places of blessing." Whether that means quality time with your children, a healthy church community, a supportive small group, fellowship with loving people, or places of beauty and awe.

Accept the fact that many people, including a prospective mate or future boss whom you haven't met yet, would love to have you in their lives, on their team, or in their business.

While some folks feel ashamed for being suddenly forsaken and others feel foolish for staying too long, another group feels ashamed for leaving their marriages too soon after intimate betrayal. That is what we will cover in the next chapter.

Chapter 9

Shame For Leaving

*Do not forsake wisdom, and she will preserve you;
love her, and she will guard you.
~Proverbs 4:6*

After discovering multiple infidelities, it took everything "Betsy" had to file for divorce. After all, she'd grown up in a family with no history of divorce. And she was a Christian who took her marriage vows seriously. However, the guilt and shame overcame her, and she halted the paperwork. She didn't want to be the one to give up on the marriage.

Then, as the lying continued and she discovered texts to another girl, she went back to her attorney and filed for divorce a second time. But her conscience continued to bother her. Initiating a divorce went against everything she believed about the commitment to marriage. What about the kids? How would she make it financially? What would people think? Surely, there was a sliver of hope for preserving their family. So, she backed out of her plans to divorce again.

It took her two more years of torment to realize their situation was hopeless. Her husband refused to change and accept responsibility for his wayward ways. She gathered her courage, smothered the condemning voices in her head, and filed for divorce a third time, this time following through.

Once life gets tough during a separation or after divorce—when financial stress mounts and the kids are struggling—betrayed spouses may start to question their decision to walk away. They wonder if they acted too hastily. Like Betsy, some reverse course and backpedal on their original intentions. Others who exited quickly may find themselves second-guessing the choice later on.

And, if they joined a recovery group for partners of sex addicts, for example, with many members still fighting for their marriages, separated and divorced spouses may feel out of place. Like losers who didn't have the gumption to try as hard as they see their companions doing.

Remember, not every marriage can or ought to survive an affair.

There are many valid reasons to leave an unfaithful, uncooperative partner. While Scripture doesn't mandate divorce after infidelity, it permits it, acknowledging the profound harm it causes to the marital bond. No one should fault you for choosing to leave a broken marriage.

Other justifiable reasons include chronic lying, repeated betrayals, addiction, abuse in any form, ingrained personality disorders, or illegal behavior. Most critically, if your children face any risk of harm, leaving becomes not just a choice but a necessity.

One woman, "Karla," in a private Facebook group for betrayed Christian women, put it this way:

> My husband kept saying things were fine and we needed to just keep doing what we were doing and everything would be okay. He made his choice: telling the marriage counselor that there was nothing wrong and that he was just there to appease his wife. Knowing this helped me make my choice: I got a lawyer that week and served him with papers. He had been cheating on me for years with other women in online relationships and refused to acknowledge that it was a problem or make any changes to give them up.
>
> He lied to me many times about it and pretended to stop, while just getting more creative in hiding things from me. I finally acknowledged reality. Our relationship was over. He left me five years ago, and I just filed the paperwork to make it legal. I didn't leave him. I didn't kill our marriage. I just signed the death certificate.[1]

Character Issues

Craig Englert, a pastor under whom I volunteered for two summers in my late twenties, challenged me to study the various character qualities discussed in the book of Proverbs and color-code them. I spent the following year studying them and highlighting each type with distinct colors. Proverbs upholds some kinds of folks to emulate and warns us to avoid others.

For example, Proverbs affirms the "wise" person, the "generous" person, the "prudent" person, the "gracious" woman, and the "patient" person.

The book of Proverbs also cautions us to avoid the "adulteress," the "unfaithful man," the "ungodly" person, the "dishonest" person, the "slanderer," the "proud" person, the "angry man," the "sluggard," and the "false witness."

However, one of the most common characters the writers of Proverbs warn us about is "the fool." The "fool" is the overarching flaw encompassing most of the negative character traits listed above. Fools do not learn from the past. They make unwise decisions. They fall into grave sin. They cheat others. They are easily deceived. They are proud. They are selfish and lazy. They are easily angered. If these qualities sound familiar, take note that the book of Proverbs warns us that if we closely associate with a fool, it will not go well for us:

> "One who walks with wise people will be wise, but a companion of fools will suffer harm" (Proverbs 13:20).

God will not likely kill your foolish spouse like he did Nabal, Abigail's husband, as described in 1 Samuel 25. However, he may release you from the bondage of such a marriage. Let's look at a few verses that indicate we should not live with or hang around people with serious character flaws.

Much like Jesus' warnings against the "leaven" of the Pharisees and the symbolic use of unleavened bread in the Eucharist, Paul teaches that the yeast of sin affects the whole loaf of a local church fellowship.

> "Get rid of the old leaven, that you may be a new unleavened batch, as you really are. For Christ, our Passover lamb, has been sacrificed. Therefore let us keep the feast, not with the old bread, leavened with malice and wickedness, but with the unleavened bread of sincerity and of truth" (I Corinthians 5:7–8).

Paul then reminds them of a letter he previously sent them regarding a man who was sexually involved with his stepmother. Paul believed that the church's tolerance of this man and his immoral activities was leaven, contaminating the body of Christ in Corinth.

> "I wrote you in my letter not to associate with sexually immoral people. I was not including the sexually immoral of this world, or the greedy and swindlers, or idolaters. In that case you would have to leave this world. But now I am writing you not to associate with anyone who claims to be a brother but *is sexually immoral* or *greedy*, an *idolater* or a *verbal abuser*, a *drunkard* or a *swindler*. With such a man do not even eat." (I Cor. 5:9–11, emphasis added)

In verse 10, Paul distinguishes between casual acquaintances in daily life and those with whom we share close relationships. He is especially firm about avoiding those who claim to be Christians but whose lives contradict Christian values. He specifies avoiding those actively engaged in destructive behaviors.

Notably, Paul's use of the word *is* highlights an ongoing state—someone who *is* immoral differs from someone who *was* immoral. Likewise, a person who *is* a drunkard differs from one who *used to be* but is now sober and in verified recovery.

Now, let's examine the types of individuals Paul instructs believers to avoid, even refraining from sharing a meal with them:

1. The Sexually Immoral (perverted sex or sex outside of marriage)
2. Greedy (selfishly materialistic to the detriment of others)
3. Idol Worshippers (worships other "gods")
4. Verbal Abusers (those who lash out or harshly put others down)
5. Drunkards (alcoholic, addict)
6. Swindlers (thief, liar, gambler, or con artist)

My Next Question

If Paul instructed the *church* to avoid those with persistent character flaws, *why should Christian spouses be expected to live with and share meals with the very individuals whom Paul warns against?* This is an important question to consider when evaluating whether to remain with or leave an unfaithful, vow-breaking, or abusive spouse. As we explore this topic, keep in mind biblical principles and personal discernment necessary for making such a difficult decision.

The Disgust Factor

The "defilement" of infidelity may be too disgusting for a betrayed spouse to overcome, especially if it involves a relative, prostitution, the sex trade, same-sex relations, incest, or underage victims. Certain degrees of sullying are too much for many of us to bear. Envisioning your spouse in sexual acts, real or imagined, with illegitimate others may be so nauseating that you can't find the wherewithal to get beyond it. There may be exceptions. But leaving in such cases may have been your wisest move.

The Lord himself was disgusted by Israel's idol worship, often associated with orgiastic rites and unfaithfulness to Him:

> "Your adulteries and lustful neighings, your shameless prostitution on the hills and in the fields—I have seen your detestable acts. Woe

to you, O Jerusalem! How long will you remain unclean?" (Jeremiah 13:27).

"You have defiled the land with your prostitution and wickedness" (Jeremiah 3:2b).

The Lord found his people's unfaithful lusts "detestable" and "defiling." You should not feel guilty for deciding not to stay in a marriage that was violated in this manner. Each of us has a limit regarding what we can or should live with.

God divorced Israel

Some religious circles treat divorce as an unpardonable sin, shaming those who experience it—regardless of the circumstances. But if that were true, how could God himself have divorced Israel?

In Jeremiah 3, the Lord addresses the prophet regarding the nations of Israel and Judah. Israel, the northern kingdom, had consistently turned to idol worship—spiritual adultery—despite God's patience. When they refused to repent, he issued them "a certificate of divorce," sending them away to be absorbed by the Assyrians, never to return as a distinct nation. Judah, the southern kingdom, witnessed Israel's fate, yet still delayed repentance. However, God preserved a remnant from the tribe of Judah, who ultimately returned to him.

This passage makes one thing clear: divorce itself is not a sin. Rather, it is the betrayal, unfaithfulness, and destruction of the marital covenant that grieves God's heart. If the Lord justly ended his covenant with Israel due to treacherous behavior, then the decision to divorce in cases of persistent infidelity, abuse, or abandonment should not be viewed as shameful but as an allowable response to disloyalty.

The Lack of Motivation Factor (a.k.a. "The Marital Sluggard")

The book of Proverbs often references the lazy person, also known as the "sluggard." If your partner lacked motivation to do the hard work of repair, you found yourself in a precarious position. You couldn't save your marriage alone. While it may take time for a strayer to "get it," it shouldn't take years.

Some people leave when they realize their unfaithful spouses have no interest in repairing the damage, especially when the betrayer remains disengaged, lazy, passive, defensive, or entitled.

> While it may take time for a strayer to "get it," it shouldn't take years.

Or perhaps your partner insisted you already knew everything, only to drip additional details over time. Your spouse's trickle-truth and lack of forthrightness undermined your confidence that your mate would ever come clean.

In other cases, your spouse may have refused to leave despite their lack of cooperation in the marriage. When an unmotivated betrayer stays, sometimes it's because he/she doesn't want to be "the bad guy" for initiating a divorce. They want to save face, save money, or maintain their wayward lifestyle *and* their families.

Rather than making amends, they make life so unbearable that their faithful partner is left with no choice but to file for divorce. I call this having to "file for divorce by default."

This doesn't mean you didn't want the marriage to work. You simply couldn't salvage it all by yourself. A stalemate, standoff, or sliding backward wasn't a viable option for you. Like Karla, whom I quoted earlier, you merely signed the death certificate.

The Chronic Lying Factor

Repeat lies and deception do not bode well for successful reconciliation. Re-establishing trust is a fragile process. Some strayers are generally truthful and only lie to conceal their affairs. Once the infidelity stops, so does their lying. In such cases, there may have been an opportunity for repair. Sometimes, a betrayer may fear losing you, so they initially have trouble coming 100% clean. But this should not continue. Yet, if the strayer has a history of lying and chronic character issues, I see little reason for a cheated-on spouse to stay. In a marriage, there is no place for repeated hiding, lying, deceit, gaslighting, or secret keeping.

If you were married to a smooth-talking con artist, you likely gained valuable discernment to avoid being deceived again. Leaving a charming yet untrustworthy partner has spared you further heartache and made you wiser in the process. Sadly, it may take you years to clean up the mess in your finances.

The Dual-Addictions Factor

Some folks with compulsive sexual appetites struggle with other kinds of addictions as well. Whether that means binging on alcohol, drug abuse, gambling, or other uncontrolled behaviors, these compulsions interfere with the prospects of recreating a safe marriage. Unless the strayer pursues long-term, specialized help to address *all* of their unmanaged habits, they are not great candidates for a future life together. Even if they make periodic efforts to get help, that doesn't mean you must stay in the marriage. When a person fails or refuses treatment for other untreated addictions, it often portends a greater danger of repeating romantic offenses in the future.

The Abuse Factor

Verbal and emotional abuse are serious issues. Infidelity is one form, but many unfaithful spouses behave in other harmful ways, such as belittling, swearing at, threatening, yelling, controlling, or neglecting their partner. If your spouse repeatedly exhibited these behaviors, it might not have been worth trying to save the marriage. Your need to feel safe was more important than saving face in the eyes of others.

Looking back, if you constantly walked on eggshells, afraid of your partner's next blow-up, I hope you know that no one should live in constant dread or fear. Remember, "For God has not given us a spirit of fear, but of power, love, and self-control" (2 Timothy 1:7). A spouse who induced such fear in you was not reflecting God's character nor his heart toward you.

Among the people in I Corinthians 5:11 whom Paul instructs the church to shun is a "verbal abuser." The original word is *reviler* (#3060 in the Greek concordance dictionary). This term is translated as *abusive, railer, or reviler.* These words are derived from Greek words that indicate *one who insults, reproaches,* or *verbally abuses* another person. To rail against someone is to *revile or scold in harsh, insolent language, scoff, and berate.*[2]

You should not have to tolerate a barrage of put-downs that make you feel horrible about yourself, whether in the church or in your home.

Jesus also strongly warned against verbal abuse in the Sermon on the Mount.

> "But I tell you that anyone who is angry with [enraged, wrathful] his brother will be subject to judgment. Again, anyone who says to his brother, 'Raca' [Aramaic for Empty-head!—a term of extreme contempt, similar to our words, "numbskull, or "stupid"] is answerable to the Sanhedrin. But anyone who says, 'You fool' [moronic, nonsensical, useless, brainless] will be in danger of the fire of hell" (Matthew 5:22, bracketed explanations added).

If your spouse repeatedly demeaned or insulted you in any of the above ways, I hope you see that both Paul and Christ take verbal abuse very seriously.

I'll never forget a woman named "Christa," who attended one of my workshops and shared a heartbreaking story. Her husband was a successful businessman whose best friend was unfaithful to his wife. During his friend's pending divorce, the buddy didn't want to divide their assets with her. So, he devised a plan: write a list of as many insulting, hurtful, and negative things about his wife as possible and hand it to her. His goal was to discourage her to the point that she would want to take her own life. Unfortunately, before their divorce was final, she did just that. His plan worked, and he and his new lover got to keep the house, the children, and all the marital assets.

That's when Christa started to cry. It turned out that her husband of twenty years had recently been involved with another woman, filed for divorce, and was using the same tactic. Her shoulders shook as she told us how her husband handed her three pages listing all her "awful" traits. The pages were filled with insults, put-downs, and reasons he hated her and believed she was an unworthy wife. He pulled out all the stops, naming every below-the-belt insult he could think of, some with a hint of truth and others completely false.

Because Christa knew about her husband's best friend's success in getting his wife to commit suicide, she suspected that her husband had similar intentions. He aimed to demoralize her with his reproachful words, hoping she would take her own life before the divorce was finalized, allowing him to keep everything. Fortunately, she was aware of his motives. However, this realization did not lessen the impact of his abusive words on her self-esteem.

I seriously doubt this man suddenly became verbally abusive once the divorce was in progress. Likely, he had malevolent tendencies, which were only magnified by his affair and conniving effort to keep all of his retirement, the kids, and their beautiful home.

Christa's story may be an extreme example, but some of you have no doubt lived with a verbally or emotionally abusive partner. This is not God's design. I don't believe he intended us to put up with someone who seeks to tear us down in such ways.

> "Drive out the mocker, and out goes strife; quarrels and insults are ended" (Proverbs 22:10, NIV).

One way to detect whether you are being abused is to consider this heartwarming verse:

> "There is no fear in love; but perfect love casts out fear, because fear involves torment. But he who fears has not been made perfect in love" (I John 4:18, NKJV).

Living in fear is the opposite of living in love. Ask yourself: Did you constantly walk on eggshells, dreading your partner's words or reactions? Did the thought of returning home fill you with anxiety, uncertain of whether you'd be greeted with warmth or hostility? Were there particular subjects you consciously avoided, fearing they might spark an explosive argument or unleash a torrent of cruel accusations?

If these scenarios resonate with you, it's essential to recognize that this is not the kind of love and respect God intended for marriage. You deserve to be cherished and treated kindly by your spouse, not subjected to fear and apprehension.

I don't have room to list all of the signs of an abusive person in this book. However, there are some excellent books and resources to assist people in recognizing signs of abuse. One of my favorites is *Why Does He Do That?* by Lundy Bancroft.

The Personality Disorder Factor

You may have realized your partner isn't just selfish—they may be a narcissist or sociopath. I will explore this further in Chapter 13, "Underlying Disorders." Personality disorders form early and are largely unalterable. While some may make minor adjustments with professional help, deeply ingrained selfishness or foolishness often remain unchanged. The Bible portrays characters like this realistically.

> "Though you grind a fool like grain with mortar and a pestle, yet his folly will not depart from him" (Proverbs 27:22).

If you recognized immovable, destructive traits in your spouse and chose to leave rather than futilely try to change them, affirm yourself for choosing wisdom over unrealistic control.

The Illegal Behaviors Factor

If your partner not only deceived you romantically but also engaged in criminal behavior without remorse, intense treatment, and accountability—that's a major red flag. Some individuals are master manipulators, unworthy of further trust. Protect yourself from someone with a "criminal mind," and don't let yourself be fooled again by an unchanged, convincing actor.

If you've been married to a slick swindler or chronically abusive person, shield yourself. Note the advice in Proverbs:

> "The prudent see danger and take cover, but the simple keep going and suffer the consequences" (Proverbs 22:3).

Another grievous illegal situation is discovering your spouse was soliciting sexual contact with minors. Pedophilia, seducing underage teenagers, and viewing porn with children is still illegal in this country (despite some efforts to reduce the stigma by calling them "minor-attracted individuals").

Even worse is the shock of learning your spouse was incestuously involved with your own child, a stepchild, grandchild, or other related young person. You must take a protective stance regarding those under your care.

Whatever the illegal behavior, there is no shame in sizing up your situation, cutting your losses, and choosing to leave an unsafe, unhealthy, lawless partner.

The Self-Respect Factor

After James broke up with the other woman and we moved back in together, he broke every promise he'd made to get me back. For weeks, he treated me with contemptuous disregard. After a weekend of him walking out of every room I entered, I was at my wits' end. As mentioned before, I joined my friend, Elizabeth, in attending a retreat for spouses of sex addicts.

At first, I felt a little out of place. While James had dabbled in porn, he wasn't a sex addict. My greater problem was dealing with the fallout of his romantic affair and his emotional distancing.

Our leader, therapist Rob Jackson, had us each sketch a "trauma egg" with pictures of various traumatic life experiences in the "cracks" in the egg from a young age up to the present. We had an hour to explain our "egg" to the group. When my turn came, I summarized the hurtful events in my life, from my childhood up to my husband's infidelity.

When I finished sharing my story, Rob asked the group, "Do you see a pattern in Linda's life over the years?" Everyone nodded in agreement. *Hmm.* I wondered what that could be.

"Did you notice that Linda tends to tolerate inappropriate behavior for far too long?" Again, the group members nodded their heads affirmatively. This revelation stunned me. Here, I believed I was admirably long-suffering. They thought otherwise. I found this feedback invaluable and empowering.

Based on some incorrect assumptions, my mother's modeling, and poor Bible teaching, I mistakenly thought I was supposed to endure mistreatment as a forgiving, forbearing, godly woman. I realized that this misbelief only caused me unnecessary misery and enabled lousy behavior in those who treated me poorly. I did no favors to them or myself by putting up with others' cruelty.

Too often, Christian people confuse tolerating the intolerable as a Christlike act of "turning the other cheek." They forget Jesus avoided those who sought to kill him until the time of his choosing. David hid in the wilderness from murderous King Saul for ten years. Jesus told his disciples that if a household refused to accept them, they needed to "shake the dust" off their sandals and leave.

What if your son or daughter married someone who treated them the same way your spouse has treated you? How would you feel? What would you say to your adult child? Next, reflect on how you think your Heavenly Father felt about the maltreatment you received. If you could hear his voice, what would he say to you?

Clinical Social Worker and Life Coach Leslie Vernick offers workshops, blogs, books, coaching, and classes on coping with a destructive marriage. She helps people develop biblically sound assertiveness skills to gain the courage to confront rather than accept a partner's mistreatment. I highly recommend her material and courses, which are primarily geared toward Christian women.[3]

I hesitate to mention this next book, as it contains a lot of f-bombs and other salty language. However, if you easily let others walk all over you, consider reading Tracy Schorn's humorous book, *Leave a Cheater Gain a Life: The Chump Lady's Survival Guide*.[4] If you still feel ashamed for leaving, you might find it an entertaining read and a boost to your self-esteem.

Returning to Betsy's story at the beginning of this chapter, she now looks back on her choice to file for divorce as her wisest option. She wishes she'd had the strength to stick with her first filing. After much reflection, she is secure that her decision was the right one, all things considered.

Hopefully, this chapter helps alleviate any lingering, misplaced shame you may feel for choosing a different path or timeline than others expected of you. If you found the strength to leave a hard-hearted, unrepentant, abusive, or unfaithful spouse, take a moment to commend yourself—for your courage, self-respect, and decision to align with God's value of you.

Next, we'll explore another common source of shame: Missing the Red Flags. Understanding why you may have overlooked the signs of spousal cheating will help you extend compassion to yourself and let go of self-blame for not recognizing what now seems clear.

Chapter 10

Missing The Red Flags

> Solid food is for the mature, who by constant use
> have trained their senses to distinguish good from evil.
> ~Hebrews 5:14

I should have known. Looking back, the warning signs were there, flashing like neon lights. But at the time, I explained them away, convincing myself they didn't mean what my gut told me they did.

With graduate school consuming my time, I asked my fiancé, James, to draft our custom marriage vows, planning to review and provide input later. When I finally read what he had written, something glaring stood out—he hadn't included a promise of faithfulness. Given his past casual remarks about fallen Christian leaders, alarm bells went off in my mind.

When I pointed out the omission, his response turned my concern into full-blown panic. He admitted he didn't trust himself enough to make that promise. The conversation escalated into an intense argument, and for the first time in my life, I found myself hyperventilating, forced to breathe into a paper bag to regain my composure.

Eventually, we reached a resolution with two agreements:

1. We would tell each other if we ever felt romantically attracted to someone else.
2. A promise of fidelity would be included in our vows.

But rather than James writing those words himself, I was the one who added them. He reviewed the final version, appeared satisfied, and I convinced myself the issue was settled.

Three weeks later, in front of 700 guests, we recited those vows during what I believed was the happiest day of my life.

I had no idea then that what I assumed was resolved was actually a warning of what was to come.

What Red Flags did you gloss over when you were dating or engaged to be married? Did your friends or family express any concerns you dismissed as irrelevant? Were there hints of a secret life or hidden issues you deserved to know?

Showing a casual attitude regarding the subject of infidelity is only one sign of trouble ahead. The other extreme is when your future spouse vehemently judges those who engage in affairs. People who manifest either overly tolerant or condemning attitudes toward folks who have affairs may be hiding similar propensities.

Shame for Missing the Red Flags

One of the most common sources of shame for Betrandoned spouses is missing the Red Flags. Like me, you may wonder, "How did I overlook this?" "Where was I when my spouse was so unhappy?" "How come I didn't ask more questions about their whereabouts?" "Why was I the last to know?" We feel like fools when we look back and realize we ignored clues of betrayal.

Rather than putting ourselves down, it helps us to learn that there are logical reasons we missed the Red Flags alerting us to danger ahead—indicators that we can only see clearly in hindsight.

I've found that many betrayed spouses overlook the warning signs for three key reasons: Assumed Trust, Skillful Deceit, and Betrayal Blindness. As you read about why spouses fail to catch the Red Flags, I hope you better understand why you missed some signals that your spouse either had the potential or began stepping outside the bounds of your marriage.

ASSUMED TRUST

Few of us marry someone we do not trust. When we fall in love, we believe our partner's expressions of affection and the sincerity behind their desire to tie the knot. Most people, particularly people of faith, consider marriage a sacred rite. And when we say our vows publicly before God, friends, and family and sign legal documents to that effect, we assume our partner meant their pledge to marital fidelity as sincerely as we did.

During the initial infatuation phase of a relationship, heightened emotions can make it easy to overlook warning signs. We instinctively give our spouses the benefit of the doubt, viewing them through rose-colored glasses. If we would never consider being unfaithful, we naturally assume the same of our partner. And if we learn of past indiscretions, we often believe that our love is stronger than their previous relationships, convincing ourselves it won't be an issue in our future together.

When reflecting on the early stages of your relationship, you might realize that you dismissed warning bells trying to get your attention. These signs might include a history of cheating, disrespectful behavior, pressuring you for sex before marriage, lying to you, anger issues, compulsive behaviors, or unresolved family issues.

Below, I'll share further examples of Red Flags that I shoved under the rug (not in chronological order) to help you know you are not alone if you missed hints of potential unfaithfulness. Your experience may differ from mine, but I share these examples to encourage you to extend grace to yourself for overlooking any Red Flags.

Red Flag #1: Partial Admissions

A few years into our marriage, James left full-time ministry to return to the business world to work with some good friends. They assigned him to oversee a company division alongside a competent woman at the office. Unbeknownst to me, he and Judy spent many freeway hours driving to different business outposts together. A few months later, he informed the company's owners that he could no longer handle working so closely with a woman who wasn't his wife. His superiors immediately reorganized his job description, so the pair no longer worked together directly.

He then pulled me aside and explained these changes and why. I felt honored by his honesty. His admission only bolstered my trust in him. I figured his transparency with me and his bosses would solve the problem. I assumed his disclosure broke the "spell" of his secret attraction toward her—a huge miscalculation on my part. I also had no idea that she was aware of his infatuation with her.

At the time, the fact that he handled everything behind the scenes before admitting his struggle to me didn't seem like a bad sign. In hindsight, however, it may have been a precursor to more instances where I would be the last to know.

A number of years later, after a big promotion, we purchased a larger home. I oversaw several major remodeling projects on our poorly constructed money-pit house. I eagerly looked forward to finishing so we could relax and enjoy our beautiful waterfront home better. I assumed James's only contact with his previous "crush" was in the group meetings he supervised. It never occurred to me to ask if he was having one-on-one meetings with her. Turns out, he was.

In September of 1999, he admitted he was struggling with an attraction toward her again, adding, "But, this time, I don't want to tell the company's owners." *Big. Red. Flag.*

Looking back, I could kick myself for not asking more questions, such as, "Why don't you want to tell the owners this time?" "What do you mean you're struggling with your feelings again?" "Does she know about this?" "How far have things progressed?" He left me under the impression he was fighting a solitary battle, one that she was unaware of. In reality, I was the one who was clueless. Their romance had already begun.

I later wondered, "Why did I take him at face value without pressing him harder for answers?" Again, I mistook his admission as a sign that he was forthright with me.

What about you? Did you only learn partial truths when there was much more to the story? Were others in the know before you were? Did you make the mistake of confusing partial admissions with confession and repentance? Did you believe your partner's lies, only to later feel foolish for trusting them?

Red Flag #2: Withdrawal and Impatience

I subtly sensed something wasn't quite right in the lead-up to James's affair. He became less responsive to me than he had been earlier in our marriage. He hid behind the newspaper to avoid talking with me, stopped inviting me to join him in the hot tub at night, and spent hours downstairs playing what I assumed were just internet games. Though his distancing hurt, I brushed it off, telling myself things would improve once the remodeling projects were completed. I assumed too much.

After he and Judy became involved, but before I knew anything, I noticed James's heightened impatience with me. I dismissed it as a result of job-related stressors. For example, when we took our ski boat on a short trip up the coast and ran out of gas—nothing I said or did was acceptable to him. "You're doing it all wrong!" he shouted at me; his mouth twisted in disgust. I shrank inside. *Hmm. Why the increased venom?* I could tell something was off-kilter, but I couldn't figure out what it was. Rather than feel bad about him, I felt bad about myself.

How about your situation? Did you notice increased distance or impatience from your spouse when he/she was wandering into the dark waters of unfaithfulness? Did he or she begin to pull away from some of his/her Christian friends? Did you detect a growing coolness or cynicism toward church, spiritual matters, or other believers?

Red Flag #3: Intuition Alert

Shortly before he crossed physical lines with Judy, I had a vivid nightmare I couldn't shake for days. In the dream, James was driving us home. When crossing a high bridge over an ocean passage, he unexpectedly turned onto an exit under construction that I knew led nowhere. As we climbed higher, I began to yell, then scream, begging him to stop. "Watch out! There's a drop-off ahead!" But he refused to listen and sped on. Without even attempting to hit the brakes, my husband drove us off the unfinished exit, and our vehicle became airborne as it shot over the edge, flying high. Then we nosedived faster than a horrifying roller coaster ride. My stomach lurched, and I gripped my seat. I'll never forget the helpless terror I felt as our car descended like a bullet toward the swirling waters below. I stiffened for fatal impact and woke up with a start, my heart pounding so hard my ears hurt.

Looking back, I believe my subconscious mind was picking up signals of pending danger. My gut somehow detected James was contemplating a hazardous wrong turn—something I'd be helpless to prevent. And, in his refusal to listen, our marriage would be destroyed.

The dream didn't make logical sense to my mind at the time. Even though I knew James could be stubborn and sometimes disregard my fears, I never dreamed he'd break his moral code of conduct as a believer. I felt secure in his commitment to me, beyond what I now know he deserved. But my body and unconscious mind detected that our marriage was on the brink of disaster.

Unbeknownst to me, three weeks after my nightmare, James and Judy crossed the line into affair territory, kissing at a work retreat.

The unraveling had begun.

I could tell something was amiss. Whenever James arrived home, his smile seemed forced. He started to pop Tums like candy and occasionally slept on the couch. He was less affectionate. As my anxiety increased, he distanced himself further, which I interpreted as, "You're too needy." So, I backed off.

After he admitted his supposed one-way attraction to her, my body registered a danger that he wasn't acknowledging. I trembled constantly, hardly slept, and had many disturbing dreams where my husband had a secret life. Despite this, during the day, my mind stayed in denial, believing the explanations he gave to cover up their romantic encounters.

One cringeworthy example is when James told me he was heading to a neighboring high school's basketball game. That seemed odd since our youngest son's team wasn't playing that night. My gut twinged. I almost followed him to the game to see if he was there. But I held back, wanting to believe him and afraid to learn otherwise. Plus, I'd feel foolish if I was wrong. I knew if he saw me there, he'd get angry, knowing I was checking on him.

Months later, after he confessed, I learned he'd lied so he could rendezvous with *her* that night. I wish I'd followed my instincts. I could have benefited from having hard evidence that he was lying to me earlier in his affair.

The longer my husband was in his affair, the more time he had to polish his rationalizations and invent a narrative to support his wayward direction. Despite noticing hints that more was happening behind the scenes, his aloofness put me in a bind. I was afraid to ask hard questions or protest intensely, fearing that I would further alienate him. So, I held my tongue when I shouldn't have and occasionally let it fly when I wished I hadn't.

Can you relate? Looking back, was your gut trying to tell you something was amiss? Were you tense, on edge, or having frightening dreams? Did you hold back from expressing your feelings or asking tough questions?

Red Flag #4: Defensive Reactions

Before I knew the fuller story, I grew increasingly uncomfortable. To tweak his conscience, I left a copy of our wedding vows on the kitchen counter. Upon noticing our vows, he accused me of being "manipulative." He fumed, "I *only* agreed to tell you if I was attracted to anyone else!" I wondered, *What about approving and later declaring our vows of fidelity at our wedding?* Boy, did I feel duped.

By the time I discovered theirs was a mutual romance, the damage to our relationship was already severe. I berated myself for missing the "signs" of their involvement, asking, *Why couldn't I see what was happening almost right under my nose? Why did I accept his excuse about wanting to get out of town for a quiet personal retreat when he actually used it to meet up with her? Why didn't I confront him more forcefully when he dismissed our premarital agreement and vows? How did I have him on such a pedestal that I believed his half-truths and lies—despite my better judgment?*

Defensive reactions beyond the norm can signal that your partner is hiding something. Some of you may have been less frozen than I was and sought to confirm (or relieve) your suspicions by pushing harder for the truth. Alternatively, you may have conducted some detective work, such as reviewing phone records. Don't let your partner's defensive reactions make you feel ashamed for your need to know more.

Here, I was a professional counselor who specialized in helping folks recover from infidelity, and I missed the Red Flags, too. Even counselors lack objectivity when it comes to their personal relationships. Assumed Trust is no guarantee of future faithfulness.

YOUR SPOUSE'S SKILLFUL DECEIT

Besides Assumed Trust, another reason we sometimes miss the signs of betrayal is that straying spouses go to great lengths to hide their actions. Skillful Deceit becomes part of the thrill, adding to the dopamine-fueled euphoria of pursuing a forbidden relationship or sexual habit. The lying, hiding, and secrecy become second nature, and most betrayers become highly proficient at it. Over time, they craft a concealed life outside their marriage—one that their spouse remains completely unaware of.

Dr. Minwalla calls this hidden world the betrayer's "Secret Sexual Basement."[1] He compares it to a house where family members all live on the main floor, unaware of a secret basement where a loved one's cheating or sex addiction occurs. Unlike substance abuse, which is noticeable, sexual infidelity is often well-hidden. Family members might sense something is wrong, but can't pinpoint it due to the careful deceit of the offender.

This secrecy harms the betrayed spouse's ability to trust their instincts, as discussed in Chapter 5, causing them to ignore their God-given intuition to seek safety. The unfaithful become masters at deception to avoid admitting details that could reveal their actions. They use gaslighting to make their partners doubt themselves, keep their betrayals secret, and leave them unaware.

It's likely that you, too, had a lingering sense of unease that you couldn't logically explain at the time. But once you discovered your partner's secret sexual activities, those faint impressions of something being off suddenly made sense.

> Learning to trust one's intuitions takes a lot of practice, especially if we were trained as children to ignore it.

You may feel foolish for not seeing this before. Keep in mind, you could only act on what you saw in the light. You are not to blame for your spouse's cleverness at keeping you in the dark. Learning to trust one's intuition takes a lot of practice, especially if we were trained as children to ignore it. Or if we live with a clever, invalidating, deceitful, cheating spouse.

Scripture encourages us,

"Have no fellowship with the fruitless deeds of darkness, but rather *expose* them" (Ephesians 5:11, emphasis added).

If your spouse was bent on keeping secrets, their cloak-and-dagger routines were an open invitation for you to do your own research. If your partner had a hidden life, you deserved to know about it. After all, your spouse's sexual behaviors had a direct bearing on you, your body, your emotions, and your station in life.

My friend, "Elizabeth," once confided in me about her suspicions that her husband was hiding something, though she had no solid proof of what it was. I suggested she obtain a credit report. Sure enough, it revealed a recurring charge for a private post office box—which she soon learned was his means of secretly communicating with call girls and brothels. This discovery gave her the clarity and confidence to take protective steps for herself.

Uncovering the truth often requires asking hard questions and following uncomfortable leads. If your pursuit of answers angered your spouse, remember that early detection may have been your best chance to address the situation before it escalated. Even if it led to conflict, that doesn't mean you were in the wrong. Hard evidence can be a powerful wake-up call, forcing a deceiver to face what they've tried to conceal.

While early detection is no foolproof guarantee of future repair, it can increase your odds of avoiding future traps. If you needed to do some sleuthing to discover what was happening, you were not out of line. Your partner's effort to hide his or her affair was the real issue—not your effort to uncover it.

And, if you missed the clues that your spouse was sexually betraying you, you are not alone. Strayers typically work hard to keep their dalliances under wraps, both to get away with forbidden pleasures and to buy time to decide if they want to run off with their lovers or not. A subversive form of control.

Rather than beating yourself up with shame, view this as a hard-earned lesson to no longer discount the niggly messages your intuition is trying to tell you. Instead, seek to listen to your gut hunches and strengthen your courage to confront uncomfortable truths you deserve to know.

Every betrayed partner I have worked with who has reflected on their past experiences has concluded that in each case of silent alarm, their intuition was 100% correct. May you learn to listen to your body's signals when something isn't right. And take appropriate action.

BETRAYAL BLINDNESS

Many of you can likely relate—wanting to believe the best despite subtle warning signs. As an honest person, you extended the gift of Assumed Trust, believing your spouse's integrity mirrored your own. Meanwhile, they employed Skillful Deceit to conceal a secret sexual world. When the truth finally surfaced, you may have felt foolish or ashamed for not seeing it sooner.

Therapists who specialize in Betrayal Trauma call this tendency to overlook or rationalize a loved one's violations *Betrayal Blindness*—a survival instinct that shields the betrayed from a reality too painful to fully process at the time.

The first researcher I am aware of who identified this phenomenon among victims of abuse is Jennifer Freyd, a clinical psychologist and retired professor at the University of Oregon. She and her coauthor explain this tendency in their book *Blind to Betrayal: Why We Fool Ourselves We Aren't Being Fooled*: "People remain unaware of betrayal when the unawareness helps them stay in a relationship they believe they need for their own survival."[2]

Denial prevents us from facing a dreadful truth that might threaten our primary relationship. As the authors state, "We remain blind to betrayal to protect ourselves."[3] And, "Knowledge of betrayal is always destabilizing."[4]

> Denial prevents us from facing a dreadful truth that might threaten our primary relationship.

Hence, we tuck in our heads like turtles to avoid rocking our relational boat. That was me.

I was afraid to know what I didn't know. It felt too dangerous. So, I remained consciously clueless, ignoring my unconscious instincts that were telling me the awful truth—truth that would have revealed my personal options sooner rather than later.

Frey and Birrell state, "The need to trust is a powerful agent, a blinding force."[5] When we need to depend on a loved one, it can feel dangerous to expose and confront any treachery in the relationship.

In my case, I was blind to the hints of my husband's betrayal in ways that replicated my family's denial regarding my father's alcoholism. My mother dutifully wanted to trust my dad to pick me up safely from school activities *because she needed him to*. Thus, she remained blind to the danger this put me in. He would leave the house reasonably sober, but by the time he reached my school, he was inebriated. This pattern continued throughout my junior high years. We all danced around the truth in a misguided effort to preserve our family.

Reflect on your early years. Did your family teach you to ignore your feelings and instincts? Was there a pattern in your family to deny the obvious? To act as if everything was fine when it wasn't? Understanding the reasons why you were prone to Betrayal Blindness will help you see why you played ostrich when your marriage was at risk.

My own Betrayal Blindness, which afflicted my family when I was growing up, also showed up in my marriage. Besides his casual attitude about affairs before we got married and the other Red Flags I've shared so far, here's another glaring example of the level of denial I was prone to. Some of you may be able to relate:

Blind to the Degrading Impact of Porn

About a year before he commenced his affair, James's buddies forced him to admit to me that he'd been dabbling in pornography for months. Being somewhat naïve about the porn industry, I assumed this was no worse than viewing the swimsuit edition of Sports Illustrated. Yes, I know. Many of you are shocked at my ignorance. While I knew sex addicts could get into some raunchy stuff, I figured James was above all that and assumed that whatever he watched was on the lighter side. Now I know that even the "light" stuff is bad, contaminating, and progressive.

I appreciated James telling me about this and let the matter drop. Again, I mistook his admission as a sign of repentance. My underreaction sent him a message: "I can get away with anything I want, and my wife won't hassle me." I also didn't realize that viewing pornography wears a person's morals down and increases the viewer's appetite for and the likelihood of extra-marital affairs.[6]

Several months later, I walked in on James downstairs, in front of the computer. When he quickly exited the screen, my gut immediately twinged. *He's hiding something.*

James swiveled toward me and said, "Oh, I was just chatting with a widow who needed comfort." Despite his earlier admission to porn, I didn't connect the dots. Afraid to challenge his lame explanation, I quickly deposited this incident into the dungeon of "don't-go-there" items where I buried scary things I couldn't afford to know. Rather than doubt him, I doubted myself.

What about you? What Red Flags did you miss before discovering your spouse's affair? Take comfort in the fact that even an infidelity specialist like me can overlook warning signs. Be gentle with yourself—you're human. Give yourself credit for wanting to believe the best about your spouse. And just because your spouse was clever in hiding their secret life, it doesn't make you responsible for it.

Let this experience serve as a valuable lesson to trust your instincts, listen to your gut, and have the courage to ask tough, uncomfortable questions.

Taking a Mental Health Break

Despite his early partial admission, I remained in denial for the next five months. I misinterpreted what my frayed nerves were trying to tell me. He denied that his one-way feelings for *her* had anything to do with his growing dissatisfaction with our marriage. After months of suffering his painful ambivalence toward me, I finally decided to take a mental health break and flew to Hawaii to stay with friends—my first healthy action. While there, I met with a church counselor, Karen Johnson, who helped me uncover what I was too scared to face.

After listening to my story, she suggested more was happening behind the scenes than he'd told me. I objected, "But he's never lied to me before!" With a knowing smile, she said, "They *all* lie." Stunned, I left our session shaken.

In the meantime, my trip to Hawaii flipped the script. Sensing new strength in me, James was nervous that I would leave him on my own terms and timing. While I was away, unbeknownst to me, he and the other woman had broken up. He began phoning me from the mainland, begging me to let him fly to Maui to walk the beach with me, holding hands. I refused. Although his voice was as tender as it was when we were engaged, I still didn't trust him. Emboldened by my counselor's objective support, I began to ask him the tough questions I'd been avoiding all this time. I finally pressed him, "I deserve the truth. After all, I'm your *wife*!"

After a fitful night, James called me the following morning, tearfully confessing his affair. I learned details such as when they crossed the line from flirting to kissing, their secret getaways, etc. Finally, it all began to make sense. I was shocked, hurt, relieved, and hopeful all at once.

Later that day, I met with my counselor, eager to share what I thought was good news—James had confessed and seemed remorseful. But she offered a measured response. "You're not out of the woods yet. He still has a lot of inner work to do."

She picked up a pen and drew two circles on a piece of paper. In one, she placed two stick figures. "The best hope for your marriage lies in his upcoming counseling," she said, pointing to James and his new therapist. Then she gestured to the second circle, sketching James and me surrounded by friends. "And in the community around you. Until he examines his motives, is transparent with those who care about him, and allows them to hold him accountable, he risks slipping back into deception."

I wish I could say James embraced this wisdom—that he engaged deeply in counseling and leaned on his friends for accountability. But neither happened. He manipulated his therapist to reinforce his justifications, refused to be honest with those closest to him, and dismissed my requests to cut all ties with Judy.

A month later, brokenhearted and exasperated, I packed some clothes and moved into a friend's cabin in protest. A few months later, they finally ended things for good. But by then, his justifications and new libertine theology had taken root. Despite our efforts to reconcile, it soon became apparent that our values were no longer aligned and that he'd permanently hardened his heart toward me. No acts of kindness or tough love on my part made a dent in his feelings.

WHAT YOU CAN LEARN

Whatever your story, I assume you can relate. You may know what it's like to overlook Red Flags, caught in a state of Betrayal Blindness. Fear of the truth kept you from acknowledging the signs, and your heart clung to the hope that the person you loved was incapable of such deception. You dismissed your body's warnings, holding onto memories of tenderness while avoiding the painful reality.

But like so many who have walked this road, when the truth finally surfaced, shame followed. You berated yourself. "How could I have missed what now seems so obvious? How could I have been the last to know?"

Yet, all is not lost. This experience, painful as it is, holds the power to teach you some valuable lessons. With reflection comes wisdom. And with wisdom, the strength to trust yourself again.

Lesson #1: Listen To Your Intuition

When your gut twinges, pay attention. When you have vivid dreams that you can't shake the next day, don't dismiss them. As we discussed in Chapter 5, your intuition is a gift from God; learning to listen can provide you with the insight and direction you need.

> "I will bless the LORD who counsels me; even at night my conscience instructs me" (Psalm 16:7).

The word translated as "conscience" is "kidneys" in Hebrew, a term that describes one's gut feelings or heart. So don't ignore it. Push yourself to ask hard questions, no matter how scared you are or how the other person reacts. Don't let your fear of hostile or defensive reactions stop you from pressing for the truth. You have a right to know.

Lesson #2: Admission Is Not The Same As Repentance

Looking back, I can see that each time he admitted something—his first crush on her in 1994, his use of porn in 1998, and his rekindled attraction for her in 1999—he left out critical information. It took me years to realize that each admission was only a partial truth. For one thing, unbeknownst to me, she knew about his attraction toward her the first time. His porn use wasn't compulsive, but he'd ventured onto more sites than I had imagined. When he mentioned he was struggling with feelings toward Judy again, they were already involved. Regretfully, my blindness to betrayal allowed him to get away with each step of moral failure and our marital demise.

I learned this the hard way. I would have discovered much more if I had followed my instincts and asked more challenging questions early on.

What about you? I hope you don't confuse admission with healthy confession and genuine repentance.

Sometimes, an unfaithful partner will confess just enough to make you believe they've told the whole truth—when they haven't. Or they'll express just enough regret to convince you they're repentant—when they're not.

Some unfaithful people withhold details out of fear of hurting you further. Or they do this to protect themselves from your anger or rejection. These are not good reasons, but they are somewhat understandable.

Yet other, more perverse strayers intentionally leave out important information, believing they are entitled to privacy apart from you—the legitimate spouse.

Lesson #3: Forgive Yourself

Rather than recriminating yourself, please know that you are not alone. Denial serves a short-term purpose: to protect you from something you are not ready to face—something that could alter the bond in your marriage, even though the real threat is your partner's outside enchantments.

It is no crime to believe the best in someone you love. Forgive yourself for being human and simply trying to survive. Let Jesus wash away the shame over how your partner fooled you.

Take heart. You know enough of the truth by now that you are no longer groping in the dark. It may have cost you a lot. But you are wiser for it. You won't be easily fooled again once you've:

- Learned to trust your intuition.
- Gained the courage to ask tough questions.
- Realized the wisdom of seeking outside help.

Hopefully, you've increased your capacity to detect and confront inappropriate behavior sooner rather than later. Consider writing down a list of the Red Flags you missed. Then, reflect on what you've learned from the last few chapters.

The betrayed often feel shame for missing the Red Flags that could have revealed their partner's betrayals sooner. It's important to understand that "Assumed Trust" and "Betrayal Blindness" are common among the deceived.

When the unfaithful skillfully hide their actions, trusting spouses are easily misled. This is not their fault. It's the result of believing the best, fear of facing unbearable loss, and the betrayer's well-concealed secret life.

Once you learn to trust your gut instincts and pursue the truth without fear of repercussion, you will be empowered to cope with whatever new challenges you face in the future, this time with the blinders off.

Now that you've better identified your shame from the divorce and for missing the Red Flags, you are ready to understand the degree of Rage you felt over being betrayed and abandoned. Such Rage is more normal than you think. We will explore the reasons behind the Rage you felt and how to manage these unpopular emotions.

Chapter 11

Shame For The Rage

Be angry, yet do not sin.
~Ephesians 4:22

During our marital crisis, I used to sit in our living room gazing out our large picture windows—seething. I imagined taking a baseball bat, swinging it with all my might, and smashing the glass into smithereens. I envisioned shards of glass flying everywhere, leaving a jagged, gaping hole in our windows, ruining the view—just like my life was in ruins.

I relished imagining the shocked faces of others over such a violent outburst. I wanted everyone—including my unfaithful husband—to know just how furious I was. Thankfully, I never acted on the fantasy, but envisioning it felt satisfying, nevertheless.

I had never experienced such searing rage until my husband betrayed me and threatened divorce. I didn't think I was capable of such intensity. I imagine it's akin to a mother's fury when her child is taken—only in this case, it was my Protective-Partner instinct roaring to life. Normally, I'm level-headed and not easily wrangled. But this threat to my security shattered my composure.

I had no safe outlet for the fury I felt.

As we explored earlier, shame in betrayal takes many forms — it can attach itself to our choices, our marriage's collapse, and even to things beyond our control. But shame rarely travels alone. It often fuels anger, creating a volatile mix. The same voice that whispers, 'You should have known better,' can also ignite fury: 'How could they do this to me and our children?' This is why shame and rage often rise together in the healing journey.

Psychologist Steven Stosny puts it this way:

Attachment pain tends to be the worst kind of emotional pain, which is why intimate betrayal is so devastating. It can make you feel unlovable and inadequate as an intimate partner, parent, child, sibling or close friend.[1]

Many spouses react with uncharacteristic animosity when they discover a partner's betrayal. They may smash wedding pictures, scream, throw cell phones across the room, or melt in agony on the floor. Some beg their spouses to stay or write nasty notes to the affair partner. When triggered, others physically kick their partners in the shins. Most of us don't take the insult of intimate betrayal very well.

One study of 297 participants in a survey on sexual betrayal trauma found that 87% reported self-blame, and 43% considered harming themselves. Results clearly indicate that betrayed partners are significantly impacted physiologically, psychologically, behaviorally, and spiritually. They also experience feelings of intense anger, with 84% reporting they experienced more intense anger than at any other time before discovering betrayal.[2]

Did you catch that? *84% experienced more intense anger* after discovering betrayal than at any other time in their lives. I hope you find consolation knowing that you're in good company.

Christian women, in particular, feel guilty about the rage they experience over romantic betrayal. They often believe it's ungodly or unbecoming for a Christian spouse to feel such intense anger. As a result, they may assume it's sinful and try to hide or deny their wrath.

I love an Instagram post from @hopeafterbetrayal:

> There is a holy rage that rises in the heart of a betrayed partner—and it is sacred, not sinful. It is the roar of a soul that knows its worth. It says, "What you destroyed mattered. What you shattered was sacred. And I will not be silent about it."[3]

Yet, instead of expressing their rage directly, many women express it passively—through silence, overspending, or excessive drinking. Keep in mind, rage is a natural response to the threat of abandonment. God never intended us to endure betrayal quietly. As the saying goes, "Hell hath no fury like a woman scorned." The same applies to men, who often feel less guilt when expressing their rage more openly.

It's Not a Sin to Feel Angry

The Bible says, "Be angry, yet do not sin" (Ephesians 4:26). I see this as the Lord permitting us to be angry but admonishing us not to lose control *in* our anger. The sin is not in feeling angry. It is acting with cruelty or harm toward others in the midst of it.

God the Father often raged about spiritual adultery in the Old Testament, and Christ became angry when the money changers violated the sacredness of the temple.

Read the Psalms if you want to see David's honest expressions of rage after betrayal. He shared his angry emotions in song or prayer. The Lord included them in the Scriptures as an example for us to know that we can express our rage to him. David even asked God to kill his enemies. He said,

> "And in Your loving devotion, cut off my enemies. Destroy all who afflict me, for I am Your servant" (Psalm 143:12).

It's therapeutic to pour out our acrimony to God in prayer. Yet, when we are angry, helpless, or desperate, we may say or do things we later regret. I remember pounding my head on a friend's wall as I sobbed in anguish, an incident that I later wished I could erase.

Intimate betrayal degrades us, and we sometimes behave in ways that further degrade ourselves. The specter of unfaithful loss is a primal threat that either empowers us to act in our own self-interest or prompts actions we later regret. Immediate righteous rage can be healthy, energizing us to stop tolerating the intolerable. But when nursed, it can harm our minds and health or lead to actions we'd like to undo.

Don't Lose Your Dignity

While rage is a normal reaction to intimate betrayal, we must remember that exercising self-control will spare us indignities that would only worsen our plight.

Part of our recovery from shame is realizing that our straying partners are not the only ones with options. We have them, too. Yet, we must find *healthy outlets* for our justified red-hot rage.

Counselors often frame anger as a secondary or umbrella emotion. The primary emotions underlying anger are hurt, shame, or a perceived threat of harm. For the betrayed, the umbrella of rage is over an intense fear of abandonment or the total devaluation of our existence.

The most effective way to process our pain is to have the chance to do so with the one who caused the offense. The problem for Betrandoned spouses is that this rarely occurs. The offending spouse usually refuses to listen or accept responsibility for their damaging actions. Instead, they blame the betrayed spouse and rebuff their feelings. Some strayers use threats of divorce, hanging up the phone, or walking away to shut their spouses down. Others, suddenly disappear or sneak off at night, as in Pastor Michael's case from Chapter 8.

When betrayers refuse to engage in a meaningful discussion about how they've injured their spouses, it only fuels the fire of a hurt spouse's smoldering angst. So, what's a Betrandoned person to do?

Healthy Ways to Cope with Your Rage

While I will discuss ways to release your angst in Chapter 23 and explore them more thoroughly in the Workbook, here are six initial suggestions for coping with your understandable rage in a healthy way.

1. Counseling. One option is to seek a professional who can equip you with tools to manage your reactions to deep emotional wounds. True healing comes from addressing the pain that fuels your rage. A trained, empathetic therapist can offer much of the comfort, validation, and guidance you need. Intense anger short-circuits a person's ability to make logical, self-controlled choices amid a threatening crisis.

As a betrayed spouse, you may need the help of a well-trained counselor or coach to help you name your feelings, calm your nerves, reconnect with your wiser self, and regain your equilibrium so you don't do stupid, knee-jerk things when seeking an outlet for natural rage.

2. Confidential Friends. In addition to finding a skilled therapist, another source of help is to find trustworthy friends with whom to share your pain. You need friends you can confide in without feeling judged. Expressing your darkest feelings in a safe environment functions like a pressure relief valve. It provides an outlet for your pent-up anger and gives you the space to process the burning pain fueling it.

It's beneficial if you can find others who've suffered some degree of interpersonal trauma in their lives. You need people who listen to you compassionately without trying to "fix" you. Those who've "been there" especially know the value of walking alongside you as a confirming, empathetic witness to your sorrows.

3. Group Support. Finding group support is one of the most effective tools to help you overcome betrayal shame. Shame's power is magnified when you suffer in the shadows. But when you share your sorrows in the light with those who get your pain, the isolating burden of disgrace is lifted. You'll feel less alone and less ashamed of your spouse's rejection when surrounded by a supportive group of people who understand your unexpected emotions and reactions to betrayal.

Support groups can also be beneficial when a newcomer arrives, and you see how far you've come in your own healing. You notice what the Lord has taught you through your pain, especially how to listen with empathy and comfort others.

I recall the time when "Loretta," a respected local leader in Bible Study Fellowship, joined our support group for the first time. We asked her to share her story. It turned out her husband had begun an affair with the instructor of the Zumba class she and her husband were taking together.

When she got to the part where she showed up at the lover's Zumba class, the support group members' eyes widened, impressed by her bravery. Loretta explained,

> After class, I delivered a copy of the note I'd found, which revealed the betrayal, to the instructor. I said, "You did this to me! I thought you were my friend!" I walked a few steps away, spun around, and looked her straight in the eye, and said, "Bitch!" I then turned back away and marched out.[4]

We all laughed and applauded. Loretta's shoulders visibly relaxed at the group's admiration for her courage and candor. I think she was surprised at her acceptance in this group of Christian women.

Loretta navigated her unwanted divorce with continued dignity, holding firm lines and receiving the settlement she deserved. Later, she led a well-attended Divorce Recovery group for her church for two years.

> *No one should have to bear the unbearable alone; we all need compassionate others to help us through.*

Remember: if your spouse swore you to secrecy, that wasn't fair. What right did they have to demand your silence while they hid devastating secrets of their own? They may have withdrawn from friends, but at least they had the comfort of a lover to confide in—you had no one. When your spouse went behind your back and plotted the end of your marriage, you lost your primary source of support. No one should bear the unbearable alone; we all need compassionate others to help us through.

4. Study God's Word. There is a reason Paul urged Timothy,

> "Study and do your best to present yourself to God approved, a workman [tested by trial] who has no reason to be ashamed, accurately

handling and skillfully teaching the word of truth" (2 Timothy 2:15, AMP).

In a crisis, we may only have the energy to glance at Bible memes on social media or scan a daily devotional filled with someone else's reflections. But true comfort and transformative wisdom come from diving into God's Word for yourself—not just skimming the surface.

The Bible contains precious promises and principles for beleaguered, betrayed spouses. The truths of Scripture are incredibly grounding—treasures to be mined like precious gold or gems.

When your world has been turned upside down, and you can't rely on those you used to trust, you need to fasten the "belt of truth" around your waist. This is what holds your spiritual armor together. Clinging to truth when hurricane winds assail will anchor your roots deep, keeping you grounded through the storm.

That is why I created the Workbook to accompany this book—so you, too, can dig for the many stabilizing truths contained in Scripture for yourself.

5. Honest Prayer. Early in my journey to recovery, I resolved to be authentic—no more phony Christian niceties to impress others, including God. I was determined to process my losses and wounds as genuinely as I knew how. My best tool for that was having frank conversations with the Lord, which were more like yell sessions or fall-on-the-floor sob sessions with him. I told the Lord exactly how I felt. How disappointed I was that he hadn't rescued our marriage. My fury over all that happened. I wrestled with God like Jacob, cried aloud like David, and lamented like Jeremiah.

After screaming *at* him, I then sobbed *with* him. I let him into my agony over my ruined life. Sharing my sorrows with the Lord allowed him to share his sorrows with me. I realized he was just as upset over my shattered marriage as I was. After all, Jesus knows betrayal like no other. While my grief took years to process, as the shock wore off, I was able to receive the comfort of my loving, compassionate, understanding Lord.

I encourage you to do the same.

Yell, scream, and get it all out of your system. But don't leave it there. Weep with him and allow him to weep with you. Like in the Psalms, conclude your rantings of hurt and rage with a small request or an expression of trust, praise, or gratitude. Then drop your tiny mustard seed of faith into his hands for him to plant and eventually grow into a large, redemptive bush.

6. Healthy Protestations. This may involve setting boundaries with your estranged or ex-partner regarding what you won't tolerate or expressing your carefully considered feelings, which are best written down and reviewed by another person for editing first. We have the right to object to sexual offenses. We should not be pressed into silence or inaction.

I must admit that I mishandled some of my early attempts to protest my husband's infatuation with the other woman. Some of these efforts were justified, while others were not. I've often wondered if I had stuck to my first red line, whether he would have awakened from his artificial bliss before it completely seared his conscience. Instead, intimidated by his pushback, I caved and dropped my boundary. My lack of follow-through reinforced his mistaken belief that he held all the rights, and I had none.

Two people made comments that alleviated some of my shame over certain reactions and inactions. One person was my counselor during my two-week hiatus in Hawaii. I shared with her a few of my failed attempts to interfere in my husband's affair. She simply stated, "You get to." I did a double-take. I thought she would gently reprimand me for some of my foolishness. But her attitude was essentially, "He did the unthinkable to you, so you had the right to protest his wrong behaviors in whatever non-destructive way you wished."

My brother was the other person who helped me rethink my shame. He said, "When your husband broke his vows to you, he threw out the rule book. You can respond however you want, as long as it doesn't cause bodily harm."

I realize neither person permitted me to exact revenge on him, such as slashing his tires (as I've known some jilted spouses to do). However, I had inadvertently reinforced James's belief that he was the only one with options. He believed his affair was no one else's business, including mine.

Yet, here he was, cavorting with a secret lover, with ramifications that hugely impacted me as well as the workplace. It took me some time to realize that it *was* my business who he was messing around with. I just needed enough light and wisdom to take action that didn't invite further indignity upon myself. Rather than freeze, as though I'd been tazed, I considered what I could do to reclaim my self-respect.

Since my husband refused to listen to my woes, I decided to confront the other woman. When I mentioned my plan to Dr. Tim, he called this a "bold new move" for me. I had three goals in mind: I wanted her to know the pain their affair had caused me, the ways the Lord met me in my grief, and to insist they have no more contact, as I still hoped for reconciliation.

Many counselors advise against such a meeting. But I think it all depends on the situation. If you choose to confront an outside lover, I encourage you to discuss it with a wise person you respect beforehand. Decide what you wish to accomplish by confronting the other person. Are you seeking an apology? Hoping to insist he or she break off the affair? Or do you mostly want them to know the pain their involvement with your spouse has caused you?

Try to assess, based on what you know about the other person, if you are more likely to regain or lose more of your dignity. And examine your motives. It will not go well if you simply want to vent some steam by verbally attacking the affair partner. You can't predict how they will react.

Fortunately, I didn't unleash my anger on her and pretty much followed my plan. I was surprised that Judy was a good listener and only said one thing that "tweaked" me. It was when she said in a condescending tone, "I'm not responsible for the condition of your marriage, Linda." I quickly responded, "I didn't *know* we had problems until you got involved with him. I was completely blindsided. Your relationship poisoned our marriage!" Looking back, I'm glad I had the chance to say that to her.

You need to pray about whether or when to have such a meeting. Affair-partner confrontations must be well-intentioned and not done in the heat of the moment. Also, keep in mind that some affair partners are so well-defended that they may say terrible things to you that you wish you hadn't heard. And you won't know the degree of lies they are telling that could torment you for a very long time.

I've also known betrayed spouses who confronted the other man or woman in a fit of rage with poor results. The confronter ended up so triggered by the paramour's defensive reactions that they lost their cool, came across as threatening to the other person, and ended up being hauled away by the police.

Some wounded spouses find satisfaction in writing a carefully crafted letter to the affair partner. However, since tone of voice doesn't come across in writing, it's important to be cautious with your wording. Letters can easily be misinterpreted and even used against you. You may not receive a response, which can leave you feeling unresolved. If you're okay with no response or a defensive one, then go ahead and write. But I don't recommend using social media or email for this, as what you write can be edited and forwarded to unsympathetic eyes.

You are in good company if you struggle with shame over some of your unpleasant or angry reactions. You've experienced a horrific ordeal that no one should have to endure in this life. God did not design you for betrayal. Nor did he plan for you to lose your spouse in such a degrading manner. Even God showed rage in the Old Testament when his people unfaithfully turned away from him. And Jesus demonstrated righteous anger when the money changers were cheating fellow Jews in the Temple. He understands. And he doesn't expect you to do trauma and betrayal perfectly. Just don't let the weight of despair paralyze you into inaction.

Ask yourself, "Will this cause me to violate my own integrity?" and, "Will I regret this five years from now?"

If your answers are "no," then, in the words of Karen Johnson, my Hawaii therapist, "You get to."

Closing Thoughts

I hope you found relief from reading **Section II**. Victims of betrayal and abandonment suffer an inordinate amount of shame in the aftermath of their spouse's unfaithfulness and rejection. It's terrible to be replaced, unwanted, and thrown away by the person we pledged our lives to, built our dreams around, and formed families with.

Since spousal betrayal is a shameful, frightening form of abuse, most of us react in unbecoming ways upon its discovery. Whatever your reactions to betrayal-shame, good or bad, nice or not-so-nice, you likely operated within the range of normal, considering the abnormal degree of trauma and shame you've experienced. However, be sure to evaluate whether future actions will complicate your recovery, further erode your already low self-esteem, or compromise your personal integrity.

As you move forward, you may need to draw and uphold lines of respect for yourself and advocate for your children when necessary. Just learn to do so in a calm and self-controlled manner.

If you're struggling with undeserved shame, I encourage you to seek counseling, confide in trusted friends, join a support group, immerse yourself in God's Word, pray honestly, and consider establishing healthy boundaries or expressing your concerns in a constructive way.

Next, in **Section III, Revealing the Source**, I offer unique insights into understanding your betrayer. This progression of chapters will help you make sense of how infidelity crept into your partner's life. These consecutive insights will also help you release even more of the misplaced self-blame and shame you feel over the breakup of your marriage.

SECTION III

Revealing the Source

"Truthful words stand the test of time, but lies are soon exposed."
~ Proverbs 12:19, NLT

Once your wounds are named, the next step is to uncover what—and who—are really behind the betrayal. All is not as it seems. Infidelity rarely occurs in a vacuum.

Until you look beneath the surface, you can't fully grasp what shattered your life. But when the curtain is fully pulled back and the hidden influences exposed, the illusions lose their grip. The image of Scorn shrinks when you see the truth behind it.

Understanding the deeper forces—such as emotional deception, rationalization, unresolved childhood issues, mental disorders, or spiritual compromise—brings clarity. And with clarity comes freedom. The more you recognize that your partner's betrayal was shaped by factors beyond you, the more shame loses its hold.

You were not the cause. You were caught in the fallout.

This section will help you identify the real drivers behind the destruction—so you can stop carrying what was never yours to bear.

Boy Meets Girl

by Linda J. MacDonald
(can be reversed to apply to either sex)

Boy meets Girl.
Boy falls in love with Girl and woos her.
Boy asks Girl to marry him.
Girl says yes, believing theirs is "true love."
Boy and Girl become Man and Wife.
Life gets hard.
Baggage between Man and Wife builds up.
Man meets Other Girl.
Man gets confused.
Man attaches to New Girl and feels like Boy again.
Boy forgets he was a Man.
Boy detaches from Wife.
Boy sees Wife as obstacle to happiness.
Wife senses detachment and starts to complain.
Boy forgets good memories.
Boy sees Wife as witch.
Boy seeks solace with New Girl.
Boy's love for New Girl has no baggage.
New Love feels more real than Old Love.
Boy decides he doesn't love Wife.
Boy can't remember ever loving Wife.
Boy rewrites marital history and tells Wife.
Wife's world crumbles.
Boy feels justified.
Boy leaves Wife to be with Other Girl.
Wife is devastated.
Boy stays Boy for a very long time.

Chapter 12

The Iceberg Below

> All these evils come from within, and these are what defile a man.
> ~Mark 7:23

Recently, while watching a fascinating documentary, "10 Mistakes that Sank the Titanic,"[1] I learned that the iceberg that sank the ship comprised one million tons of ice, 90% of which was below the waterline. As it had melted slightly, it formed a dangerous, jagged edge below the surface—the ledge that cut through the mighty Titanic's hull on its maiden voyage in April 1912.

The show also described an unfortunate series of errors that combined to cause its sinking, some of which resulted from human hubris. For example, Captain Smith liked to travel fast, so the ship steamed ahead at 22 knots instead of the usual 18–19 knots of most ocean liners. Had he been going slower, the ship would not have been on the path of the large iceberg, or at least the captain might have been able to maneuver around it.

The crew concealed the fact that a fire in Boiler Room #5 had weakened one of the protective bunker walls, which were meant to create watertight compartments, causing it to leak water that later flowed into other bunkers. The wireless operators were so busy relaying and receiving passenger radio messages that when they received an alarming notice about an iceberg field from a nearby ship, the Californian, they ignored it and replied, "Keep out, old man." So, the Californian's wireless operator stopped trying to warn them and went to bed.

The cruise line believed that having new wireless equipment to contact a nearby ship for help was enough, so they vastly underestimated the number of lifeboats needed on board.

Soon, the Titanic struck an unseen iceberg, which tore a hole in its hull. That damage, combined with a series of human errors, led to the ship sinking, resulting in the deaths of 1,500 out of its 2,224 passengers and crew.

I liken the factors that precede infidelity to an iceberg, with 90 percent of them existing below the surface, ready to tear into a relationship with destructive force. The hidden issues within the betrayer play a larger role in the demise of a marriage than the ten percent that many people, including therapists, often focus on. And, like Captain Smith of the Titanic, it is human pride and denial that hinder taking steps to prevent such a tragedy.

The Brokenness Below

It's easy for counselors, betrayed spouses, and their wayward partners to concentrate on surface issues like couple communication or immediate conflicts instead of the deeper ones beneath the surface. Often, the betrayer blames the faithful spouse or the state of the marriage as the reason for seeking comfort outside the relationship. This is a superficial view of a much more complex problem.

Like Gwen in the movie *Ghost Town*, you may have wondered, "Why wasn't I enough?" when the question had little to do with a straying partner's choice to engage in an extramarital relationship. As I said before, your spouse had many other options for coping with whatever emptiness, distress, or boredom that made them susceptible to an affair at this time in their life.

> In my thirty-three years as an infidelity therapist, I've concluded that the real factors behind infidelity usually predate the marriage.

In my thirty-three years as an infidelity therapist, I've concluded that the real factors behind infidelity usually predate the marriage. Knowing this can help both partners shed their shame and stop focusing on the surface ten percent that distracts them.

Battling and blaming one another over the visible, above-the-surface issues is futile when more pressing matters must be addressed. The real message of your marital crisis was to draw attention to and seek healing for the ninety percent of causal factors that lay below the surface, often outside the purview of both the betrayed and the betrayer.

Family Background

When betrayers explore their past histories and identify the origins of their unhealthy coping strategies, they pull the curtain back so they can view and correct their misbehaviors. And when they realize their misconduct had a deeper root cause, they feel less shame and may be motivated to rectify their misapplied coping methods. They gain hope that if they address and process these pre-existing conditions, they can overcome their tendency to seek comfort or validation from an unhealthy addiction or outside romance.

The same is true for betrayed spouses. Once they understand a straying partner's history and its role in driving their partner's sexual or romantic compulsions, it can soften their hearts toward their betrayers and reduce the shame they feel for "not being enough" to make up for the strayer's painful or sordid pasts. Even if the pair never reconciles.

As you read on, I trust you will see how these earlier influences had little to do with you.

Infidelity Runs in Families

Like alcoholism and depression, infidelity tends to run in families. The children of adulterers often repeat the behaviors of their parents or marry someone who has affairs. Parental modeling and attitudes play a huge role in these generational patterns.

Author and psychologist Bonnie Eaker Weil believes that "adultery is an inherited emotional and biochemical pattern of emptiness passed down from generation to generation..."[2]

In her clinical experience, she estimates that 90% of people who have affairs had a parent or grandparent who stepped outside their marriage.[3] I'm uncertain that every clinician would find the same statistical results. Still, Dr. Weil has examined the family histories of hundreds of clients and has determined this to be true, often without the adult child being conscious of parental treachery before entering therapy. Children or grandchildren of infidels tend to either repeat these untoward behaviors or marry and tolerate the antics of someone who does.

The classic example of generational infidelity is the Kennedy clan. After reading several books on the Kennedys, I drew a diagram of the family's infidelities, going back to Rose Kennedy's father, the oldest family member, who reportedly had an affair. His daughter, Rose, went on to marry Joseph Kennedy, Sr., a serial adulterer (with five known affair partners).

Out of Rose and Joe Sr.'s four sons, at least three (Joe Jr., President JFK, and Senator Edward Kennedy) had multiple affairs.

A few tabloids insinuate that the fourth son, Senator Robert F. Kennedy, also had several affairs.[4] Whether true or not, it is more well-known that four of Senator Robert Kennedy's adult children had at least one affair.

Entitlement

One of the dominant attitudes that fosters infidelity is entitlement. People with an attitude of entitlement believe they *deserve* certain privileges, including having an affair with someone else's spouse. And they assume they can get away with it.

As noted in the Kennedy family, Joseph Sr. instilled in his sons a strong entitlement mentality. His modeling taught them that enhanced masculinity means accumulating outside lovers who fawn over them and build their egos. After all, they were wealthy, privileged, and above the fray of ordinary folks.

This attitude is reflected in the story of how, during the reception of his younger brother Edward's wedding, John F. Kennedy was overheard leaning over and saying to him, "Just because you're married doesn't mean you have to be faithful."[5]

Attitudes of entitlement can emerge from other types of family backgrounds. One is from growing up as the golden child, where parents think their child can do no wrong. These parents allow youngsters to get away with sneaky acts or give them privileges that make them think they are superior to others. When wrongdoing is met with little to no consequence, the child learns they're the exception to the rule—free to violate others' rights because their family excuses and even enables their conduct. They live under the illusion that being "special" grants them permission to be selfish.

One betrayed spouse, "Gayle," shared that her husband—widely regarded as the golden child in his family—was nicknamed "Teflon Don" because no consequences ever seemed to stick. Whenever he colored outside the lines, he would excuse, avoid, or outright evade the consequences. Accountability slid off him like water on a slip-and-slide, and the same held true when he was unfaithful to Gayle. His parents and siblings met the news of his affair with a shrug and even welcomed the new lover with open arms. Shockingly, his company's co-owners, despite the affair being with a fellow employee, turned a blind eye. Gayle was left feeling abandoned on all sides, with no advocate to confront or challenge her husband's betrayal.[6]

While some people develop an attitude of entitlement from being allowed to get away with too much, others feel entitled due to a sense of deprivation experienced in childhood. As adults, they seek to compensate for what was previously withheld by grasping for everything they can obtain, whether financially, emotionally, or relationally. Their belief is: "Since I was deprived as a child, the world owes me..." including a string of lovers not their own.

Certain families inadvertently cultivate an attitude of disrespect towards individuals of the opposite gender. When fathers mistreat their wives, they set a precedent for their sons to follow, potentially leading them to mistreat their own wives in adulthood. Similarly, daughters may learn to tolerate disrespect from their male counterparts, as this behavior was modeled for them within their own family.

Likewise, mothers who frequently criticize their husbands may unintentionally teach their children to disrespect their future partners. One of the most profound indicators of disrespect for either gender is the act of infidelity. It is crucial to understand the impact of these behaviors, as they can perpetuate a cycle of mistreatment in relationships.

As you reflect on your partner's family of origin, do you see any similar reasons they felt entitled to an extramarital liaison (or two or three) in ways that violated your rights as a life partner? Or did you learn to tolerate such attitudes due to the modeling in your own family?

Early Trauma

Dr. Kathy Nickerson suggests that infidelity sometimes fits what she calls the "Affair as Anesthesia" Model, suggesting that individuals who engage in affairs often feel lost or are attempting to numb a deep-seated emotional wound.

> "Affairs are often not about thrill or sex, but about relief," she explains. "People don't betray their partners because they lack a moral compass; they betray their partners because they're trying to numb a wound that feels unbearable."[7]

Yet I've found that once someone tries to mask an unhealed injury or persistent internal discomfort by engaging in an affair, they can lose touch with their moral compass, at least temporarily.

Childhood trauma can create a deep need for reassurance and comfort that no one person can satisfy. For example, parental suicide attempts are very traumatic for children. Or sex abuse by a trusted family member or neighbor. Or the sudden death of a close friend. These traumas can leave a wound that festers below the surface if they don't find the comfort they need. Unmitigated traumatic experiences can cause a person to pursue unhealthy, soothing, or thrilling experiences to distract from unresolved pain from their past.

> Childhood trauma can create an excessive need for reassurance and comfort that no one person can satisfy.

In their coming-of-age book, *American Leftovers*, adult children Heidi, Shaun, and Eric Wilson recount the story of their upbringing by parents who had each been emotionally harmed in their own families of origin. Their father,

Mark, was raised by an emotionally unavailable, alcoholic mother and a harsh, unpredictable father. Older neighbor kids sexually abused him as a child. As a teenager, he got into trouble with the law, impregnated his girlfriend, and married her. Mark later found Christ, which revolutionized his life. While his winsome personality paved the way for many people's admiration, his early experiences remained unresolved.

After years of thrilling work smuggling Bibles into communist countries, serving as a beloved pastor of a thriving church in the States, and raising three children into young adulthood, Mark finally cracked under the weight of his demanding ministry and struggling marriage. To everyone's shock, he ran off with an 18-year-old girl—a friend of his teenage daughter—claiming they were in love and that his actions were justified.

These siblings, now adults, came together to share their unfiltered tales. In the book, they take turns describing their experiences growing up in a flawed yet adventurous family deeply rooted in ministry. As a therapist, I appreciated their insights into the origins of their father's midlife crisis, recognizing that much of it was tied to his unaddressed early trauma and the pressures of a demanding ministry.

Like the sad instance of Mark Wilson, I get frustrated when Christians with childhood trauma ignore their need for outside help. While I believe that the Lord can use a variety of means to bring healing to peoples' lives, when an abused believer thinks they can handle these matters on their own or simply alone with God, it's only a matter of time before their unhealed childhood brokenness catches up with them in the form of infidelity, addiction, or other unhealthy coping mechanisms, much to the harm of their families and others in the body of Christ.

Statistically, people who become addicted to pornography were exposed to porn at an early age, with the average start being 11 years old. When budding adolescents discover both the pleasure and shame of secret indulgences, they often develop a cycle of self-soothing and self-punishment to cope with life's pressures. Instead of learning to express their needs and let another person into the vulnerable spaces of their hearts, they turn to the quick, isolating dopamine hit of onscreen gratification, seeking relief in secret and later hiding their true selves from their partners, whom they keep at arm's length.

Regarding early exposure to pornography, one researcher made an interesting observation: "In my opinion, it is a form of sexual trauma, just like witnessing a car accident or parental domestic abuse can be traumatic for the observer."[8]

Perhaps your spouse felt assaulted by the shocking discovery of porn at a tender age, when children don't understand sexuality. Or maybe they felt abused by a loved one who introduced porn to them in a way that made them feel both fascinated and creepy at the same time.

If you've ever wondered what led to your partner's unfaithfulness, unresolved childhood trauma may have been a hidden factor. Trauma has a way of eroding self-worth, weakening boundaries, and fueling anxiety or emotional instability, making the thrill of an affair feel like an appealing escape, even if it goes against their values or merely masks deep, unhealed shame.

Trauma Repetition

Often, when I probe an unfaithful client's life history, we uncover unresolved early trauma. Freud's theory of "Repetition Compulsion" has been used to understand the behavior of pedophiles. In 35% of cases of an adult molesting a minor, the adult was sexually abused as a child.[9] Freud believed some people try to work out their unsolved pain by reenacting the same mistreatment that was done to them in a maladaptive way. Such individuals mistakenly believe they can gain mastery over their own abuse in this manner.

You'd think their personal experience of abuse would give them compassion for a vulnerable child whom they would seek to protect rather than inflict the same trauma they endured growing up. However, regrettably, some individuals find destructive ways to cope with their unresolved issues by reenacting them.

The same holds for adult children of the unfaithful. Their parents' infidelity injured them more deeply than they recognized. Sometimes, they sympathize with an admired yet offending parent. And rather than avoiding the same mistakes, they repeat them, as though the unfaithful parent gave them unconscious permission to do the same. Perhaps this was also the case in the Kennedy clan. The notion that parental modeling carries more weight than a parent's words fits the modern proverb, "More is caught than taught."

Some young people, especially those who empathize with the betrayed parent, vow never to repeat their parents' mistakes. Sometimes, those vows hold. But other times, unresolved wounds resurface later, leading them to mirror the very behaviors they once despised—often in moments of stress or emotional vulnerability. This cycle can be broken, especially when a trusted, nurturing adult offers a safe space to share, or when therapy helps them process the pain. But it takes time and intentional healing to undo the deep imprint of a parent's dysfunctional example.

Unprocessed Grief

Another iceberg ledge that can doom fidelity is unprocessed grief. Many of the unfaithful people I've worked with suffered a major loss, such as that of a job or relative, and sought the antidepressant effect of an exciting affair. So, they sometimes seek comfort from an idealized lover as a substitute for working through the grief of a disappointing loss.

One such person, "Christopher," shocked everyone when he left his wife and daughters for a younger woman. Unbeknownst to his wife, "Sara," the illicit pair had previously connected as teachers who enjoyed running on the school track. Sara had assumed his hours upstairs on the computer were related to his teaching job. Instead, he was corresponding with his girlfriend.

He'd been alienated from his father for years, who'd left his mother for another woman. So, when his beloved mother died, rather than share the pain of his loss with his wife, he confided in his running partner. Layers of unprocessed grief set the stage for their emotional affair to become sexual.

When he announced to Sara he was leaving her for "Kari," she was aghast. He used the excuse that she had not been there for him when his mother died. Christopher failed to take responsibility for withholding his sentiments from his wife, who would have gladly lent an empathetic ear had he given her the chance.

The fallout from the demise of this Christian family reverberated for a long time. His adolescent daughters chose to avoid him as much as possible into early adulthood and struggled with male trust issues for years. The wife later remarried a great guy, but Christopher's betrayal and rejection remained an enduring source of grief for her.[10]

Discontent

Besides trauma, parental disapproval and verbal abuse can create a sense of discontent within a child that they carry into adulthood. Because they never felt they could live up to the expectations of a distant or critical parent, they often struggle to find contentment as adults. They frequently change jobs, houses, and spouses because they are difficult to satisfy. No one person can ever be enough for someone with chronic discontent or unresolved issues beneath the surface.

I remember a time during our marriage crisis when my husband was sleeping on the couch, and I was a total mess, needing multiple medications to get any semblance of sleep. Disoriented and hazy, I stirred from a chemical slumber around 2 a.m. Despite my fuzzy brain, one clear thought pierced my mind as sharp as lightning:

"He is a discontent man, and I am not his problem."

Suspecting this message was important and I'd forget it by morning, I scrounged the top drawer of my nightstand, seeking a pen. All I found was a blue highlighter and a wrinkled envelope. I scribbled the phrase for what I later came to view as a divine revelation and drifted back to my usual fitful sleep.

That envelope became a note of sanity for me.

Since then, many insights have confirmed this truth: I wasn't responsible for my husband's discontent, which led him to seek a mood-boosting heart-throb outside our marriage. His unresolved grief and early trauma—rooted in his parents' emotional distance, infidelity, suicide attempts, and alcoholism—long predated me. Realizing these deeper wounds held more weight than my shortcomings helped lift the burden of misplaced blame.

The Gaps We Can't Fill

Whether your spouse's emptiness or discontent came from unprocessed childhood trauma, parental disapproval, attitudes of entitlement, or some other family dysfunction, you could not make up for your partner's emotional or psychological deficits.

Researchers Balswick and Thoburn surveyed pastors who were unfaithful and found that the following family backgrounds heavily correlated with marital infidelity:

- 91% of cheating pastors came from chronically dysfunctional families.
- 83% of the families [they grew up in] had chronic emotional disorders.
- 66% of families had experienced substance abuse.
- 58% of families were involved in affairs that resulted in having illegitimate children.
- 50% of families had episodes of physical violence.
- 25% of families were troubled with incest.
- 8% of families had problems with chronic gambling.[11]

If this is true of pastors, I think it's safe to say that these statistics may also apply to non-clergy individuals.

These insights don't mean that betrayed spouses don't have their own issues. But the primary cause of partner infidelity usually lies deep within the straying spouse, not within the betrayed. There are plenty of people in less-than-ideal marriages who never stray.

I share all of this to help you understand that prior family histories, attitudes of entitlement, exposure to porn, unprocessed trauma, unresolved grief, and parental disapproval have a larger effect on a person's choice to commit adultery than having an unsatisfying marriage.

Difficulty With Conflict

Well-respected psychologist Emily Brown theorizes that two precursors to infidelity are avoidance of conflict and intimacy. When one or both partners tend to ignore or overlook hurt feelings or offenses, they allow resentments to build up over the years until someone decides to express them in a big way. I recall several marriages where a secretly annoyed spouse chose to jump into a new romance rather than deal honestly with their existing spouse.

One man, "Jonathan,"[12] was married to a woman who criticized him daily. He explained that she never apologized for her harsh words. In his effort to gain her approval, Jonathan did everything he could—doing most of the housework, preparing meals, and running a successful business—except for expressing his hurt feelings.

Meanwhile, he grew close to a neighbor who had witnessed his wife's mistreatment and showed him welcome compassion. He soaked in her praise and affirmation. One weekend when both their spouses were away, they became sexually involved.

In counseling, we dug into the roots of Jonathan's conflict avoidance. He grew up with a critical mother and was terrified of confronting her. Any attempt to express his feelings only estranged her further. As an adult, he feared upsetting his wife, just as he had feared upsetting his mother. And the more he tried to please his wife, the more critical she grew.

When his wife learned of the affair, she was devastated. She hadn't seen it coming. We only met three times, once as a couple and twice alone. While I held Jonathan accountable for the wrongness of his affair and his avoidance of conflict, she was reluctant to explore her own issues underlying her tendency to be overly critical. Sadly, their marriage ended before we could address their individual struggles with conflict and emotional intimacy.

While some people are drawn to a partner who shares their tendency to avoid difficult emotions, others are attracted to someone who is more expressive than they are.

That was the case with "Tonya."[13] She was lively, open, and honest, with no hidden agendas. Her husband, "Darin," found her personality fascinating and her frankness an attractive strength compared to his family growing up. His parents never fought openly, and the underlying message regarding sharing honest feelings was, "Shove them under the rug." Consequently, Darin had difficulty being honest with his wife when he disagreed, which led her to believe they were always in agreement, even when they were not.

To make things more complicated, after seminary, he became a pastor who delivered powerful sermons and gained a sizable following. The praise from his parishioners made him feel as if he couldn't be vulnerable with anyone about his personal struggles. He isolated himself despite others reaching out to him. As Tonya later discovered, Darin allowed his resentment of her outgoing personality to grow. Instead of exploring how his tendency to avoid conflict caused negative feelings to build up, he secretly blamed his wife. She spoke her mind, and he did not. But she believed he did.

That's why Tonya was caught off guard when the man she trusted and respected most became involved with a needy, younger woman from church. By the time they sought counseling, she realized he'd been privately building a case against her rather than addressing his difficulty with conflict. (More on this story in Chapter 21, "When Helpers Harm.")

Affairs Magnify Marital Discontent

Regardless of pre-existing factors, the affair itself brings a host of new problems. The artificial glow of an extra-marital relationship creates a fantasy world that no real-life marriage can match. The illusion fuels restlessness and exaggerates minor marital frustrations, deepening the divide.

I liken this to someone who's genuinely content with their sporty Subaru Crosstrek. It handles well in the snow, has a tight turning radius, plenty of space for camping gear, and a look they enjoy. Then one day, they ride in a friend's brand-new Jeep Grand Cherokee—complete with leather seats and all the latest technology. Suddenly, the Subaru feels inadequate. It's too noisy. It doesn't accelerate fast enough. That subtle itch to upgrade begins to grow.

The once-satisfied driver starts fixating on everything the Subaru lacks. He talks to a few advisors—his best friend or a family member—who affirm his dissatisfaction. Eventually, convinced that the Subaru just isn't enough, he trades it in.

At first, he's thrilled. The new car smell, the sleek interior, the feeling of finally owning something that reflects how special he thinks he is—it's intoxicating. But the high wears off. The steep car payments sting. A few door-dings show up. Maintenance costs rise. And the shiny new Jeep loses its luster.

The same happens in relationships. Comparing a real-life spouse to baggage-free, untested love is an unfair and costly exchange.

That is why I listen skeptically to the woeful tales of an unfaithful partner. The real source of the person's dissatisfaction usually goes much deeper than the current marriage. There's an iceberg of other factors below the surface that are the real culprits.

> Comparing a real-life spouse to baggage-free, untested love is an unfair and costly exchange.

And the affair itself has magnified whatever flaws exist in the relationship and within the faithful spouse.

The Midlife Crisis

Depending on your former spouse's age, the subjects I've discussed in this chapter can pave the way for a classic midlife meltdown. Unfinished business from our past tends to catch up with a person by midlife and, if not dealt with healthily, may strike the family yacht enough to make it sink.

Midlife Crises are often preceded by burnout—when a person becomes exhausted from trying to please and appease spouses, bosses, the corporate ladder, or a congregation, or from trying to survive a significant loss such as the death of a parent, the loss of a job, or a seemingly unsolvable financial hardship. At other times, a person reaches the pinnacle of success in a career or child-rearing, only to find that it doesn't satisfy them the way they had anticipated.

When pressures from the past clash with perceived pressures in the future, the one caught in the middle may get in touch with their mortality, knowing they can't keep going the way they are. Something has to give. And that is when a person is most vulnerable to accepting the temporary reprieve of a mood-lifting extramarital affair.

I've never quite figured out whether the drive to lose weight, buy a fancy sports car, start wearing the latest fashions, and hit the gym is what leads up to an affair, or if it's the result of one. I suspect it's often the latter.

The next set of "Iceberg Issues" involves Mental and Personality Disorders. These conditions can be difficult to identify before marriage and may emerge during it. Either way, they exist on a continuum from mild to severe. If you're unfamiliar with these disorders, the next chapter will offer a solid starting point and may lead to some enlightening "lightbulb" moments for you.

Chapter 13

Underlying Disorders

*He who isolates himself pursues selfish desires;
he rebels against all sound judgment.*
~Proverbs 18:1

One former client, "Janice,"[1] had just dropped her youngest son off at college with her husband. On the long drive home, ready to talk about their future as empty nesters, she heard the unthinkable: "I've found someone else and want a divorce." Trapped in the car for four more hours with an unsympathetic partner, she later admitted she seriously considered jumping out. "How could he tell me this right after we said goodbye to our son? I had nowhere to escape, no space to process my devastated emotions!" The rest of the trip home, her husband seemed occupied with his own thoughts, oblivious to the wreckage he'd just caused.

As Janice reflected on their past relationship, she remembered feeling abandoned when he frequently left for the weekend to pursue his beloved sport of surfing, leaving her to care for the kids alone after they'd both had busy weeks at work. She'd been afraid to admit how hurt she'd been over his refusal to stay home despite her appeals to have him engage with the family instead of pursuing his solo activities. He seemed ensconced in his own world. She realized his traumatic childhood may have contributed to his selfish tendencies, which only worsened with his affair.

Similar to Janice, some of you may have been married to someone with narcissistic traits that only surfaced more clearly during your crisis. You remember being swept up by their initial "love-bombing," only to find yourself later criticized, devalued, and emotionally drained. You may have felt confused by how much admiration they seemed to require just to show you basic kindness. And when they got involved with someone else, their glaring selfishness became unmistakably obvious.

Narcissistic Personality: Enduring Trait or Temporary Phase?

Public awareness of narcissism has gained greater visibility in recent years, and for good reason. According to Ruffing et al. (2018), evidence indicates that levels of narcissism have been rising in Western society over the past few decades. This condition often manifests in politicians, pastors, and business managers, as those with narcissistic traits are attracted to leadership positions.[2]

There's been an explosion of books on narcissism and its impact on relationships, marriages, and divorce. From my perspective, unfaithful people exhibit a higher rate of narcissism than the general population.

Since narcissists tend to think of themselves as more special than others and impose high expectations on their mates, they tend to be less satisfied with their romantic partners. Respected researchers in the Netherlands note:

> It is widely known that narcissists are more likely to be unfaithful to their partners, and they report low relationship satisfaction in their romantic relationships if the necessary conditions are not provided to meet their expectations.[3]

The Dutch study also concluded,

> Narcissism has positive significant correlations with low relationship satisfaction and a high possibility of intentions towards infidelity.[4]

Other writers suggest that a narcissistic person's constant need for affirmation heightens their inclination to search for the perfect partner. Such individuals often turn into philanderers, which refers to engaging in multiple affairs, either sequentially or simultaneously.[5]

This means that spouses high in narcissistic traits are harder to please and naturally prone to infidelity—another indication that their romantic escapades had little to do with their spouses.

Yet, we need to be careful about labeling everyone who is unfaithful as a narcissist. A person can have narcissistic traits without having the full-blown personality disorder. Let me explain.

The term "narcissist" was adopted by psychologists based on the Greek myth of Narcissus, who spurned other lovers, saw his reflection in a pond, and fell in love with himself.

Recent research shows that narcissism exists on a spectrum ranging from mild to extreme. Every person possesses some degree of narcissism, often referred to as "normal narcissism," due to our inherent self-interest and sinful nature.

Individuals who score higher on the Narcissism Personality Inventory (NPI) are referred to as "escalated narcissists." In contrast, someone with the actual personality disorder is categorized as a "pathological narcissist."

Most experts seem to agree that there are three basic types of narcissists:

- High-functioning/Grandiose
- Covert/Vulnerable
- Malignant[6]

With concentrated therapy, a small degree of change is possible for the first two categories, but unlikely if someone has the most pathological personality disorder, often referred to as "Malignant Narcissism." The typically quoted statistic for rates of NPD in the United States is 6.2%, somewhat higher in men.[7] However, in clinical settings, the diagnosable disorder ranges as high as 15% of the population.[8]

The High Functioning Narcissist is outgoing and charming and comes across as having an exaggerated sense of self-esteem, which hides their deep-seated insecurities. They are incredibly self-centered and exploit others for their own personal benefit. High-Functioning Narcissists have a lot of charisma, excessive outward confidence, and a desire to rise above the crowd. They know how to draw admirers to themselves from a position of self-interest rather than with genuine empathy. ("If I can get you to think I care, you will adore me and fulfill my needs for admiration and attention.")

The Covert or Vulnerable Narcissist is usually shy and is less likely to be the life of the party. They may use passive-aggressive tactics and are highly sensitive to criticism. Like other forms of narcissism, the Covert Narcissist is self-centered, entitled, has a fragile ego, and lacks genuine empathy.

At the high end of the spectrum is the Malignant Narcissist, who bears similarities to the High-Functioning Narcissist. However, the Malignant Narcissist has a bottomless need for affirmation and exploits others even more heartlessly for their own gratification. Malignant Narcissists are the ones who check most of the boxes for the full-blown personality disorder: remorseless, devoid of empathy, and often counted among criminals and serious abusers.

All ranges of narcissists tend to:

- Be charming
- Have a false self
- Lack genuine empathy
- Show a lack of remorse when wrong
- Exploit others

- Be self-absorbed
- Be perfectionistic
- Idealize a lover, then harshly criticize them when disappointed
- Become enraged when feeling neglected
- Seek kind, thoughtful people as partners (to serve as their "narcissistic supply")

Discussions on narcissism often note a pattern of initial "love-bombing," where narcissists overwhelm their targets with romantic gestures and affirming compliments. They paint their partners as the answer to their dreams, charming them into a relationship under the guise of deep affection. But this flattery is often a manipulative tool to satisfy the narcissist's own needs. Once the spouse fails to live up to the idealized image, or the narcissist finds a new admirer, the affirmations quickly turn to criticism and blame.

A narcissist's need for adulation is endless—no one can fulfill it. Their unfaithfulness stems from unrealistic desires, not your imperfections, and may be triggered by an affair's temporary euphoria.

Temporary Adolescent Narcissism

I would like to propose a name for one more category of narcissism that I have witnessed among the unfaithful: "Temporary Adolescent Narcissism." If you are a teacher or a parent of teenagers, you know adolescents are often self-consumed and think they're invulnerable to natural consequences. They tend to be impulsive and driven by hormones.

When a spouse engages in a secret, forbidden affair, they experience a dopamine high with an adrenaline rush that resembles the hormonal energy and self-centeredness of a teenager. They take risks they ought not to take, are obsessed with their lover, and base decisions on immediate emotions rather than logic. The ecstasy overtakes their conscience like that of a substance abuser. In other words, they regress to an adolescent phase of self-absorption.

In mature marriages, when a partner is experiencing a midlife crisis, they often seem to have reverted to a temporary, much younger stage of life. The flashy car or motorcycle, the new clothes, the weight loss, and the sudden desire to work out like they did in high school are signs that they have a new heartthrob in their lives whom they want to impress.

While some people's fear of growing old may lead them into a midlife crisis, the typical cause of a midlife meltdown for an otherwise stable adult is an extramarital affair, which incites a form of narcissism that leaves much destruction in its wake.

Underlying Disorders

I remember when my husband, James, believed he was in love with Judy. He lost weight, became unusually focused on his appearance, and radiated a new confidence—while mine plummeted. Even before I knew they were mutually involved, he showed little empathy for how his romantic fantasizing was affecting me. But the clearest clue to how self-absorbed he'd become came near the affair's end, after I had learned most of the truth.

I was house-sitting to escape the constant tension at home, still holding out hope for reconciliation. Judy had left the company and taken another job, but her husband, still unaware, continued working alongside James.

Restless dreams haunted me, fueling my fear that the affair hadn't ended. Desperate for clarity, I decided to confront Judy, as I mentioned earlier. The next day, while running errands, an unfamiliar word kept popping into my mind: *supplantress*. I had to look it up to see its relevance. The word "supplanter" was first used to describe Jacob, who stole his brother Esau's inheritance by trickery.

In the book of Proverbs, it is in the list of "three things under which the earth trembles, under four it cannot bear up...a maidservant who supplants her mistress" (Proverbs 30:21, 23). In other words, a maid who underhandedly replaces her mistress's wifely role and position.

I called my friend Tammy to tell her about my conversation with Judy and the strange term that kept coming to mind. Tammy asked, "Well, did you ask her if they were still seeing each other?" *Hmm*. I had forgotten to ask Judy the most important thing I needed to know.

That evening, I mustered the courage to call Judy. "I'm not going to keep calling you," I said. "But I forgot to ask something last night. Are you and James still seeing each other?"

She sucked in her breath and paused. I started to tremble.

"It... It's not what you think."

"I don't care what it is! I told you last night that I need you to have zero contact, and I meant *zero*. It's obvious that you two can't control yourselves. I'm going to give you twenty-four hours to tell your husband the truth. After that, I make no guarantees as to what I'm going to do." I hung up, still shaking.

I knew that if I told her husband, it might not go well for them as a couple. It was better for her to admit it to him than for him to learn about their affair from me.

I don't know how much she confessed, but it was enough. Apparently, he was livid. And with the company owners out of town, James had to face him alone at work the following week.

A few days later, I called James to see how he was doing, hoping to see some evidence of humility. His response?

"That was the *meanest* thing anyone has ever done to me!"

The *meanest* thing anyone had ever done to *him?* After everything he'd done to *me* the previous nine months? After betraying not only me but also Judy's husband? I understood that consequences sting. But sometimes, the truth is the kindest and most necessary wake-up call a person needs.

When I shared James's reaction with Rob Jackson, who'd become a colleague at my office, Rob paused thoughtfully.

"He's either a narcissist," Rob said, "or he's fallen into a narcissistic sinkhole."

A narcissistic sinkhole. Hmm. I pondered this notion for a while. Certainly, his reaction was horribly selfish rather than appropriately remorseful. While I didn't believe James was a true narcissist, during his affair, he slipped into an adolescent mindset with self-indulgent behavior.

For example, he portrayed anyone who spoke the unwelcome truth as the "bad guy." His temporary state of narcissism caused him to think only about himself rather than his wife, kids, friends, or bosses. He seemed to view himself as the victim rather than the victimizer. Once I recognized his current self-centeredness as a sign of narcissism, the lights came on for me.

Like my former husband, some people only fall into this sinkhole when they are caught up in the euphoria of an affair. Life becomes all about them. While some individuals manage to emerge from this condition once the excitement fades and they awaken from their temporary stupor, others do not.

Sometimes, a person's infidelity may have made them more selfish than usual. Yet, for others, an affair may have revealed a deeper form of narcissism. In such instances, once your spouse became involved with an affair partner and withdrew from you, their underlying selfishness became more apparent. Looking back, you might recognize hints of their self-absorption over the years. However, their involvement with an outside lover magnified this tendency like an enormous balloon.

Narcissists Reverse the Role of Victim and Offender

This leads me to a hurtful tactic that narcissists, deep-seated or temporary, use to defend themselves. They tend to act as if they're the victims and treat the ones they've offended as if they were the offenders. This concept was developed by Dr. Jennifer Freyd, whom I quoted earlier. She refers to it as DARVO.[9]

D – **D**eny (deny the abusive behavior)

A – **A**ttack (attack the victim for speaking the truth or confronting the betrayer)

R – **R**everse (reverse who is the Victim and who is the Offender)

V – **V**ictim (the self-absorbed offender)

O – **O**ffender (you, the actual victim)

In other words, a self-absorbed offender **denies what they've done and then attacks** the victim for being hurt or objecting to the offense(s). In the process, the **Offender** (abuser/betrayer) accuses the **Victim** (you) of being the **Offender** instead of the other way around (hence **Reversing** who is the true **Victim** and who is the **Offender**). What this might look like:

Betrayed Spouse (Victim): "It really hurt my feelings when you defended your affair partner."

Strayer (Offender): "What are you talking about? I never did that."

Betrayed Spouse (Victim): "That's what it sounded like when you told me she 'needed' you, which justified your affair with her."

Strayer (Offender, Attacks spouse): "For crying out loud! You just keep making things up in that screwed-up head of yours. Besides, don't you have any compassion?"

Betrayed Spouse (a fair request): "When you defend her, it makes me feel like my need for you matters less to you than *her* 'need.'"

Strayer (Offender): "There you go again. Making everything about you. I'm sick of this! You *always* complain and hound me to death. I can't say anything right!" (The Offender stomps off, making himself out to be the Victim when, in fact, the Betrayed Spouse is the real Victim.)

Such responses are another form of gaslighting, which narcissists are adept at.

Here are three true stories from our virtual group members that further illustrate how a strayer may use DARVO to turn the tables on an injured spouse.

When "Terilyn's" husband discovered she had spoken with his affair partner—the woman he was secretly trying to rekindle things with—he flew into a rage, threatened to take the kids away from her, minimized his actions, and blamed her for holding him accountable.

After his mistress refused to take him back, he began sulking and sought attention in disturbing ways. He played "their" songs on the piano—music that once symbolized his betrayal—where his wife and children could hear. Without Terilyn's knowledge, he even bought a flashy sports car and named it after a poet the other woman used to read to him. The children, oblivious to the hidden meaning behind these actions, became a vessel of pain to Terilyn as they sang these songs and called the car by its pet name.

When Terilyn calmly said, "I understand you're grieving and feeling sad, but when you play those songs—especially around the kids—it hurts me," he angrily exploded. "I can't even play music in this house! Yes, I miss her, and now she is a ghost."

Do you hear the DARVO pattern here? He flipped the script, cast himself as the victim, and turned Terilyn into the offender for feeling hurt by his offensive actions. But his wife figured out what he was doing, even in front of the kids, and it tormented her. She was the one who deserved empathy, not manipulation or mockery.

Here's another example:

"Meredith"[10] and her husband of 23 years, "Ray," ran a small farm. When their 24-year-old farm employee suddenly lost her apartment, they opened their property and hearts, offering her the little house out back. She wasn't a believer, and Meredith thought, *Maybe we can show her what a Christ-centered marriage looks like.*

At first, it seemed harmless. But within six months, Meredith started noticing subtle changes—lingering glances, quiet conversations that ceased when she entered the room. Her gut tightened.

When she finally asked Ray about it, his reaction was swift and convincing: "*Nothing* is going on." Later came the insults. "You're just jealous and angry!"

But the signs piled up until the truth could no longer be ignored. Still, Ray denied the affair.

The breaking point came when he refused to let the young employee go. The emotional strain was crushing. Meredith packed her things, moved into a cheap rental with their daughter, and held onto the one hope left—that the agreed-upon counseling would bring him back. But Ray never followed through.

Then, in a letter during their failed reconciliation, he made a late confession to her in writing: yes, they'd had an affair. Later, he revealed that his now live-in girlfriend was pregnant. Meredith moved forward with the divorce. One year after the divorce was finalized and the baby was born, Ray married his younger lover.

Meredith's three children were devastated. One still lived with her, trying to make sense of it all. Then came the cruelest twist: Ray denied to his kids that he had had an affair. He told his extended family the same story, adding that Meredith's "anger" and her decision to "abandon" him were the *real* reasons for the divorce. He painted himself as the long-suffering husband who'd finally found happiness after enduring an "angry and controlling" wife. All of which made future family dynamics painfully awkward for Meredith.

This was DARVO in action. In his rewritten story, he was the wronged party, and Meredith was the villain. And in his quest to protect himself, he lied about how his new relationship began and blamed the divorce on his wife's "anger" rather than his refusal to admit and give up the affair.

Here is another true story by a lovely woman named "Melanie":

> My husband, "Jerry," had invited a single mother from his workplace, "Starla," and her daughter to join us for Thanksgiving dinner. Our tradition was to welcome those with nowhere else to go during the holidays. As the evening unfolded, I couldn't help but notice Jerry's unusual attentiveness towards Starla and her daughter. I found myself observing their interactions from the food line, a sinking feeling in my stomach suggesting that something was amiss. I felt like an outsider in my own home. A feeling I will never forget.
>
> A few days later, Jerry casually mentioned his plans to assist Starla with something at her place. I pointedly asked him if there was anything more to their relationship. He shook his head in denial. Tears welled up in my eyes, and he held me close, reassuring me that there was nothing to worry about. His words brought me temporary relief. But confusion set in when he proceeded with his plans to meet up with Starla. It was as if our conversation had been about something mundane like the weather, not a potential affair.
>
> In the days that followed, my emotions were in turmoil. I was increasingly disoriented and confused. When I questioned him again, Jerry was quick to insist on his fidelity, defend Starla, and chastise me for my suspicions.
>
> "How could you label her a homewrecker when she's a grieving single mother who lost a child to brain cancer!?"
>
> I recoiled in guilt for questioning their integrity. I even found myself apologizing to Jerry for accusing them of such a heinous act despite my intuitions screaming otherwise.
>
> Shoving down my misgivings, I agreed to host the company Christmas dinner on December 9th, which Starla attended. At the end of the evening, I recall bidding her farewell with a warm hug and heartfelt Christmas wishes—a memory that now gives me the creeps.

Twelve days later, I couldn't stand the internal chaos anymore. Late at night, while Jerry was asleep, I stealthily picked up his phone and snuck into the bathroom. My hands shook as I discovered a series of vile, sexual text messages exchanged between him and Starla on December 17th—the very night we'd celebrated our 22nd wedding anniversary over a romantic candlelit dinner.[11]

Did your partner try to make you feel guilty for suspecting something was amiss? If you confronted your betrayer, did he or she Deny or minimize the truth? Then, did your partner proceed to Attack you as if you were the "bad guy?" Were you falsely accused or belittled for your apprehensions? Did they follow this by Reversing who was the Victim and who was the Offender, when speaking to you, your children, or others?

Whenever an unfaithful person tries to play the victim when they've actually been the victimizer, they sink to using the DARVO tactics of a narcissist.

Betrayed spouses regain sanity when they recognize narcissistic maneuvers by a straying partner. This knowledge helps them stop blaming themselves for their partner's hurtful, self-absorbed behaviors and attitudes.

Bipolar Disorder and Adult ADHD

People with Bipolar Disorder and Adult Attention-deficit Hyperactivity Disorder share a common struggle: *impulse control*. Their brains function differently from those of the average person.

Bipolar Disorder, once called "manic-depression," is marked by alternating episodes of mania and low mood. During mania, individuals may experience intense energy, impulsive behaviors, rapid speech, sleeplessness, reckless spending, bouts of gambling, dangerous driving, or extramarital affairs. Though the high feels exhilarating, it often damages relationships due to poor impulse control and trust violations.

Many people with Bipolar Disorder resist medication because they enjoy the manic highs, believing that this version of themselves is their "true self." Unfortunately, when the cycle shifts to depression, they may self-medicate with pornography, marijuana, or risky sexual behavior to escape their low mood.

Sometimes, a doctor may mistakenly prescribe a single medication suitable for major depression when the patient is actually experiencing a downturn in their mood cycle. Bipolar disorder often requires anti-cyclic mood stabilizers or a combination of medications, rather than the typical treatments used for clinical depression. Misdiagnosed or untreated bipolar disorder is an unfortunate condition that can fuel a partner's inclination toward unfaithfulness when their mood swings in one direction or another.

Lack of impulse control is also common in adults with ADHD, even without the hyperactivity component. Since wise choices require access to the brain's executive control center, untreated ADHD often impairs emotional regulation and increases the risk of sexual acting out.

If your spouse struggled with one of these disorders and refused treatment—whether counseling, medication, skills training, or one of the new brain therapies—understanding this may help ease any misplaced guilt you carry about your former spouse's behavior.

Oppositional-Defiant Disorder and Anti-Social Personality Disorder

While severely misbehaving children are typically the ones diagnosed with Oppositional-Defiant Disorder (ODD), Dr. Omar Minwalla also identifies this disorder in sexually addicted adults. These individuals tend to be uncooperative, defiant, and hostile toward any authority or legitimate partner. The precursors of this disorder often begin in childhood.

Some children grow out of it. Yet about forty percent of children with this disorder carry it into adulthood, and unfortunately, the symptoms continue to show up in their social interactions. Sometimes, ODD transitions into Antisocial Personality Disorder in adults (commonly known as a Sociopath)—a terrible dysfunction to develop.

People with Antisocial Personality Disorder are cruel to animals, show no conscience when they hurt other people, engage in criminal behavior, and sometimes end up in prison. If your spouse exhibited either of these tendencies, Oppositional Defiant Disorder or Anti-social Personality Disorder, you had your hands full. They needed specialized help. Personality disorders are deeply ingrained and not temporary tendencies. Apart from establishing firm boundaries and insisting they get professional help, if they refused, there was nothing else you could do.

> Personality disorders are deeply ingrained and not temporary tendencies.

Brain Injuries

Every once in a while, I hear about a partner who has had an extreme personality change due to a brain injury. This can result in cruel or violent behavior. Other times, a severe head injury can disconnect the person from their emotions, so they no longer feel empathy toward their spouse. Another result of a brain injury can lead to inappropriate sexual advances.

An impaired person's heightened sexual interest can be especially stressful and embarrassing for families and caregivers. Lacking an adequate filter, the individual with a brain injury may make crude remarks, flirt with a married friend, attempt inappropriate touching, or demand sexual attention from a spouse or significant other in public.[12]

Depending on the severity of the damage, it might signal serious trouble ahead in the relationship. For example, a friend of mine's husband suffered a critical brain injury that severed his ability to feel empathy. She told me that one psychiatrist advised her, "Don't walk. Run." Heartbroken, she ended up divorced from the love of her life, who was no longer an emotionally safe person for her.

When a spouse can't feel or show empathy toward a partner, either due to Narcissistic Personality Disorder, Anti-social Personality Disorder, or a brain injury, you are in danger of further emotional and possibly physical abuse than you've already suffered. It's okay to accept this reality and move on.

What About My Marital Vows?

As a follower of Christ, you may wonder, "What about my vows to stay married 'in sickness and in health?'" While some conditions are mental "sicknesses," there's a difference between physical or cognitive illness (like Alzheimer's) and deeper spiritual or character-related disorders. Your spouse's troubled conscience, distorted thinking, or disordered personality may not have been clear when you married them.

Most of these individuals still have a choice. If your spouse refused medical, psychological, or pastoral help to address their distorted thinking, that's not the kind of "sickness" you're required to endure. A mental or personality disorder, or even an abusive childhood, may explain their behavior, but it doesn't excuse it. It means they need help. This chapter is meant to help you recognize the issues often linked to unfaithful behaviors, not to stir so much sympathy that you feel obligated to stay with someone who refuses to change. Remaining with a morally unwell partner at the cost of your own well-being is not healthy.

Consider David's relationship with King Saul. Saul began as a humble leader and mentor, but as pride and jealousy grew, so did his rebellion against God. This opened the door to tormenting spirits, perhaps akin to mental delusions. Though Saul depended on David's music to calm his troubled mind, he eventually turned abusive. God did not expect David to stay. What began as a blessing became a source of danger—so David wisely fled.

So far, in Section III, we've examined Iceberg Issues that lie beneath the surface and threaten the sanctity of marriage. Unfinished business from childhood, unresolved trauma, buried grief, midlife stressors, personality disorders, and mental illnesses are often the unseen ledges that rip into our lives and cause a marriage to sink. However, there is one more category that opens the door to sin—**Footholds** in a person's life. This is what we will discuss next.

Chapter 14

Footholds

> But if you refuse to do what is right, sin is crouching at your door;
> it desires you, but you must master it.
> ~Genesis 4:7

> And do not give the devil a foothold.
> ~Ephesians 4:27

When my oldest son developed a chronic illness that interfered with his capacity to run hard or play certain sports, he took up rock climbing to keep in shape. I admired his fortitude as he practiced on a gym's climbing wall so he could take on steep cliffs in the wild, which he did. His arms became so strong that he even won a Ninja competition.

Rock climbers look for protrusions to stand on or grasp to pull themselves upward. Ledges are beneficial for rock climbers searching for a grip to ascend a steep incline and conquer a mountain. However, ledges can be detrimental if the devil seeks a foothold to seize, exploit a weakness, and use it to take control of your life.

Paul warns fellow believers, "Do not give the devil a foothold" (Ephesians 4:27). The word *foothold* literally means "place" or "ground" in Greek, warning us to avoid giving the devil a ledge of access in our lives.

I believe there are three fundamental footholds that Satan uses to ensnare us, even as believers:

- Unrepented sin
- Bitterness toward God
- Pride

Before your spouse ever strayed, one of these ledges likely allowed Satan to worm his way into their hearts and lead them astray. Such footholds in your partner's life may not have been visible to you. However, upon reflection, you may recognize them. The Lord likely provided many off-ramps that they could have taken to avoid the sin that later entangled them, but they ignored those opportunities and continued their harrowing path.

Unrepented Sin

Any unconfessed sin can lead to moral failure, but secret sexual sins often erode the soul, weaken moral resolve, and eventually erupt as infidelity.

For example, research has shown that people who indulge in pornography have a 300% greater chance of having a physical affair than someone who avoids porn.[1] When we entertain sordid instincts, they gain power over us. And the more attention we give them, the more these debasing influences expand.

I remember attending a professional seminar by a national expert on affair recovery, who recommended the use of porn in certain situations. When I subtly shook my head in disbelief, my Christian colleague, Ted Brackman, leaned over and whispered, "Porn is not benign." He was right. Much like a malignant tumor, the influence of pornography spreads beyond its starting point and penetrates a person's soul with debilitating effects on the host's mental, physical, and relational life.

> "Porn is not benign."
> ~Therapist, Ted Brackman

Perhaps the use of pornography or suggestive romance novels whetted your partner's appetite for increasingly taboo pleasures. Or maybe the crude joking at the office sparked a growing connection with someone at work. Most affairs begin with a minor boundary infraction: a comforting hug, confiding in a colleague, exclusive lunches that no one else knows about, or social media communication that crosses the line. Once the temptation shifts from fantasy to opportunity, involvement is not far behind.

Even secular research confirms that premarital promiscuity increases the likelihood of infidelity in marriage.[2] Satan exploits unconfessed sin to harden our hearts toward God and sabotage our relationships. But even more dangerously, he uses it as blackmail to lure us deeper into sin, one poisonous drip at a time.

The devil is extremely patient. He plants seeds of sensual compromise in people's hearts. If they start to feel guilty about it, he reminds them that they've already messed up and might as well give in again or reoffend later.

Was your spouse involved with porn during their teenage years? Or behind your back during your marriage? Did your spouse cheat on you or anyone else before you were married?

These indicate signs of a disordered conscience. Even if they experience a degree of shame, unless they have acknowledged their violations and engaged in a healthy process of repentance, they likely rationalized these sins, which opened the door to other unfaithful activities.

If their porn habit devolved into an actual sex addiction, they needed more than willpower to overcome their compulsions. They needed professional help. There are many resources these days for folks struggling with sex addiction, the best being specially trained Certified Sex Addiction Therapists and therapist-guided group therapy.[3]

Secret Sins

One key flaw is a lack of mental discipline. A person may maintain a polished exterior while moral compromise quietly takes root in the heart.

The saying "our true character is what we do when no one is looking" holds true, and nothing is more hidden than our private thoughts. Was your spouse a fan of erotica in books, online, or movies, or did they withhold their truest feelings from you, seeming to foster a secret life to which you had little access?

This leads to another character flaw that may pave the way for unfaithfulness—dishonesty. Did your partner sneak around or lie to you about anything before the affair? Did they show no guilt for stealing from a store or cheating on their taxes? Did they refuse to admit to a gambling problem, misspend money, or make business deals without your knowledge? Any of these secret sins can weave their way into our partner's heart and remain dormant, only to explode into an affair during a vulnerable time in their life—much to the surprise of friends who believed your spouse was above reproach.

The news of my husband's moral failure shook many people. His former college roommate could hardly believe it. Steve and his wife, Cindy, decided that if James could fall this way, anyone could. As a result, they developed an adult Sunday school class based on Jerry Jenkins' book, *Hedges: Loving Your Marriage Enough to Protect It*. This book explores the boundaries and heart attitudes that couples must cultivate to safeguard their marriages against missteps, such as infidelity. The class was well-attended and held several times, which may have helped a few individuals avoid falling into the same trap.

Thinking through matters of conscience ahead of time can help people avoid falling into temptation. For example, I suggest folks consider what Dr. Janice Abrams-Spring calls "The Well-lit Room Test." Ask yourself, "How would I feel if my spouse saw me with so-and-so and could overhear our conversation right now?" This simple tool can be an effective gut check and help prevent further entanglement with a coworker, friend, or neighbor. At some point, your unfaithful spouse failed to guard their heart.

The enemy will exploit any initial slip-up to either deceive us into downplaying wrongdoing or shame us. He seizes on our weaknesses to encourage us to excuse our sins or to discourage us in our walk with God. Such opportunities give the devil a foothold to lead us into further sin. God warns:

> "Guard your heart with all diligence, for from it flow springs of life ...
> Do not swerve to the right or to the left; turn your feet away from evil"
> (Proverbs 4:25, 27).

That's why it's vital to keep short accounts with God and stay transparent with a few trusted friends. Hidden sins, the little lies, and minor compromises often snowball into major failures.

Solomon suggests to his lover, "Catch for us the foxes—the little foxes that ruin the vineyards—for our vineyards are in bloom" (Song of Songs, 2:15). In other words, it's the little sins that eventually overtake and ruin the fruit of our spiritual and marital lives.

Bitterness

Another foothold that may pave the way for infidelity is when a person harbors feelings of bitterness. Bitterness has a corrosive effect on our spiritual and relational lives. Buried resentment hardens our hearts and blocks the Holy Spirit from keeping our attitudes soft toward God and others.

A woman, "Alice," in our support group told us how her husband, "John," went from a faithful follower of Christ to an adulterous man. He'd been a general contractor with ten homes finished and ready for sale when the Great Recession of 2008 hit. None of his homes were selling. He met with other Christian builders to pray over their projects, hoping the Lord would rescue them from their desperate circumstances. Rather than relying on home sales, the Lord answered their prayers by having the banks agree to take back their houses and not foreclose on them. This spared the builders from the bankruptcy that other contractors were suffering.

The Subprime Lending Crisis forced John to switch from building new homes to renovating existing homes, which Alice said was a better fit for him. His new business took off, and they survived the financial meltdown in better financial shape than before.

However, John could not see this as the Lord's answer. He became embittered toward God for not selling his ten spec homes. This blinded him to how the Lord got him through the financial crisis. Disillusioned, he dropped all his Christian friends, stopped attending church, and fostered a growing resentment toward God. Alice believes this paved the way for him to turn away from the Lord, get involved with another woman, and leave their marriage.[4]

When we use bitterness to protect our hearts, we barricade ourselves emotionally from loved ones. And, more importantly, bitter feelings erode our faith in the Lord. We may blame him for not preventing or intervening in whatever misfortune or injustice we feel wounded by.

Resentment toward God is often hidden, which is why Scripture calls it a "root of bitterness" (Hebrews 12:15). It spreads quietly underground, then surfaces unexpectedly. Disappointment with life circumstances frequently masks an even deeper disappointment with God. When we feel let down by the Lord, we're more tempted to take matters into our own hands—like justifying an affair with, "I've lived for everyone else. Now it's *my* turn!"

Looking back, do you suspect your partner harbored bitterness? Did they have a hurt or misfortune that planted doubts in their minds about God's goodness and caused them to question his wisdom and resist his Lordship?

A person who strays is essentially shaking a fist at God and saying they know better than the Lord does. When people are privately angry with God, they erect barriers that silence the whispers of the Holy Spirit, who is trying to draw them back into a right relationship with him.

Pride

> "Pride goes before destruction, and a haughty spirit before a fall" (Proverbs 16:18).

The third foothold that grants the devil access to an unfaithful person's life is pride. Similar to the hubris among those who contributed to the sinking of the Titanic, pride obstructs our ability to address issues before they arise. The troubling aspect of pride is that we often fail to recognize it in ourselves. Unless you've been humbled on multiple occasions or permitted a few honest friends to speak into your life, unhealthy pride can hinder your spiritual journey and damage your relationships.

Narcissists aren't the only ones who suffer from excessive pride. From my observations, other potential sources of pride are:

- Superior intelligence
- A winsome personality
- Physical beauty or handsomeness
- Exceptional athletic talent
- Musical or artistic talent

- Business success or financial acumen
- An unwillingness to admit a need or fault
- A cover-up for underlying insecurity

It's not a crime to be beautiful or smart. I know many attractive, exceptional people who don't let their physical and mental advantages go to their heads.

However, when individuals depend on external attributes for their identities, they may neglect to cultivate other essential character traits such as empathy, compassion, and kindness. As a result, they struggle with Imposter Syndrome, convinced that their outward gifts deceive others into believing they are better people than they genuinely are.

Deep down, some people fear that their flaws will repel others if they are fully seen. To guard against rejection, they cling to good looks or exceptional talent, using them as their main source of value. However, this outward focus often comes at the expense of developing the deeper character traits necessary for genuine self-acceptance and intimacy.

Outward power and charm can also attract people seeking to elevate their own status—such as the groupies who flock to celebrities, frequenting their hangouts in the hope that physical closeness or sexual favors will boost their personal star value. It takes a grounded, inwardly strong person to resist these temptations and remain faithful.

The adulation that power brokers receive tricks them into believing they are superior to others. They think they can get away with behaviors that others cannot. After all, they are smarter, cleverer, and shinier on the outside in ways they believe will protect them from accountability for their wrongdoings.

These individuals develop a certain hollowness from over-focusing on the constant pressure to perform well in the eyes of others. They seldom reveal their true selves to those close to them, fearing exposure. Their exceptional external traits may lead to financial gain, awards, promotions, admiration, and even adoration from others, including a romantic partner. This compulsion to uphold a false persona heightens their fear of being exposed as merely average, vulnerable to the same rejection and scorn they privately project onto others.

Pride in one's superficial gifts is a cover-up for insecurity. Such people must appear superior to others. Otherwise, their façade would collapse. They may outwardly appear mature beyond their years. At the same time, their inner selves remain underdeveloped due to hiding their unseen wounds.

Another form of pride can develop when a child is forced to mature too quickly. For example, children who grow up in an addicted or dysfunctional home may take on the role of Family Hero—someone who steadies the ship amidst the chaos, neglect, or instability in the family. Coming home to an unsafe environment can cause a child to sharpen their "antennas" to scan the room for danger, paying close attention to the moods of others. Is Dad in a bad mood? Is Mom emotionally available or ready to pounce on me? They become excessively aware of others' feelings while being less aware of their own.

Such youngsters become premature adults at an early age, responsible for keeping things even-keeled at home, which stunts their personal emotional development.

Their role as a Hero may continue into adulthood, causing them to develop a façade of "I can handle anything." These individuals often become the seemingly mature bosses, pastors, and community leaders whom everyone holds in high esteem. No one would guess that there is a hurting child deep inside who never learned to care for himself or process their inner pain. That's why it's so shocking when one of these admirable people dashes off with the secretary like a rebellious teenager.

Prideful people work hard to conceal their true selves. The more someone builds a false persona of superiority, the more fragile it becomes—until, in a moment of vulnerability, when temptation aligns just right, the mask cracks, and their moral compass falters.

Pride can also blind a person to their need to process early abuse or trauma. They don't want to admit that their childhood unprocessed pain is somehow affecting them in the present. It takes humility to admit one's need for counseling or the assistance of others. Yet, when a person's trauma remains unprocessed, it gnaws away at their self-esteem in ways that may cause them to compensate by engaging in unhealthy behaviors that, at minimum, hurt themselves and those who love them.

The Example of Darryl Strawberry

I appreciate the honesty of famed baseball legend Darryl Strawberry, who exhibited all three footholds. He grew up in a home broken by his abusive, alcoholic father, who often told him he was worthless and would never amount to anything. Inwardly bitter, he defied the Lord despite encountering his Spirit at a crusade. He compensated for his low self-esteem by excelling at baseball.

Once his athleticism thrust him into money and fame with the New York Mets, his ego got the better of him. Unaware of his buried hurts, he considered himself above the limits of others. Straw began to use drugs and carouse with the many women attracted to his stardom.

His false pride blinded him to the destructive nature of his misbehaviors and got him into trouble with the law, as well as with his three sequential wives, who divorced him, primarily due to his unfaithfulness. It wasn't until he married his fourth wife, dealt with his inner demons, and got his life straightened out with the Lord that he began to thrive in his personal life. Today, he has matured, lives on a modest income, shares the gospel of Jesus wherever he goes, and runs a charity to support children with autism.[5]

The Ripple Effect

Influential people who suffer from blinding pride often wound those close to them. They use people for their own gratification and decimate their families. My heart aches whenever I hear about another respected Christian leader whose moral failures are exposed. It distresses me to think about the damage they've caused, particularly to their family and close friends. The ripple effect of an influential person's unfaithful acts reaches far and wide. Such downfalls are poor reflections of our Lord. Failures by prominent Christians disillusion those who are weak in their faith and bolster unbelievers' excuses to resist coming to Christ.

Even if your straying partner wasn't well known, they still had a sphere of influence that affected you, your children, and anyone close to the situation. Infidelity is not the private matter that unfaithful people often claim it to be. Its impact reverberates for generations.

To broaden your perspective, it may help to consider the role that spiritual warfare played in the downfall of your once-loyal spouse and the subsequent breakup of your family.

The Real Enemy

Scripture is clear that "our struggle is not against flesh and blood, but against the rulers, against the authorities, against the powers of this world's darkness, and against the spiritual forces of evil in the heavenly realms" (Ephesians 6:12). This verse provides another reason for you to see that the forces seeking to destroy your marriage were not a reflection of you. More players were involved than you, your spouse, and some seducer at the office. Evil forces were at play, attempting to oppose God and his plans for the world. You and your partner likely ended up in the crossfire.

Here is an example of how Satan's role became clear in my marriage crisis. One of the owners of my husband's company was a friend and longtime believer who sensed something nefarious was going on with my husband. One weekend, the owner, "Carl," was praying and fasting for James and had a disturbing vision. I reported this in my journal:

> As he [Carl] prayed, the face of a temporary employee whom Carl hardly knew kept coming to his mind, along with the term "Spirit of Seduction." He prayed about the matter almost all night. The sense he got was that the woman was a "plant" assigned by Satan to put a "curse" on the company.

He did some checking around the next week. It turned out this temporary employee had been hired on August 23, 1999, and now her term was almost up. Some of her coworkers had discovered she was into witchcraft, were uncomfortable with her "vibe," and reported this to their supervisor. Given the input from her coworkers, the supervisor felt hesitant about rehiring her and let Carl know around the time he was making his inquiries.

Carl later reported all this to James, and it weirded him out. It turns out James knew the exact date he and Judy crossed the line from flirting to kissing—the first day of a company retreat, August 23.

Whether you discover evidence that suggests that Satan was targeting your spouse, the workplace, and family, or not, I have no doubt more was going on in the spirit realm than met the eye. Your partner's temptation was likely plotted, planned, and staged by the enemy of their soul, even years in advance.

A few months later, my husband attended an extended counseling retreat with Psychologist #2, who combined Christian beliefs with Eastern philosophy. The night after he returned home, he found himself in the spiritual battle of his life. Here is another journal entry of mine from that time:

> James startled me by whimpering in his sleep. He began calling out to Jesus for help. I shook him awake. He'd had a nightmare. He told me he had felt an evil presence in the room and was being "levitated" in his dream. He couldn't tell if the evil was emanating from the dark-haired woman in the dream (I presumed this represented Judy) or the white cat that he called "Snow Cat" sitting in the corner (a creature he felt represented God's presence in his dreams while on his intensive retreat). This was confusing to him. We prayed together, and he seemed to feel better and drifted back to sleep. (I've often wondered since then if Snow Cat was actually a demonic "spirit guide," similar to the spirit beings people encounter through occult practices.)

To me, this dream revealed the intensity of the spiritual battle over James, which shouldn't have come as a surprise. My husband had been a powerful Christian influence in the lives of hundreds of people—a significant target for Satan to take down. If you and your spouse were serious about your commitment to Christ and involved in some form of ministry, your family may have been a threat to the evil one and his minions. One of the greatest tools Satan uses to take influential Christians out of commission or thwart potential ones, such as your children, is intimate deception, leading to moral failure.

I remember a client who would sense a dark, creepy presence sweeping through her home at night, like a stream of smoke—something she couldn't comprehend until she became aware of her husband's deep involvement with pornography. Like her, perhaps you have sensed an evil presence in the house during your spouse's affair or sexual compulsion.

Infidelity can open the door to evil spirits. Perhaps you noticed that once the dominoes started falling, it felt like the odds were stacked against you. Nothing seemed to go your way. Maybe a string of minor mishaps kept going wrong, like a dozen bowling balls rolling down your lane, knocking over every pin you tried to stand upright, leaving you feeling helpless and confused.

In such instances, the resistance seemed so powerful, you sensed you were battling something formidable, sabotaging your efforts to save your marriage. Forces from without and within crushed you, tearing your family apart. This suggests a deeper cause than you realized—a malevolent force amplifying your spouse's deception beyond the natural pull of an affair.

I share all this with you to suggest you consider the potential role that spiritual warfare may have played in your marriage's demise. This will broaden your picture of what transpired, help you pray more effectively, and encourage you to guard your heart. If the enemy came so vociferously for your partner, he was also coming for you.

> "Be sober-minded and alert. Your adversary the devil prowls around like a roaring lion, seeking someone to devour" (1 Peter 5:8).

The enemy sought to "steal, kill, and destroy" the sanctity of your marriage, target your children, and bring you down, too. Although he may have influenced your spouse, don't grant him the satisfaction of undermining your faith, self-esteem, and future ministry.

The good news is, "Greater is he that is in you than he that is in the world" (I John 4:4, KJV). As a believer, the Holy Spirit resides in you, able to empower you against the "wiles of the devil" (Ephesians 6:11). Just because your former spouse has become a casualty of Satan's designs doesn't mean you have to succumb as well. As destructive as this season has been for you, it is not the end of your story. It can lead to a new beginning where fresh and deeper fruit will develop despite the enemy's schemes.

Don't forget Myrna Larson's statement, from the Introduction: "There isn't anything beyond God's ability to redeem. He can redeem anything!" Even Satan's wiles.

You must have been a threat to the enemy for him to attack you in this manner. You matter to God and the kingdom. Otherwise, the devil wouldn't have bothered. May the battle you've just come through give you a clear perspective and strengthen your resolve to forge a spiritually dedicated path.

Did your unfaithful partner have any footholds, as discussed in this chapter? Were you aware of past dishonesty or prior sexual/romantic infractions? Did your spouse have lingering bitter feelings that left them secretly angry with God? Or was your spouse smart, attractive, talented, or successful in ways that may have fed their pride and contributed to their downfall?

Now that I've pointed out some ways Satan may have gained a foothold in your betrayer's life, I hope you will stop blaming yourself for the poor choices and attitudes that got him/her in hot water.

If your former mate had any of the underlying "iceberg" issues we've discussed, I hope these insights have been helpful.

Now, I'm eager to explore **Section IV** with you. The upcoming four chapters will reveal the secrets behind your spouse's reckless actions. You'll understand how the affair evolved from emotional confusion to cognitive dissonance, how and why they rewrote your marital history, all of which caused them to become someone you no longer recognize.

By reading these chapters in order, you'll understand how each stage led your partner down a destructive path, hurting both your marriage and your well-being. More importantly, you'll learn how to reject the harmful messages that each phase leaves behind.

SECTION IV

Rejecting The Lies

> When he lies, he speaks his native language,
> because he is a liar and the father of lies.
> ~John 8:44

Liar on the Loose
By Jamie Owens Collins
(excerpt)

Do you know a lie when you hear one
Can you tell the false from the true?
When you hear the song of a stranger
Do you know who's singing to you?

A tempting voice in the darkness
Sweet words that tickle your ear
But he mixes honey with poison
Don't believe everything that you hear

'Cause there's a liar on the loose
Yeah, there's a liar on the loose
But he'll run from the fire of the Truth
Well, there's a liar on the loose
Don't let him lie to you

©1981 Fairhill Music, used by permission
From the Album *Straight Ahead*
https://fairhillmusic.com/shop/straight-ahead/

Chapter 15

Emotional Distortion

The Great Lie

Stolen water is sweet; food eaten in secret is delicious.
~Proverbs 9:17

When we went out to dinner for our anniversary in early July 1999, James said, "This has been our best year ever!" I was a little surprised. Although it had been more peaceful, aside from a few arguments over our house remodel, I still felt we lacked adequate quality time together. I looked forward to finishing the remodel so we could finally unwind, relax, and enjoy each other's company more. Or so I thought.

Our oldest son, who had been away at college, was back home and oversaw a large high school Bible study group over the summer. He asked me to give one of the talks near the end of July. I looked forward to the opportunity to speak on a topic close to my heart: learning to walk by faith rather than by sight.

On July 16th, a week before my planned talk, some terrible news grabbed the headlines. While piloting a small plane to a family wedding on Martha's Vineyard, John F. Kennedy, Jr. (President Kennedy's son) crashed into the ocean, killing himself, his wife, and her sister. Having been fascinated for years by the Kennedy clan, I was glued to the television and news accounts regarding the crash, the search for the bodies, and the theories behind why it happened.

After learning that Kennedy was not "instrument-rated," I asked a friend who was a professional airline pilot to explain the term and how it contributed to JFK Jr.'s accident. The more I learned, the more I believed this story to be a sad but perfect illustration for my talk. I re-titled my message "Trusting God in the Dark."

After my son led the worship time and introduced me, I held up the latest Time Magazine, with a photo of JFK Jr. splashed on the cover, featuring the story of his accident. I described the conditions that contributed to his crash: fog, darkness, and his lack of being instrument-rated. To become instrument-rated, a pilot needs enough flight hours and to pass specific tests before qualifying for the license to fly beyond weather and visual minimums. The goal? To demonstrate that he has learned to trust the dials on the plane's instrument panel more than his subjective perceptions.

I explained that when haze or darkness obscures a pilot's visual reference points, such as land, building lights, or the horizon, his body's auditory system can become "spatially disoriented." This means his senses are confused, causing him to misjudge his direction and altitude. When the pilot's vision is limited, his other senses may take over and give him false impressions about his flight positioning. In such conditions, if a pilot hasn't learned to rely on the objective instrument panel more than his own feelings, he can become disoriented, lose control of the plane, and plunge to his death. As a risk-taker, JFK Jr. flew beyond his certification and took a shortcut to his destination despite the darkness and haze.[1]

Using JFK Jr.'s experience as a metaphor for life, I suggested that everyone goes through difficult times that can cloud our vision and skew our perspective. Then I asked, "What sorts of experiences do you think might 'fog' your minds and cause you to lose your bearings?" After considering a few suggestions, I had the kids break into small groups to discuss further situations that might cloud or darken their observations and mess up their lives. The room hummed as they tossed around various ideas among themselves.

After gathering the kids back together, I asked for their opinions on what could cause them to lose sight of land and distort their perceptions. They suggested ideas such as "tragedy," "a painful breakup," "lust," "the death of a loved one," "rejection," and "disappointments in life or God."

Now that I had their attention, I emphasized the importance of Christ's followers becoming metaphorically instrument-rated. In other words, they should become so familiar with and trust the instrument panel of God's Word that, regardless of what life brings their way, they will be prepared.

I said, "Trials will come. Darkness and haze may block our vision. But if we've practiced trusting the dials of God's Word more than our fluctuating emotions, we'll be prepared to weather any hardship that might otherwise throw us off course."

Looking back, I believe the Lord orchestrated the timing of my talk to brace me for what lay ahead for James and me. A dark and violent storm was brewing that would knock both of us off our feet.

In my case, I was on the verge of losing sight of where I was, who I was, and where God was. Up was about to feel like down, and down like up. I desperately needed to grip the controls and, by faith, rely on the dials of God's Word to guide me through the pending storm despite my messed-up emotions. He knew that relying on my usual sensations wouldn't cut it.

Within a month of my presentation on "Trusting God in the Dark," James crossed the line from emotional to physical with Judy. That single act changed everything. Although I didn't learn the details for months, I immediately sensed James's heart shutting down toward me. I went from feeling secure in my marriage to being terrified. From being sure of myself to questioning my sanity. From solid in my faith to thinking God was less powerful than Satan. From looking forward to the future to utterly dreading it.

In hindsight, the JFK Jr. metaphor helped me when my whole world felt like it was spinning out of control. I kept repeating to myself, "Trust the dials! Trust the dials! No matter how you feel right now, the Word of God is the one thing you can rely on."

JFK Jr.'s unfortunate story not only helped me endure the greatest trial of my life but also enabled me to understand how the fog of my husband's affair affected him so profoundly. This seemingly sensible man cast aside his prior wisdom, former trust in the Lord, and principled conscience all for the sake of an unrealistic, exhilarating romance he believed would resolve his midlife crisis.

As the two of us awkwardly fumbled in the dark, we hurt one another more deeply than I ever thought possible. While I adored him, I also wounded him with my desperate attempts to awaken him and regain his love. As we lay separately, emotionally bleeding, I can imagine heaven's angels watching us closely, wondering, "Will these humans choose to trust the reliable, loving words of God? Or will they rely on their storm-tossed, finite feelings to guide them through this terrible time?"

As the clouds rolled in, James and I experienced a crisis of faith in the months and years that followed, taking us in very different directions.

Clouded Emotions

As a therapist, I spend a significant amount of time helping clients identify and explore their emotions. However, this is only the first step in gathering information. Our feelings can provide essential insights into the sources and reasons behind our distressing conflicts.

Emotions can lead us to necessary truths, or they can mislead us if we give them more credence than they deserve. Various situations can skew our perceptions and steer us toward faulty conclusions. For example, a season of depression can cause a person to feel hopeless and conclude that life is not worth living. Alcohol use can alter a person's mood, ranging from cheer to self-pity, resulting in reckless behavior.

We need to take our mental health, substance use, faulty beliefs, and brain chemistry into consideration when assessing whether our feelings are on target or off-base.

Like pilots facing spatial disorientation in darkness or adverse weather, the exhilarating highs from secret indulgences can create deceptive illusions, cloud judgment, and prevent recognizing a deviating path. Heightened passions may cause individuals to ignore warning signs, leading them further astray. This is especially true in cases of infidelity.

Brain Chemistry in Ordinary Infatuation

Scientists have found that mood-lifting neurotransmitters, such as dopamine, norepinephrine, vasopressin, and endorphins, play a fundamental role in fueling romantic highs. Brain scans have revealed that dopamine lights up the pleasure centers of the brain when someone is feeling passionately in love.[2]

The excitement of falling in love is also intensified by a lesser-known hormone called phenylethylamine, or PEA. This neuroamine, which is also found in small amounts in chocolate, is released during new infatuation. It adds energy to the mixture of dopamine and endorphins, acting on the brain's opioid receptors.[3]

You likely felt elated by these biochemicals when you met, dated, and got engaged to your partner. God designed this initial attraction to bring a man and woman together, desiring the commitment of matrimony. But he didn't expect us to throw prudent counsel and good sense out the window.

Couples need to balance their emotions with wisdom when considering a life partner. Marriage involves much more than good feelings and sizzling sex. Before tying the knot, couples must evaluate whether they share values, have a warm companionship, demonstrate maturity, possess the ability to give and take, and have the capacity to work through conflicts together.

The Increased Power of Forbidden Romance

The unique thing about affairs is that they heighten these euphoric feelings to a fervor beyond what is experienced in a regular public romance. Researchers have since developed new theories about the heightened power of an alluring affair, surpassing the ordinary attraction people feel when falling in love.

You've likely encountered various labels for the emotional states triggered by infidelity, such as Limerence, La La Land, The Affair Bubble, Affair Fog, Affair-Derangement Syndrome, and Fantasy Land. These terms exist for a reason.

Social scientists have found that the greater the barriers, the greater the thrill. Secrecy, lying, and getting away with wrong create an adrenaline rush that boosts hormone levels beyond the excitement of a non-secretive relationship or a typical marriage.

The temporary delirium induced by the neurotransmitters produced from a forbidden affair (or pornography) stimulates the pleasure centers of the brain in ways that resemble the effects of morphine. For a spouse caught in infidelity, nothing in real life feels as tangible, desirable, or worthy of sacrifice as an illicit entanglement. This can lead some individuals to act more like desperate drug addicts than rational, loving partners.

Adversity and mystery elevate romantic cravings. As Pat Love explains in her seminars, the more forbidden the relationship, the more intense the effect these hormones have on the brain. When spouses engage in a web of secrecy, intrigue, and breaking all the rules, these barriers can bring a person's emotions to a peak that is not possible in normal, everyday life with a spouse. What your unfaithful spouse experienced with his or her affair partner was the sneaky pleasure of stolen goods. It is simply not realistic to compare a secret, outside romance with a legal, seasoned marriage.[4, 5, 6]

Similarly, researcher Dr. Fugère notes that *obstacles* and *secrecy* can unnaturally intensify a romantic relationship. Regarding *obstacles*, she says,

> Forbidden relationships can take many forms ... we may fall in love with a coworker, supervisor, or someone who is already committed to a serious relationship. The obstacles to these relationships may be explicit or implied, but these obstacles may actually serve to *strengthen* our forbidden relationships (emphasis hers).

Regarding *secrets*, Dr. Fugère goes on to say,

> Sharing secrets with one another increases a sense of intimacy. Secrecy also guarantees that the couple is not "socially tested." And, without that reality-testing, secrecy fuels much idealism that they can project on each other.[7]

This idealistic distortion can persist until the bubble bursts when the affair is exposed or the couple actually live together.

VULNERABILITY TO AFFAIRS

The various factors that contribute to a person's vulnerability to having an affair are beyond the scope of this book. However, I have identified a few powerful dynamics that helped me understand how good people, such as my former husband, were lured into the trap of infidelity, leading them to leave their marriages in search of the impossible dream.

When I mention factors that can make a person vulnerable to infidelity, I only mean more vulnerable. Given our sinful nature, every one of us is just one decision away from going off the rails. I appreciate what Kay Arthur says in her talks: "Godly character is built by a series of right decisions." We need to develop strength of character over time to protect ourselves from sexual or romantic temptation. Yet even the sincerest Christians can stumble if they are unprepared.

No wonder Scripture warns, "Guard your heart above all else, for it determines the course of your life" (Proverbs 4:23, TNLT). In other words, we must protect our hearts from the influence of the world, unethical friends, and a libertine culture at the office. It is beneficial to establish healthy boundaries and surround ourselves with godly friends. However, the most salient advice comes from the Word of God, as Scripture is full of warnings about avoiding infidelity.

Airplane pilots must follow strict protocols to ensure safety. The FAA manual advises, "Most importantly, [you should] become proficient in the use of flight instruments and rely upon them. *Trust the instruments and disregard your sensory perceptions*" (emphasis added).[8]

If only your spouse had trusted God's Word in the same way.

Let's review some factors that contributed to JFK Jr.'s tragic crash,[9] which offer parallels to those who become entangled in affairs.

Unfinished Business

JFK Jr. likely carried the heavy weight of grief from his father's assassination at a young age, compounded by the loss of his uncle and other family tragedies that haunted the Kennedy family over the years. The pressure to live up to the family legacy may have also shaped him during his formative years, possibly fueling his reported impulsive nature. It's likely that he had unhealed wounds and sought solace in exciting yet sometimes reckless behaviors.

Similarly, individuals with buried emotional wounds are often the most susceptible to the fleeting relief that an affair can bring. The temporary lift from infatuation or a sexual encounter can offer an escape from both overt and covert psychological distress, but the long-term consequences are destructive.

Circumstances

JFK Jr.'s fatal flight began with a series of unfortunate circumstances. Due to New York traffic congestion, he and his passengers arrived at the airport later than expected, which delayed takeoff. By then, fog and darkness were setting in. In a hurry, he took a shortcut in flight, which took him further away from the shoreline. Each of these conditions hindered his ability to see the visual cues that would have helped him maintain his sense of balance.

When considering external situations that contribute to increased opportunities for infidelity, one is the increased number of men and women working together in the workplace. Forbes magazine reported, "58% of employees have engaged in a romantic relationship with a colleague."[10]

Business travel, conferences out of town, and working closely with others on projects can give people an artificial sense of closeness and camaraderie that is greater than what they share with spouses at home. If someone hasn't set appropriate professional boundaries with coworkers or supervisees, these relationships can turn romantic, given the right situation.

The atmosphere of societal moral decline seems to have also set the stage for an increase in wayward behavior. Whether in movies, television, or music, a wave of normalizing extramarital sex has descended upon Western civilization. These influences can undermine a person's resistance to temptation. Rather than repelling immoral cultural messages, they unconsciously absorb them as their own.

Many people who have affairs blame their behavior on circumstances beyond their control. They claim it happened by accident. They may feel like they couldn't help themselves, as if they were victims of fate (or chemistry). Yet even so-called accidental affairs do not occur by happenstance. Their resolve to remain faithful has been subtly weakened by allowing permissive cultural sexual norms to penetrate their psyches. So, when the opportunity presents itself and their hormones race, the tempted one easily chooses to succumb, one rationalized micro or macro step at a time.

Risk-takers and Novelty Seekers

From reading about the Kennedy men, it's clear that risk-taking was a common trait among them. JFK, Jr. was no exception, reportedly possessing a "risk-taking" gene that led him to believe he was invincible. His love for novelty and adventure was apparent. His mother even tried to dissuade him from learning to fly because she knew her son had a "limited attention span, a high threshold for risk, and an attraction to danger."[11] Despite this, he ignored his mother's concerns.

On the day of his cousin's wedding, he dismissed the advice of experienced professionals, violated National Transportation Safety Board guidelines, and declined his flight instructor's offer to accompany him. He disregarded the wisdom of others, relying instead on his own judgment, which ultimately led to tragic consequences.

Similarly, research has shown that people who thrive on the adrenaline rush of risk are more likely to engage in affairs.[12] Like JFK Jr.'s disregard for caution in flying, these individuals often dismiss the advice and concerns of others. Their craving for novelty and excitement, coupled with their tendency to seek risky ventures, can lead them down the destructive path of infidelity.[13]

As Vincent Fitzgerald, LCSW, also notes,

> By virtue of newness alone, affairs are more attractive options because they are a new world, and we worship newness. In this world, bills, fights, or diapers do not exist, and the part of the brain most stimulated is the same as the one stimulated by heroin.[14]

Was your former spouse attracted to risk and novelty? If not, I would wager that the person who pursued your spouse may have possessed these traits.

Arrogance

> "Pride leads to disgrace, but with humility comes wisdom" (Proverbs 11:2).

I've already noted that JFK Jr. refused to heed the advice of others. He seemed to believe he was a cut above the need to heed their wisdom. Despite his limited training, he presumed he could navigate the airplane through haze and darkness.

He overestimated his skills and experience, taking a shortcut to his destination, which placed him and his passengers in even greater danger. Apparently, he thought he was invulnerable to the phenomenon of "spatial disorientation" that other pilots sometimes encounter. He hadn't yet learned to trust the plane's instrument panel over and above his internal radar.

Scripture says,

> "The way of a fool is right in his own eyes, but a wise man listens to counsel" (Proverbs 12:15).

Did your wayward spouse refuse to listen to you or the counsel of others? Like JFK, Jr., did they appear to think they knew better than everyone else?

When I was housesitting for friends during one of our separations, I came across a book by Steve Farrar, *Finishing Strong: Finding the Power to Go the Distance*. I knew James had studied it with a group of his buddies the year before he got involved with Judy. Curious as to its contents, I read it with interest. The more I read, the angrier I got. The purpose of Farrar's book was to challenge men who follow Christ to avoid moral failure in the latter half of their lives. He cited numerous examples from Scripture and contemporary culture of those who either faltered or finished strong in the faith.

Steve made it his personal goal to "not screw up" his marriage, his relationship with his kids, or his integrity (p. 51). The book was filled with wise principles to ponder and inspire men to finish their lives strong in the faith and faithful as husbands and fathers. Near the end of his book, he wrote,

> In order to finish strong, we must have vision. Vision for what is really important, vision for what our kids really need, and the vision to steel ourselves against the strategies of the enemy to destroy everything near and dear to our hearts.[15]

One example he cited was King Uzziah, who accomplished great things for the kingdom of Judah. Yet, later in life, his pride got the better of him, and he flagrantly disobeyed the Lord by assuming the role and privileges of a priest. When the actual priests confronted him, Uzziah became angry. Farrar points out how pride can blind a person to the point that they believe they deserve privileges that don't belong to them, and they tend to resist healthy accountability.

Knowing that my husband had seriously discussed the tenets of this book with close Christian friends, I realized two things. First, the Lord was trying to send him a message: Anyone can fail a moral test, even those who have followed the Lord for most of their lives. And second, I realized he hadn't listened. He missed the book's point: It's not about how we begin—it's about whether we persevere and finish strong.

Looking back, do you see any ways the Lord tried to get your partner's attention? Did God use the example of others, good or bad, to encourage faithfulness or to dissuade them from making their own blunder? Were there friends or bosses or sermons or other advance warnings where the Lord was trying to caution your spouse of danger ahead? Did your spouse react with anger or refuse to listen?

It can be frustrating to know if your spouse proudly ignored God's promptings. But it can also be a source of comfort, knowing that God tried to prevent or intervene in their wayward direction, even if your spouse resisted his prodding.

When Perceptions Drift Off Course

> "Trust in the LORD with all your heart, and lean not on your own understanding" (Proverbs 3:5).

Had JFK Jr. trusted his instructor and early training, he would have known that when pilots lose their visual cues, they can become disoriented. When flying without a view of the horizon, their auditory system and sense of balance may indicate one thing, while the instruments indicate something different. Had he become instrument-rated, he would have learned to trust the dials on the cockpit dashboard more than his inner senses. Instead, as the fog and darkness rolled in, experts believe he relied on his subjective sensations, which deceived him regarding his altitude, positioning, and direction.

Similarly, people who become entangled in affairs lose their good judgment. They ignore the warning lights of Scripture or the "Uh-oh" of their consciences. The neurohormones generated by their illicit involvements seem more real to them than the objective tools available to them.

Temporary ecstasy tricks the unfaithful into believing their outside lovers are more wonderful, more exciting, and more fulfilling than they really are. They veer off course when they mistakenly allow these enthralled feelings to be their guide. Soon, blissful emotions override the straying person's head knowledge about right and wrong, their marital commitments, and their prior understanding of God's moral laws.

The emotional high induced by infidelity artificially insulates a person from considering the impact on a loyal spouse or anticipating real-world outcomes on themselves and other loved ones. It dulls their conscience.

Scripture is filled with warnings about the consequences of unfaithfulness. One such passage is in the book of Proverbs:

> "Can a man take fire in his bosom and his clothes not be burned? So is the one who goes in to his neighbor's wife; Whoever touches her will not go unpunished" (Proverbs 6:27, 29).

Fooled by a Feeling

> "The heart is more deceitful than all else and is desperately sick; Who can understand it?" (Jeremiah 17:9, NASB)

During his time of "spatial disorientation," my husband, James, went to lunch with a friend, "Arnie," whom he had ironically helped extricate from an affair several years earlier. He asked his friend, "Looking back, do you think your attraction to 'Denise' was because she was a better match for you, personality-wise, than your wife?" Arnie leaned forward, looked him straight in the eye, and said, "It was pure deception!"

That response shook my husband. As we lay in bed that night, James told me about his conversation with his friend. He tenderly held my hand while praying aloud to be released from deception. But, much to my heartache, he reverted to his ambivalent self within a couple of days. I begged the Lord, with tears, to pierce through the darkness that blinded him and hovered over our home.

Some people, like my husband's friend Arnie (and many of my clients), are humble enough to embrace biblical truth over immediate feelings. They submit to a process of accountability, truth-telling, counseling, and guided self-reflection. Other people refuse to do the hard work it takes to escape the allure of romantic titillation or undo the damage. Unfortunately, you and your kids were likely the casualties of that refusal.

Infidelity Skews the Relationship

I rarely find that an unfaithful person's initial complaints about their marriage reflect the real issue. More often, they use a list of grievances to deflect attention from the truth: Many of their marriage problems emerged *because* of the affair, not the other way around.

Strayers underestimate the extent to which unfaithfulness injures their faithful partners. The distance, slights, and dissatisfaction with their spouses increase as they are drawn toward a shiny new heartthrob.

When betrayed spouses sense their partners pulling away, they often notice a shift: Quirks that were once endearing are now met with eye-rolls or irritation. This impatience often stems from the betrayer's emotional detachment and the unfair comparisons they're making between their steady, familiar spouse and a captivating affair partner.

When betrayed spouses sense their spouse's disapproval or disengagement, they may complain about their absences or strive harder to connect with their wayward partner, all to no avail. This gives the unfaithful person a manufactured excuse to blame the innocent spouse for encroaching on their space. Hurt spouses, in turn, blame themselves for their inability to regain their partner's attention and affection.

This common pursuer-distancer dynamic develops around infidelity, even before it is discovered. Unfaithful individuals often avoid their rightful spouses due to feelings of guilt and a desire to pursue their lovers. They close themselves off emotionally, work long hours, and are generally unresponsive to their puzzled partners. When the unfaithful withdraw, betrayed spouses move toward their partner in ways the wayward person typically resists.

Even as I write these words, memories of rejection emerge, reminding me that I was in a no-win situation. No matter what I attempted, my enamored husband seemed impossible to win back. Perhaps you can relate to the same feelings of powerlessness.

However, instead of acknowledging the role the affair has played in this unpleasant dance, strayers often accuse their spouses of trying to control them. This leads betrayed individuals to question their own motives as if they should feel ashamed for wanting to connect more closely with their distancing partners. When both partners accept the avoidant partner's narrative of "you are trying to control me," betrayed spouses recoil in shame for supposedly alienating their secretly unfaithful partners. Meanwhile, strayers feel justified in seeking consolation in the arms of an idealized, uncritical lover.

The magnetic pull of an outside love interest acts as an invisible third force that throws the dynamic of the marriage off-kilter. And once the marriage takes a negative turn, it skews the couple's perceptions of each other.

> The magnetic pull of an outside love interest acts as an invisible third force that throws the dynamic of the marriage off-kilter.

Couples often fail to account for the role the affair itself has played in their uncomfortable disconnect. So, the blame game continues until the infidelity is fully revealed, and the affair is exposed for the power player it is. If they focus on repairing the surface ten percent (i.e., marital distress) and ignore how the affair has altered their marital dynamic, they will miss the villainous ninety percent lurking beneath the surface, waiting to finish sinking their ship.

My purpose in discussing how forbidden, secret liaisons can hijack a person's emotions is to help you understand how heightened neurochemicals contributed to your partner's deceived state.

When the affair fog rolled in, your unfaithful spouse was in over his or her head and perhaps too proud to recognize it. The fact that illicit affairs generate hormones that mimic the effects of morphine should bring you a degree of relief. Your partner's irrational downward spiral was not all about you. The bubble of ecstasy distorted their perceptions and poisoned your marriage.

Knowing the neuroscience behind affairs will hopefully help you take your spouse's misbehaviors less personally. Much like JFK Jr., your loved one strayed from reality and lost their bearings. Therefore, your partner's betrayal and decision to go off course stemmed from following their misguided senses rather than as evidence of your unworthiness.

Emotional Distortion

If your spouse, like mine, never emerged from the emotional distortion that pulled him or her away from you, you likely endured the bewildering effects of living with a deluded partner. Your spouse's confusing emotions misled him or her, which engulfed you in a disorienting fog of your own.

Betrandoned individuals are often thrown off balance by their partners' words and actions. We ask, "What is real? What is true? Who am I? Where was I? Where is God in all of this? Has the Lord forsaken me, too?"

This is not the time to abandon your faith in Christ. Instead, now is the moment to grasp your plane's steering mechanism and trust the instruments provided in Scripture. Unlike your disoriented spouse, you can stay on course despite the lack of visual cues in your life right now. Your spouse may have spun out of control, but you don't have to go down with him or her. You need the light and wisdom offered by the objective truths in God's Word and the voice of reason to stabilize your life so you don't crash and burn, as well.

When our beloved spouses enter a season of emotional distortion and make foolish choices that shake our foundations and threaten our existence, we must stand on the solid rock of Christ and his Word amid confusing times. Few experiences can overwhelm us as fiercely as losing a beloved spouse through the painful vehicle of infidelity. Just because your spouse has fallen for "The Great Lie" of emotional distortion and twisted hormones doesn't mean you must follow suit. Instead, remain steadfast in your secure foundation.

> "Therefore everyone who hears these words of Mine and acts on them is like a wise man who built his house on the rock. The rain fell, the torrents raged, and the winds blew and beat against that house; yet it did not fall, because its foundation was on the rock" (Matthew 7:24–25).

I assume that since you are reading this book, the storm of Betrandonment has assailed your house like nothing you've ever experienced before. Now is the time to dig through the sand and find the rock-hard truth. We need to give more than mental assent to Jesus' words; we must act on them. That means following his will, regardless of how you feel or what anyone else is doing or saying to you.

Rely on the Lord, cling to him, and press into him, no matter what your troubled emotions (and deranged spouse) may tell you. A friend of mine, Debbie, once shared a quote by Rev. Arthur Finlayson that I found comforting: "I may tremble on the rock, but the rock does not tremble under me." [16]

I love that.

No matter how your world and your faith may shake, I encourage you to rely on the sturdiness and reliability of Christ. Your spouse's delusional mindset has tossed you about, but Jesus—his character, solidness, power, love, and truth—will not budge.

I hope you now have a better understanding of how your partner's feelings misled them, turning your life upside down. They lost their direction and succumbed to "The Great Lie," as ancient as the Garden, and fell under its influence. Their journey into La La Land wasn't nearly as personal as it seemed. The truth is, no one can stay suspended between right and wrong forever. Those who play the emotional game of *Truth or Dare* eventually choose a side.

In the next chapter, we will explore how your partner's Emotional Distortion set them up for a dilemma known as "Cognitive Dissonance." Once you understand its dynamics, you will recognize why *Dare* often wins.

Chapter 16

Cognitive Dissonance

*He who walks in integrity walks securely,
but he who perverts his ways will be found out.*
~Proverbs 10:9

Rick,[1] a full-time leadership trainer, invited my husband to speak to a group of 25 youth leaders staying at his parents' enchanting waterfront home for a weekend retreat. Once everyone had settled on the floor, cross-legged, and sang a few robust worship songs, Rick introduced James as a business executive with extensive experience working with teenagers and training youth workers.

My heart swelled with pride as he opened with a few lighthearted jokes to ease the room. As always, I watched James's warmth and natural charisma draw his listeners in. With confident ease, he transitioned to his favorite topic—integrity.

"Integrity," he began, "comes from the Latin word *integer*, meaning whole, intact, complete. In math, it refers to a whole number, undivided, not a fraction. When applied to people, integrity describes someone of sound moral character. Someone thoroughly honest in all their dealings."

He paused, then added, "To walk in integrity means we live the same on the outside as we are on the inside—whole, consistent, above reproach. The person others see is truly the person we are."

James emphasized the importance of followers of Christ becoming more whole, with their outward lives in harmony with their inner selves. "We are most at peace and glorify the Lord best when our external conduct matches our inner convictions."

James then shared the story of when his father looked him in the eye and said, "Never sell your integrity, son." This motto made a considerable impression on James growing up. He later adopted it as his own.

As he scanned their faces, his eyes narrowed. "I say the same thing to you: never sell your integrity. Nothing is worth trading your integrity for. Strive to be whole, honest, and consistent, inside and out. Make sure your outward behavior matches your inner life with Christ."

I don't remember the other illustrations or the Scripture he referenced. But this was the essence of his message.

James always had a way of convincing people of his sincerity and the rightness of his words. He possessed a gift of persuasion, which he utilized effectively in both ministry and business.

Over the years, I had heard James speak on integrity several times. But this one felt different. It struck a deeper chord. Maybe it was the audience—young adults in their early twenties, standing on the threshold of their futures, wide-eyed and eager to absorb wisdom. Or perhaps it was the setting—a pristine home surrounded by breathtaking beauty, lending a quiet, sacred quality to the moment.

But more than anything, I believe it was divine timing. As if the Lord himself had prompted James to revisit this message, planting seeds the Holy Spirit could later water—right when James needed them most.

Later, I also wondered if this talk had left such a strong impression on me because I would need to hold on to my own integrity, even if imperfectly, when my world was spinning out of control. Or maybe God knew I needed this memory to remind me of the person James used to be, so that I wouldn't come to hate him as much as I loved him.

I never could have imagined that a little more than two years later, I'd be house-sitting in this same home—alone—waiting for my beloved to awaken from the stupor of an affair, while I quietly weighed my own options.

Maybe you, too, have wondered, "How on earth did my spouse change from a loving, principled, God-honoring person into someone capable of stepping outside our marriage for another person or even a shameful habit?"

You may have asked yourself, "Where did my spouse's ethics go? Their values? The promises they made? Was it all a lie—or did something inside them change when the affair began?"

If you're anything like I was, you're stunned by the drastic character shift your once-trusted partner displayed while living in La La Land with the very person who helped unravel your marriage.

Why do people who know better ditch their values to "follow their hearts" in the heat of an affair? As discussed in Chapter 15, the Emotional Distortion that occurs during acts of unfaithfulness is powerfully deceiving. People lose all perspective when engulfed in the fog of infidelity with no visual cues to reorient them.

The Battle of Cognitive Dissonance

Initially, most people feel conflicted when contemplating an illicit attraction. Their prior beliefs suggest they flee, avoid, or escape. Yet their hormones and emotional cravings may drown the voice of reason and drag them over the edge of no return. When people face a dilemma between what they know is right and a sensual, pleasurable option, their minds are conflicted. Their consciences tell them, "Don't go there," but their emotions tell them, "Don't pass this up!"

In 1957, the social scientist Leon Festinger published a book explaining a new theory about the human mind's workings, known as "Cognitive Dissonance."[2] It is considered one of the most significant contributions to 20th-century social psychology. He conducted several experiments to show that people will go to great lengths to avoid the discomfort of holding two contradictory beliefs simultaneously. He went on to demonstrate that people in mental conflict often choose the belief they want to believe to avoid remaining suspended between two opposing options. Despite contrary evidence, they will seek reasons to justify a biased position. He used the example of smoking.

People who like to smoke or find quitting difficult may be torn for a while when they learn how harmful it is to their health. But, to rationalize their choice to continue smoking, they will minimize the health risks and tell themselves such things as, "If I quit, I will gain weight, and that would be unhealthy, too."

Most people struggle to endure opposing beliefs, pulling them in different directions. It's like hearing jarring, discordant music—unsettling and hard to ignore. When sensual desires clash with moral values, inner tension builds like a pressure cooker. Eventually, something must give. Relief only comes when the steam escapes and harmony returns.

Though many claim to live by strong values, when emotions run high and resistance weakens, feelings often win. But once a person gives in, dissonance grates like fingernails on a chalkboard. To quiet the noise, they must resolve the conflict—either by changing their behavior or adjusting the beliefs that stand in the way.

The tension of moral indecision is so uncomfortable that most people can't hover long between their former values and their lusty longings. They find the balancing act too strenuous to maintain. They must choose one side of the fence or the other. The only problem is that most people lean toward what *feels* good rather than what *is* good. And once they give in, their Cognitive Dissonance clangs louder.

This presents a new dilemma: how to justify what they know is wrong so they can live with themselves and quiet their internal conflict. The solution?

Rationalization

As Dr. Festinger pointed out, *rationalization* is the process by which someone makes internal excuses for doing something they intellectually know is harmful or unethical. When people lose the war against choosing what is right, they seek ways to justify what they once believed was wrong.

When it comes to infidelity, the unfaithful need to come up with reasons they are entitled to have an affair. They must change their beliefs to align with their sinful actions. That way, what they once considered immoral somehow becomes understandable and okay. When these rationalizations take hold, their minds relax, and they think, "Now all's right with the world." At least in their made-up world.

Over the years, I've heard numerous justifications from spouses who stray and their partners. I even compiled a list of these rationalizations and conducted surveys with betrayed spouses—both in my workshops and on my website—to see what excuses they had heard from their unfaithful partners.

From the 81 people who filled out the surveys, I tallied the most common to the least common rationalizations their unfaithful spouses used to "explain" their affairs and/or marital rejection. I then divided the rationalizations into categories, noting the number of applicable answers given:

- **Blame** (193 answers) which suggests, "My affair/porn addiction is *your* fault!"
- **Entitlement** (92) refers to attitudes that make them believe they are exceptions to the rule.
- **Minimizing** (76) where betrayers make light of their wrong actions.
- **Rewriting the Marital History** (69), including notions like "I am not sure I ever loved you" and "I married you too quickly" (as covered in depth in Chapter 17).
- **Religious Excuses** (44), like "God will forgive me" and "People in the Old Testament had concubines" (as will be covered in Chapter 19).
- **Hero Syndrome** (10), a rationalization driven by the ego's need to rescue an outside lover.

(Check out **Appendix D** to compare your partner's rationalizations with the answers of others.)

I hope reading the excuses that other betrayed spouses have endured helps you feel less alone. Human nature and Satan's tactics haven't changed much since the Fall. Remember, these rationalizations, which range from simple to elaborate, are the lies that straying partners adopt to reduce Cognitive Dissonance and rationalize their affairs.

An Embattled Mind

I like how authors Tavris and Aronson address the path to and beyond Cognitive Dissonance. "How do you get an honest man to lose his ethical compass? You get him to take one step at a time, and self-justification will do the rest."[3]

The Bible says, "A double-minded man is unstable in all his ways" (James 1:8, KJV). And no one is more double-minded than a person in the throes of Cognitive Dissonance over an affair.

If you've lived with a double-minded partner, you know the torment of walking on eggshells, wondering if your mixed-up spouse will choose you or their new delirious lover or habit. One day, your spouse gives you a warm, reassuring hug, and your nerves calm down; another day, your spouse stiffens, won't look you in the eye, and avoids you like the plague, scaring you out of your wits.

Sadly, strayers often prioritize their fleeting emotions over sound judgment, inventing justifications for their harmful behaviors to soothe their conscience. Once they convince themselves that what's wrong is acceptable, their distorted thinking only deepens.

Tavris and Aronson note,

> "Dissonance reduction operates like a thermostat, keeping our self-esteem high. That is why we are usually oblivious to the self-justifications, the little lies to ourselves that prevent us from even acknowledging that we made mistakes or foolish decisions."[4]

Innocent spouses may sense something has changed within their mate, but can't yet put their fingers on it. Even if faithful spouses suspect their partner's inappropriate relationship, they would be shocked to discover the straying partner's entirely new, fabricated reality.

A self-justifying spouse's secret, internal dialogue doesn't usually come to full light until the wayward person is on the brink of leaving. By then, no amount of cajoling can penetrate the upside-down worldview of the unfaithful. The prophet Isaiah warns,

> "Woe to those who call evil good, and good evil;
> Who substitute darkness for light and light for darkness;
> Who substitute bitter for sweet and sweet for bitter!
> Woe to those who are wise in their own eyes
> And clever in their own sight!" (Isaiah 5:20–21)

Can you think of a better description of a rationalizing strayer? I would add, "And woe to those who love such a person, for they will suffer unspeakable sorrow and heartache."

Scripture demonstrates that sin deceives people and hardens their hearts from accepting the truth.

> "But exhort one another daily, as long as it is called today, so that none of you may be hardened by sin's deceitfulness" (Hebrews 3:13).

You need to understand that your wayward spouse's sexual sin has hardened their heart—both toward God and toward you. You may have heard accusations from your partner that shocked you; thoughts you never imagined they would have, let alone believe. The lies, half-truths, excuses, blame-shifting, defensiveness, and gaslighting can deeply undermine a betrayed spouse's sense of reality.

Connecting the Dots

Betrandoned spouses must understand the role emotional distortion played in their partner's illegitimate choices. Once feelings led them astray, the internal conflict of Cognitive Dissonance set in. Desperate for relief, instead of turning back as conscience invites, they clung to Rationalizations—like mental permission slips that made their behavior seem acceptable or at least justifiable.

Most people in the thrall of an affair find it easier to reshape their beliefs than redirect their actions. They justify each compromise, step by step, until the new beliefs feel like lifelines—helping them stay afloat amid emotional chaos and outside disapproval. They silence their consciences, distance themselves from protesting spouses, and cling tightly to their invented narrative as if their survival depends on it.

> Most people in the thrall of an affair find it easier to reshape their beliefs than redirect their actions.

As the authors of *Mistakes Were Made but Not by Me* write,

At the simplest level, memory smooths out the wrinkles of dissonance by enabling the confirmation bias to hum along, selectively cause us to forget discrepant, disconfirming information about beliefs we hold dear.[5]

Selective memory helps a person dismiss good memories of a marriage and string together the unpleasant ones to create a confirming narrative that justifies their wayward actions.

A strayer's need to solve their moral quandary may leak out during an argument. Once they express their off-base reasons out loud, your partner may work hard to convince you that their new "truths" are valid (saying things like "If you weren't so_____, I never would have____"), fully expecting you to accept their lame excuses.

If your betraying spouse can't convince you to agree that you are the problem, they will find a friend, lover, or an easily manipulated therapist who only knows part of the story to accept their woeful tale. If they successfully persuade a friend or two to affirm their maligned beliefs, it can make you doubt yourself even more.

As discussed in Chapter 5, "Betrayal as Abuse," rationalizing partners use gaslighting to throw you off track. They lie, deny, and want to control if, when, or whether you discover some portion of the truth. These combined tactics drive an uninformed spouse to the brink of crazy.

The Progression from Infidelity to Abandonment

No wonder it felt like your heart and mind might explode. Your spouse moved through increasingly dark stages—justifying the affair and even considering leaving you for greener pastures.

Sensing them slipping away, you may have responded with desperate attempts to save the relationship: involving others, sinking into depression, begging for another chance, offering more sex, being overly kind, or lashing out in anger.

All these appeals likely increased your partner's disrespect for you—after all, they knew deep down that they would not put up with what they were doing to you. Like a drowning person, you may have clung to your spouse for dear life, which only bolstered their belief that you were "controlling" and not good for their emotional health. In truth, they were the controlling one, managing you by their secrecy in ways that were not good for *your* emotional health.

Whether your partner took off with the other person/habit or not, you painfully learned that their heart toward you was permanently closed. And if you were still in love with them, this mutation frightened you and shredded your heart. You wondered, "How could this happen to us?"

Here is another story by "Alice" that illustrates a spouse's progression from a Loving Christian to a Heartless Betrandoner.

> My husband experienced physical and mental abuse, parental unfaithfulness, early exposure to porn, and personal discontent—all of which he later blamed on me. He totally rejected God when he started the affair and actually kind of blamed God for his discontent—God did not answer his prayers the way he wanted for his construction business.
>
> After I found out about the affair and confronted him, he completely changed his behavior towards me. He showed a lot of contempt and kept telling me he had been unhappy for a "very long time" (of course, he neglected to tell me this). He was angry that I even found out about the affair and asked me not to contact the affair partner's husband, as he did not want her to be afraid (she should be afraid!). Along with the contempt he showed me, he was very rude, interrupting me during conversations and sometimes walking away from me and closing the door. I think those were the hardest things to deal with besides the affair.
>
> Before the affair, he was kind, generous, protective, loving, a Bible study leader, and very involved in our church. Once he began his affair, he became someone I did not know anymore.[6]

As you can see from Alice's example, extramarital affairs do not happen in a vacuum. Earlier factors and conflicts within the offending spouse contribute to the deterioration of a marriage. And, besides pre-existing conditions, affairs can, in themselves, change a person for the worse.

Your spouse chose emotional elation over you and reshaped their beliefs through rationalizations to make "following their heart" seem permissible. Even if the affair fizzled or the habit shifted, they clung to a web of justifications that propped up their desired fresh start. This distorted mindset temporarily validated their betrayal and fueled their continued slide into deception.

If your spouse appeared to find relief in pursuing an outside lover or leaving you, it did not mean it was their best course of action. It only meant that the unfaithful person "solved" their once-tormenting Cognitive Dissonance. They were no longer in limbo. Their temporary sense of relief was fueled by the anticipation of either pursuing their affair partner or escaping the daunting task of repairing the damage they had caused.

Cognitive Dissonance

Do not confuse your partner's apparent transient respite after making an immoral decision with the penetrating peace of the Holy Spirit. Fantasy will not match reality. It's a counterfeit serenity from the natural relief of jumping off the fence of indecision—often onto the most expedient but destructive side of the equation.

In the following two chapters, we will discuss further reasons behind your spouse's distancing spiral. Once you understand the next factors that caused your marriage's demise, your partner's unfamiliar alterations will make more sense. This knowledge will empower you and bring you considerable relief.

First, let's dive into how your spouse created a distorted narrative about your marital story that left you dazed and confused.

Chapter 17

Rewriting The Marital History

*Keep me from lying to myself; give me the privilege
of knowing your instructions.
~Psalm 119:29, TLB*

Freckle-faced 25-year-old "Jeremy Richards," the organizer of a group of college-age Christian leaders, asked James and me how we met and fell in love. I lit up. I always enjoyed the opportunity to share our love story over the years. Having dated a lot in my twenties, I was passionate about encouraging young people to wait for the right life partner and not settle for second best.

After downing delicious cheesy chicken over rice, the college students eagerly gathered around us to listen.

James seemed hesitant, so I jumped in first, telling our romantic love story from the beginning. Recounting the events and feelings that transformed our relationship from casual acquaintances to a loving couple always warmed my heart.

As I talked in my usual animated way, James remained quiet. When it became his turn to chime in with his side of the story, I noticed a slight strain in his tone of voice. He used the usual illustrations but with less earnestness and detail. Something didn't seem quite right.

The students were enthralled with all the little coincidences that unfolded on our path to engagement, the description of our magical wedding, and the ways God had blessed our subsequent marriage. I beamed as I explained our story of true love, shared values, and a vision for serving Christ together. When we finished, Jeremy commented on how inspiring our story was. The other students nodded affirmatively.

As the last guest waved goodbye, my back wilted against the door. *What's wrong? Why wasn't James as enthused as usual when discussing our romantic journey?* I was sure the students didn't pick up on it, but I sensed something was amiss. *Could it be that his recent admission of struggling with an attraction for that woman at work was having a greater effect on him than I knew?* He said it was just a one-way attraction. *Surely, a passing fancy,* I'd thought to myself. But now, I wondered.

A couple of weeks later, driving on a date night together, I worked up the nerve to ask James how he was handling his feelings toward Judy. He replied, "Not so well." My heart sank. He explained, "I've concluded that my real issue has nothing to do with her. It's about our *marriage*."

My mouth turned to cotton. How could I have missed this? Surely, he's kidding, right?

James cleared his throat. "I've decided the trouble is that we don't do enough active things together," he continued. "You're just not playful enough. Since we moved, I haven't had any buddies to do stuff with. Sitting around talking isn't enough for me."

While I could understand his need for more shared recreation, I had never heard this complaint from him before. We had always enjoyed going to movies, having dinner with friends, attending our kids' sports events, participating in joint ministry endeavors, and brainstorming ways to remodel our home together. At least, I thought so.

Now that we are on the cusp of being empty nesters, perhaps he is right. I swallowed hard. "How about if we take up line dancing, ballroom dancing, or swing?" He shook his head. "I could work on my golf game." He gave a mild nod. However, he quickly shot down every other idea I suggested. Nothing but the notion of golf even slightly appealed to him. *If our lack of shared activities was the real problem, why is he so unreceptive to my ideas?* Then it hit me full force. My thoughts and feelings no longer mattered to him, something I had never felt before.

The unraveling continued over the following weeks. As I mentioned in other chapters, I heard everything from "I love you, but I'm not in love with you" to "I'm not sure I ever loved you" to "It's not about *her*, it's about *us*!" to "You're boring," and "I don't think God really brought us together."

I struggled to sleep all night, replaying his disorienting pronouncements. *What happened to our beautiful love story?* According to him? Gone. *His loving feelings for me?* Never happened. My perception of our loving marriage? He must have faked it all these years. *Our shared sense of purpose?* A figment of my imagination.

In the months that followed, James's emotional withdrawal turned our once warm, love-filled home into a torture chamber. I was at a loss for how to respond—everything I did seemed to invite more disdain. Bound by his demand for secrecy, I found myself alone with only rejection and fear for company.

Weaving together a shared story of love is one of the most love-affirming tasks a couple can do for their marriage. It gives the pair a sense of meaning and creates a cherished duo-biography in honor of their relationship. Remembering how they met, what drew them together, and how their love evolved over the years reminds the couple of their love and the purpose behind being together. Even the hardships and how they were overcome give meaning to their story. They are lovers. They've weathered family storms. They belong together. They stayed committed to each other through thick and thin.

Positive selective memory and storytelling go hand in hand. We cannot share everything which would make the story too long. So, we choose highlights representing all the other experiences along the way.

When we love someone, we naturally filter out some of the negative data. For example, most parents view their children through rose-colored glasses. We feel protective and biased in our defense of them.

However, in non-biological relationships, we require more than just good feelings to maintain a sense of positive regard for one another. In a marriage, once the initial infatuation dies down, we must consciously focus on what is good and lovely about the beloved. Dr. John Gottman and Professor Robert Weiss refer to this as "Positive Sentiment Override,"[1] —the concept that selective positive memory helps us maintain our sense of love despite minor irritations in the relationship. When we give our spouses the benefit of the doubt and emphasize the good in our life partners and marriages, it is a sign that we are loving people.

Not that we should completely ignore hurtful and negative behaviors. Troublesome issues must be addressed if a couple is to have an authentic, healthy relationship. Love is a choice, and part of that choice involves accentuating the positive highlights of your life together, acknowledging the challenging ones, and weaving them together into the story of your marriage. The "warts" become endearing, or at least fade into the background, compared to the goodness we appreciate in our partners.

Our loving feelings decline when the negative data outweigh the positive data. As marriage researcher John Gottman says, a marriage can only thrive when the positive feedback outweighs the negatives by at least a ratio of five positives to one negative.[2] I believe that includes our internal attitudes as well. When we foster private, pessimistic beliefs about our partners to the exclusion of the positive ones, especially to justify an illicit entanglement, it can throw shade on our spouses and, by extension, unfairly tinge our view of the marriage.

When couples revisit the meaningful parts of their journey and share that story with others, they reaffirm the value of their relationship and remember why they chose each other. Their story is like a co-authored book full of joys and sorrows—providing the glue, context, stability, and strength to get them through the hard times.

Many clients have told me that their shared history is what kept them from walking away. The time invested, mutual friendships, laughter, tears, intimacy, kids, and challenges they overcame—wove a story uniquely theirs. It brought them a sense of connection and security, even in crisis.

The Realities of Marriage

The importance of a shared story reminds me of one of the last scenes in the popular movie, "The Story of Us."[3] Actors Bruce Willis and Michelle Pfeiffer are driving to pick up their children from summer camp, discussing how to tell them of their plans to divorce.

When the moment arrives, and the kids pile into the van, Michelle falls apart as she reviews their shared memories as a couple—the good and the bad. They get out of the van to discuss this away from the children. Here are a few excerpts of what she says to her husband:

> "...we are an 'us.' There is a history here, and histories don't happen overnight. You know, in Mesopotamia or ancient Troy or somewhere back there, where there are cities built on top of other cities, but I don't want to build another city; I like this city.

> "I know where we keep the Bactine and what kind of mood you are in when you wake up, by which eyebrow is higher. And you always know that I am a little quiet in the morning and compensate accordingly. That is a dance that you perfect over time. And it is hard. It is much harder than I thought it would be, but there is more good than bad, and you don't just give up.

> "Let's face it—anybody is going to have traits that get on your nerves. I mean, why shouldn't it be *your* annoying traits? And I'm no day at the beach—but I do have a good sense of direction. So, at least I could find the beach, which is not a criticism of yours—it is a strength of mine...

"Haven't we hit the essential paradox? Give and take. Push and Pull. Ying and yang. The best of times. The worst of times.

"I guess what I am trying to say is ... I love you."

In her monologue, Michelle Pfeiffer overturns their plans to divorce with a plea to stay together, recognizing the significance of their shared marital history.

Maintaining a united view of the marriage—including the good and the not-so-good—is crucial. It is part of what binds a couple together through life's storms. As Michelle said, "Anybody is going to have traits that get on your nerves. Why shouldn't it be *your* annoying traits?" That is reality.

Trying to Make Sense

Nothing is more divisive to a couple's story than when one member romantically attaches to an outside, idealized person. When the straying spouse attaches to Mr. or Ms. New Love Interest and detaches from the faithful partner, their prior rosy lenses toward their mate glaze over. Suddenly, the unfaithful person feels increased irritation and impatience with the real spouse, who can't compete with the euphoric feelings associated with the outside paramour.

Wayward spouses often search for ways to justify their change of heart. They brood over their confusion, grappling with intense feelings for their lover and growing indifference toward their spouse. This mental churn brings buried doubts and resentments to the surface, crowding out the good memories of their marriage.

They ask, "Why am I drawn to this outside person?" "Why do I feel so disconnected at home?" Over time, these private questions produce answers that harden into new "truths." Many conclude they must have married the wrong person or perhaps never truly loved their spouse. "Otherwise," they reason, "how could I fall so deeply for someone else?"

These illicit feelings toward the new heartthrob displace the good that once existed between the marital couple. Wayward spouses who switch allegiances rewrite the marital history to favor the alluring lover over the dejected, existing spouse. This may lead them to leave the marriage for the love object or in search of greener pastures.

As authors Tavris and Aronson say,

> Those who travel the route of shame and blame will eventually begin rewriting the story of their marriage. As they do, they seek further evidence to justify their growing pessimistic or contemptuous views of each other. They shift from minimizing negative aspects of the mar-

riage to overemphasizing them, seeking every bit of supporting evidence to fit their new story.[4]

Personal Stories

Here are a few examples from the women in our Betrandoned support group, starting with "Melanie:"

> He described our marriage as "a mistake." He told me I was "no fun," that I dressed too modestly, "like a teacher," and that he could never follow the rules all the time like I did. When he would say things like this, it would confuse me deeply. For decades, he had set a conservative tone in our home and in our relationship. He was a leader in the churches we attended, taught Sunday School, occasionally spoke from the pulpit, doled out marriage advice, and gave copies of the movie *Fireproof* liberally to the servicemen he mentored. It has been difficult for our sons and me to process the rewriting of our marital history. His "rewrite" tricks our minds, steals our memories, and leaves us questioning reality.[5]

Another woman, "Evelyn," married for 27 years, freshly separated, told us about a time when she was trying to reach her husband by phone to confirm an important breakfast meeting the next day.

> He must have hit the wrong button on his Apple watch, so I heard him bash me to a room full of people at a bar. I am not sure if the affair partner was there or not, but I could hear women laughing as he told them he "had been unhappy" with me "for the last 10 years." I couldn't believe my ears. Ten years earlier, we had celebrated our 17th anniversary in Jamaica, and we were super happy. Everything I heard him say at the bar was shocking and untrue. During his affair, he complained that I 'like to read too much.' For Pete's sake, he married me, knowing I was an English major![6]

Our support group members laughed at this ridiculous complaint, agreeing that liking to "read too much" wasn't grounds for infidelity or divorce. Another member, "Terilyn," said,

> When my husband was justifying his affair, he rewrote our history and minimized his former feelings, moments of love, and all that we supported each other in. He said he never felt "like this" [blissful] with me like he did with her. He even told our daughter that it was a "movie

> moment" when he met his girlfriend and that they were "soulmates." I had difficulty working through what he said about our relationship. But the biggest hurdle for me to overcome was what he told our daughter.[7]

Hearing such glowing words about an affair partner cuts like a knife. Besides idealizing an outside lover, a straying spouse may unfairly denigrate the spouse. I have heard or witnessed many others make excuses for their choice to abandon their marriages.

One male client told me that his wife accused him of being "manipulative" in his efforts to save their marriage. (Didn't many of us behave desperately when our partners threatened to leave?) When she emotionally withdrew from him, he scrambled to win her back. Then, she blamed his "intrusiveness" as the reason she needed to divorce him.

Ironically, the real manipulation was her concealing an affair she was having with a fellow church staff member—an important detail she conveniently omitted when venting to others, including her divorce attorney.

It's astonishing how often betrayers invent flimsy excuses to justify leaving a marriage wounded by infidelity. They repeat these stories so often that they start to believe them.

In their book *Mistakes Were Made (but not by me)*, authors Carol Tavris and Elliot Aronson suggest,

> Memories are often pruned and shaped by an ego-enhancing bias that blurs the edges of past events, softens culpability, and distorts what really happened.[8]

They go on to say,

> As the new story takes shape, with husband and wife rehearsing it privately or with sympathetic friends, the partners become blind to each other's good qualities, the very ones that initially caused them to fall in love.[9]

Do these stories resonate with you? Have you endured the pain of a stolen past, felt the mind-bending detachment and false accusations from a spouse you once trusted? Has your wayward partner invalidated the love you shared, blamed you for their unfaithfulness, or exaggerated the difficulties in your relationship? If so, you know the deep hurt of having your love story distorted, denied, or erased.

A Common Phenomenon

Having your marital history robbed or twisted by a recalcitrant spouse rips a gaping hole in your past. It pulls the rug of reality out from under you and shreds your sense of trust in others, yourself, and the world. You no longer feel grounded. To re-ground yourself, it helps to understand how common this occurrence is and the forces at play.

Infidelity expert Dr. Shirley Glass[10] and other researchers have identified the common tendency of unfaithful spouses to rewrite the marital history in ways that are unrecognizable to the faithful spouse. She states, "Involved partners, as happens frequently, may negatively rewrite the marital history to justify an affair."[11]

As an infidelity therapist, I saw this pattern both before and after my personal experience. Two clear signs of an affair are when one partner grows hard-hearted toward the other and their accounts of the marital history differ drastically. The longer the affair lasts, the more elaborate the unfaithful spouse's self-justification becomes. Initially, there may be only a few complaints, but over time, the straying partner's negative view of the marriage often deepens, distorting their perception of the past. As a result:

- Inconveniences become roadblocks.
- Small obstacles become mountains.
- Irritants become deal breakers.

As discussed in prior chapters, the elements that contribute to strayers' tendencies to reinvent the story of their original marriages are:

- The ecstasy of forbidden love.
- The betrayer's biased motivation to write a new narrative to "explain" these good feelings.
- The faithless person's need to rationalize their wrongs to calm a nagging conscience.
- The secret life that allows self-deception to grow in darkness.
- The lack of reality associated with living in a secret affair bubble.
- To gain sympathy from the affair partner.
- The tendency to view the spouse as an obstacle to their happiness.
- All of which foster a strayer's need to blame the marriage or demonize the betrayed partner.

Wayward spouses often engage in historical revisionism to justify their feelings, quiet their consciences, and make their misconduct seem acceptable.

So, you may ask, what's a betrayed spouse to do? How does one upright a narrative that has been turned upside down? If you are like me, you must first examine how your former spouse's version of your story has damaged your psyche. Then, you can begin to sort the truth from the lies and construct a more accurate picture of yourself and your life together.

The Impact On You

Devastated spouses who hear a distorted version of their marital past often feel blindsided and overwhelmed with self-doubt. They question where they went wrong, wondering, "How did my partner fall out of love without me noticing?" They ask themselves, "Was I really so difficult to live with that their only options were to have an affair or leave?"

Betrandoned spouses have a terrible time understanding the reasons for the leaver's change of heart. Not knowing which came first, the partner's marital unhappiness or the temptress, can torment abandoned spouses for years. We often blame it on our lack of attractiveness, lovability, or worth.

> There's nothing like a heart-involved affair to lure a strayer's affections away from a decent, loving spouse.

Many issues in a marriage could be resolved with professional help. But once the magnetic force field of an illicit romance pulls someone's heart away, it's hard to reverse. It takes a near miracle to break the spell and restore a betrayer's sensibilities. There is legitimacy behind the old "Alienation of Affection" laws. There's nothing like a heart-involved affair to lure a strayer's affections away from a decent, loving spouse.

Reconstructing The Truth

No marriage is perfect. After all, it comprises two imperfect people. However, just because your spouse betrayed and abandoned you does not mean you deserved it. Yet, since your delusional spouse is someone you used to trust and respect, it can be difficult to sort fact from fiction.

How do you regain your sense of reality when a rationalizing spouse has undermined what you knew to be true? It took me hundreds of journal pages, prayers, wise counsel, friends, blogs, good books, and Scripture study to heal from the damage of having the story of our marriage rewritten.

When a love-crazed, vitalized betrayer forsakes the marriage, the Betrandoned feel discarded, heart-stricken, and alone to make sense of what happened and pick up the shattered pieces of their lives.

Dr. Shirley Glass explains the injury of unanswered questions from a Post-Affair divorce this way:

> Psychologically, one of the greatest difficulties is the lack of closure… The one who is left must formulate the story alone, without the input of the central character in the drama. It's like trying to build a building without ever having seen a blueprint.[12]

Betrandoned spouses need to reconstruct a more realistic version of their relationship's history: the good, the bad, and sometimes the ugly. This involves:

- Identifying and dispelling your spouse's lies and distortions.
- Reclaiming the good you know was true.
- Admitting any deficiencies in the relationship that you may have minimized or ignored, so you can learn from them.

Even if you glossed over a few Red Flags, it still didn't justify your spouse's affair or the rejection that followed. Nor does having an imperfect relationship make infidelity okay. As we covered in Chapter 6, "The Double Humiliation," your spouse had a lot of other options at his/her disposal to address any troubling issues in the marriage or complaints about you, other than an affair.

COUNTERING HURTFUL LABELS

Here are a few ways the Lord helped me overcome the hurtful labels and unfair judgments my unfaithful husband used to justify his affair and abandon our marriage. I needed an outside perspective to counter the negative programming James tried to impose on me.

Unfair Judgments

During one of our separations, I drove 80 minutes to visit the pastor who officiated our wedding. I had served with him as a volunteer church staff member for several years. He and his wife patiently listened for hours as I sobbed through my story. When I mentioned that my husband had told me I was "boring," Pastor Lee threw his head back and laughed. "That is the *last* word I'd use to describe you!"

Instantly, relief poured over me. I realized James's accusation was ridiculous. Of course, I was not a boring person. *Any* spouse seems boring compared to the thrill of an exciting, secret affair. My former pastor's laughter helped me override my husband's stilted perspective.

Have you told a few safe friends about your spouse's unfavorable judgments about you? What did they have to say? Betrandoned spouses need the objective feedback of others who know them well to counter the jaded views of an unfaithful partner and bring peace to their embattled thoughts.

Who is the Betrayal a Reflection of?

Near the end of our meeting, Pastor Lee said, "He walked away from the Lord before he ever walked away from you." I thought about this phrase all the way home.

His statement sparked two realizations: first, that my husband had likely been struggling spiritually long before he crossed the line with Judy; and second, that James's infidelity and threats to leave were symptoms of his spiritual condition, rather than a reflection of my worth. Had his heart stayed aligned with Christ, even in hardship, he wouldn't have drifted so far from the Spirit's promptings or his former convictions.

What about you? Looking back, do you see any signs that your spouse was in a spiritual battle before he or she acted out? Perhaps some past hurts bubbled to the surface, or recent pressures or disillusionment caused them to question God's character. Or maybe they fiddled with pornography or otherwise compromised their conscience in a way that distanced them from the Lord.

As discussed in Chapter 14 on "Footholds," unprocessed sin and unbelief are significant barriers to an unfettered walk with God. These can cause anyone to take matters into their own hands and leap into an outside affair rather than trust God amid a difficult situation or temptation.

Your spouse's choice—and it was a choice, not an accident—to romantically step out of your marriage first damaged his or her relationship with God. That act, in essence, raised a middle finger to God before it did so to you. Like Pastor Lee said to me, I say to you: Your spouse walked away from the Lord before he/she had the nerve to walk away from you.

God takes it very personally when a rebellious person deeply wounds individuals who matter to him (i.e., you).

Imagine a bully attacking your child—throwing him down, kicking and hitting him until he bled. As you rushed to lift your battered child and get him to the hospital, the anger, anguish, and heartache you'd feel would be overwhelming. That's how the Lord feels about your wounds. You are his child. He knows the cruelty of spurned love and longs to carry you to the Father's throne for intensive care, where you can rest in his healing love.

Distorted Perspective

After we'd been divorced for a few years, I suspected my husband had presented a slanted perspective to gain our adult kids' sympathies for his affair and justify divorcing me. I confirmed this during a discussion with one of my sons. My dating-skittish son admitted an underlying fear that he might marry the wrong person. "I just don't want to make a *mistake* like Dad did." Ouch! I didn't blame my son, but the fact that my ex-husband had told our kids that marrying me had been a *mistake* made my blood boil.

After I hung up the phone, I fumed. "How dare he tell our kids that marrying me was a mistake!?" Looking up, I snapped, "You can't possibly know what it's like to be called a *mistake*!" After venting, I sensed the Lord quietly respond. "I understand." "Well?" I asked. Then he reminded me—people once accused Jesus of being Mary's illegitimate son, a huge scandal in his day. That reminder calmed my heart. At least he knew what it was like.

And then he whispered, "And just because others accused me of this, didn't make it *true*." I began to weep. I knew that Scripture was clear that Jesus was *not* illegitimate. He was God in the flesh, conceived of the Holy Spirit. The Old Testament predicted his immaculate conception (Isaiah 7:14), and the New Testament affirmed it (Matthew 1:20-23, Luke 1:35). Just because some folks promoted the lie that Jesus was born illegitimate didn't make it true. This insight brought immense peace to my heart.

Another story from our Betrandoned Zoom group illustrates this point.

"Tonya" was shocked to learn that her unfaithful pastor husband was telling friends, "I had an affair, but I won't go into the 27 years of [her] mental and emotional abuse." In his divorce papers, he conveniently left out his affair and listed her "abuse" as the reason for their divorce, accusing her of "multiple affairs." Exasperated, she asked herself, "Where was I when I emotionally abused him? And I'd like to know the names of these men I supposedly had affairs with!" All were lies and projections.[13]

Has your spouse falsely accused you or burdened you with an unfair label? Did they twist the story of your marriage in ways that don't match reality? Jesus knows what that's like. And just because your wayward partner made false claims doesn't make them true.

John Lawless, a schoolteacher and history buff, once shared a story about Abraham Lincoln that encouraged me. Although we see him as a popular president today, during the Civil War, journalists filled newspapers with slanderous accusations about him. One reporter asked him, "What are you going to do about all the terrible things being said about you?" His reply? "Well, my closest friends won't believe them. And the rest of them don't matter anyhow." What confidence! Many of us need that kind of security within ourselves and among our friends. Keep in mind the following verse:

> "Like a fluttering sparrow or darting swallow, an undeserved curse does not come to rest" (Proverbs 26:2).

No matter what your ex-spouse may say about you, if you are falsely accused or lied about, it won't stick. Your true character will shine through to those who know you best. And, like President Lincoln said, "And the rest of them don't matter anyhow."

Sorting Facts from Fiction

We lose perspective when we experience the double betrayals of infidelity and rejection, not just about ourselves but about our marriages. Most likely, there were many good times associated with your relationship that your unfaithful spouse discounted or that you buried beneath a pile of hurt. Much like after a hurricane's destruction, it helps to revisit the scene and search for treasures to reclaim and restore. Your relationship probably wasn't all bad.

I knew I needed to recall some of the good times. I may have married late, but I was a quick learner and grew significantly over the years. We were united in our hearts for ministry and shared many similar values. We had terrific vacations, conferences, family ventures, and joys investing in our kids and watching their sporting events. I loved him and felt loved by him most of the time. At least until his outside entanglement.

At one point, James told a friend about his doubts about our marriage without mentioning his ongoing affair. The friend, a groomsman in our wedding, asked James, "How would you rate your marriage? Great? Good? Crumby? Terrible?"

James thought for a moment and said, "Good."

His friend said, "Whoa. I'd think *twice* about throwing away a 'Good' marriage!"

When James arrived home, he reverted to his usual warm self, which I relished. At least until he went back to work around *her* the next day. Yet it helped me to hear that he rated our marriage "Good" to his friend, even during his affair.

What about your relationship? Can you look past your recent hurt to identify the good that was there before things went sideways? If so, consider writing down the positive aspects of your marriage and the lessons you learned.

Don't allow the affair to overshadow your entire past. Salvage the moments you felt loved and learned to be more loving. This might be painful now, but tuck the good memories away for future reference so that once you are more healed, you can share them with your children without wincing.

Admitting the Deficiencies

Sometimes, those of us who have a bent toward optimism may have been in denial about our partner's downsides or the weaknesses in our marriage.

In my case, James had been so charming and persistent when we were dating that he captured my heart and unwavering loyalty. I assumed he'd always love me as intensely as he did early on. Even after learning his heart was elsewhere, I still believed in our "meant-to-be" marriage, expecting him to wake up and return to me. My unrealistic view of him and our relationship kept me from honestly assessing our marriage—past, present, and future.

One way for us overly loyal individuals to recognize our marital blind spots is to keep a journal. Writing about our honest feelings helps us develop a more sensible perspective regarding the fault lines in our marriages. I know mine had many more cracks before the affair than I was willing to admit.

When you write about your pain, believe it. Your wounds are trying to tell you something. Did your romantic idealism cause you to ignore troubling issues bubbling below the surface? Did you put up with some put-downs you didn't deserve? Were you too tolerant of inappropriate behavior? Or did you fail to insist upon some much-needed couples counseling a long time ago?

Heightened hormones and brain chemistry often trick unfaithful people into giving more credence to their temporary delirium than to their memories of you and the marriage. One of a betrayer's survival tactics is to remake the story of the marriage, with you as the villain, so they can feel better about their affairs and the choice to abandon you.

Don't buy it. Your imperfections may be areas for growth, but they are not justifications for unfaithfulness and are only rarely a reason for divorce.

The combined factors of Emotional Distortion, Cognitive Dissonance, and Rewriting the Marital History often lead to another mind-bending experience for the Betrandoned—when your spouse morphs into someone you don't know—better known as The Alien Syndrome. Once you identify this startling condition, you can make more sense of your spouse's strange transformation.

Chapter 18

The Alien Syndrome

> He who is the Glory of Israel does not lie or change his mind;
> for he is not a man, that he should change his mind.
> ~ I Samuel 15:29

Gary[1] and Mary left their previous church after their pastor had an affair and resigned. They happily found a new church where Gary could once again serve as a worship leader. Ron, the associate pastor, took a liking to them, and soon they spent recreational time together as families. Gary quickly got along with Ron and considered him his new best friend.

After a few years, Mary found she had some discretionary time beyond homeschooling their four children. When Ron invited her to work part-time for him as his administrative assistant, she gladly accepted his offer.

While Gary liked Ron, he was bothered by Ron's use of foul language, smoking habit, and his spiritually lax attitude—different from what he would expect from a person in vocational ministry.

One day, as the two men drove to Montana to pick up their respective kids from a YWAM camp, Gary began to feel some misgivings about Ron. He realized he didn't fully trust him. He comforted himself with the thought that even though his wife worked for Ron, he had no concerns about her loyalty or faith. "I knew if Ron ever made a pass at her, she would never respond." So, he shrugged off his strange foreboding.

Yet that gnawing feeling wouldn't go away. Finally, Gary asked to meet with the Senior Pastor. After some casual chatting, Gary asked him, "Do you trust Ron?" The pastor paused and said, "We should probably meet."

The next evening, Gary and Mary met in the pastor's home with another couple in leadership at the church. Although Gary was curious about what

The Alien Syndrome

they would say about Ron, he calmly settled into the couch, figuring his wife was in the clear.

The pastor began with, "You asked me if I trusted Ron. Well, just last night we put him on a plane to fly to California for several months of counseling."

When Mary learned Ron had been flown out of state, something in her snapped. Her entire tenor shifted before Gary's eyes—she fell apart.

Gary was totally caught off guard. He told me, "I suddenly didn't recognize her. Her whole demeanor changed. She went nuts—her voice was sharp with fury, and her face twisted with grief. As she sobbed uncontrollably over losing Ron, the anguish poured out of her like a tidal wave I never saw coming."

That's when the truth surfaced: Mary had been having an affair with Ron for months. And the moment she realized she'd lost her lover, he realized he'd just lost his wife.

Back home, Gary gently suggested counseling. But Mary wanted no part of it. Her focus was singular.

"I don't *want* you anymore!" she retorted. "I don't want the kids. I don't want the house. I just want *out*."

Soon thereafter, when she was sound asleep, he gently touched her shoulder and prayed for her. His wife began eerily squirming and writhing in her sleep, as if he were fighting a demon.

Dazed, the next day, he called around to see if any friends would take Mary into their home for a while. No one was interested.

He arranged for his wife to move into an apartment and bought her a used car, all the while in deep grief over the pending loss of his 20-year marriage. He scrambled to get the kids into public school and, out of necessity, had his 16-year-old daughter care for the younger ones when he was still working. He signed them up for sports activities and met with their teachers, searching for ways to help his children flourish in the midst of great upheaval.

It turned out that Mary only wanted to have the kids one weekend a month. He could hardly believe the change in her, from devoted Christian wife and home-schooling mom to crazed adulteress.

Upon Ron's return to Washington, he left his wife and kids to take up with Mary again. Once their respective divorces were final, they got married, much to the sorrow of their shell-shocked families.

I know all too well how mind-bending it is to go from Cherished Spouse to Disposable Dishrag so quickly. Like in Gary's situation, the affair changed my spouse into someone I no longer recognized. Perhaps you can relate.

Same Body, Different Person

A year after my unwanted divorce, at a professional workshop on infidelity, I sat near "Misty," a friendly, engaging therapist. During the lunch break, she shared the heart-wrenching story of losing her husband of 25 years to an extramarital affair. As she described the drastic, robotic transformation he underwent, I couldn't help but ask, "How did you cope with the changes in your now ex-husband?" Her response was both poignant and unexpected.

> "The only explanation I've been able to come up with," she said, "is that aliens descended from outer space, abducted him, extracted his soul, and replaced it with a foreign entity that subsequently took control of his body. The man he's become is unrecognizable to me. Externally, he looks the same, but internally, he's inhabited by an alien."[2]

Inhabited by an alien? I could relate. It seemed like the man I knew had vanished, and some other strange creature had taken his place—same body, different person.

This fascinating metaphor describes the profound heart shift that transpires when a partner attaches to a new lover and detaches from their original spouse. Misty's experience resonated with me and echoed similar narratives I've heard since.

Sudden Change

One of the most painful aspects of a pending Post-Affair Divorce is the sudden change in a beloved spouse's demeanor and attitude. Whether the shift occurs soon after the wedding or 40 years into the marriage, when a trusted spouse loses interest in their partner because of an outside sexual habit or lover, it destabilizes the still-loyal, attached spouse. Betrayed spouses often panic when they notice their partner's heart slipping away. Even if the faithful spouse doesn't know about a secret affair or a partner's clandestine encounters, they often detect an emotional drift on the part of the unfaithful one.

Straying partners who once showed care for their spouse's concerns can become shockingly disconnected, callous, and even cruel, leaving the betrayed spouse bewildered. Those who fall headlong for a captivating paramour often seem like strangers to their families. Tragically, many never return to the loving selves they once were.

Symptoms of an Alien Invasion

As a friend and therapist, I have heard countless stories from abandoned spouses about the phenomenon of what I now call "The Alien Syndrome." Many lamenting people describe affectionate partners who abruptly switched into uncaring people they scarcely recognize. In every case of loving-spouse-turned-stranger, the person was involved with someone outside the marriage, whether known by the faithful partner at the time or not. This is especially true when the unfaithful one can't compartmentalize enough to love two people simultaneously.

Along with this strange revolution, the straying partner often seems to live in another realm, oblivious to the impact of their choices on loved ones. The intoxicating nature of an illicit affair cocoons the betrayer in a blanket of elation, self-centeredness, and unreality. The character changes could easily be the title of a movie: *The Dawn of the Clueless Alien*.

The transformation feels even more jarring when it coincides with a midlife crisis. The wanderer makes a complete 180 ° turn, abandoning formerly held values, goals, language, behaviors, and beliefs—often drastically, and usually for the worse.

Some compromised individuals lose focus and rationalize their poor choices to the degree that they become a shell of who they once were. As their morals decline, a type of sclerosis of the heart takes over, and these people sadly remain oblivious to the devastation left in their wake. Over the years, I have heard many wrenching stories from their previous spouses and adult children who feel rejected and estranged from a formerly loving parent or ex-spouse they no longer recognize.

Out of Touch

For example, one former client of mine lamented with tears,

> After my dad left our family for the other woman, he became a different person. He expected us to be happy he'd found this lover. He forced us to spend time with them as a couple, which I absolutely hated. It was as if my feelings didn't matter to him. Over time, he grew increasingly distant. Then he stopped trying. When I saw him at my grandmother's memorial many years later, I barely recognized him. And he stared through me with empty eyes as if he no longer remembered I was his daughter.[3]

I've heard similar stories over the years.

Another woman in our Zoom group, Tonya, described her Alien experience this way,

> It's similar to when a daytime soap opera wraps up for the year, and the next season, they replace the lead actor with a similar but new actor in the same role, continuing the series as if nothing has changed. When the 'swap-out' is never acknowledged by the producers, the viewer finds this a startling adjustment.[4]

Similarly, in her personal life, everything had undergone a change. Her husband was not the same person. And no matter how often he goes by the same name, wears the same clothes, and even repeats the same lines, she can tell a new inhabitant has taken his place.

A real-life swap-out routine occurs for those whose spouses leave for another person. Not only has the unfaithful partner changed, but it appears, at least on the outside, that the paramour gets to pick up where the original wife or husband left off. The new couple forms a "family," and life continues as if nothing is wrong with this picture. Sadly, no one files a missing person's report on behalf of the original spouse and children whose husband and father have emotionally disappeared.

Unfaithful people are usually so self-absorbed that they don't grasp the impact their behaviors and words have upon their betrayed spouses.

A friend from my Zoom support group, "Bonnie," wrote recently:

> Well, tonight is my ex-husband's wedding to one of the women he had an affair with. We've been separated for six months. He announced his engagement on the day our divorce was final—two weeks ago. It's been a long two years of me trying to repair our marriage while he was continuing the affairs behind my back. This woman lasted the longest.
>
> He introduced our daughter to his fiancé this week and told her she was "getting a new mom"—the first time she met the OW. Our daughter is understandably very upset and confused. And to top it off, he is claiming to be a Christian again and telling everyone how "God blessed him" with the OW.
>
> Now the OW [his new wife] is sending me scathing messages from his phone anytime our daughter expresses sadness or I say 'no' to my ex-husband about anything. I'm just exhausted and so incredibly sad. I wish they would leave me alone long enough for me to heal.[5]

Such is the insensitivity of a former spouse-turned-alien.

Affairs Make Matters Worse

There are plenty of people in unhappy phases of their lives or relationships who don't get involved in outside romances. You probably know a few. It's called having mature love and personal integrity. (For further reading, I highly recommend Christine Meinecke's *Everybody Marries the Wrong Person: Turning Flawed into Fulfilling Relationships*.)

When problems arise in marriages, secret romantic or sexual behaviors only exacerbate matters. They are often the spark that burns down an otherwise salvageable marriage. When debating which came first, the marital troubles or the affair, many times, it was the affair that came first, rather than the other way around. Therapist Linda Riley states,

> Frequently, we only fall out of love after having an affair not before. The affair breaks the bond and makes us feel no longer in love with our spouse. [6]

And that changes everything.

I remember friends telling me they admired the warm affection in my relationship with James. Yet, a few months into his affair, he announced he was "miserable" in our marriage. I asked him when he realized that. He said, "Well, I didn't *know* I was miserable until I fell in love with Judy." Funny how that happens.

> "Frequently, we only fall out of love after having an affair not before."
> ~Linda Riley

Young marriages aren't immune to Alien Invasions, either. One woman, "Sherry,"[7] shared how she dated a man who "love-bombed" her, convincing her she was his one and only. Flattered, she fell in love and agreed to marry him. Yet soon after the thrill of their honeymoon faded, he strangely withdrew. Having caught his "prize," he lost interest in her. Had they not gotten pregnant right away, the marriage might have dissolved sooner.

Tortured by his emotional detachment and wanting to provide their child an intact home, Sherry kept trying to rekindle his affection. By the time their daughter was born, he had already engaged in several affairs. After four years of marriage and on their way to divorce court, he showed little interest in their child. During their separation, he impregnated his last affair partner and married her the day their divorce was finalized.[8] You can only imagine the heartbreak Sherry endured, having been so completely won over by a man who turned out to be so self-absorbed.

Intimacy Issues

As therapist Rob Baker says, "Folks who seek sexual expression outside of their marriages show they suffer with an intimacy disorder. They have difficulty with real-life, emotional closeness and vulnerability."[9]

He traces this difficulty to a lack of emotional safety growing up. He's found that those who seek extra-marital relationships often fear further abandonment and shame for feeling unwanted, which drives their real selves underground. A false, prideful self develops, and such people cover up their deeper needs by engaging in behaviors that make them temporarily feel good, such as pornography, promiscuity, or serial infatuations. Since no one person can fill their childhood voids, when they marry, they keep their spouse at a safe emotional distance. At some point, the former dysfunctional ways of coping with unprocessed grief emerge, and the dissatisfied person seeks other sexual mood-altering behaviors to mask the emptiness inside.

Sometimes, the evasion of intimacy surfaces immediately, as in Sherry's case. For others, undercurrents of dissatisfaction brew quietly for years, only to erupt dramatically in midlife. Most betrayed spouses I counsel tell me that their partners' struggles with emotional vulnerability were long-standing issues. Yet, they didn't fully grasp the extent of the problem until they discovered their spouse was involved with another lover or a compulsive sexual habit.

Of course, a real-life marriage can't compete with the titillation of a fresh, baggage-free, forbidden romance. The resulting switch of allegiances causes many straying partners to detach from the original spouse in cold, uncaring ways. Once an unfaithful spouse bonds with an outside person, they may blow up their lives—and their families' lives—to pursue the temporary elixir of "true love" or the elusive soul mate.

Altered World Views

Regardless of any pre-existing circumstances, the crisis of infidelity often profoundly shifts the betrayer's worldview. Their efforts to justify these newfound, euphoric feelings mark the beginning of a new, and usually less conscience-driven, chapter in their life. As discussed in Chapter 16, they typically discard long-held beliefs in favor of ones that better align with their current feelings and actions. The wayward spouse often adopts a certain cynicism about faith and morality. Strayers typically seek a more permissive worldview that renders their forbidden behaviors acceptable.

Others continue their illicit affairs and mask their immoral choices with a veneer of heightened religiosity. They may suddenly expound on their newfound spiritual insights or attend a new church with their affair partner, presenting themselves as a legitimate couple seeking Christian fellowship, without acknowledging the circumstances that birthed their relationship.

Soon after his affair ended and our marriage was on the brink of divorce, James often told unsuspecting friends, "I'm doing better than ever, spiritually!" Given his persuasive nature, some accepted his words at face value without knowing about his affair, plans for divorce, and growing skepticism toward traditional Christianity.

The betrayer's harmful behaviors and beliefs profoundly alter their life and the lives of their spouse, children, extended family members, and closest friends. Ignoring their conscience, the straying person often morphs into a home-wrecking nightmare that family members no longer recognize.

Some wayward spouses who previously appeared mature beyond their years suddenly behave like rebellious adolescents or giddy teenagers in love who throw caution to the wind. Others unexpectedly become self-absorbed and unsympathetic during an affair, revealing flaws previously held in check or ignored by an overly gracious spouse.

Most clients recovering from a Post-Affair Divorce share how stunned and heartbroken they are by the character decline they witness in their former spouses. Many describe a selfish streak they never noticed before. I've heard countless stories of once-caring partners behaving in shocking, unrecognizable ways. Offended spouses and children often tell me things like:

- "I don't recognize him/her anymore."
- "How could he/she *do* that?!"
- "He seems so aloof. Like a stranger."
- "He wants us to double date. Did you hear that? He wants me to find a boyfriend and go on a date with him and his new lover!"
- "She brought him into our home and had sex on our bed while I was away!"
- "How could he tell our son how much happier he is with the other woman and expect our son to be happy for him?"
- "Why did Daddy bring _____ (the other woman) with us to the park? I just want to be with him."
- "I married my wife because she seemed so sweet. Now she's become an Ice Queen."
- "I thought he was more special than that (to be sleeping around)."

Have you noticed such an evolution in your betraying spouse? These changes are often linked to affairs, particularly when the betrayer refuses to seek help, continues their wayward path, and abandons the marriage. Sometimes, the pendulum swing is temporary, but for those who persist and justify their actions, the changes tend to become long-lasting.

People who engage in heartfelt affairs often detach from their original mates once they bond with a new heartthrob. That's how you can tell that the Alien Syndrome has taken over—when you, the original spouse, no longer count. You feel invisible. You have no vote. No place. No rights. And this new creature inside the body of your once beloved life partner acts like you don't belong in your own home, let alone in his or her life.

> That's how you can tell that the Alien Syndrome has taken over—when you, the real spouse, no longer count.

When Your Spouse Decides He or She Is Transgender

The following example illustrates the connection between Rewriting the Marital History and The Alien Syndrome.

Christine Benvenuto, a Jewish writer, was married to "Tracey" for over 20 years. They had three children together. About 18 years into their marriage, he admitted to her that he couldn't stop thinking about changing his gender. She said, "For two years I watched my husband die." [10]

She goes on to say,

> "I thought we were forever...Once he'd embarked on his transformation, he told me we were never." "He said the person I had loved for so many years was not him. In fact, he never existed at all. Erasing his own past, he re-wrote the whole of my adult life as a love affair with a phantom.[11]"

> "You lose your partner and your access to his memories." She continues, "He tells you that he has been posing as your partner, a fictitious character of his own and perhaps your invention throughout your relationship. Tells you every memory you've stored needs to be rewritten. This person, the one standing before you now, who looks and sounds and moves in a manner that strikes you as being just about as authentic as a child playing dress-up, tells you: I'm real. The man you knew was not ... It's like losing a part of one's mind."[12]

Some of you may relate to Christine's mind-bending experience: loving and building a life with someone who later decided they were no longer the gender you thought you married. Such drastic changes can trigger an identity crisis of your own. In some cases, a partner's Alien-like shift isn't due to an outside affair, but to adult-onset male transgenderism. One form, known as *autogynephilia*, can be described as a man falling in love with or turned on by the imagined female version of himself.[13]

Alienation From Yourself

When you realize that your partner has withdrawn their heart from you, it's natural to attempt to recapture their love. You might think, "If I always agree with him/her and ignore their emotional distance, perhaps they will lower their guard and feel a renewed closeness to me."

However, when you turn into a chameleon to gain acceptance from an unfaithful spouse, you betray yourself and accept your partner's negative perceptions of you.

When you notice the faraway look in their eyes, the contempt in their voice, and their resistance to connection, you begin to wonder, *Am I the problem? Maybe I'm too difficult to love. Maybe I don't deserve their affection.* Over time, you start to believe they are right. *I must be a terrible, inadequate partner for them to seek fulfillment outside our marriage.*

Their excuses and dismissiveness begin to seep into your self-perception, and you start to reject yourself in the same way your unfaithful partner has rejected you. The distorted reflection of who you are in their eyes convinces you that you somehow deserve their withdrawal.

This is how spousal disconnection can estrange us from ourselves. When our identity has been deeply intertwined with our spouse's, their emotional departure leaves us feeling lost. We were once beloved husbands or wives—now we feel like a ship torn from its moorings, drifting without anchor or direction. Reclaiming a sense of self after such disorientation takes time, gentleness, and grace.

One Zoom group friend, Wendy, put her self-alienation this way,

> I had always promised myself that if anyone cheated on me, I would leave them. Now I was betraying my own values and feeling really bad about doing that. I also became hypercritical of my rejected self. Still unconsciously taking his side, I rejected myself too. I looked in the mirror and saw all my imperfections the same way he did. As the only one betrayed, I felt the isolation and alienation of being out of sync with all those who hailed him as "such a great guy." I was humiliated at being the scorned woman and didn't want that identity. I also experienced a painful lack of validation from his family. His brother even asserted that "he didn't do anything wrong." I doubted my own emotions and reactions. I doubted myself and asked counselors if I

had overreacted. I descended into a downward spiral of grief, alone and vulnerable to all my enemies, both internal and external.[14]

Betrandoned spouses need help to undo the spell cast by the long shadow of an alienated partner's distorted perspective. It would have been more humane for our spouse to either drag us into counseling to grapple with genuine difficulties together or mercifully divorce us for legitimate reasons (such as our adultery, addiction, or abuse) than to escape our relationship via the lure of an unrealistic, euphoric affair.

Underlying Issues

Emotionally mature, genuinely loving people understand that love is more than just a feeling. They don't discard their core values when faced with disillusionment, disappointment, or a temporary loss of affection for their spouse. Instead, mature adults do everything they can to restore and repair their committed relationships; they don't seek comfort in another's arms.

If an outside friendship begins to drift toward romance, healthy individuals recognize the risk, reestablish firm boundaries, and seek support. They don't sprint headlong into an affair. They reinforce their lifetime values in times of crisis, pulling back from the flames rather than leaping in and tossing their beliefs aside to "follow their hearts."

Once a person has swallowed the poison pill of infidelity, they face a choice: either seek an antidote and work like crazy to make amends, or else feed themselves lies to justify their wrong behaviors. The latter decision results in the deterioration of the unfaithful one's character in ways that usually render them unrecognizable to their once-intact families.

Practical Application

Watching your once-caring partner devolve into someone you no longer recognize is painful. Hopefully, you will find comfort in knowing other spouses have had the same unfortunate experience. Heart-based infidelity often transforms the unfaithful partner into a Clueless Alien—someone who is intrinsically different from the person you thought you married. It is vital for you to realize that this negative transformation was not your fault.

The grief you feel is real and valid. In many ways, your spouse—as you knew them—is truly "gone." Unfaithfulness robs you not only of a partner but of the shared life, loyalty, and love that once bonded your family.

Barring the miracle of radical repentance—which I've occasionally witnessed—you can no longer rely on them to be trustworthy or compassionate toward you. A stranger took their place. Though they may look the same on the outside, they've changed inside. Like something out of *Invasion of the Body Snatchers*, a different mind and heart now reside where your spouse once was.

Despite resembling your spouse, the person who walks up to your door to pick up the kids—with their lover sitting in the car you once owned—is an alien. Internally, he or she is an impostor inhabiting your ex's body—incapable of charitable treatment of you or feeling your pain. Even if he or she shows occasional tears of shame, it is more likely from self-pity than healthy guilt or empathy for you.

Facing the Alien Syndrome is a key step in your recovery process. You need to allow your image of the former spouse to "die" and do your best to stop hoping he or she will resurrect back into the caring, committed spouse you once knew. Reducing expectations will help you grieve the old, let go of what was, and accept your new reality.

Recognizing this alien switch-out routine during the divorce process is crucial. You may assume you're still dealing with your original, caring spouse—someone who will sympathize with your need for a fair settlement. You're not. Assume your future security is no longer their concern. You must become your own advocate and protect yourself. While I don't recommend being unfair or engaging in emotionally destructive battles over assets, I do advise clients to stay firm and treat divorcing spouses like unreliable business partners. Keep it all business.

Look deeper if your alien spouse acts as if he is doing you a favor. There's a good chance that the terms he or she is pushing for are primarily favorable to him/herself (and perhaps the new lover). Anyone who would abandon his or her family to pursue an outside romance is not worthy of your trust right now. Be cautious and proceed with care. Scripture teaches us to be "Wise as serpents, harmless as doves." Now is the time to put on your wisdom hat with the help of a skilled attorney.

I have worked with many idealistic abandoned spouses who gave up too much in their divorce settlements and later regretted it. They either hoped that being nice to their stubborn spouses would increase their chances of future reconciliation or feared that standing up for themselves would further antagonize an already hostile partner. Expecting a detached spouse to have your best interests in mind is usually unrealistic.

While it may seem counterintuitive, I have noticed that spouses who take firm stands during the divorce process often maintain the scant respect they have for one another. Standing firm helps them achieve a more manageable financial settlement and fosters a more respectful relationship with their ex-spouses in the future.

Rethink What You Want for Your Future

Now is the time to reconsider the type of people you wish to relate to in the future. Ask yourself the following questions:

- Would I have married _____ if he/she were the person back then that he/she is today?
- Are the character changes in my ex-spouse ones I respect and admire?
- How much of myself did I compromise when attempting to save the relationship?
- What hints of difficulties with emotional intimacy did I gloss over in my partner, either before we married or over the years before the affair?
- What red flags must I watch for in a potential future mate?
- What ritual can I devise to bury old expectations of my ex-spouse and come to terms with the new version of my former life partner—the Alien?

These questions can serve as writing prompts in your journal for further processing.

I hope this exercise has helped you realize that hoping for your once-loving spouse to reappear is futile. As hellish as your life became during your spouse's wayward and rejecting season, you would have likely experienced even worse had you stayed together. Living with an ambivalent, detached, untrustworthy spouse would have kept you on edge for years, worn down your health, and been an unhealthy example for your children.

It may not feel like it now, but if your former spouse fits the description of the Alien Syndrome, parting ways ultimately did you a favor. Once your spouse's soul was hijacked and replaced, their true self, at least towards you, vanished. Post-divorce, as painful as it is to deal with an alien version of the person you once cherished, they no longer exist. They've been vaporized. What remains is a stranger with altered character and values. As hard as it is, it's in your best interest to release what was and let the shared dreams dissolve.

This is a time to remember that even though your estranged or ex-spouse has changed, your Lord will not. He is faithful and consistent and does not lie or swerve in his love for you. Christ is committed to you for life. Knowing this should help you relax.

You don't need to retaliate; that will only change your character for the worse. Assertiveness, yes; revenge, no. It's better to invest your energy in healing, becoming the parent your children need, uncovering new purpose, and growing more confident in the Lord's unfailing love for you.

> "For great is your love, reaching to the heavens; your faithfulness reaches to the skies" (Psalm 57:10).

Despite the overwhelming deception and rejection you've endured from a spouse who now seems like a stranger, rest assured—they won't escape the long-term consequences of their choices. In contrast, you have God's unwavering presence. His character is constant, his love unchanging. He will never leave you or betray your trust. You are safe with him. Unlike your wayward spouse, God has no hidden agenda—only faithfulness.

> "Don't be deceived, my dear brothers. Every good and perfect gift is from above, coming down from the Father of heavenly lights, who does not change like shifting shadows" (James 1:16–17).

I've worked with many unfaithful folks over the years. After trading one spouse for another, a few finally realized there is no perfect mate who can keep them in a continual state of bliss. Someday, your former spouse may wake up to the same realistic conclusion.

One friend of mine, Steve, told me that his dad, near the end of his life, after having four marriages, three of which began as affairs, confessed, "I never should have left your mother (his first wife). She was the best thing that ever happened to me!"

Most of us won't have the satisfaction of hearing such an admission this side of heaven. But I find comfort in knowing that God sees it all. He knows. And someday, perhaps your straying spouse will see the light as well.

> "For there is nothing hidden that will not be disclosed, and nothing concealed that will not be brought to light" (Mark 4:22).

When we face a series of painful life disappointments, it's easy to question our faith—in God, ourselves, and others. **Section V** explores how your trust in the Lord may have been shaken: through your partner's religious justifications, the collapse of long-held spiritual assumptions, or wounds inflicted by those who should have helped but didn't.

If your spouse claimed to be a person of faith, you may have noticed unsettling shifts in their beliefs. Worse, they may have twisted Scripture to excuse their actions. For many, this kind of spiritual manipulation is deeply wounding, shaking your faith to its core. I've seen this happen so often that I devoted an entire chapter to it—and that's where we're headed next.

SECTION V

Restoring Your Faith

"Let your roots grow down into him, and let your lives be built on him. Then your faith will grow strong in the truth you were taught, and you will overflow with thankfulness."
~ Colossians 2:7 (TNLT)

Betrayal doesn't just break your heart—it can shake your faith. Disillusionment can leave you questioning God, your beliefs, and what you thought was true.

But this is not the time to cling to shallow formulas or walk away in frustration. It's an invitation to go deeper—beyond surface religion—into a faith rooted in truth, not performance. This season is about:

- Letting go of harmful theology that added to your pain.
- Silencing the false judgments of your ex and well-meaning but misinformed voices.
- Rediscovering the steady, unchanging character of God—even when others failed you.

You may feel like your spiritual foundation has cracked—but beneath the rubble is solid Rock. This is your time to dig down, clear away the debris, and rebuild a faith that's stronger, wiser, and more alive than ever before.

So grab your shovel and put on your hard hat. Truth is waiting beneath the surface.

THE LIGHTHOUSE...GOD'S WORD

By Linda J. MacDonald

A beacon that leads us to all that is true
The Lighthouse shines hope to the shadowed and blue.
It flashes a warning when sharp reefs are near
And leads us to safety, away from all fear.

The fixed point of reference through turbulent storms
Its beams show the course and protect us from harm.
Though pride bids us judge by our own eye and ear
Only the foolish press on with a sneer.

Refusing to trust the Lighthouse to guide
The proud come to ruin with no place to hide.
Yet, seasoned sailors fix their eyes on the light
No matter the gale or blackness of night.

When raging storms die and the morning is new
The faithful awaken, intact ship and crew.
For once raging waters are calm and serene
The treacherous coral and rocks can be seen.

Yet strewn into shambles are ships that ignored
Trustworthy guidance the Lighthouse affords.
Though roughed up and weary your vessel may be
Trusting the Lighthouse bars shipwreck at sea.

If, wisely, you look to the Lighthouse to guide
Your boat to safe harbor with Him by your side,
Resisting the lure of your own senses' charms,
You'll find yourself resting in God's loving arms.

Chapter 19

Religious Excuses

Religious evil is the worst kind of evil.
~Ron Enroth, PhD

I will never forget the day, shortly after Christmas, when James came home from a two-day sabbatical at a local hotel. He had read Philip Yancey's book *What's So Amazing About Grace?* (one of my favorite authors), and also, unbeknownst to me, spent eight hours with his affair partner.

He mentioned three new insights he'd gained from his time away. He began with what he gathered from Yancey's cautions about the harm of legalism and our need for grace. So far, so good. However, James used the book's premises to develop a new truth of his own.

"After all, Jesus allowed his disciples to pick grain on the Sabbath, and David and his men seemingly broke the Law when they ate the showbread reserved only for the priests." Tears welled in James's eyes as he said, "You see? God is willing to break his rules to meet a need." *I could see where this was going*. He continued.

"And, since God is a God of grace, he will forgive you, no matter what you do. Therefore, you can do whatever you want." *The knife in my gut began to twist.*

He also said, "God told me I could choose." I was never sure if that meant God gave him permission to choose between me and the other woman or between staying married to me or leaving.

I gripped the edge of the couch as the room began to spin. Something felt terribly off, but I couldn't name it yet. All I knew was that James had misused God's Word, added to a well-known Christian author's words, and claimed a spiritual impression to justify his attraction to the other woman. These declarations hit me like a hammer. After all, who was I to question the Bible, a respected Christian author, and the supposed voice of the Holy Spirit?

Why Religious Justifications?

If your unfaithful spouse was a person of faith, they may have merged their religious beliefs with their errant actions to alleviate feelings of guilt. They might have made statements like, "God told me..." or "I've prayed about it," as a precursor to delivering a noxious blow to you. While some Christian betrayers wouldn't dare use a religious alibi, I wrote this chapter for hurt spouses who were subjected to the misuse of faith words by a wayward partner who did. If this doesn't apply to you, feel free to skim through this chapter.

Some unfaithful people appeal to a higher authority, not to seek truth, but to quiet their conscience and outmaneuver opposition. They hide behind God like a child behind a powerful parent when confronted by playground bullies. Only this time, the so-called bullies are you, Scripture, and the truth standing in the way of their self-serving desires.

Dr. James Dobson calls an unfaithful person's claims of God's approval for their unethical decisions "the ultimate rationalization." After all, "... who can argue that point further? The conversation is over."[1]

You undoubtedly felt hurt by some of your straying spouse's excuses for his or her affair. But if they added the dagger of spiritual rationalizations, their injurious words may have penetrated you to a whole new depth. One friend told me, "Of all the wounds my former husband foisted upon me during his season of unfaithfulness, his spiritual excuses were the worst."

Religious strayers sometimes invent pious excuses to ward off anyone who might object to their inappropriate behaviors. Betrayed spouses, children, and friends experience these justifications, framed in "Christianese," as harsh attacks on themselves and their faith.

When a strayer uses God's words against God's people, recipients suffer a nasty form of spiritual abuse.

> When a strayer uses God's words against God's people, recipients suffer a nasty form of spiritual abuse.

I've spoken with many betrayed followers of Christ who've been similarly wounded. Remember, you have the Bible, Christian history, the Holy Spirit, and common sense on your side. I hope this chapter helps you dispel any lingering doubts about your faith stemming from past interactions with a religiously defended spouse.

Typical tactics of a spiritually deceived strayer include using Scripture out of context, relying on subjective feelings, and lobbing religious accusations at anyone who opposes them.

USING SCRIPTURE OUT OF CONTEXT

Betrayers with a history of religious faith may consciously or unconsciously resort to cunning tactics to twist the truth and justify their emotionally driven beliefs. One common strategy is cherry-picking Bible verses out of context. Rather than embracing the full counsel of Scripture, they selectively choose phrases that align with their desires and overlook the rest. Below are several Christian concepts that betrayers commonly twist to support their wayward activities.

"God is Love"

Religious betrayers may overemphasize God's love while downplaying his righteousness. They use the phrase "God is love" (1 John 4:8) to reinforce false beliefs, such as:

1. Mistaking Loving Feelings as a Sign of God's Endorsement.
A strayer's faulty logic often sounds like this: "God is love. This other person makes me feel deeply loved. Therefore, God must have brought them into my life." Those who equate "this feels like true love" with "it must be from God" fall into a dangerous fallacy—one that has misled many. Emotionally charged, hormone-infused feelings are a poor substitute for mature, righteous love.

2. The Permissive Love Excuse.
"God's love is unconditional. That means he will love and accept me no matter what I do, even if I have an affair." This portrays God as an all-loving and no-discipline sugar daddy—pure nonsense. No loving parent would let their child eat ice cream for every meal or bully their sibling without consequences. In the same way, God's love includes correction. He sees the bigger picture and knows what harms his child or those they love.

When you examine the phrases surrounding "God is love," you'll notice the context often revolves around loving one another. God is the source of love, and when we truly know him and are infused with his love, we will naturally love those closest to us unselfishly. God's love should lead us to a virtuous form of love, not a selfish or illegitimate one.

Did your partner justify their wrong behaviors using the "God is love" argument? God's love should have resulted in your partner choosing to love you, not betray and abandon you in search of a more enchanting partner.

Likewise, consider the Lord's second greatest commandment, "Love your neighbor as yourself." Then ask yourself, "Who is or was your spouse's closest neighbor?" The answer? YOU. You were your partner's closest neighbor. What your straying partner has done to you (and your children) is the antithesis of love. Instead, it is one of the greatest examples of *un*love one spouse can do to another.

If your ex-mate used the idea, "God is love," to justify following their heart into an affair, believing God wouldn't condemn them—they distorted that truth.

God's love never condones sin. In the context of 1 John 4 and the entirety of Scripture, God's love is never a license to break faith and harm others.

When we grasp Christ's love for us and genuinely love him in return, we seek to obey—not resist, resent, or rebel—even when his commands are difficult.

> "For this is the love of God, that we keep His commandments. And His commandments are not burdensome" (1 John 5:3).

Infidelity does not reflect the nature of God's love. Infidelity destroys, and God's love heals. Infidelity shatters loved ones, but God's love embraces them. Infidelity focuses on pleasing oneself, while God's love is about blessing others. Infidelity inflicts shame, while God's love heals shame.

Don't let a delusional spouse convince you that their waywardness is sanctioned by an all-loving, unconditionally accepting God. Such illusions insult the Lord, reducing him to a Fairy Godmother who grants your every wish, regardless of the damage left behind. That is not the Christ I have come to know. And I trust it's not the Lord you've come to know and love, either.

"God's Grace"

A similar rationalization I encounter with religious Betrandoners is their appeal to "God's Grace." Strayers sometimes say, "God is a God of grace," suggesting that obedience is irrelevant. Others dismiss moral boundaries with "Those 'rules' were for Old Testament days—we're under grace now!"

But when you study God's grace in Scripture, you will often find it paired with the words "truth" or "righteousness." For example,

> "The Word became flesh and made His dwelling among us. We have seen His glory, the glory of the one and only Son from the Father, full of *grace* and *truth*" (John 1:14, emphasis added).

Christ is filled with the perfect balance of both.

One of my former pastors, Gino Grunberg, uses a train track analogy to underscore the necessary balance of Grace and Truth in our spiritual journey. He explains that these two elements must run in harmony, much like parallel train tracks, to ensure a smooth ride and a balanced spiritual life. However, if Grace parts ways with Truth, it is akin to a pair of tracks diverging, which will cause the train to derail, leading it—and our lives—into chaos and destruction.

As respected author Larry Crabb notes,

> Our Christian culture has weakened our understanding of the holiness of God by introducing too soon the idea of grace. We now talk about grace in a way that changes our view of God from holy to paternal, from justifiably enraged to strict but understanding.[2]

He illustrates his point by telling the story of a discussion he had with a married young man, who said,

> "I know I'm wrong to continue my affair, but you're wrong to insist I end it. God doesn't want me to continue it, but I know He'll forgive me. I sense only judgment from you. God is a God of grace."[3]

Do you see how this young man distorted God's Word? He presumed upon God's forgiveness and grace, twisting Dr. Crabb's message and labeling him as judgmental—a common tactic of the guilty.

In my situation, James often spoke of God's "scandalous grace" (a phrase popularized by Brennan Manning, another author he liked to quote out of context) as a cover for continuing his affair and thoughts of divorce. He became adept at using grace-talk to evoke my sympathy. At times, I even thought, "How could a loving and gracious God expect him to stay married to someone as 'boring' as me?" Then I'd snap out of it and berate myself for falling for his bent reasoning *again*.

His new love affair with a warped version of grace became my personal hell.

If your unfaithful spouse played the grace card, consider what Paul explains in Romans 6. These verses offer clarity and truth to counter this spiritual manipulation.

> "What then shall we say? Shall we continue in sin so that grace may increase? *Certainly not!* How can we who died to sin live in it any longer?" (Romans 6:1–2, emphasis added.)

In other words, just because the Lord offers grace does not give us permission to indulge in further sin. Paul's emphatic phrase, "Certainly not!" has been translated as "God forbid!" or "By no means!" My current husband, Dan, a pastor and devoted student of Romans, likes to put it bluntly: "Hell, no!"[4] We are not to continue in sin to maximize God's grace.

To put it into perspective, misusing God's grace is like a compassionate friend selling his business to purchase a house for a bankrupt friend. But instead of using the $400,000 for the home, the friend gambles it all away.

When we squander God's grace on selfish pursuits, it's as if we "*trampled on the Son of God, profaned the blood of the covenant that sanctified him, and insulted the Spirit of grace*" (Hebrews 10:29, emphasis added).

We should not presume on the grace of God by sinning on purpose. Yet that is exactly the intent of those who misuse God's grace as a cover-up to engage in wrongdoing. Theologians have names for when we exploit the grace of God: "Grace Abuse," "Counterfeit Grace," "Prostituted Grace," or, as Dietrich Bonhoeffer calls it, "Cheap Grace." Larry Crabb refers to it as "Assumed Grace" and states, "*Assumed grace can never be transforming grace*" (italics his).[5]

I appreciate Mark Gaither's statement from his book, *Redemptive Divorce*:

> "The misuse and abuse of grace is not new. People always have and always will look for an opportunity to twist grace into something grotesque."[6]

The person who continues an affair under the guise of grace dishonors both God and the family members they once held dear. The outcome is a self-serving grace: "Grace for Me, abuse for You." This twists the true intent of God's costly gift—undeserved favor—meant to lead us to repentance, not excuse rebellion.

> The outcome is a self-serving grace: "Grace for Me, abuse for You."

Those who recklessly pursue extra-marital activities or initiate a baseless divorce, assuming they will be covered by divine grace, are gravely mistaken. Their dulled conscience, numbed by emotional euphoria, won't shield them from the ripple effects of their choices.

Here is a New Testament verse that reinforces that even in the era of grace, there are still consequences for disobeying the Lord.

> "Marriage should be honored by all and the marriage bed kept undefiled, for God will judge the sexually immoral and adulterers" (Hebrews 13:4).

I am not saying God's grace is insufficient for sins like unfaithfulness. Indeed, the Lord will forgive a penitent strayer. But when we presume upon God's grace, we take advantage of him and will suffer the natural and logical consequences of disobedience. If your spouse used this excuse to continue in such a sin, be assured, they will not get away with it forever. And, if or when they repent, they have a long road back to a pure mind and restored character.

"God Will Forgive Me"

The next common religious rationalization I encounter is the "God will forgive me" excuse. In my survey of 81 betrayed partners, 22 of them reported hearing this line from their straying spouses (**Appendix D**). I wonder how many of their unfaithful partners ever turned around, truly repented, and genuinely sought God's forgiveness?

It's a farce to continue to sin and plan to ask for God's forgiveness later. In many cases, later will never come.

Yes, when asked, God will forgive them. However, they will not be truly cleansed from their unrighteousness without agreeing with God that their waywardness was wrong, turning away from their sinful path, and making amends with those they've harmed. Their repentance won't lead to lasting change ("fruit") unless they dismantle the rationalizations behind their unfaithfulness and allow the Lord to transform their minds and character.

No one engages in such wrongdoing without consequences. Scripture repeatedly warns about the corrupting impact of sexual sin. It's never worth defying God's commands under the guise of his love, grace, and forgiveness.

In Yancey's chapter on "Loopholes," a friend of his, who was embroiled in an extramarital affair, asked Philip if God would forgive him if he left his wife and family for another woman. After some thought, Yancey replied,

> What we have to go through to commit sin distances us from God—we change in the very act of rebellion—and there is no guarantee we will ever come back. You ask me about forgiveness now, but will you even want it later, especially if it involves repentance? [7]

At the time of his writing, his friend had turned away from God and dismissed the Christian friends who disagreed with him as "narrow-minded" and "judgmental"—classic accusations from an unrepentant Betrandoner.

It is also ludicrous for the unfaithful to emphasize God's love, grace, and forgiveness while ignoring the 228 verses on obedience,[8] 147 verses about repentance,[9] 151 warnings against harlotry, 92 verses forbidding unfaithfulness or going astray, 85 verses on adultery (128 in the KJV),[10] and the 53 verses prohibiting sexual immorality.[11]

The Example of Bible Figures

Besides using Bible verses out of context, Christian betrayers sometimes look to imperfect people in the Bible to justify their wrongdoings.

You may have heard your straying spouse use one or more of the following comparisons to excuse their behaviors:

- "People in the Old Testament had concubines."
- "King David did it (committed adultery)."
- "Solomon had many wives and concubines."
- "Jacob had two wives and two concubines."

They use the ancient practices and misbehaviors of Old Testament characters to justify their actions. Nine betrayed spouses in my Rationalizations Survey (**Appendix D**) received similar comparisons from their wayward partners. However, there are significant flaws in the misapplication of using biblical figures as models for living.

Descriptions vs. Prescriptions

There is a distinction between the Bible's honest *descriptions* of significant figures in biblical history and its *prescriptions* for how we should live. Just because someone committed wrongful acts and God did not instantly strike them dead does not mean the Lord endorsed their behavior. Scripture's portrayals of well-known followers with character flaws testify to the Bible's reliability. The writers presented facts as they were, without whitewashing the blemishes in Jewish history. Even though Scripture records the culturally accepted practices of some heroes of faith, it does not signify that God approved of everything they did or that their lives ended faithfully. God has chosen to accomplish his purposes through imperfect people.

Cultural Norms are Not Necessarily Godly

I can't explain why the Lord tolerated polygamy within ancient cultures. But it's important to understand that these practices were not universal among the Jews. They were typically limited to the wealthy—those who could afford multiple wives or concubines, the latter often being maidservants or war captives. While God allowed certain cultural customs, that doesn't mean they reflected his original design. From the beginning, as seen in Genesis and later reaffirmed by Jesus, God's intent for marriage was one man and one woman

(Genesis 2:24, Matthew 19:3–6). This standard continued in the early church, as seen in qualifications for leaders (1 Timothy 3:2, 12, and 5:9) and has generally been upheld by Christians throughout the centuries.

Consequences

In most cases, the Bible shows how the Lord chastened the very people your partner may have held up as models to imitate. For example, consider David's sin of adultery with Bathsheba and arranging the killing of her husband. One consequence David suffered was the death of the baby from his illicit relationship. Despite his human frailties, the Lord continued to use this man because he was miserable with conviction during the year he kept his secret (Psalm 32). And, when confronted by the prophet, Samuel, he repented with genuine contrition. All along, he maintained a soft heart toward the Lord.

God didn't cancel his plans to bring the Savior to the world through his lineage. But he didn't intervene to prevent some of the natural consequences of David's character deficiencies, either. His sons and grandsons were a moral mess, filled with so much strife that it eventually caused the Jewish kingdom to split in two. Yet, David's life and writings are included in the narrative of Scripture to encourage us. God uses flawed people to accomplish his ultimate, divine purposes, particularly among those whose hearts remain tender toward him despite their human failings.

Regarding Solomon, over time, his fame and fortune got the better of him. He formed alliances with other tribes and kingdoms by marrying foreign wives and acquiring an overabundance of concubines. But that doesn't mean God approved. As the Lord previously warned future kings of Israel, "He must not take many wives for himself, lest his heart go astray" (Deuteronomy 17:17). Eventually, that is precisely what happened.

> "When Solomon grew old, his wives turned his heart after other gods, and he was not wholeheartedly devoted to the LORD his God, as his father David had been...Now the LORD grew angry with Solomon because his heart had turned away from the LORD, the God of Israel, who had appeared to him twice. Although He had warned Solomon explicitly not to follow other gods, Solomon did not keep the LORD's command" (1 Kings 11:4, 9–10).

This illustrates that the Lord did not approve of Solomon taking many wives and concubines, who then contaminated his religious beliefs.

Yes, there were disobedient figures in the Old Testament who strayed from God's original design for marriage—but they didn't escape the consequences.

Some, like David and his predecessor, Judah, repented. Others, like Solomon, apparently did not. Yet in every case, their compromised choices bore bad fruit, even if the fallout took time to appear. In Solomon's case, the idols he built to appease his pagan wives ultimately led to the spiritual downfall of Israel and influenced many of the kings who followed.

Many Bible Figures Honored God

What about the positive examples in Scripture? Take Joseph, for instance. When Potiphar's wife tried to seduce him, he refused and fled. His godly response to her was clear: "He [Potiphar] has withheld nothing from me except you, because you are his wife. So how could I do such a great evil and sin against God?" (Genesis 39:9). He identified two evils: sinning against her husband and sinning against God. And he did everything possible to resist and escape temptation. Did your spouse look to Joseph as an example of how to respond under pressure?

And what about other Old Testament characters? "We don't see any of the twelve sons of Jacob having multiple wives, [nor] Moses, Joshua, Caleb, the Judges (not even Sampson), or the prophets. It simply was a rarity." [12]

Did your spouse consider New Testament stalwarts of the faith, such as Paul, Peter, Timothy, Priscilla, Aquila, Barnabas, James, and others who were either celibate or had only one spouse? Don't let your ex-spouse's appeals to the poor behaviors of Bible figures be used to coerce you into accepting his or her unfaithful actions. Sinful people seek consensus and the poor example of others to feel less guilty about their behaviors. The age-old "everybody's doing it" is a well-worn excuse that's laughable. You have the Lord, godly followers of Christ, and hundreds of Scriptures to back you up.

> "For the time will come when men will not tolerate sound doctrine, but with itching ears they will gather around themselves teachers to suit their own desires. So they will turn their ears away from the truth and turn aside to myths" (2 Timothy 2:3–4).

In contrast, Paul encouraged Timothy to "Make every effort to present yourself approved to God, an unashamed workman who *accurately* handles the word of truth" (2 Timothy 2:15, emphasis added).

Correctly interpreting God's Word involves effort, study, and setting aside our biases—the opposite of those who misuse the Bible to justify their wrongs.

RELYING ON "IMPRESSIONS"

The Subjective Feelings Error

The Subjective Feelings Error, widespread in our culture, is the tendency to let emotions dictate our actions and decisions. Popular mantras "You've got to do what's right for you," "Follow your truth," and "If it feels good, do it" reflect this mindset. Rather than relying on objective truth, many people let feelings guide their choices.

In religious circles, some even attribute these emotions to divine guidance, such as the Holy Spirit, without the necessary discernment and balance. This error can affect both straight and non-straight spouses and reveals a lack of spiritual maturity in how feelings are processed. When we give too much weight to our emotions, we risk being led astray.

As author and same-sex attracted believer Rachel Gilson, who has chosen to align her life with God's Word instead of her feelings, wisely states, "He is clear throughout Scripture that our desires are not a compass for goodness because they are broken."[13]

When we base ethical decisions on subjective perceptions and fluctuating emotions, we lose reliable markers to distinguish right from wrong, especially when hormones are involved.

I remember one professor in therapy school joking, "When the hormones go up, the IQ goes down." Unfortunately, it's an especially fitting description of extramarital attractions.

Subjective measures rely on internal feelings and opinions, which are easily swayed. In contrast, objective standards, like company policies, laws, marriage vows, and Scripture, exist outside of us and offer steady guidance. Paul encourages Timothy to use his faith and an uncontaminated conscience to guide him in doing what is right.

> "Holding on to faith and a good conscience, which some have rejected and thereby shipwrecked their faith" (1 Timothy 1:19).

Although we must pay attention to our feelings, they should not be the primary basis for major life decisions. We need objective indicators, like a pilot needs an instrument panel, to gauge our options, motives, and direction. Otherwise, when we disregard these guides and prioritize our feelings over our faith, or twist our beliefs to accommodate them, we may lose our once-dearly-held trust in Christ and the Bible.

Regrettably, the shift in our contemporary society away from objective truth has led many individuals to rely on emotions and personal perceptions.

All too often, truth is seen as a subjective matter—uniquely experienced within the individual. Phrases such as "Your truth is your truth, and my truth is my truth" suggest that all truth is a matter of personal, private interpretation. While some "truths" are not really truths but matters of differing sentiments, applying this concept too broadly undermines reality and the necessity of objective facts.

This post-modern influence has even permeated the church. In Christian circles, such notions may lead individuals to confuse their emotions and wishful thinking with the voice of the Holy Spirit.

The Subjective Feelings Error often begins with:

1. "God told me..."
2. "I've prayed about it and..."
3. "God wants me to be happy, therefore..."

Misguided Christians under the spell of an affair may complete spiritual-sounding phrases in ways that reflect personal bias rather than biblical truth.

When my husband, James, in his delusional state, said, "God told me I could choose," I was stunned. At first, given his background in theology and former walk with the Lord, his preface of "God told me" sounded plausible to me. I am grateful for the solid Bible teachers and mentors in my life who reminded me that the Holy Spirit will never contradict the Word of God. Just because someone cloaks a lie in Christian language doesn't make it true.

Likewise, if you heard, "God wants me to be happy," followed by, "and my lover makes me happy," suggesting the Lord's approval of the relationship—you heard a lie. Deep down, you knew it wasn't right. But for a moment, you may have hesitated, thinking, "Who am I to question?" Or "How can I argue with God?"

Such situations can undermine your trust in the Lord and his love for you. You may have asked yourself, "How could my spouse, whom I believed to be a Christian, say such a thing? And how could my Savior, whom I thought loved me, support behaviors that have inflicted such profound pain upon me?"

"Evelyn," an aggrieved Christian spouse told me:

> I truly hoped Daniel would come to his senses before being unfaithful again. But here we are after 23 years of marriage and two wonderful kids—separated and on the brink of divorce, and he still has not come to his senses.
>
> Instead, he told our 18-year-old daughter, Sharalyn (who is uncom-

> fortable spending time with him and "them") in a text the other day that he prays about it all the time, saying, "God just keeps telling me, 'Be patient.'"
>
> I am struggling with this. How can he not hear God telling him to leave his affair partner? How can he not hear God telling him to leave his sin? How can he not realize that he has brutally abandoned his family? Instead, he believes God is telling him to be patient, and the kids will eventually come to terms with his affair and betrayal. And then what? They will become one happy family with him, his affair partner, and her kid? I have no idea what he's thinking in that warped mind of his.[14]

Just because Evelyn's husband said he had "prayed about it" and claimed he heard God telling him, "Be patient" doesn't mean his motivations were pure or that this message came from God. More likely, this impression originated from wishful thinking. Wayward people often attempt to remake God in their own image and "hear" him in their own voice.

Had he truly been listening to the Lord, he more likely would have heard, "You need to fall on your knees in total contrition and apologize to your daughter for having an affair, abandoning her mom, and breaking up her family." Not, "Be patient and your daughter will come around to embrace your new lifestyle."

Remember, it is difficult to remain unbiased when our emotions are involved. Even worse with hormonal highs. All "words," "messages," or "impressions" from God must align with the Bible and be interpreted in context. God will never contradict himself.

You are not alone if you have heard similar religious proclamations from a recalcitrant spouse. And if you find it challenging to figure out "What's wrong with this picture?"—don't forget that temporary emotions can deceive anyone, especially a hormone-crazed, unfaithful person.

The Holy Spirit will never lead us to violate God's clear commands. While the Lord gives us freedom to make our own choices, that freedom exists within the boundaries of his moral law. As long as we remain within the moral guardrails of Scripture, we have wide latitude to navigate our decisions.

> While the Lord gives us freedom to make our own choices, that freedom exists within the boundaries of his moral law.

Paul makes the point,

> "For you, brothers, were called to freedom; but do not use your freedom as an opportunity for the flesh. Rather, serve one another in love" (Galatians 5:13).

In other words, we are not to use our freedom in Christ as an excuse to indulge our sinful nature. Instead, we are to use that freedom as inspiration to serve one another in love.

So, if your betraying partner sought sexual "freedom" through an outside romantic relationship, that so-called freedom was actually the opposite of love. It leads only to bondage and eventual chaos.

If your wayward spouse claimed divine approval for an illicit habit or relationship, you can be certain: *It was not from God.*

LOBBING RELIGIOUS ACCUSATIONS AT YOU

Religious Accusations

Wayward spouses who use religious rationalizations to justify themselves often up the ante by intimidating you through verbal attacks.

For example, you may have heard phrases like, "You're just vindictive!" "You're just jealous!" "You're selfish!"—qualities that no serious Christian would want to possess. And if character assassinations aren't enough to silence you, a religious rationalizer may throw more insults your way: "You're unforgiving." "You're such a Pharisee!" "You're so self-righteous!" "You're just judgmental!"

Some even use Scripture out of context to deflect blame and attack others. When my friend "Meredith" confronted her husband about his ongoing affair, instead of humbling himself, he fired back, "The Bible says, 'An angry person stirs up conflict, and a hot-tempered person commits many sins' (Proverbs 29:22). You're just an angry person!" Do you see the deflection? He shifted the focus from his infidelity to her (rightful) anger, painting her reaction as the problem.

He pulled the same tactic with their 14-year-old daughter. When she begged her father to spend time alone with her, apart from his lover, he said, "You're just unforgiving!"—as if her desire for a personal connection with her father was a spiritual failing.[15]

As a Christian, these kinds of accusations can shake us. Unrepentant offenders use these below-the-belt strategies to make you doubt yourself, avoid accountability, and change the subject.

This tactic can be particularly difficult to dismiss if your spouse was a pastor or served in ministry. Christian leaders are often endowed with the gift of persuasion and know how to use faith words against their trusting spouses. If this happened to you, discuss your partner's insults and excuses with someone you respect. An outsider's perspective can help you reject the distorted logic so you can begin healing.

Recognizing the Shepherd's Voice

When a deceitful spouse resorts to religious put-downs, it represents the height of manipulation. A guilty partner's religious accusations can set us back on our heels, make us question our motives for protesting their immoral behavior, and cause us to feel ashamed for wanting to preserve our marriages—as if we are the ones in the wrong.

An essential key to your healing is cultivating the ability to recognize the voice of the Good Shepherd. Jesus said, "My sheep know my voice" (John 10:27). Religious attacks to defend wrong behavior do not reflect the heart of God toward you. Like a wounded lamb, allow him to carry you in his arms, close to his heart, so you become so familiar with his voice that you can quickly reject a voice that does not sound like his. [16]

Just because we are his lambs doesn't mean we should remain weak in spirit. Jesus told his disciples to be "wise as serpents and harmless as doves" and to "put on the full armor of God." We must mature into warriors equipped to battle the lies of our enemy. And by "enemy," I do not mean our partners. There was something darker afoot in the breakup of your family. We need to call upon the power of the Holy Spirit, wield the truths in Scripture like a sword, and take a stand for what is right on behalf of our children and the cause of Christ.

> And by "enemy," I do not mean our partners. There was something darker afoot in the breakup of your family.

> "For though we live in the flesh, we do not wage war according to the flesh. The weapons of our warfare are not the weapons of the world. Instead, they have divine power to demolish strongholds. We tear down arguments and every presumption set up against the knowledge of God; and we take captive every thought to make it obedient to Christ" (2 Corinthians 10:4–5).

Scripture is powerful. I encourage you to find solace in God's Word to tear down ungodly arguments unfairly used by your rationalizing ex-spouse. If you've been spiritually abused by a partner who used religious words to defend their affair, or their choice to leave, or to put you down, next are some further takeaways for you to consider.

Equip Yourself To Detect Distortion

Just as bank tellers are trained to detect counterfeit cash from handling thousands of real dollars, the more familiar you become with God's Word, studying it in context—the quicker you can identify what is false. You'll learn to discern the tone of God's voice from the harsh tone of the Tempter. Your deceived spouse was merely a tool in Satan's arsenal, aimed at weakening your faith and making you question God's love for you. Decide today: You will no longer allow yourself to fall for Satan's lies.

Strengthen Your Reliance On The Lord

Hopefully, this storm has compelled you to send your roots deeper into the soil of your relationship with the Lord, drawing from his resources to nourish your battered, depleted, thirsty soul. As a result, you are learning to trust in Christ more profoundly despite the heat of betrayal and the drought of abandonment. Reflect on this promise,

> "But blessed is the man who trusts in the LORD, whose confidence is in Him. He is like a tree planted by the waters that sends out its roots toward the stream. It does not fear when the heat comes, and its leaves are always green. It does not worry in a year of drought, nor does it cease to produce fruit (Jeremiah 17:8–9)."

You've just weathered an emotional hurricane followed by a year (or more) of drought. Use this time to deepen your roots in Christ and the Word of God, enabling you to withstand all future adverse winds and weather that may challenge your faith.

You Are a Threat to The Evil One

This awareness can protect you from falling for Satan's tactics. It will also affirm the Lord's call on your life and strengthen your resolve not to let the enemy win. You matter deeply to God and his kingdom—otherwise the devil wouldn't have bothered.

May the battle you've endured draw you closer to God's heart and fuel your determination to forge a new, Christ-glorifying path forward.

There's nothing quite like the trauma, grief, and shame of Betrandonment to shake your faith and leave you disillusioned with life. You may wonder, "If the

Lord answers prayer, why didn't he answer mine?" and "Why would the Lord lead me to marry someone only for it to end like this?"

If you're wrestling with tough questions during and after your crisis, it may be time to re-examine some of your beliefs and reinforce others. In the next chapter, we will explore a few core truths to help you shore up your foundation after the earthquake of a Post-Affair Divorce.

Chapter 20

Shattered Beliefs

So do not throw away your confidence; it holds a great reward.
~Hebrews 10:35

Donna[1] grew up in an abusive home, endured a disastrous first marriage, and was grateful to have fallen in love with "Jim," an upstanding Christian man. The stress of her first divorce had brought her to her knees and resulted in a dramatic conversion to Christ. Her new relationship with God ushered in a season of joy. Now that she had found a man who shared her new values and beliefs, she felt a fresh sense of emotional security and began new artistic business endeavors.

Donna enthusiastically shared her faith with others and led her mother and father to the Lord before they died. She was assured that as long as she was faithful to God, he would always shelter her with his protective hand.

But her optimism started to fade a few years into her second marriage. Jim struggled with periods of depression. During these times, he withdrew and became verbally harsh. Donna went out of her way to please him and reduce his stress. Although she was disheartened by his defensiveness and tendency to blame her for his problems, she remained confident that, despite the challenges, God was in control.

Over coffee with a friend, she remarked, "No matter how difficult things become, at least I know he will never have an affair." Knowing his moral convictions and that he understood how deeply her first husband's unfaithfulness had wounded her, she felt certain about that one thing. She could endure nearly anything as long as she had a faithful man.

In the meantime, Jim developed some unusual habits, such as not feeling hungry for dinner, coming home late at night, and behaving as if his comings and goings were none of her concern.

One night, unable to sleep, she stared at the clock—1 a.m. Jim was out later than usual. Tossing and turning, she waited to hear the garage door open. When he still wasn't home by 3 a.m., she panicked, fearing he'd been in a car accident. She crawled out of bed and called the police and several hospitals, trying to locate him. Shaking and unnerved, she finally heard the garage door rumble at 4 a.m.

When he stealthily slipped under the covers, she turned on the light and pelted him with questions. "Where were you? Why didn't you call? I was worried sick about you. Are you all right?"

He mumbled a few lame excuses, turned his shoulder away from her, and went to sleep. The next day, Donna refused to let the matter drop. She insisted he tell her where he'd been the night before. After 10 minutes of evasion, he broke. Nothing could have prepared her for the words that tumbled out of his mouth: "I was with Nina."

Stunned, she asked, "Who's Nina?"

It turned out that Nina was a woman he had met a few weeks earlier while out with his buddies. After a couple of late dinners, the relationship progressed into a brief affair. Jim insisted it was over. He explained that the reason he was home so late was that it supposedly took some time to convince the other woman he meant it.

Donna's limbs froze, and her mind whirred. How could this be? Jim had been so adamant about his morals when they first met. He knew this was the worst thing he could do to her. Surely, she wasn't hearing right. It must be a nightmare.

However, her nightmare did not dissipate. As the reality of her beloved husband's betrayal became clear, she sank into despair. How could he? He *knew* what would hurt her the most. Surely, he wasn't capable of such treachery. Or was he? Where was God? Why didn't he intervene?

After weeks of trying unsuccessfully to elicit his apology, she had her annual medical exam. When she returned for the test results, her doctor informed her she had an STI. From the hallway, she could hear the nurses gossiping about her unfortunate news. Donna's face flushed with shame.

She stammered, "But I haven't been unfaithful ... it was my husband." The doctor gave her a paternal look—gentle but unreadable. She left her appointment feeling devastated.

Not only had her husband torn her heart out, he had also left her with a shameful health consequence for his betrayal. Donna raged over the unfairness of it all.

She asked herself, "What have I done to deserve this? *He* was the one guilty of adultery. Not me! I thought as long as I followed the Lord, he would protect me from evil. Yet here I am, suffering from my husband's misdeeds. It's not fair!"

Donna was reeling—not just from the emotional impact of her husband's infidelity, but from the shame of a consequence that only he should bear.

Her tidy belief system began to unravel. She no longer knew what to believe. She thought that once she became a Christian, God would shield her from misfortune.

In her misery, she sought the counsel of her pastor. His advice? She needed to be more submissive to win back her husband's affection. His parting words were, "Jim wouldn't have wandered elsewhere if he were getting enough at home." Ouch. His only tone of sympathy was for her unfaithful husband.

Donna's mind and emotions swirled in confusion. Dazed, she didn't know whether to trust his advice or stomp out in disgust. Her sister reinforced the same view: the affair was Donna's fault and her responsibility to repair.

Donna sank into a depression. She tried harder to please her husband, which invited further disrespect from him. Finally, his abusive attitude translated into physical abuse. She only gained the courage to leave after he nearly strangled her to death.

Four years after their divorce was final, Donna slumped into my office, worn down by one hardship after another. She suffered panic attacks and severe anxiety. What made it worse was watching her ex-husband thrive financially while she struggled to make ends meet.

Disappointed that God hadn't "come through" for her. Donna wrestled to reconcile her beliefs with her painful reality and came up short.

She read every book I recommended and diligently worked to process her pain. After making some progress, we encountered her deepest wound: God didn't protect her. Even her pastor, God's representative, let her down. She wasn't sure she could ever trust the Lord again.

She wondered if she deserved the affair and STI. What about the emotional and physical abuse? Did she deserve that, too? And if not, then why did it all happen to her? She had been faithful to God. So why was her unfaithful, abusive ex-husband prospering while she scraped by?

It wasn't until we began to explore Donna's childhood that we found clues to her longing for predictability. Her father had been emotionally distant and explosively angry. He would suddenly knock her off her chair at the dinner table for no apparent reason. She lived in fear, never knowing what would incite his next outburst.

No one in the family came to her defense. To avoid becoming targets themselves, her siblings either stayed silent or joined in. Her mother never intervened. Donna was left to absorb the abuse alone and unprotected.

No wonder, I mused aloud, that when she met the Lord, she clung to him as the safe, loving Father she'd never had. She needed God to be everything her earthly father was not. So, when she found verses about God's blessings and protection, she latched onto them and posted them around her house. The more she focused on those promises, the more predictable and safer God seemed. And she needed that predictability—desperately.

After her conversion, given her own chaotic background, she constructed philosophical boxes for how God treats his children.

- Bad things only happen to bad people.
- As long as I am faithful, good, kind, honest, and loving, I will insulate myself from evil.
- God controls everything that happens in my life.

Donna's traumas annihilated her belief system. She no longer felt safe. The formulas weren't working. If God was not predictable, whom could she trust? If there were no guaranteed principles to safeguard her from harm, what protection did she have?

As long as she loved and obeyed God, Donna felt a false sense of security beyond what the Bible guarantees. But when her faith formula failed, she grew terrified of trying anything new, including relationships. Maybe her abusive family was right: She was bad and deserved whatever hardship came her way.

Her former optimism gave way to seething rage. Life was *so unfair*. Why were her husband's injustices allowed to go unchecked? Was God blind and deaf? Did he not care? Was her husband's rejection a sign of God's disapproval? Why was her unfaithful ex flourishing while she struggled? Nothing made sense. As Donna's beliefs crumbled, she became increasingly afraid to venture into an uncertain world.

Donna's Dilemma

Donna faced a dilemma. If she gave up her prior cherished beliefs, her way of making sense of the world would be shattered. Yet, if she held onto them, *she* would be shattered.

For example, if she clung to the belief that bad things only happen to bad people, she would have to conclude that she was a terrible person. But if she let go of that belief, then why bother being good? Both options led to futility.

How could she explain her wayward husband's apparent success? And her own ongoing hardship? Jim didn't seem to face any consequences for his cruel choices. What good had her integrity gained her? Her belief system no longer aligned with the painful reality she was living.

As we talked, she recognized that her need for predictability had restricted her understanding of God and how he works. She had focused on the appealing promises of blessings for those who follow God while overlooking the passages that address believers' trials and hardships. Can you relate?

My Own Struggle

After my husband's betrayal and our unwanted divorce, I struggled with a few spiritual formulas of my own. During my single years, a respected Sunday School teacher told me, "You've been faithful to God. He will be faithful to you." I assumed that meant God would honor my desire to find a godly, faithful man with whom to build a family and grow old. I counted on that as if God had spoken these words to me. Yet, that was not how things turned out.

One Sunday morning after my divorce, my current pastor praised a woman who chose to stay with her still-wandering, same-sex-attracted husband. I couldn't leave the service fast enough. Bursting into my condo, I tossed my Bible on the kitchen table and slumped in disgust. The pastor's illustration sounded less like Christian maturity and more like unhealthy co-dependency. I resented his using her commitment to a repeatedly unfaithful man as a model of trusting God.

The following Sunday, I couldn't bring myself to go back to church. Instead, I stayed home and read the book of Job from beginning to end in The New Living Translation. That one sitting was life-changing. It began to dismantle the formulaic thinking that had left me stuck in spiritual limbo after my painful Post-Affair Divorce.

Job sought comfort from his closest friends after enduring numerous recent tragedies—losing his children, his farm, his income, and his health. They sat with him and grieved in silence for a week. No advice. No fixing. Just offering their presence, care, and empathy. I appreciated that. But soon, the friends he sought for solace turned on him.

Job's trials threatened his like-minded buddies, prompting them to find an explanation. They launched into all the reasons why these terrible things happened to Job, expounding on their most cherished formula for successful living: "Bad things only happen to bad people."

Since bad things happened to their good friend Job, they theorized that he must have done something "bad." In their minds, there was no other explanation for the tragedies that struck him. They were too afraid to think otherwise.

If his troubles were *not* deserved, then his friends knew they, too, were vulnerable to calamity. They felt safe as long as they clung to their recipes to explain misfortune.

Reading their misguided explanations and the Lord's responses to Job was eye-opening. I realized that Job's suffering was not his fault. He hadn't done anything wrong to deserve the tragedies that happened to him. It struck me that living in a fallen world means even faithful, sincere, yet imperfect followers of Christ are not immune to disaster.

> Job's suffering was not his fault. He'd done nothing wrong to deserve the tragedies that befell him.

I also noted the greater battle over Job's life in the heavenlies. Satan, the arch-enemy of our souls, seeks ways to undermine our faith through discouragement and hardship. Job's famous declaration, "Though he slay me, yet will I trust in him" (Job 13:15, KJV), took on new meaning for me. His honesty with God and continued trust despite unimaginable loss—have comforted and strengthened generations of suffering believers, including me.

A few of my takeaways from the life of Job were:

- God is still God, no matter how dim things appear.
- We don't deserve everything that happens to us.
- God sets limits on evil.
- Remaining faithful in suffering glorifies God.
- Knowing God and his character is more valuable than having tidy answers to life's hardest questions.
- In the end, whether now or in eternity, God will bring redemption, even if it looks different from what we imagined.

Illusion of Safety

Like Donna and I, most of us construct a worldview that offers the illusion of safety. We convince ourselves that if we do things "right," we can avoid the pitfalls that others face. But when trauma crashes into our lives, that illusion shatters. Old beliefs no longer work for us. Up feels like down, and down feels like up. Well-meaning friends offer simplistic answers that sound hollow or even maddening. We're left carrying a deep sense of injustice, with no clear way to make things right.

Most of us feel indignant when our sense of fairness and justice is violated. Upon realizing that more events are beyond our control than we wish to believe, our instinctive response is to fight. We plead with God, rail, fume, and kick as hard as possible to rectify our unjust situation, sometimes to no avail.

Our next response is to recoil in fear. How can we move forward in a world so unsafe and out of our control? If we remain frightened, our confidence and our very world will shrink.

That's what happened to Donna. She quickly gave up when encountering roadblocks while trying new things to improve her situation. She withdrew from trying anything new for fear the rug would be pulled out from under her.

Many betrayed and abandoned people get stuck in this frozen state for years, unwilling to take another chance at love and relationships. They know something has to change, but they either cling to their old beliefs or toss them aside because they didn't work.

We don't need to abandon all our beliefs. However, we may need to *reframe* some of them to account for life's unpredictable sorrows or difficulties.

Shattered Windows

Everyone develops a framework for interpreting the world and how it works. This outlook is often referred to as a "schema." For those of us who believe in God, we form a set of spiritual principles that help us make sense of life. We build these beliefs to feel safe, trusting that God's ways are ordered and consistent, allowing us to navigate life with a degree of confidence.

In her book *Comfort in the Ashes* about the life of Job, author Michelle R. Keener, PhD, masterfully explains how trauma can shatter our schema. She likens it to a window through which we view life, until something crashes through it and leaves our perspective fractured.

> My belief in God shapes how I interpret those experiences. It is part of the window through which I look at the world. Trauma shatters that window. Trauma shakes and breaks the fundamental beliefs that make up our worldview window. When it falls apart, we lose our window. We no longer have those basic assumptions that helped us interpret and understand the world around us.[2]

I've sadly watched Betrandoned spouses deconstruct their once-solid faith in God as their feet bled from stepping on the broken shards of glass in the aftermath of betrayal and spousal desertion. Yet I've observed others who, rather than walk away from their faith, allowed the Lord to salvage the broken pieces of their lives to reconstruct a lovely stained-glass window through which they viewed the world and their faith.[3]

When my husband abandoned our relationship, I experienced a cascade of losses that shook the very foundation of my faith. It forced me to re-examine the theological beliefs I long held.

What follows are some of the ways I reshaped my understanding—anchoring my beliefs, not in simplistic formulas, but in the whole counsel of Scripture. I pray these insights bring you the same lucidity and comfort they brought me.

SPIRITUAL TRUTHS TO UNPACK

The most radical shift in my thinking was learning to embrace *mystery*. It took me a while. But the day I read about the life of Job, I began to accept that God is divinely all-knowing, and I am not. I know. Not exactly a novel idea.

God's Mysterious Ways

> "For My thoughts are not your thoughts, neither are your ways My ways," declares the LORD. "For as the heavens are higher than the earth, So My ways are higher than your ways and My thoughts than your thoughts" (Isaiah 55:8–9).

In other words, God's thinking is far beyond what our finite minds can conceive. So, when we go through trials, it is best not to second-guess him. Better to cling to him instead.

> "Now we see but a dim reflection as in a mirror; then we shall see face to face. Now I know in part; then I shall know fully, even as I am fully known" (1 Corinthians 13:12).

Our vision is hindered now, like trying to peer into a cloudy mirror that limits our view and reflects things in reverse. But in heaven, we will have a direct view of God and see things clearly, just as he does.

> "O, the *depth* of the riches of the wisdom and knowledge of God! How *unsearchable* are His judgments, and *untraceable* His ways!" (Romans 11:33, emphasis added)

The word "untraceable" is the word *anexichniastoi* in Greek, which is also translated as "unfathomable" and "past finding out" in other Bible versions. In other words, not only are God's ways higher than our ways, but they are so far beyond us that they are outside our ability to grasp.

When I questioned the Lord's wisdom and power during my devastation, in the end, like Job, I had to admit, "Surely I spoke of things I did not understand" (Job 42:3).

On earth, we see shadows and impressions of certain spiritual realities without complete lucidity. Only in eternity will we see the whole picture with crystal clarity. Much like the famous poem "The Weaver," God sees the beautiful upper side of the tapestry he's creating from the bright and dark threads of our lives, but down here, we only see the messy "underside."[4]

As mere mortals, we are incapable of fully grasping the extent of God's work in the cosmos. His ways are past our understanding. The sooner we accept that we only see a fraction of God's ways, the less we will doubt him when life throws us a curveball. After all, he is God, and we are not.

Like Job, we are often unaware of the spiritual battles waged over our lives and the broader picture unfolding in the heavenly realm. Yet, we can follow the example of Job and other greats of the faith who chose to trust God despite their confusing circumstances. Some answers won't come until heaven.

Accepting the unknown and unknowable is a vital part of walking by faith. When we demand comprehension of every detail, we elevate ourselves to a place we were never meant to occupy. Acknowledging our limits isn't weakness—it's humility. And wise.

God has revealed plenty about his nature through Scripture and most clearly through Jesus Christ. Our role is to walk by faith, clinging to what we know and surrendering the rest to him.

Another reality that smacks us in the face when our families fall apart is:

We Live In A Fallen, Broken World

> "I have told you these things so that in Me you may have peace. In the world, you will have tribulation" (John 16:33).

"In the world, you *will* have tribulation." No one is exempt. Just because something horrible has happened to you doesn't mean you are being singled out for calamity. To maintain a healthy outlook on life, we must accept that tribulation is an inevitable part of life in a fallen world.

Trouble is not personal—it's part of existence. If we are alive in this world, we will encounter difficulties. The gift of experiencing the joys of life also comes with the risk of pain.

I can't explain why some people are spared from atrocities while others are not. Yes, obeying the Lord can help us avoid certain consequences. But not all. Many writers have wrestled with the problem of pain. The truth is that sin has entered our world and will not be expunged until the end of the age. Sin has contaminated every aspect of life on Earth. Humans are the worst perpetrators of evil, but even nature bears the weight of the Fall. Creation itself is groaning, and not entirely friendly to Earth's inhabitants.

Scripture states, "For he gives his sunlight to both the evil and the good, and he sends rain on the just and the unjust alike" (Matthew 5:45). I am uncertain whether "rain" signifies something positive, like rain that nourishes the land, or negative, like a stormy day. Part of being human is being an equal recipient of the laws of nature, the laws of sin, and the laws of death.

Our Western culture is particularly averse to the notion of "dis-ease." After all, as stated in the Bill of Rights, we are entitled to "life, liberty, and the pursuit of happiness." But what do we do when someone steals the heart of our spouse? They've pursued their happiness, but we've been robbed of ours.

Just because someone obtains what they want doesn't mean they had God's blessing. The psalmist said, "For You are not a God who delights in wickedness" (Psalm 5:4), and "Love takes no pleasure in evil, but rejoices in the truth" (1 Corinthians 13:6).

Suffering is not a sign that we are unworthy of God's blessings. In fact, according to Scripture, it may indicate the opposite.

> "Indeed, all who desire to live godly lives in Christ Jesus *will be persecuted*" (2 Timothy 3:12, emphasis added).

Just look at the life of Paul, the Apostle—imprisoned, beaten, whipped, starved, and eventually killed. Why? For preaching the gospel. For refusing to renounce his faith. For serving God with all his heart, soul, mind, and strength.

The writer of Hebrews salutes those who were made "destitute, oppressed, and mistreated" for their faith with an incredible compliment: "The world was not worthy of them" (Hebrews 11:38). Perhaps that is the Lord's view of you as well—that this fallen world is not worthy of you. In other words, you are worth more than the terrible circumstances you may experience.

This is not to suggest that everyone who suffers emotional harm is being persecuted for their faith. Some of us weren't following God at all, but he used our suffering to draw us into his embrace.

We must release the unrealistic expectation that we are entitled to special treatment or exempt from the trials faced by the saints before us. Suffering isn't always personal. It's not a reflection of our worth to God. We do well to admit that, like other believers worldwide, we are "foreigners and strangers on earth" (Hebrews 11:13, NIV).

So, like me, I hope you can let go of the idea that life must be fair. Or that you deserve more ease and comfort than others. This world is a hostile, foreign place filled with people who defy the will of God. And if they defy him, they will undoubtedly defy you, too.

The Gift of Free Will

> "Live in freedom, but do not use your freedom as a cover-up for evil; live as servants of God" (1 Peter 2:16).

I remember being devastated when my marriage fell apart. There had been so many confirmations the Lord had brought us together before our wedding that I was confident our relationship was God-ordained. Therefore, I assumed he would help us sustain our marriage over the long haul.

But now, all those hopes and expectations seemed laughable. Why would the Lord lead me to marry someone who would later betray and forsake me? And if he is "all-knowing," didn't God know this beforehand? Doesn't the concept of God's sovereignty mean he is in control of all the events of my life? If not, what does my spouse's rejection say about my value, or lack thereof, to God? Does he not care?

I wondered, "Why doesn't God give my hard-hearted husband a Damascus road experience like Paul the Apostle, striking him with a bolt of light from heaven to bring him to his knees?" We could have a beautiful, redemptive story encouraging other limping couples seeking recovery. Since that didn't occur in one form or another, I questioned God's power.

Disheartened after our divorce, I wondered, "Why wasn't God able to turn James's heart back to himself? And why did my prayers go unanswered? Was I unworthy of the Lord's effort to save our marriage?" I had prayed hard and firmly believed the Lord would move my husband's heart. When that didn't happen, I questioned whether God was powerless or unwilling. If he was impotent, why bother to pray? And if he was unwilling, that meant he didn't care. Both options seemed dreadful to me.

Did you feel that way, too? Were you holding out hope for a redemption story—one like you've seen God write for others? And when it didn't happen, did doubts about his goodness and power creep in?

The concept of God's sovereignty is beyond the scope of this book, but it's worth mentioning in reference to free will. Maybe you believed God orchestrated your marriage, or that—even if it began imperfectly, he would still bless it. But the collapse of your relationship may have shaken that faith. This is where we must learn to accept that while human free will is a gift, not everyone chooses God's ways, and we can get hurt in the crossfire.

Although God desires for us to align with his will, he respects our freedom of choice. He guides and prompts us, but generally, will not override our decisions. We are not puppets controlled by strings from above, nor are we robots programmed merely to do God's bidding. We are created as free moral agents.

Obedience or defiance toward God, acceptance or rejection of salvation, and the decision to love or betray a life partner all stem from individual choices.

You might wonder, "If I accept that trusting God entails embracing mystery, that his ways are past finding out, that I live in a fallen world where bad things happen, and that I will sometimes suffer the consequences of another person's (sinful) free will, what am I left with?"

Jesus Has Overcome The World

Returning to John 16:33, before warning the disciples of troubles in this world, he assured them that "in Me you may have peace." In other words, in a relationship with Christ, we can experience peace regardless of what happens in our lives. Why?

"Take courage, *I have overcome* the world" (John 16:33, emphasis added). In Christ, we can have peace and courage because he has conquered all the ugliness in the world—the devil, sin, and death. There isn't anything that he can't somehow redeem according to his values and goodness.

Jesus' death on the cross was not the end but a new beginning for suffering humanity. Jesus conquered sin, evil, and death. He died so we could live. He rose again as proof that he is greater than all the world's sin and sorrow—including the evil committed against you, including the betrayal of a spouse.

We have hope because this world is not our final home. There is more to life than what we see, feel, and experience on this planet. Some spiritual realities carry more significance than what meets the naked eye.

No matter what we lose down here on earth—our health, our families, our spouses, our dignity, or our status—nothing can rob us of what God has reserved for us in heaven or what he has deposited in our hearts. Someone might steal your spouse or your temporary happiness, but no one can steal your soul, salvation, integrity, worth, ability to love, or spiritual rewards beyond your natural sight.

> "He has given us new birth into a living hope through the resurrection of Jesus Christ from the dead, and into an inheritance that is imperishable, undefiled, and unfading, reserved in heaven for you" (1 Peter 1:3–4).

The living hope we receive due to Christ's resurrection means we have a precious inheritance awaiting us in heaven that no earthly sorrow or tragedy can destroy.

Leave The Consequences Up To God

I don't know about you, but I was very frustrated that my unfaithful husband got away with so much. He'd held several leadership positions and was the head elder in our church. Yet it seemed like no one knew enough about the depth of his actions and attitudes to hold him accountable. He managed to slide out of town to avoid the fallout. The only ones left to bear the consequences were my teenage children and me.

I stayed in the same community, surrounded by constant reminders of him, her, and our past life, wherever I drove, went to church, and met people while walking downtown. I wondered, "Why should I be the one to suffer the most when he's the one who strayed and left? Doesn't the Lord care about me?" Have you ever asked the same questions?

If your mate never faced any correction or public reproof, God is still working behind the scenes. For example, I later learned that several people privately confronted James. My best friend met up with him for coffee to challenge his decision to divorce me.

One person he'd supervised in ministry wrote him a tough letter about how he'd disappointed her. When his former boss, "Carl" (a close friend), fired him, he earnestly tried to have him reconsider his direction. Of course, that is difficult with someone who is already hard-hearted. But I have also seen situations where an honest, early confrontation—before the wayward spouse is too far gone—has helped bring about a change in the person's direction.

Although betrayed spouses may cry out for justice, seemingly to no avail, we must trust that God hears our prayers. After all, he will not turn a blind eye.

> "For the LORD loves justice and will not forsake His saints" (Psalm 37:28).

> "God will not be mocked. For whatever a man sows, he will reap" (Galatians 6:7–8).

All of us, including your betrayer, will be held accountable. However, there are several caveats to this promise. The reaping will be according to God's perspective and judgment, not ours. The timing, the method, and the visibility may not fit your preconceived notions. Keep in mind that some infractions are naturally more damaging than others. So, the reaping varies accordingly. Let's examine what Scripture has to say about how God works.

God's Timing

A person doesn't always reap the consequences of sin right away. God's perspective is long and wide. He is patient with sinners (sometimes frustratingly so) because he allows them time to repent. However, he will hold your betrayer accountable even if earthly repentance never occurs. Whether in this life or before the judgment seat, God's light will expose every hidden deed.

It is not a matter of *if* but *when*. So, if your betrayer is getting away with murder (so to speak), be patient. Trust God with the timing. It will be vital for your personal healing to surrender the timing to God.

> "God says, 'At the *time I have planned* I *will* bring justice against the wicked'" (Psalm 75:2, TNLT, emphasis added).

Although your spouse may not be inherently evil, their actions certainly were.

Among the gems tucked into the book of Job are the words of his previously silent fourth and youngest friend, Elihu, who saw past the judgment of his other friends and affirmed God's higher plan.

> "God is leading you away from danger, Job, to a place free from distress. He is setting your table with the best food. But you are obsessed with whether the godless will be judged. Don't worry, judgment and justice will be upheld" (Job 36:16–17, NLT).

Did this thought ever occur to you? That despite your painful situation, God has better things ahead for you. And that he is leading you "away from danger" to a new place that will be free(er) from distress. You can be assured that God's ultimate judgment and justice will be fulfilled. If you knew and believed this, what difference would it make in your life?

God's Method

Too often, when we've been wronged, we long to witness visible consequences for the offender's actions: circumstantial hardship, financial woes, relational problems, or other visible difficulties. However, God's way of allowing consequences is often less visible and more internal. What we can't always see are the spiritual and emotional tolls: the lack of peace, inner torment, strained relationships, or the heaviness of a hardened heart. An offender may appear outwardly cheerful while hiding inward agony.

Ask yourself: Would you rather have money or peace of mind? While most of us want both, no amount of money is worth losing our peace of mind. Peace of mind and soul are far more valuable than external signs of success. That is

> There is no substitute for a clear conscience and the peace of the Holy Spirit.

what most betrayers lack when they have not repented and made restitution for their wrongs. There is no substitute for a clear conscience and the peace of the Holy Spirit. And no impenitent person can experience that. They can only drum up cheap thrills or distractions as poor substitutes.

God's Vantage Point

Scripture states that "Man looks on the outward appearance, but God looks on the heart" (1 Samual 16:7). Since your offender is not likely to confide in you these days, you don't know what is happening inside of him/her. All you can go by is outward appearance. And don't forget, appearances can be deceiving.

You may think your ex-spouse is waltzing carefree through life, but you do not know what he or she feels in the dark. You can't see the quiet torments, insecurities, or guilt that lie beneath the surface. Nor are you likely to hear how God is trying to get their attention. You won't see the sleepless nights, the friendships strained or lost, the self-doubt, or the ache stirred by news of your healing or newfound strength.

Even the most seasoned rationalizer cannot outrun the chilling effect of ignoring God. As the famous poem "The Hound of Heaven"[5] testifies, it is impossible to escape the convicting pursuit of our heavenly Father.

People try to insulate themselves with distractions—money, alcohol, achievements, new lovers, endless work, or entertainment. Still, these will not feed their soul.

God Boundaries Evil

Even when we can't see it, God has his limits. As awful as our circumstances may become, things could be much worse. Just as God set limits on Satan's afflictions of Job, the Lord imposes limits on the afflictions that come our way.

Back to Donna's story. One day, while walking her dog, she passed an elderly man walking his dog as well. He mumbled something kind, but Donna froze. Panic surged. She averted her eyes and quickened her pace, desperate to get home.

In my office, we unpacked her reaction. When she closed her eyes, the memory of her ex-husband strangling her throat flooded her mind. I suggested we pray and see if God might reveal his perspective to her.

As soon as we bowed our heads, Donna experienced a flash of insight. In the privacy of her heart, God revealed to her, in no uncertain terms, that he had been in ultimate control. He had given her the strength to say, "Get your hands off my throat!" even though she could hardly breathe. God had protected her from death.

Donna's body relaxed, and she broke into a smile. When her eyes met mine, I knew the fear was gone. Donna nearly floated out of the session with new confidence.

At our next session, she informed me that she no longer needed therapy. She had received what she came for: a renewed trust in God and freedom from fear. Her faith was now rooted in something deeper than formulas. She understood that suffering can happen to undeserving people. But even then, God is present. His boundaries for evil may not align with our ideals, but he will never forsake us, even in the worst circumstances.

Regarding You

I encourage you to commit your situation to the Lord, no matter how confusing or hurtful your circumstances. There is no other way to benefit from his promises and allow him to complete his work in your life.

I've seen many betrayed spouses lose heart and turn away from their walk with Christ. Instead, they either dismantled their faith, adopted some worldly philosophy or off-beat religious beliefs, numbed their pain through substance abuse, or tossed their morals to the wind and slept around in an attempt to feel sexually valued again, all of which only made them feel worse.

Don't do that! Hold steady. As the writer of Hebrews suggests,

> "So do not throw away your confidence; it holds a great reward. You need to persevere, so that after you have done the will of God, you will receive what He has promised" (Hebrews 10:35–36).

I've met many faithful spouses who trusted the Lord despite their flagging self-esteem and weary battles. Rather than give up, they grew into pillars of the faith, allowing God to shape their characters and deepen their relationship with the Lord, enabling others to lean on them for encouragement. I admire them immensely. Keep in mind, you never know who is watching you and has been encouraged in their faith.

Spiritual disillusionment can come through many avenues. One is when a straying spouse uses religious justifications to explain their betrayal and abandonment of the marriage. Another is the deep disappointment we feel when our once-reliable faith formulas no longer work.

But perhaps most jarring is the heartbreak that comes when someone we've looked to for godly wisdom—such as a pastor, counselor, mentor, elder, or coach—breaks our sacred trust. Because of their authority, influence, and the vulnerability we offer them, their words carry great weight.

In the next chapter, I will share a few stories to illustrate how misguided "helpers" can cause harm that is difficult to recover from. If you've ever been wounded by someone you trusted with your soul, you are not alone. We will explore that pain together to discover vital lessons it can teach us.

Chapter 21

When Helpers Harm

> It is better to take refuge in the LORD than to trust in man.
> It is better to take refuge in the LORD than to trust in princes.
> ~Psalm 118:8–9

Seven months into our crisis, I decided to take a mental health break and stay with friends in Hawaii, as I've mentioned before. James suddenly worried that I was going to leave him, so he broke up with Judy for a while and admitted to me by phone that it had been more than a one-way attraction. They'd been mutually involved since their first kiss in August. He begged me to let him fly to Maui to hold hands and walk the beach with me, but I was still wary.

Once I arrived back home, he nearly cancelled his plans to begin meeting with Psychologist #2. But, remembering my Hawaii counselor's concern that he needed to reflect on his deeper issues, I encouraged him to keep his appointments. Three weeks in, after a lengthy therapy session, James arrived home with a big smile on his face. Curious, I asked him how his counseling session had gone.

He told me he had discussed his worries with the psychologist about whether God was still loving him, back when he was messing up (for the previous seven months). His therapist reportedly said, "God still loved you."

James asked, "But how? How was God loving me?"

Mr. Psychologist said, "Through *Judy*."

After this reveal, James nodded with a grin, expecting me to be happy for him about his new insight. Instead, I felt punched in the gut, realizing this bolstered his excuses for the affair.

I couldn't believe my ears. *God was loving James through Judy? The woman who usurped his heart from me? What was this therapist thinking?* I also wondered how James manipulated this supposedly Christian professional into suggesting such a disgusting idea to him.

I tried to stay calm as a wave of revulsion washed over me. James seemed oblivious to how warped his justifications sounded. The idea that God was somehow expressing his love through an immoral relationship with another man's wife sickened me. And his lack of concern about how this so-called revelation might devastate me felt surreal—like I was watching it all happen outside my body. Could he really believe this?

I excused myself for a long drive to sob and scream in private. How could my seminary-trained, once-godly husband be so deceived? I used to admire his love of truth and dedication to Christ. What had happened to him? I railed at God for over an hour.

That's when the ramifications of his words hit me in full force, causing my self-doubts to creep in afresh. What if *I'm* the deceived one? What if it's *true*? What if God really *was* loving James through Judy? What did that say about me? About us? And what did that say about my worth to God and his love for me?

The only conclusion I could draw was that, if true, God must despise me and wish the absolute worst upon me. The fact that this suggestion came from a reportedly Christian psychologist who should know better only made it worse.

I shook my head to regain my good sense. *No, this can't be true. The God I've loved and served most of my life would never do that.* Nothing about this lined up with God's Word or his character. Still, the internal battle raged on as I slid my car into the garage and, for the sake of our still-at-home teenage son, put on a brave face through dinner.

That night, as we were getting ready for bed, I could no longer suppress my anguish. I began to sob. James gently touched my shoulder and asked me what was wrong.

Between tears, I told him how devastated I was over his belief that God was loving him through the other woman. At that, he stiffened. The brief flicker of empathy vanished. I wept from my toes for a good half hour without letup. James said nothing and offered me no comfort or reassurance. It was clear he had no intention of reconsidering his maligned new views. His heart had turned another corner.

Two weeks later, his mother called. I picked up the phone, and we talked briefly before she asked me, "What happened during those therapy sessions?" She said, "He went into them feeling guilty, but he came out of them *defiant*."

While her observations validated my recent experience with him, I still clung to a thread of hope that he would remember the fog-lifting effect he reported after ending things with Judy while I was in Hawaii.

In the meantime, I obtained James's permission to meet alone with Psychologist #2. When I entered his office, I was surprised by the man's peaceful, warm demeanor. He was very likable.

He said a few things that I appreciated. However, when I questioned him about his "God was loving you through Judy" intervention, he paused, looked up, and then back at me and answered. "It was a *transitional* truth to lead him to a higher truth." Dumbfounded, I left the meeting, frustrated with myself for not challenging his nonsensical reasoning.

That single devastating phrase caused me and our marriage more turmoil than all of the other hurtful things James said to me combined. It's a sobering reminder that even well-meaning but ill-equipped therapists can inflict deep harm.

Mistakes in Therapy

I, too, have made mistakes as a counselor in my work with clients. I learned how easy it is to be fooled by the complaints of an unhappy, wayward spouse. Most of these misjudgments occurred early in my practice.

Straying partners often use their spouse's extreme reactions to bolster the "controlling spouse alibi" and justify their two-timing behavior. They rationalize to themselves, or a best friend or counselor, that they need to find relief from the stressors at home. They, along with inexperienced therapists, sometimes fail to recognize that their intimate disloyalty has triggered a horrified spouse's primal survival instincts, similar to a drowning person grasping for anyone within reach. Rather than view themselves as the instigators of panic, the unfaithful use their partner's frantic behaviors as an excuse to leave.

A FEW HELPFUL THINGS TO KNOW ABOUT THERAPISTS

Therapists, like pastors, hold positions of influence that must be stewarded with care. Those of us in the helping professions are still human, with our own preferences, wounds, and blind spots. That's why self-awareness is essential. We need to recognize when our biases might either support or harm those entrusted to our care. For this reason, I typically worked alongside a team of Christian colleagues and sought regular input from counselors outside our clinic. Every helping professional needs wise, trusted voices around them in order to grow and serve well.

Many of Us Are Hopeless Romantics

Some of us in the marriage-saving business are hopeless romantics at heart. I know I am. So, when an unfaithful spouse comes in by themselves, describing their current partner as a bore, abuser, witch, or warlock, it's easy to empathize. In our effort to connect, we may start to feel sorry for them—sometimes even overidentifying with their pain. Then, when they talk about an admiring outside lover, their new thrall can tug at our heartstrings—even though we intellectually know better.

You may understand this human tendency. Have you ever watched a romantic movie and sympathized with the cheating protagonists who were enraptured with one another? Have you seen a film where the main characters experience a magical encounter that leads to a steamy affair, are forced to part ways, and wistfully never forget their "true love"? You know, the ones who found their mythical soulmate who fulfilled all their dreams. Mentally, you know it's wrong, but emotionally, you get swept up in their on-screen chemistry and idealized passion.

The saying, "Everyone loves a lover," rings true. Hollywood often glorifies affairs by appealing to our romantic fantasies, as seen in award-winning films such as "The Bridges of Madison County" and "The English Patient."

As infidelity expert and Psychiatrist Frank Pittman, III says,

> [The unfaithful] should seek out therapists who do not fall in love with their patients' fantasies of escape from reality and will not stand by in an "ethically nonjudgmental" state as patients sacrifice their lives and the lives of their loved ones on the fires of their passion.[1]

Like you, counselors who aim to assist couples can fall into the same romantic traps as the general public. If we are not careful, we can be manipulated into sympathizing with the tempted and find ourselves inadvertently rooting for the wrong couple against our better judgment.

Not All Therapists Are Trained to Work With Couples

Some therapists advertise themselves as marriage counselors without having the proper training. Marriage and Family Therapists must undergo supervised clinical training in what is called "Systems Theory" to recognize the relationship patterns and dynamics of couples or families.

A well-trained marriage counselor helps couples engage in real-time interactions that shift their relationship in a healthier direction. In contrast, therapists trained solely in individual work may lack the skills necessary to guide couples effectively.

I have spent years picking up the pieces after a misguided, individually-focused therapist gave harmful advice to struggling couples. One new client approached me after seeing a well-known psychologist in town. During his first appointment with her, after hearing about his affair, her parting comment was, "Well, the best you can hope for is an amicable divorce." That was not the advice he wanted or needed. I worked with him as he extricated himself from the illicit relationship, brought in his wife, and jumped through hoops to save his marriage successfully.

An Outside Influence Alters the Dynamics

Most counselors learn that effectively working with a couple is impossible if one partner is under the influence of drugs or alcohol. For a relationship to mend, the addict must be clean and sober before the marital issues can be properly addressed.

However, some therapists fail to recognize that the elevated neurohormones associated with a forbidden affair mimic the effects of morphine on the brain. Like any chemical substance, the external foreign influence must be addressed and neutralized before working with them as a couple.

If a counselor fails to address the need for the unfaithful partner to "sober up" first (i.e., cut off all contact with the affair partner 100%, stop feeding their distorted emotions, and explore their underlying issues), they may mistakenly jump into doing marital therapy, hoping that better communication will somehow make the affair magically "go away." This almost never happens.

Symptom or Cause?

The "Symptom or Cause" debate is like the familiar "Which came first, the chicken or the egg?" Some therapists treat infidelity as a symptom of an already troubled marriage. Others view it as the cause of the breakdown. So, how do you determine which came first—the dissatisfaction in the marriage or the affair?

It is a myth that all affairs are the result of an unhappy marriage. Infidelity expert Dr. Shirley Glass notes that "Affairs can happen in good marriages."[2] She also says, "Sometimes an affair can be understood by exploring the deficiencies in the marriage, but often it cannot."[3]

> Many therapists miscalculate the destructive impact an affair has on an otherwise decent marriage.

While an affair can be *both* a Symptom and a Cause of trouble in a couple's relationship, it is more often a reflection of unresolved issues within the strayer than between them as a couple. An affair is best understood as a fundamental cause of trouble in a marriage, no matter the pair's other dynamics. Many therapists miscalculate the destructive impact an affair has on an otherwise decent marriage.

Family therapists working to help couples repair their marriages must recognize that an affair, like a chemical addiction, functions like a powerful magnetic force that *creates a life of its own*. It pulls the marital system out of alignment, much like the moon affects Earth's tides. And like a hidden moon behind clouds, an affair can alter the seasons of a marriage long before it's discovered.

Whatever the pre-existing issues, most were likely repairable *before* this third, disruptive force entered the picture.

If the therapist fails to account for the affair's impact, they may wrongly blame the marriage or the uninvolved spouse, and underestimate how the affair itself has destabilized the relationship.

Once the affair has been neutralized, the emotional distortion is dismantled, and firm boundaries in place, a skilled therapist can often guide the couple through recovery. With intentional work, this process can become a turning point—building deeper empathy, greater emotional tolerance, and a stronger foundation for the future.

Did you have a negative experience with a counselor during or after your crisis? If the counselor was unprepared to handle your situation, they may have unintentionally caused more harm than good. However, despite a counselor's experience, a stubborn spouse may still be unyielding. Your partner may have only agreed to counseling so they could claim they tried therapy and it "didn't work." Or they might have intended to leave you in the care of a counselor and then disappear.

Pitfalls of Well-Meaning Therapists

If you went to a therapist who was not trained in infidelity or sex addiction recovery, you may have been additionally traumatized if:

- Your counselor fell into the "romantic love" trap and, knowingly or not, sympathized with your straying partner over you.
- They focused on improving communication without confirming the affair was fully ended or addressing the deeper issues driving your spouse's behavior.
- They treated the affair as merely a symptom of a troubled marriage, downplaying the affair's actual harm.
- They reinforced your spouse's unfair judgments of you and your reactions. As Dr. Pittman notes: "Therapists who see their function as

guilt reduction can always find some marital imperfection on which to hang the infidelity."[4]
- They prematurely labeled you as "co-dependent," even before you knew about the affair.
- They failed to recognize your trauma and misdiagnosed you.
- They were duped into buying some of the betrayer's rationalizations.
- They lacked training in how to treat sex addicts and their partners.
- They allowed a manipulative betrayer to get away with damaging narratives and unchecked behavior.

Pastors and Other Leaders

Pastors must wear many hats, and most are not trained counselors. I've found that some preachers have a greater gift of gab than of listening, leaving those seeking help feeling disappointed or dismissed. Sadly, church leaders may subscribe to uninformed myths, like Donna's pastor in Chapter 18 ("He wouldn't be looking elsewhere if he were getting enough at home"). Pastors are notorious for similar kinds of victim-blaming. Elders and friends may fall prey to other misguided beliefs, such as pinning the "problem" on the faithful spouse for not offering quick forgiveness, further deepening the betrayed partner's pain and sense of being judged.

One friend of mine, "Elizabeth," recently confided that her husband had an affair early in their marriage. As new believers, they sought counsel from their pastor. Rather than address her husband's affair, he insisted that the most important thing was for her to immediately forgive him. This allowed her husband to evade personal responsibility and avoid his underlying issues.

While she sensed his emotional distance for many years, she didn't discover his repeated involvement with prostitutes for another 25 years. A few years after their divorce, she ran into the daughter of this same pastor and learned he had lost his pastorate due to unfaithfulness to her mother. I was not surprised.

I've counseled many people in abusive marriages who attended rigid churches that prioritized the institution of marriage over the well-being of the person. In such environments, pastors and leaders can become additional sources of harm. Sadly, some churches are like big, dysfunctional families rather than safe havens.

One client likened her church experience to the story of the Good Samaritan. Her husband had emotionally abused her, robbing her self-esteem, to the point that she was metaphorically bleeding on the side of the road. Yet the religious leaders she turned to either looked away or crossed to the other side—just like the priest and the Levite in Jesus' parable. It was only the unlikely figure—the Samaritan, someone the religious elite despised—who showed true compassion. Jesus used this example to teach what it really means to love your neighbor.

While Jesus is our ultimate Good Samaritan, it would help if a few of his shepherds and disciples would dress the wounds of an abused person and make sure they get to a safe place rather than judging the injured party.

While we all want to trust our friends, siblings, pastors, and elders to protect us (and sometimes they do), they are imperfect and can be constrained by church polity, teachings, and personal biases in ways that may hurt wounded parishioners.

It is vital to find a safe place to fellowship with other believers. You need people who will support you and provide solace and encouragement. If you don't already have a loving church family, this may take time. But don't give up. A healthy, grace-filled church often includes:

- A high view of Scripture without rigidly enforcing debatable doctrines.
- Small groups and/or recovery ministries for deeper connection and healing.
- A culture of grace that still upholds biblical truth.
- Mature leadership that serves with humility rather than control.

The last thing we need after betrayal and abandonment is to remain in an unhealthy church that reinforces our feelings of shame regarding a Post-Affair Divorce. On the other hand, we should not isolate ourselves from fellowship because of that shame. Healing happens best in community.

I always encourage wounded spouses to attend a small recovery group such as Divorce Care or other divorce recovery ministries, a therapy group for betrayed partners, Celebrate Recovery, or a Betrandoned group based on my Workbook. Even an online support group run by a qualified therapist or coach can be helpful. (I keep a list of these on my website.)

Another Helper Nightmare

My friend, Tonya[5], met her husband, Darin, in high school, and they attended Bible college together. They had been married for nearly 28 years, working as a team, with him serving as a pastor and her as a worship leader for the church they were affiliated with. She loved him and believed they had a strong marriage.

When Emily, a needy young woman in her twenties from their church, was discharged from a mental health ward, she had nowhere to stay. Out of compassion, they allowed her to live with them for a few months to help her get back on her feet. However, Tonya grew uncomfortable with her pastor-husband's relationship with Emily—specifically, the looks exchanged between them, the time spent together, and the favorite meals they prepared for each other—all of which made Tonya feel uneasy. She insisted that Emily find another place to live, which she did. Nonetheless, Pastor Darin continued to show excessive concern for her even after she moved out.

One day, he announced that he had made an appointment to see "Dr. Kim," a mutual friend they had known for 20 years. She was the go-to person to whom they referred parishioners, most recently including Emily. Darin and Tonya had served on Dr. Kim's non-profit board for years, attended retreats with her, and supported her ministry in various ways. Due to their many connections, Dr. Kim offered to see him for free.

Tonya had wondered why Dr. Kim had relinquished her professional counseling license to focus on "pastoral counseling." When asked, she claimed she'd done this to lower her fees and have more freedom to incorporate Scripture. At the time, this seemed reasonable to Tonya.

Soon after Darin returned from his first private session, he and Tonya fought over his ongoing attention toward Emily. He blurted, "Dr. Kim said you might even be a narcissist and a liar and that you don't have an empathetic bone in your body! I think we *both* need to see her." Stunned, Tonya stumbled to find words. Darin spun around. "This conversation is over!" Then he stormed off.

Despite being thrown by his harsh words, Tonya looked forward to meeting with her trusted friend and counselor. *Surely, she hadn't said such things to him. He must be making this up.* Setting aside the tightness in her stomach, she agreed to meet with Dr. Kim. After all, they desperately needed marriage help, and this was their most affordable option.

When they entered her office, Tonya sensed a chill in the air and noticed a look of contempt on Dr. Kim's face. Instinctively, she thought to herself, *This is not going to go well.*

Rather than discussing their mutual goals for counseling or addressing the suspected affair, the counselor allowed Darin to dive right into complaints about their sex life. He claimed that his wife often rejected him. Tonya was flabbergasted. He had never mentioned this to her before. The only time she recalled pulling back was during her mother's illness and subsequent death. He also grumbled that she was unwilling to engage in oral sex.

Dr. Kim raised her eyebrows, looked incredulously at Tonya, and asked, "You've never given him a blow job?"

Tonya shrank into the couch, intimidated by her counselor's accusatory tone, her husband's anger, and the unexpected denunciation.

"N...No...I've never given him a blow job." Tonya began to cry in shame.

Dr. Kim appeared disgusted. "You were not fulfilling your 1 Corinthians 7 wifely duties!"

She continued, "You stood before your church, preaching and leading worship, with your marriage in this condition?" She shook her head. "You need to confess, right here and now, that your ministry was a *fraud*."

Shocked and broken, Tonya and Darin complied, kneeling and praying aloud. Afterward, Tonya collapsed onto the floor in a fetal position, sobbing. Her friend dispassionately handed her a tissue.

Instead of guiding them toward healing or addressing the glaring issue of the suspected affair, Dr. Kim pivoted to the topic of divorce and co-parenting, pulling books off her shelves.

Shaken at the sight of her 27-year marriage spiraling down the drain, Tonya began to tremble and dissolved into tears. She said, "But I...I don't have a job! How am I going to feed the kids? And how can I afford to stay in the house?"

At this, Darin turned to Dr. Kim and said, "See? How am I supposed to deal with *this*?" Pointing to his wife on the floor, he added, "*This* is how she gets!" Tonya was stunned. *This?* Sobbing in a fetal position wasn't typical of her. And it certainly wasn't typical of her usually even-keeled husband to show such disdain.

Clutching the divorce and co-parenting books from Dr. Kim, Tonya stumbled out the door in a daze. The session had blindsided her, leaving her reeling—betrayed by both her husband and their counselor friend, and abandoned with no one left to stand for her or their marriage.

Within a month, Tonya discovered undeniable proof of her husband's affair with Emily. She tried to meet with Dr. Kim to show her the evidence, but she refused to meet alone with her. Pastor Darin submitted a vague resignation letter to the elders, who then sent a brief message to the church. Darin ended the relationship with his young lover and relocated 90 minutes away. Tonya and the kids were left to fend for themselves without a husband, father, church home, or compassionate therapist to support them.

Thankfully, despite limited finances, Tonya found what she called a "real" counselor—someone who gently walked her through the layered grief of betrayal, abandonment, and the secondary trauma caused by Dr. Kim's unethical conduct.

Rather than allow her disappointments to jade her view of God, Tonya pressed deeper into her relationship with Christ. She found a new church fellowship, survived financially by working three jobs, supported her kids and all their sports activities, deepened some of her friendships, and finally found the strength to relinquish the hope that her now ex-husband would come to his senses and seek to reconcile.

I asked Tonya what advice she would give others who may have had a bad experience with a misguided counselor. She said,

- Don't allow one off-base person (pastor, therapist, coach) to make you assume the entire industry is tainted.
- Examine a counselor's credentials to determine if they are certified or licensed in your state.
- Look for someone who is a good fit, honors your faith, and understands the emotional distortion accompanying affairs.
- If you don't know where to start, ask your friends who they would recommend, or else ask a pastor or a doctor you trust.
- Seek a counselor who validates you, helps you unpack your pain, and allows you to grieve your losses properly.

I would add:

- Avoid seeking counseling from someone with whom you wear multiple hats, such as a friend, board member, worship leader, and counselor. There's a reason licensed therapists are prohibited from counseling friends and family; it's nearly impossible to remain objective within a personal relationship.
- Look for a counselor with specialized training in infidelity recovery or sex addiction, depending on your circumstances.
- For your personal healing, choose someone who understands betrayal trauma and uses a trauma-informed approach with trauma-focused therapy.

The average person may not be aware of the ethical guidelines that licensed counselors must follow. In the Christian community, we often look to a person we know who seems spiritually wise for advice or prayer. Sometimes, that works out just fine.

However, for in-depth counseling, you need someone who is trained in infidelity recovery or sex addiction and credentialed in their field. Without that expertise, a counselor may be easily swayed by a straying spouse's rationalizations, as we saw with Psychologist #2 and Dr. Kim. Worse, if the counselor isn't held to a professional code of ethics or lacks proper oversight, as in Dr. Kim's case, after relinquishing her license, clients lose protection and recourse for boundary violations. Had Dr. Kim still been licensed, Tonya likely would have had grounds to file a formal complaint with her state's licensing board.

Ultimately, it's the responsibility of helping professionals to know their limits and uphold ethical standards. If a pastor or counselor crossed a boundary with you or operated outside their expertise, that failure was not your fault.

How I Overcame My Obsessive Thoughts

It's difficult to understand when a respected spouse turns into someone you no longer recognize. When they betray their values, disrespect us, and choose another person or way of life, merging who they were with who they've become can be a struggle, especially when a therapist or pastor appears to validate their harmful actions.

Complicating matters is if you, like Tonya and I, were married to someone you admired who was particularly smart, persuasive, or theologically trained. Their words can carry extra weight.

The most damaging effect of their rationalizations is how they cause us to question our reality and self-worth. We may wonder, *Did I deserve to be forsaken? And what if my partner's rejection reflects how God sees me, too?* When a counselor seems to affirm their delusions, it can deepen the fear that even God has turned his back on you.

In my case, I wondered what I could have done differently to save my marriage. I berated myself for missing the red flags and for my desperate behaviors.

However, the most tormenting thought of all was the idea that God was loving my husband through Judy. I didn't know how to shake such a gut-wrenching belief. I needed input from other objective people who understood the delusional effect of intimate betrayal.

Three Bolts of Light

After a women's meeting for church, I felt the need to share my secret torment with a close friend, Tammy. When I learned she wasn't there, I chose her best friend, Keely, to confide in. Sitting on the hall floor by ourselves, I shared my agony over the therapist's intervention and James's belief that God was loving him through his affair partner. Her response?

"That's B*** Sh**!!"

I jumped. Her frankness both jolted and relieved me. *Hmm. So I wasn't making a big deal out of nothing after all.* I later learned her father had had a string of affairs when she was growing up, and she had zero tolerance for a betrayer's excuses. I found her no-nonsense approach therapeutic for me.

Hers was the *first bolt of light* to pierce my confusion.

However, I was still stumped. Intellectually, I knew my husband's belief was off-base, but that didn't stop me from obsessing over the therapist's words and James's enthusiastic acceptance of them. I couldn't reconcile the respect I once had for his spiritual wisdom with such an extreme level of self-deception.

If it were true that God was loving James through Judy, it meant God must hate me, given the ruinous impact of their affair on my life. But this didn't make sense to me, either. Intellectually, I knew God loved me. But I didn't *feel* loved by God, as the lie still had a grip on my soul.

At my wits' end, I wrote an email to Welby O'Brien, author of *Formerly a Wife*, one of the few books I found at the time written by a betrayed and abandoned Christian spouse. I did my best to describe what happened and poured out my consternation via email. She replied with the following sage advice:

"Stop trying to make sense of the insanity of sin."

That simple phrase was the *second bolt of light*.

It struck me that I was indeed trying to make sense of the insanity of my husband's sin and Psychologist #2's poorly devised intervention. It didn't make sense because it wasn't supposed to. Her words shone a bright light on a lie that kept me tied in knots.

Soon thereafter, I found the *third and final bolt of light* that freed me from the last vestiges of my obsession—from God's Word.

> "Stop trying to make sense of the insanity of sin."
> ~Welby O'Brien

> "When tempted, no one should say, 'God is tempting me.' For God cannot be tempted by evil, nor does He tempt anyone. But each one is tempted when by his own evil desires he is lured away and enticed. Then after desire has conceived, it gives birth to sin; and sin, when it is full-grown, gives birth to death" (James 1:13–15).

There it was—straight from God's Word. *No one,* not even a psychologist or a deceived seminary graduate, should ever claim that an illicit temptation came from God. Scripture is clear: the Lord cannot be tempted by evil, nor does he tempt anyone. Our temptations come from our own sinful desires and broken places. Period.

I finally saw the truth. There was no way God had sanctioned James's affair, let alone expressed his love through another man's wife. I was free! No more obsessive rumination. No more forcing a puzzle piece that never belonged.

If you're still battling lies or harmful words from a straying spouse or misguided counselor, don't give up. Keep seeking the truth. Ask for wise counsel. And above all, anchor yourself in the promises of God's Word.

> "So He said to the Jews who had believed Him, 'If you continue in My word, you are truly My disciples. Then you will know the truth, *and the truth will set you free*'" (John 8:31–32, emphasis added).

Scripture holds the power to penetrate our hearts and minds, shattering the enemy's lies like nothing else can. In my case, God used three distinct bursts of truth to free me from a falsehood that nearly destroyed my faith.

The first came through a friend's blunt, eye-opening words—a jolt that awakened my senses. The second came from an author who had faced a similar battle and exposed the futility of fixating on lies. Each breakthrough chipped away at my confusion until God's truth flooded my weary mind and brought lasting freedom.

Perhaps, like Tonya, you've been haunted by an unfaithful spouse who weaponized a therapist's words, quoted accurately or twisted, to condemn you. Or maybe you endured a counseling session where your partner attacked you while the therapist sat silently by. You may have encountered a pastor, counselor, or even a well-meaning friend who didn't understand how infidelity distorts a betrayer's reality, and their words injured you.

I hope you have level-headed truth-tellers around you to help you redirect your obsessive thoughts away from trying to solve the unsolvable. Sin is not a jigsaw puzzle piece that you should forcibly jam into the canvas of your life. Trying to make sense of the insensible only leads to confusion and destructive lies about your worth.

If you are fixated on certain aspects of your spouse's misbehavior or the damaging words of a pastor or therapist, do what I eventually did: *Let it go.* It doesn't make sense because it's not supposed to.

Instead, soak yourself in the truth of God's Word. Don't legitimize the lies Satan used to sideline you or distract you from the work of rebuilding your life. Treat those deceptions like an ugly, mismatched puzzle piece that doesn't belong: Throw. It. Out.

> "Without wise leadership, a nation falls; there is safety in having many advisers" (Prov 11:14, TNLT).

The key here is having "wise leadership." That means experienced and knowledgeable folks to guide us, as I've hopefully outlined in this chapter.

We also need the safety of having "many advisors" to provide checks and balances in case any one of them is unsound. That's what Tonya did. When her unwise counselor and pastor-husband let her down, she sought a well-qualified therapist and a healthy, new church.

At the same time, no helper, counselor, pastor, or spouse should be given a higher place in our lives than the Lord himself. Trusting completely in the arm of flesh will only lead to disappointment. Re-read the verse I quoted at the beginning of this chapter:

"It is better to take refuge in the LORD than to trust in man. It is better to take refuge in the LORD than to trust in princes" (Psalm 118:8–9).

Only God deserves to be on a pedestal in our lives, including "princes" (i.e., people in positions of authority or leadership). Respect, yes, when earned. Pedestal, no. That honor should be reserved for God alone.

In **Section VI**, we will explore ways to "Remove the Angst" over the injustices you have endured. This won't be easy, nor will it be completed just by reading the next few chapters. But I hope to equip you with practical tools to help you continue the difficult path toward emotional freedom.

Letting go of angst is a process—not a quick fix. Don't be discouraged by Christian platitudes that slap a Band-Aid over deep wounds and dishonor your pain.

The first step is learning to recognize the difference between Pseudo-Repentance, Shallow Repentance, and Genuine Repentance. Understanding these distinctions will help you see what you're really dealing with and how best to respond. That's where we'll begin next.

SECTION VI

Removing The Angst

*"Why is my pain unending, and my wound incurable,
refusing to be healed?"
~Jeremiah 15:18*

Healing from the twin bombs of spousal infidelity and abandonment is no easy feat. Well-meaning friends who've never been through Betrandonment may suggest that you quickly forgive to be done with your sorrow. Others may advise you to "let go and move on."

Not so fast.

Letting go of the anger, resentment, and aggravation of an unwanted divorce involves so much more than mouthing Christian cliches. Your entire world has been turned upside down. It takes mountain-moving faith and a lot of blood, sweat, and tears to emerge from the rubble of destroyed dreams, financial hardship, and broken relationships.

You need time. Time to assess the damage. Time to explore and remove all the landmines left behind. Time to retrace how you lost yourself and rediscover who you are, so you don't lose yourself again.

Your Faithful Redeemer can patiently show you how to entrust these burdens to him, when and how you are ready.

Chapter 22

Is It Charm Or Contrition?

> The sacrifices of God are a broken spirit;
> a broken and a contrite heart,
> O God, You will not despise.
> ~Psalm 51:17

When James and I were discussing our tax returns before our divorce was final, I remember saying to him, "I want you to know that if you ever want to apologize to me for what you've done, even if it's ten years from now, I will forgive you." He immediately quipped, "I will *never* do that!"

His defiance revealed how deeply his self-justifications ran, which helped me begin to face the hopelessness of our situation. Before that, I had clung to his earlier suggestion that perhaps after we divorced, we would remarry again.

How does a person determine if such hopes are realistic or futile?

False Hope

Perhaps you, too, hoped for a sincere apology, or even reconciliation, after your partner's betrayal or your unwanted divorce. For most of us, that kind of closure never comes, at least not soon enough to repair what was broken. And if your spouse was especially winsome, you may have found yourself clinging to promises of change that never materialized.

I've known spouses who repeatedly offered second, third, and even sixth chances to a charming but wayward partner. No matter who files first, a betrayed spouse may wonder if they should have held out hope for repair.

Facing the direness of your situation is the first step toward your healing. False hope will only keep you stuck in quicksand, unable to find resolution or the capacity to move forward. Before you can begin to let go of your angst over your spouse's offenses, you must assess the condition of their heart toward you and toward the Lord. After all, you couldn't save your marriage with an unwilling, unsorry, unmotivated partner.

Upon reflection, how could you have known if your unfaithful partner, or a future one, turned a reliable corner or not? What follows are some guidelines and examples for you to discern the difference between:

- Pseudo-Repentance
- Shallow Repentance, or
- Genuine Repentance

Let us look at some personal and Scriptural examples of each kind of repentance to decide which heart condition best explains your former spouse's attitude. This will guide you toward the kind of forgiveness you may someday consider, both toward your ex-spouse and yourself. It will also sharpen your ability to discern who is safe or unsafe when assessing future relationships.

Pseudo-Repentance

Typically, pseudo-repentance is feigned remorse—insincere, self-focused, and often for show. The offender may still believe the lies they've told themselves to justify their actions. They might express regret when caught or threatened with serious consequences, such as divorce, exposure, or job loss. They may even break down in tears and plead for forgiveness, but their regret is rarely for the people they've hurt. Instead, their grief is rooted in self-pity—"Poor me!" rather than "Poor you!" Deep down, they still enjoy their sin and have no real intention of changing once the heat dies down.

This fake repentance is usually seen in people with strong narcissistic tendencies. They don't like bumping into walls (a.k.a. consequences). They detest the disapproval of others (hence feigning regret) while secretly treasuring their libertine lifestyle.

My current husband's favorite uncle, "Chad," was one of those men everyone seemed to admire. Handsome and charismatic, with a winsome sense of humor, he lit up any room he entered. When he taught adult Sunday School, tears of gratitude for God's love would stream down his cheeks. He and his wife were well-respected members of their church community.

Chad was a clinical psychologist with a thriving practice, serving many patients referred by their large church and from his wife's classes on Christian Womanhood. It took years for the truth of his unethical sexual misconduct with friends' wives and his female patients to come to light. After the licensing board received complaints from exploited women and their distressed husbands, the state revoked his license to practice psychology.

After convincing his wife, through tears and promises, that he was sorry, they moved to Washington State for a fresh start. My husband, Dan, unaware of his uncle's full history, invited him to speak at a Christian retreat for high school students. Dan marveled at Chad's compelling talks. The kids were drawn to his charisma, and many were moved by his testimony.

Later, Dan was gravely disappointed to learn that his favorite uncle had continued seducing women in his new church, causing further heartache for his wife and now grown children. At one point, Chad even boasted to my father-in-law that he could "get any woman into bed." This is the tragic nature of an unrepentant heart—one that refuses to dismantle its rationalizations and hides behind charisma and charm rather than confronting the truth.

Consider King Saul in the Old Testament. When Saul was first chosen to be king, he appeared humble, hiding behind the luggage to avoid drawing attention to himself. Yet, deep down, he harbored hidden pride and jealousy, which grew as he gained more power, prestige, and riches.

Saul occasionally suffered depression and mental anguish, which he attributed to evil spirits tormenting him. He invited David to play his harp and sing to him, which soothed his troubled mind. Saul relied on David for his personal comfort and to help him win against the kingdom's enemies, especially the Philistines and the Amalekites.

But as David's battle skills increased, Saul grew jealous of all the accolades he received: "And as the women danced, they sang out: 'Saul has slain his thousands, and David his tens of thousands'" (I Samuel 18:7).

Soon, the king began to plot ways to eliminate David. When his son Jonathan, David's best friend, spoke to Saul, he swore an oath that he would not kill David. Yet only a short time later, Saul attacked David and threw a spear at him twice (1 Samuel 13:11, 19:10). Fortunately, the spear struck the wall, and David fled.

David spent ten years hiding in the wilderness while Saul relentlessly pursued him. At one point, Saul learned that David had spared his life when he found him sleeping in a cave. Saul wept and called David "my son," feigning a change of heart. But David wisely kept his distance.

Later, after David again withheld vengeance, Saul repeated the charade—calling David "my son," confessing, "I've sinned," and promising not to harm him. Yet David remained cautious, and rightly so. Saul never stopped scheming to kill him (see 1 Samuel 18–31).

Saul wept, swore oaths, made emotional appeals, and admitted sin—only when it suited him. His repentance was not genuine but manipulative, as proven by his ongoing efforts to destroy David.

May this be a lesson for us all: true repentance isn't proven by promises, sweet talk, eloquent words, or even tears. If you once believed your former spouse's show of remorse, you're likely wiser now after enduring the painful aftermath of a Post-Affair Divorce. You've seen firsthand the futility of trusting someone who loves their sin more than what is right. As Scripture says,

> "In their own eyes they flatter themselves too much to detect or hate their sin" (Psalm 36:2, NIV).

My friend Elizabeth says, "Don't listen to their words. Watch their feet." In other words, actions matter more than polished speech. Once you recognize Pseudo-Repentance for the façade it is, you can stop blaming yourself for not doing enough to win them back. Their refusal to change wasn't about you or yours to fix. Lasting change is an inside job—within the offender.

Shallow Repentance

Unless an unfaithful spouse has completely seared their conscience, most experience some degree of guilt or shame over their actions. But guilt and shame alone are not enough to bring about the kind of transformation a betrayed spouse can, or should, depend on.

Scripture uses a specific Greek word for this shallow level of repentance: *metamelomai* (Strong's 3338), meaning "regret," "a change of mind," or "remorse." It refers to sorrow that stops short of true heart change and reform.

For example, after Judas betrayed Jesus, we read: "When Judas, who had betrayed Him, saw that Jesus was condemned, he was filled with remorse *[metamelomai]* and returned the thirty pieces of silver to the chief priests and elders" (Matthew 27:3).

Although Judas confessed to sinning and returned the bribe, his sorrow was rooted in self-pity, not genuine transformation. Instead of turning back to Jesus and dedicating the rest of his life to Christ as a redemptive testimony, he took his own life. His remorse never became true repentance.

THE SIGNS OF SHALLOW REPENTANCE

Avoiding the Topic of the Affair

Those who stray often carry so much shame that they avoid discussing what they've done. They resist sharing details with a pastor, counselor, or especially their spouse. Common deflections include, "I don't remember," "That was too long ago," or "We're having such a nice time—do we really need to talk about this now?"

As author Emily Brown notes, avoiding conflict or emotional intimacy can make individuals and marriages more vulnerable to infidelity. But secrecy and evasion only block the path to repentance and healing. The resistance typically stems from a mix of pride and fear—both of which hinder true restoration. Without humility, a half-sorry strayer will continue protecting themselves rather than fully coming clean.

I recall a Christian acquaintance, "Francine," who once shared her story with me. After discovering her husband's affair, she reached out to their pastor, desperate for help. The pastor sent an elder to their home. When the doorbell rang, she let her husband answer it, hopeful that someone was finally coming to speak truth into the devastation.

But as the elder stood on the porch, grinning, he declared to her husband. "You are forgiven!" Her husband, visibly relieved, clung to those words as if he'd been absolved of all wrongdoing. In the days that followed, he used it as a defensive shield: "Why do you keep bringing this up? I'm forgiven!" And "If God forgives me, why can't you?"

And just like that, the door to any meaningful conversation about the betrayal slammed shut.

Years later, when she confided in me, the no-talk rule was still in effect. The wound, though old, remained unacknowledged—hanging between them like a wall of dry ice: untouchable, numbing, and emotionally dangerous.

She felt obligated to play the role of the forgiving Christian wife on the outside. But on the inside, her agony remained alive and unresolved—frozen beneath the surface, where no one dared to go.

Francine is not alone. Sometimes, other fearful, betrayed spouses go along with the avoidance—hoping that keeping the peace will somehow save the marriage. This is especially common among believers who deeply value their marriage vows. But there's an important difference between *pleasing God* and *appeasing an unfaithful spouse*. In truth, the opposite is often true: God never minimizes unfaithfulness—and neither should we.

Without bringing the full truth into the light—and examining it with the help of a wise, objective professional—the unfaithful partner is likely to sidestep true repentance and derail any meaningful repair. Excuses go unchallenged. Patterns remain unbroken. And the deep work of healing gets stalled. Unless the roots are uncovered, false narratives exposed, and healthy boundaries put in place, neither spouse can heal as fully or deeply as God intends. "Pretending" is not a healthy coping strategy. It defeats repair.

Lack of Commensurate Consequences

While initial exposure can serve as a wake-up call, the fog of an affair rarely lifts immediately. True clarity takes time and requires spiritual insight, Scripture's conviction, outside support, and meaningful consequences. The disappointment of a betrayed spouse or others' disapproval is typically not strong enough to penetrate the conscience of someone who has spent hours justifying their actions in their own mind.

I remember working with a couple where the wife, "Alicia,"[1] kept saying she felt her unfaithful husband wasn't "getting it." In hindsight, I regret not empowering her to set and enforce firmer boundaries from the outset. After enduring several revelations of betrayal, her breaking point wasn't another affair. It was him lying to her about something entirely different.

Later, Alicia confided that she'd made it too easy for him after the truth came out. Instead, she'd bent over backwards to preserve stability for the kids, while neglecting her own need for healing and respect. She wished she had asked him to leave, to give him the space to truly grasp the severity of his behavior, the pain he had caused, and the fragile state of their marriage. That "brush with death"—the threat of losing it all—might have shaken him out of his complacency. His most recent lie only confirmed what she feared: he still had a propensity for deceit and didn't grasp the gravity of his offenses.

Sometimes, it takes strong consequences for a deluded partner to be broken enough to awaken from their tendency to blame others and make excuses for themselves. Again, it was not her fault that he hadn't shown evidence of more profound regret. There was no guarantee that a temporary separation would have made a difference. But it might have. Either way, he deserved and needed the strong medicine of firm consequences to break the spell of his ill-chosen, destructive behaviors.

A Lack of Contrition

Whenever I hear an unfaithful person claim their spouse's flaws—or life's stressors—drove them into the arms of a lover, I know they're still caught in emotional distortion. Until they take full responsibility for their own choices—without blaming others—they won't gain the insight or heart change needed to heal their marriage or grow spiritually.

I'm not talking about self-recrimination; most betrayers feel some degree of that. And I'm not denying that difficult circumstances can set the stage for temptation. But what is needed is Holy Spirit-inspired conviction—a conscience awakened to the weight of one's personal sin. Romans 12:9 reminds us: "Detest what is evil; cling to what is good" (NASB). Real change begins when someone sees their sin for what it is, recognizes the pain it has caused, and learns to hate it more than they hate the guilt. Without that, like Judas, they may simply seek a way out—not a way through.

I'm not saying that change is impossible for the irreligious without the work of the Holy Spirit. However, in my experience, a true metamorphosis most often follows a meaningful encounter with God, accompanied by ongoing accountability through professionals, mature believers, and those who are further along in their recovery.

Another attitude associated with a lack of contrition is having an entitlement mentality, as mentioned in Chapter 12. Therapist Rob Jackson says, "The one caught in sexual sin needs to wave a white flag and allow the injured spouse to set the terms of surrender."[2] A truly repentant spouse will not make demands, insist on their rights, or attempt to control the conditions of reconciliation. They will ask, "What must I do to rebuild your trust?"

Even when there is no hope for reconciliation, a contrite offender won't fight for their "fair share" of the assets. Instead, they will offer the betrayed spouse a generous settlement as a means of making amends. They won't resist paying for state-mandated child support or seek to put you in a disadvantaged financial position. A truly remorseful spouse won't keep dragging you to court to make your life miserable. Instead, the unrepentant may force you to keep dragging *them* back to court to make them live up to their obligations.

Repeat Unfaithful Behaviors

I've seen unfaithful people express regret, only to relapse into the same behaviors. Sometimes, there's an addictive pull rooted in deeper issues. Other times, the needed healing is short-circuited—whether by poor counsel, a family death, pressure from the affair partner, or an unplanned pregnancy. Willpower alone won't break addictive patterns. Long-term change requires multiple guardrails, and most importantly, a genuine heart shift—often brought on by therapeutic insight or a spiritual awakening.

Many who find lasting freedom from addiction attribute it to God's intervention. For example, actor Dennis Quaid, raised in a Baptist church, struggled with cocaine addiction early in his career. Even after rehab, he felt an inner void—until he returned to the Bible. He describes the words of Jesus as transformative and attributes his recovery to building a personal relationship with Christ.

Of the unfaithful people I've observed who did a successful U-turn and stayed committed to their recovery, nearly all pressed deeply into their relationship with God. Unless your spouse is softened toward the Lord, you have little hope for lasting change from sexual misbehavior. A person's trust and reliance upon God can make all the difference, as it adds a deeper layer of motivation for a former strayer to remain faithful and true.

Sometimes people cloak their sin in religious language to convince others—and sometimes themselves—that they're on the right path, when in reality, they're in denial about the grip that sin has on their hearts. As psychotherapist Rob Jackson states, "Adultery is a malignant tumor that requires deep surgery to remove."[3] That surgery involves skilled counseling, a supportive healing team, and, most importantly, the convicting work of the Holy Spirit. Genuine, lasting change requires deep emotional and spiritual transformation.

This doesn't mean a sincerely repentant person won't ever stumble, especially if they're battling sex addiction. Recovery is often jagged. But a surrendered believer will be motivated to return to the process, seek God's mercy, and continue the hard work of reform and rebuilding trust.

EVIDENCE OF GENUINE REPENTANCE

Deep Regret and Abhorrence

Genuine repentance is a beautiful thing. I have witnessed it in my counseling practice when an unfaithful partner's eyes are opened to the depth of their transgressions and the devastation that their selfish actions have caused their spouse and children. The tears, sincere grief, the efforts they make, along with the long-term compassion they show towards their betrayed spouses, are some of the highlights of my work with affair-injured couples.

So, you may wonder, "What does genuine repentance look like?"

The word "repent" originates from the verb *metanoeo* (Strong's 3340) or the noun form *metanoia* (Strong's 3343), which means "to think differently or afterward, i.e., reconsider (morally feel compunction), repent." In other words, repentance is much deeper than mere mental assent. It's not just a change of mind but a change of heart. It's where we get the term "metamorphosis," such as when a caterpillar transforms into a butterfly.

My favorite definition of repent, based on Thayer's Greek Lexicon, is found in the Amplified Bible. It describes the immense joy in heaven over one "person who repents—changes his mind for the better, heartily amending his ways with abhorrence for his past sins" (Luke 15:10, TAB).

Let's take Thayer's biblical definition apart, piece by piece, so you can evaluate whether you saw this in your former spouse. Ask yourself:

- Did your partner truly "change his/her mind"? (i.e., demonstrate a real turnaround in thinking vs. continued rationalizing)?
- Was this change "for the better," rather than a backward slide?

- Did your spouse do so "heartily" (with sustained heartfelt enthusiasm rather than begrudgingly)?
- What efforts did he/she make to "amend their ways" (correct the damage as best as possible and make restitution)?
- Did your partner show "abhorrence" for his/her past sins? (i.e., show obvious disgust and hatred for his/her betrayal and harm of you, rather than doing more of the same or engaging in self-pity, hating himself, or making excuses.)

Did your spouse show *this* kind of regret for their sexual or romantic wrongdoing? With most strayers, true repentance takes time and much self-reflection. However, if you didn't see your partner soften toward you and the Lord and eventually exhibit the above attitudes and actions, then you likely didn't witness genuine repentance.

Tears of regret are not enough. A person can hate the guilt, shame, or even themselves without being truly repentant over the sin. Self-loathing only magnifies a person's drive to use unhealthy coping strategies. A person needs to hate the sin itself and see it from God's vantage point—as damaging to their spirit, as well as their relationship with God and loved ones.

> A person can hate the guilt, shame, or even themselves without being truly repentant over the sin.

There is a reason we are told in Scripture, "Love must be sincere. Detest what is evil; cling to what is good" (Romans 12:9).

Abhorring the sin of infidelity, instead of merely hating the guilt, can motivate the unfaithful to undertake the deeper work necessary for lasting change.

John the Baptist challenged his listeners, "Produce fruit in keeping with repentance" (Luke 3:8, NIV). Other translations say to bring "fruit consistent with" or "worthy of" repentance. This means there should be *tangible evidence* of authentic heart change, not just words or tears.

Vertical Repentance First

Jesus expands on true repentance in Luke 15 with the parable of the Prodigal Son. The son demands his inheritance early and squanders it in a "distant country" on reckless living—likely including sexual sin. When a severe famine hits, he's left broke and desperate. Reduced to feeding pigs—a deeply shameful task for a Jew—he still finds no satisfaction. In recovery terms, he had "hit bottom."

"Then when he came to himself" (Luke 15:17, TAB) (other translations say "came to his senses"), he faced the reality of his situation and realized how much better he had it when he was in right relationship with his father.

A truly repentant person needs to have such a progression. They must hit bottom, see the wrongness of their pursuits, and desire to repair the damage. In the son's case, he awakens from his empty fantasy and gets in touch with who he truly is—the son of a loving father, the person God intended him to be.

He decides to "get up" and "go to my father." This signifies that he does more than think about his options. He *acts on* his conviction by rising out of the grime and embarking on a journey toward his father. In other words, he leaves behind his desperate, sinful life and sets out on a long journey to reconcile with his dad.

Along the way, the son rehearses what he wants to say to his father: "Father, I have sinned against heaven and in your sight" (vs.18). He admits that what he's done is sinful. It was wrong. Bad. Terrible. In God's eyes and his father's eyes. No mere "I made a mistake" or "I slipped up." A truly repentant person names what they've done for what it is. They are humble and contrite.

Notice that the Prodigal first expresses repentance toward God (in heaven) before addressing the father he betrayed. This order is significant. Lasting and meaningful repentance must begin vertically, with God, before it can truly impact horizontal relationships.

The son also admits he no longer deserves the rights of a son and humbly plans to ask for a place as a hired servant. His attitude reflects true contrition—the opposite of entitlement.

Sincere Heart Change

Once a Betrandoned spouse truly distinguishes Genuine Repentance from fake imitations, they experience a measure of freedom. They realize that genuine repentance must begin with their partner's relationship with God, which is not something a betrayed spouse can control. All we can do is be honest about our feelings, set appropriate boundaries, and wait and see. No efforts to be perfect or shame the betrayer would have done the trick.

I remember casually speaking with a family law attorney at a church event as our divorce drew near, hoping for some guidance. He told me, "I never see these situations work out unless the unfaithful one is totally broken and willing to do whatever it takes to rebuild the marriage." I saw no such spirit in James. Though his words weren't what I wanted to hear, they forced me to face reality and doused my lingering hopes for a last-minute change of heart.

It is helpful to understand that unless an unfaithful spouse experiences a sincere change of heart, your chances of further heartbreak are all but certain. Therefore, instead of remaining in turmoil over feelings of betrayal and abandonment, you can embrace the old saying, "Not Rejection—Protection."

I hope this discussion helps you overcome that lingering longing for someone who no longer exists. If your spouse never fully repented, accepted personal responsibility, sought in-depth healing, and made a heartfelt turn-around, God wants you to see what he sees—a partner with a hardened heart. God can use this reality to deliver you from an unsafe person and direct you toward new purposes for your life. You've been spared the bondage that would have ensued had you remained tied to an unloving, unrepentant spouse who refused to grow.

Example of the Corinthian Church

Another powerful example of genuine repentance appears in the Corinthian church. Paul discovered that the church was tolerating blatant sexual sin—a man who was involved in an incestuous relationship with his stepmother. Rather than confronting him, the church turned a blind eye, allowing him to continue his double life unchallenged.

While Paul may not have known the man personally, he had a close relationship with the church. He sternly rebuked them for enabling such behavior, warning that unchecked sin can spread like a virus, giving others silent permission to do the same. He also recognized how dangerous it was for the man himself to persist in sin, presuming he could still maintain right standing with God.

How about you? Were you too tolerant of a partner's signs of cheating for fear of inviting an adverse reaction from your spouse?

Paul wrote a stern letter rebuking the Corinthians for allowing a brazenly sinning man to remain in their fellowship without objection. His words struck a nerve. Confronted with their tolerance of immorality, the church responded with repentance and took Paul's bold but necessary advice: they removed the man from their midst, hoping it would prompt his own repentance. It was likely an uncomfortable decision both for Paul and the congregation. However, they accepted the correction and took the necessary action. Paul later learns of their obedience and writes:

> "And now I rejoice, not because you were made sorrowful, but because your sorrow led you to repentance. For you felt the sorrow that God had intended, and so were not harmed in any way by us. Godly sorrow brings repentance that leads to salvation without regret, but worldly sorrow brings death" (2 Corinthians 7:9–10).

He distinguishes between *godly sorrow* over sin, which brings true reformation and relief without regretting the decision to repent, and *worldly sorrow,* which reflects the gloom that accompanies not being right with God. See the difference in the chart below:

GODLY REPENTANCE	SHALLOW REPENTANCE
Earnestness	Lackluster Attitude
Eagerness to apologize	Reluctance to admit fault
Indignation toward the sin	Indignation toward victim/accuser
Alarm over seriousness of offense	Dismissive re: seriousness of offense
Longing to repair the damage	Dragging their heels
Zeal to make things right	Little effort to make things right
Vindication - getting right with God	Self-justification

What about your ex-spouse? Did they demonstrate the attitudes associated with Godly Repentance as described in 2 Corinthians 7:10, or Shallow Repentance? If you did not observe these efforts in your former partner, it may take time to accept, but you will be better off not living with someone whose heart has not changed.

The good news is that later, the man in question repented of his ways, stopped living in sin, and the church accepted him back into its fold.[4]

Example of David's Repentance

Another example of genuine repentance is King David, who describes his feelings when his sin remained hidden.

> "When I kept silent, my bones became brittle from my groaning all day long. For day and night Your hand was heavy upon me; my strength was drained as in the summer heat" (Psalm 32:3–4).

This passage reflects the conviction of the Holy Spirit and a person's openness to God. Justified sin hardens the heart, but David couldn't escape his guilt. He was miserable carrying his secret, and in Psalm 51, he pleads with God for mercy and cleansing. He calls his actions "evil" and prays, "Create in me a clean heart and renew a right spirit within me" (v. 10). David describes the proper posture of repentance: a broken spirit and contrite heart (v. 17). In summary:

- He was miserable in his secrecy.
- He begged for mercy.
- His strength was drained.

- He named his sin "evil."
- His spirit was broken.
- He had a contrite heart.

If your spouse was not remorseful towards you and the Lord in these ways, you were heading for more suffering than you've already endured. One day, you will be grateful for the Lord's gracious deliverance.

I hope you can see from the examples of the Prodigal Son, the Corinthian church, and King David what Genuine Repentance in mind, heart, and attitude looks like. May you find peace knowing that unless you saw evidence of the heart changes in your ex-spouse as described in this chapter, you've been spared a life of misery. Your emotional efforts are best focused on finding a way to move forward with your life.

Empathy and Amends: The Example of Judah

Finally, I want to highlight two other important qualities of genuine repentance: *empathy* for the wounded one(s) and an effort to *make amends*.

One Christmas, I was curious as to why God the Father chose to send his Son through the lineage of Judah. Why not Joseph, the brother who saved his family from starvation and preserved the Jewish people? That question led me back to Genesis to study the life of this lesser celebrated brother.

Judah's transformation—from scheming betrayer to a compassionate advocate—offers a powerful picture of redemptive change.

To set the stage: Jacob had two sons from his favored wife, Rachel—Joseph and Benjamin. Judah and his half-brothers grew jealous of the special attention their father gave to Joseph. When Joseph was still a teenager, the brothers plotted to kill him. But at the last moment, Judah intervened. Rather than shed his blood, he suggested they sell Joseph to passing merchants headed to Egypt (a hint of Judah's leadership potential, even while participating in wrongdoing). After the sale, they slaughtered a goat, dipped Joseph's multicolored coat in its blood, and tricked their father into believing a wild animal had killed him.

Years later, when Joseph rose to power in Egypt, a famine struck the land, and ten of the brothers went to Egypt to trade goods for grain.

Joseph tested them to see if they had changed their ways. The final test resulted in Joseph demanding that Benjamin be kept as his slave.

The brothers were filled with horror, assuming Joseph's tough testing was a sign of God's judgment on them for betraying Joseph and lying about it to their father. This is where Judah's true change of heart really shines. Judah requests a private meeting with Joseph and says:

> "Now therefore when I come to your servant my father, and the lad is not with us, when his *life is bound up in the lad's life*, and *his soul is knit with the lad's soul*, when he sees the lad is not with us, *he will die*; and your servants will be *responsible* for his death and will bring down the gray hairs of your servant our father *with sorrow* to Sheol (the place of the dead)" (Genesis 44:30–31, TAB, 1965, italics added).

Do you see Judah's empathy toward his father here? He explains how devastating it would be for his father to lose Benjamin, the son of his favored wife, after enduring so much pain from losing Joseph. He recognizes Jacob's deep attachment to his surviving son, Benjamin, without a trace of jealousy. He shows concern for his father's emotional state and empathizes with his father's grief. He emphasizes that if Jacob were to lose Benjamin, he and his brothers would bear the weight of their father's immediate demise.

Rather than cause Jacob further heartache, Judah offers his own life in exchange for Benjamin's, volunteering to become a lifelong slave in Egypt—a tangible act of restitution for his past wrongs.

Joseph, already deeply moved after overhearing his brothers express regret and now seeing Judah's empathy for their father, had undeniable evidence of true heart change. When Judah offered to give up his freedom for Benjamin's sake, Joseph could no longer hold back. He broke down and wept so loudly that everyone in the palace heard him.

When I re-read this story, I, too, wept. Judah's sorrow for his past betrayal and sincere compassion for the father he had once deceived were so profound that he was willing to sacrifice his freedom in place of his younger brother's potential bondage. This is genuine repentance in action.

No wonder, despite Judah's earlier failures, God chose to send the Messiah, Jesus, through his lineage. Judah's offer was a foretaste of Jesus, who offered his life "as a ransom for many" (Mark 10:45).

The Holy Spirit in Action

Sometimes, an unfaithful spouse eventually experiences a "come-to-Jesus" moment. By that time, you may have already been divorced and lived with the grief and consequences of a Post-Affair Divorce for an extended period, regardless of whether you remarried or not.

I had the privilege of attending a meeting with "Carol" (the pastor's wife from Chapter 8) and her ex-husband, "Michael." He was initially dismissive about the gravity of his adultery. He attempted several times to re-enter the ministry with his new wife, the affair partner. He even made gestures of shallow repentance, sending less-than-meaningful letters to the many people he had let down.

However, ten years later, he experienced an encounter with the Lord that forced him to feel the full weight of his sin. He reported that the Holy Spirit overwhelmed him with his presence, instilling a deep sense of remorse and horror over what he had done years before. He broke down and wept, finally admitting to God and himself how wrong he had been. Shortly thereafter, he asked to meet with his ex-wife to allow her a chance to express her hurt regarding what he had done to her. He suggested that she decide who she would like to have present. She invited her pastor and me.

Carol and I met two weeks beforehand to discuss what she wanted to say to him. I encouraged her to write out her thoughts so she wouldn't become overwhelmed and unable to express herself. She put a great deal of thought into crafting her letter.

I wasn't sure what to expect at the meeting. He invited her to say whatever she needed to. After she tearfully read her letter, he validated her pain and told her she'd been "a good wife" who didn't deserve what he'd done. In fact, he wanted her to know that he didn't deserve forgiveness; he "deserved hell." He shared the story of the Holy Spirit's conviction of him and showed her much compassion. As we walked out of the church office, the pastor quietly said to me, "I've never had a meeting like *that* one before," indicating it is rare to see an adulterer offer sincere apologies so many years later.

I'm not claiming that this remedied all the harm he inflicted on his wife, children, and parishioners. I share this story to illustrate that only the Holy Spirit can pierce the delusional thinking of a self-justifying strayer enough to bring them to their knees, convict them of their sin, and produce the kind of brokenness that leads to genuine repentance.

> Only the Holy Spirit can pierce the delusional thinking of a self-justifying strayer enough to bring them to their knees.

You Never Know

Back to the story of when James swore he'd never ask for my forgiveness. Twenty-two years later, we found ourselves seated next to each other at a nephew's wedding reception. As we joked about a few silly disagreements from our early marriage, he suddenly turned to me and said, "I'm sorry I hurt you." I nearly fell off my chair. He then got up to mingle with other guests he knew.

It wasn't the in-depth apology I might have hoped for, as he had no real understanding of how much I had suffered. To my knowledge, he was unaware of my PTSD, nightmares, inability to work, suicidal ideation, or the depth of my grief. So, I didn't mistake his words for deep, heartfelt repentance. But still, it was something—a gesture I didn't expect. And for that, I was grateful.

After that, I felt comfortable enough to start praying for him again, as I had stopped praying for him for many years because it had occupied too much of my mind. I had a new husband, kids, friends, clients, and parishioners to focus my attention and prayers upon.

I imagine many of you would welcome a sincere apology from your betraying spouse, even if it came years later. The sting of rejection and abandonment can linger for a very long time. And any word of regret from an offending ex-partner would help.

Sadly, most of us will never hear the words of sorrow, compassion, or concern from our former spouses that we deserve. At least not in this life.

You may feel pressured in Christian circles to quickly forgive your betrayer, under the illusion that this will resolve all your woes and make your hurts disappear. Yet, how can you pardon your wayward spouse for all the wrongs that have negatively altered your life and your children's lives forever? If you're like me, you understand that it isn't that simple. Not for such profound and personal injuries.

Only God can absolve such sin. In the meantime, to find peace, we must find ways to release our angst and allow the Lord to repurpose our emotional energies for more productive uses.

You may wonder how to cope with the damage caused by an unchanged betrayer. The next two chapters will guide you toward finding peace within yourself, without minimizing or dishonoring your pain. But first, we'll explore the kinds of forgiveness that can be unrealistic or even harmful.

Chapter 23

Misconceptions About Forgiving

> He who conceals his sins will not prosper,
> but whoever confesses and renounces them will find mercy.
> ~Proverbs 28:13

Betty slinked into my home office, smiling, yet brows furrowed. Ten years earlier, she'd discovered evidence that her husband had been sexually involved with a woman at work. She left him a voicemail, letting him know what she'd found. That evening, he waltzed through the front door the day of her anguished discovery, faking eagerness to see her. Betty's first words to him were, "I forgive you!" Eyebrows raised, he paused momentarily, then wrapped her in his arms, relieved he hadn't had to face her well-deserved wrath.

Grateful for his warm response to her pronouncement, she sucked in her breath and said nothing more. Nor did he invite further discussion on the painful subject. She had done her Christian duty and forgiven him. On his part, he broke things off with the other woman and remained faithful over the ensuing years. And that was that.

Only "that" became an unseen, festering boil beneath the surface—tender, painful, and ever-present. It flinched when pastors mentioned "adultery" in sermons and throbbed during TV shows that romanticized office affairs.

Their delicate "no-talk" dance maintained the peace of their superficial interactions. Yet, over time, the infected boil swelled and became unbearable. Depressed internally but appearing cheerful externally, she deceived everyone into believing she was fine, including her husband.

When she could no longer bear the pain, she sought my counsel. Over several sessions, I assisted this sweet, conflict-avoidant woman in unpacking her accumulated unprocessed sorrow and validated the unspoken anger she'd buried underground for many years. She sobbed as the hurt poured out of her.

When she was ready, I encouraged her to invite her seemingly clueless husband to join her in therapy. But he wasn't as unaware as she'd assumed. I'll never forget when a newly empowered Betty finally voiced the pain she had carried for so many years—and how her quietly attentive husband listened.

He had sensed the weight she bore but had been too afraid to "poke the boil," fearing the eruption of molten pain that might follow. As she spoke, he broke down in tears. He, too, had been living in torment—not from her silence, but from the unspoken guilt and shame over what he'd done.

Instead of reacting with defensiveness, he melted with relief. I had to blink back my own tears as he gently held her, whispering words of empathy, understanding, and regret. I gently excused myself, giving them space to embrace the moment—and myself a chance to cry.

This was the first time I witnessed the unnecessary harm caused by Premature Forgiveness. This couple had deprived themselves of ten years of closeness and repair simply because they were too frightened to speak the uncomfortable, messy truth to one another. Fortunately, they still loved each other enough to mend the damage and learn to communicate with each other more authentically.

Not all such stories end like this. However, when a betrayed spouse forgives too quickly, it reinforces unhealthy avoidance dynamics that lead to depression, distance, and tension, often resulting in a cold-war stand-off, further infidelities, and/or the end of the marriage.

THREE KINDS OF FORGIVENESS

I have more than 60 books on the subject of forgiveness on my office bookshelves. I can't fully address such a complex topic in just two chapters. However, to explore this aspect of recovery for Betrandoned spouses, I have distilled the act of forgiving intimate injuries into three basic categories:

1. Premature Forgiveness
2. Reconciling Forgiveness
3. Unilateral Forgiveness

What follows is designed to help you discern the difference between healthy and unhealthy ways of responding to the natural, lingering resentment that betrayal often leaves behind. The chart below provides a visual overview of these three paths.

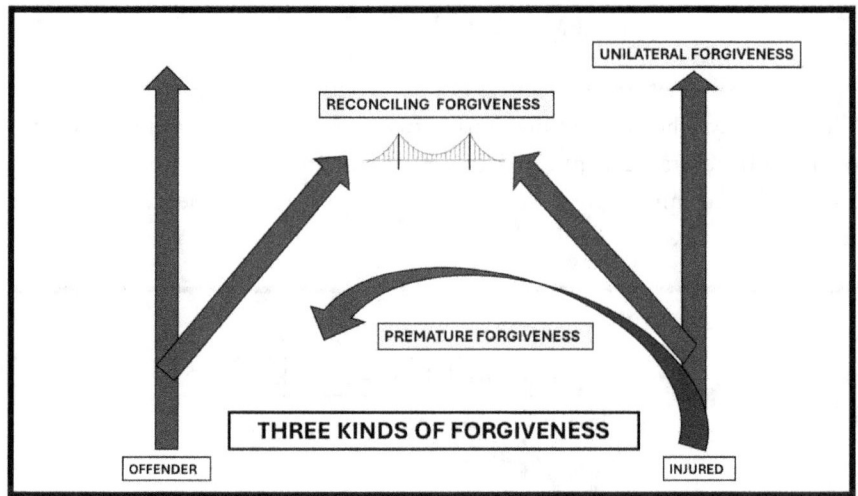

Notice how the arrow for *Premature Forgiveness* reflects an overreach by the injured party—stretching toward reconciliation before it's safe or warranted. The arrows for *Reconciling Forgiveness* converge, eventually meeting to rebuild a bridge of trust and connection. In contrast, the parallel arrows for *Unilateral Forgiveness* never intersect. This kind of one-way forgiveness means the offender and the injured party are on separate journeys, with no restoration of trust or relationship.

My aim in this chapter is to clear up common misconceptions about this all-important topic—without downplaying its healing power. As a follower of Jesus, I deeply believe in the call to forgive as Christ has forgiven us. Yet, forgiving "those who trespass against us" isn't a simple formula to apply without wisdom and care. When it comes to serious offenses between intimate partners, forgiveness is often mishandled—especially in Christian circles.

As forgiveness researcher Beverly Flanigan states, "To be betrayed by a stranger is one thing. To be morally wounded by one you have loved is quite another."[1] These wounds penetrate deeper than most other offenses. Moral injuries violate spoken or assumed agreements between intimate people.

She defines an "unforgivable injury" as "a profound and irreversible assault on the fundamental belief system of the person who has been injured."[2] She explains that this kind of offense shatters our belief in our partner, ourselves, and our beliefs about God and how the world works.[3]

This is why intimate injuries are so difficult to resolve.

In Betty's case, Premature Forgiveness caused her to gloss over her husband's offense, leading to a decade of personal misery and a serious disconnection in their marriage. Let's take a closer look at what it really means to forgive too quickly—and why it can do more harm than good.

PREMATURE FORGIVENESS

In my view, Premature Forgiveness is a dysfunctional application of what the Lord intended when he instructed us to forgive serious sins committed against us. Some believers treat quick forgiveness as a cure-all for wounds, assuming Jesus endorsed immediate forgiveness in every situation. They view it as the noblest, most obedient choice.

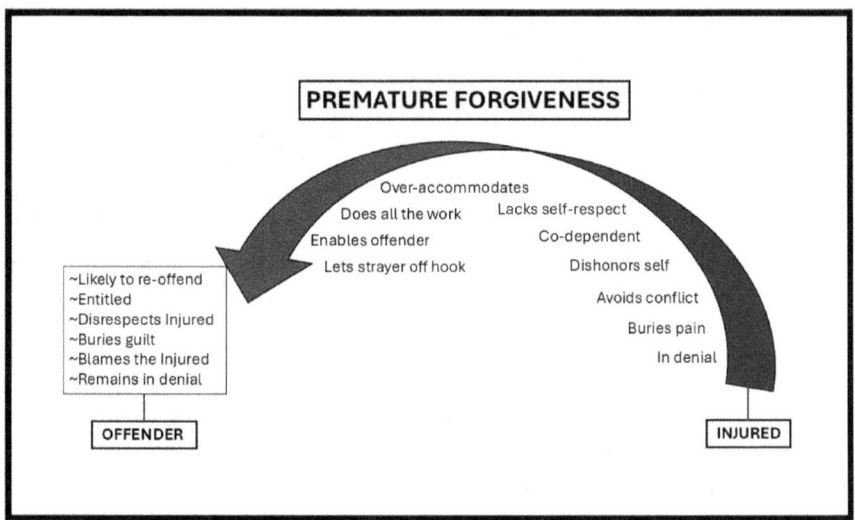

Quick forgiveness is best reserved for minor infractions, small "mistakes," unintentional offenses, personality quirks, or faults of neighbors and acquaintances. Over the years, hopefully, you've developed the discipline of extending grace and forgiveness to the imperfect people in your life.

However, when it comes to major, intimate, and intentional transgressions, the parties must engage in a more measured process, either together for Reconciling Forgiveness or separately for Unilateral Forgiveness. In my view, both the offended and the offender are short-changed when a seriously violated person puts on the Band-Aid of Instant Forgiveness—a suppressant that merely shoves the pain underground.

Premature Forgiveness often reinforces unhealthy dynamics like codependency, denial, and inauthentic relating. As shown in the previous diagram, the Premature Forgiveness line nearly spans the entire chart—symbolizing the injured spouse doing 90% of the work while the offender contributes little. When wounded partners over-function like this, no one wins. Both individuals and the relationship suffer.

Too often, well-meaning Christian communities pressure victims to forgive prematurely, shifting the responsibility for healing onto the injured party and giving the unrepentant offender a free pass. This not only deepens the wound but also undermines the betrayer's accountability.

THE DAMAGE CAUSED BY PREMATURE FORGIVENESS

DAMAGE TO THE INJURED	DAMAGE TO THE OFFENDER
Minimizes the injury	Keeps offender in denial of damage caused
Damages self-respect	Reinforces disrespect for the offended
Buries feelings – leads to depression	Remains in deception about nature of offense
Robs injured of processing grief and hurt	Robs offender of healthy repentance
Reinforces co-dependency	Likely keeps acting out, hurting others
Teaches to ignore or deny feelings	Allows a lack of accountability
Overaccommodates for offender	No avenue to relieve conscience
Fails to restore dignity	Feels self-pity rather than true remorse
Enables bad behavior	Believes own rationalizations
Reinforces pleasing/appeasing of others	May sear conscience
Damages self-esteem	No outlet for own grief or sorrow for wrongs
Lets offender off the hook	Lacks self-reflection
Feels false guilt/responsibility for offense	Doesn't accept personal responsibility

Not only does Premature Forgiveness undermine each person's need to grow and achieve true emotional maturity, but it also deprives them of the skills they need to re-bond and move forward together as a couple in a healthy way.

The chart below contains some of the damage that Premature Forgiveness causes to a marriage after a serious infraction:

DAMAGE TO THE RELATIONSHIP
Robs a couple from taking steps toward genuine repair
Reinforces conflict avoidance in both parties
Maintains a lack of authentic relating
Leads to a lack of resolution
Often results in distance and eventual divorce

If you tried to mend your spouse's breach with quick forgiveness, you may have unintentionally covered over their wrongdoing, buried your own anger and grief, and sent a message that their betrayal was tolerable. Looking back, I know I did exactly that.

In my eagerness to accept James's initial yet temporary re-engagement with me after his first break-up with the other woman, I extended total forgiveness too soon—before I had fully processed my rightful anger and grief. I returned from my hiatus to Hawaii still wearing my "understanding therapist" hat, which made it harder to access my voice as the "violated spouse."

My quick extension of grace spared him a clear-eyed view of my agony and the harm he had caused me and our children. Looking back, I saw almost no evidence that he fully embraced his responsibility in the matter, faced the depth of the wrongness of his choices, was broken before the Lord, or had explored the roots of his misbehavior.

Deep down, I sensed that he still felt justified by what he'd done and blamed our marriage (i.e., me) for the reasons he sought an outside romance. Consequently, his temporary regret didn't last long, plunging me into more profound grief and trauma than before.

Don't let others, including a pastor, pressure you into quickly "forgiving" (i.e., re-trusting, absolving, or reconciling with) an unfaithful spouse without holding out for genuine change. It's wise to adopt a "wait and see" attitude before deciding whether to pursue Reconciling or Unilateral Forgiveness with your spouse.

RECONCILING FORGIVENESS

While Premature Forgiveness requires little to nothing from the betrayer, Reconciling Forgiveness is a transactional process that requires mutual engagement from both the offender and the offended. This does not mean the offended one has no faults in all aspects of the relationship. But when it comes to major fractures in a marriage, such as infidelity, the serious breach must be addressed first before the smaller issues can be effectively resolved.

Still, as believers, how do we merge the challenge of taking time for a healthy process with the many Scriptures that command us to forgive those who sin against us?

Let's examine some of these Scriptures in their original context.

Assess the Betrayer

As we discussed in the previous chapter, the book of Genesis recounts how Joseph was betrayed by his jealous half-brothers when they threw him into a pit and planned to murder him. Instead, and nearly as awful, they sold him to slave traders heading for Egypt and lied to their father that an animal had killed him. Some 20 years later, when a famine struck the land, the brothers went to Egypt to buy grain. They didn't recognize Joseph, who had been carefully groomed to resemble an Egyptian ruler.

Rather than immediately forgiving their terrible betrayals, he put them through a series of tests to determine whether they had truly repented for their wrongs against him and their grieving father. Only after witnessing their sorrow, hearing their admissions of guilt, and observing tangible signs of repentance did Joseph reveal his identity, weep, and offer forgiveness.

This account stands in direct contrast to Premature Forgiveness. Joseph waited and watched for genuine heart change before making himself vulnerable, extending forgiveness, and reconciling with his brothers.

No instant forgiveness here.

Confront the Betrayer

Matthew 18 instructs the offended one to begin by having a serious private conversation with the offender. Notice all the "*if's*":

> "*If* your brother sins against you, go and confront him privately. *If* he listens to you, you have won your brother over.

> "But *if* he will not listen, take one or two others along, so that 'every matter may be established by the testimony of two or three witnesses.' *If* he refuses to listen to them, tell it to the church. And *if* he refuses to listen even to the church, regard him as you would a pagan or a tax collector" (Matthew 18:15–17, emphasis added).

"*If* he listens to you..." Jesus' words imply that immediate forgiveness is not demanded when the offender refuses to listen. Heartfelt listening involves hearing you out, validating your pain, and taking personal responsibility for the wrongness of their offense(s). If that doesn't happen, Jesus encourages us to bring in others. And if the offender still refuses to listen, Scripture says the person should be treated like an unbeliever.

Applied to infidelity, if your straying spouse refuses to listen with humility and contrition, it is right to involve trusted others. And if they still won't admit fault or take steps toward meaningful change, it is biblically acceptable to treat them as an unbeliever—and ask them to leave.

> Heartfelt listening involves hearing you out, validating your pain, and taking personal responsibility for the wrongness of their offense(s).

Did this happen in your situation? Or do you wish it had? Every unfaithful, unrepentant person needs to be lovingly but firmly confronted by people courageous enough to risk the relationship by speaking the truth. Sometimes this kind of confrontation awakens a wayward spouse. But if their heart is already hardened, they will likely resent anyone who challenges them. In that case, Scripture permits us to regard them as we would an unbeliever.

That is a common theme in many parables about forgiving others: We should confront our offenders and offer forgiveness to those who listen to us, accept personal responsibility for their offenses, and show evidence of repentance. Otherwise, we should not tolerate serious sins like sexual betrayal and abuse.

Now ask yourself: did your unfaithful spouse show contrition and beg you for mercy? Did he or she accept responsibility for the "debt" owed to you? Did your wayward spouse offer to work hard in therapy and make it up to you in both tangible and intangible ways? And did they follow through on their promises? Did your partner humbly examine themselves and listen to your sorrow with compassion and empathy? Did they demonstrate a tender heart toward the Lord and a willingness to get right with him?

Or did your spouse merely display self-pity, dismiss you and others, and then blame you or the marriage for his or her actions? Or, even worse, did they stonewall you or suddenly leave without providing any explanation?

The Necessity of Repentance for Repair

Similar to Matthew 18, there is a corresponding passage in Luke where Jesus, again, includes three significant "*if's*."

> "*If* your brother or sister sins against you, rebuke them; and *if* they repent, forgive them. Even *if* they sin against you seven times in a day and seven times come back to you saying 'I repent,' you must forgive them." (Luke 17:3–4, NIV, emphasis added).

From these verses, Jesus makes it clear that we must forgive an offender who responds to our rebuke and sincerely repents. However, repentance involves more than merely stating the words, "I repent." As I mentioned in the last chapter, the offender must genuinely mean it and "produce fruit" (evidence in attitude and deed) of their repentance. As John the Baptist said,

> "So produce fruit that is consistent with repentance [demonstrating new behavior that proves a change of heart, and a conscious decision to turn away from sin]" (Matthew 3:8, AMP, brackets included in the translation).

I'm not suggesting that the phrase "if he repents" gives us permission to withhold forgiveness indefinitely. Holding onto long-term grudges eventually harms us more than those who hurt us. For the sake of our own mental and spiritual health and our relationship with our children, we will need to release resentment in time. But that release doesn't lead to a restored closeness.

In truth, unrepentant people are not suitable candidates for Reconciling Forgiveness.

The diagram for Reconciling Forgiveness shows two lines, representing the paths of the Offender and the Injured one, angled at approximately 45 degrees toward each other. Moving upward to the bridge of repair requires a collaborative effort from both individuals.

While we examined true and false repentance in Chapter 22, the upward "repentant" acrostic in the following diagram offers a straightforward way to recall some of the elements of genuine repentance that we should observe in a reasonably "safe-to-re-trust" spouse before we even consider the path of repair.

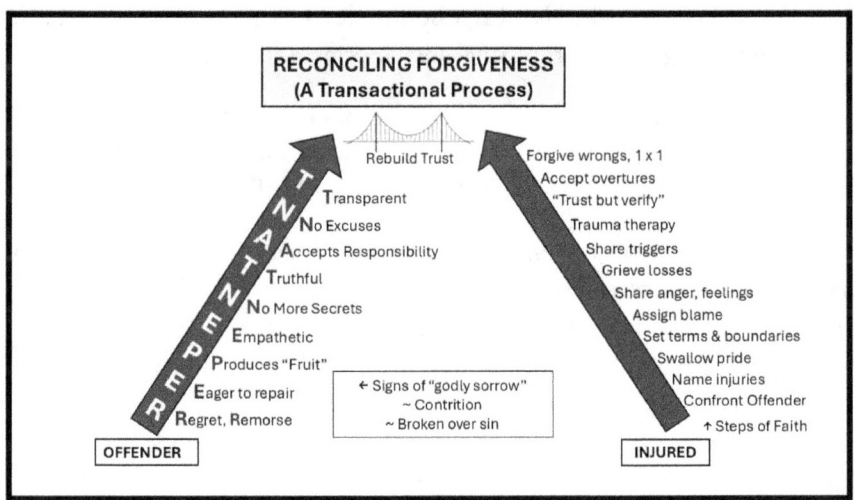

The betrayed Christian spouse needs to adopt attitudes of self-respect (such as, "I didn't deserve this" and "I'll guard my heart until I see budding evidence of repentance") without resorting to abusive rage ("I hate you, you dirty rotten pig!"), undignified capitulation ("Okay, I'll do whatever you want"), or begging ("Please stay with me! I promise I'll change!").[4]

The most successful reconciliations after infidelity are those in which the betrayed spouse establishes firm boundaries—and holds them—and the unfaithful partner responds with compassion and a willingness to meet those requests without resistance.

If you struggled to hold the line on things like zero contact with the affair partner, eliminating social media, requiring professional counseling, requesting a full disclosure of the betrayal, or even asking for a polygraph in the case of sexual addiction, you may feel shame or regret. The truth is, a genuinely repentant spouse would have agreed to do these things freely, without needing to be pushed.

I know how difficult it is to stand up to a defiant, rationalizing spouse. And, if you lacked sufficient information about the betrayal, you may have underestimated the effort required to combat an invisible adversary.

> If your spouse had been genuinely repentant, they would not have resisted you so strongly.

For those who were too afraid of rejection to be firm with your wayward spouse, don't be too hard on yourself. You were more attached to your partner than they were to you. If your spouse had been genuinely repentant, they would not have resisted you so strongly. Use this lesson to develop greater trust in your intuition and strengthen your spiritual and emotional resilience for the future.

> "Therefore take up the full armor of God, so that when the day of evil comes, you will be able to *stand your ground*, and having done everything, to *stand*" (Ephesians 6:13, emphasis added).

Reconciling Forgiveness is only possible when both partners commit to an open, honest, and respectful journey—one step at a time. I've helped many couples reach this place. When a couple approaches the healing process with humility, receptivity, and outside support, the relationship can often be restored and even strengthened.

Since you're reading this book, I assume you didn't witness sincere, lasting repentance from your unfaithful spouse. I share the requirements for Reconciling Forgiveness and the dangers of Premature Forgiveness, so you can better understand why you couldn't mend your marriage alone.

What's a Betrandoned Spouse to Do?

How do you forgive a deceitful spouse who abandoned your marriage and isn't sorry? Or who shows little concern for the damage they've caused? It's painfully difficult to extend forgiveness to someone who refuses to accept responsibility—or who disappears instead of helping you carry the weight of your grief.

It can feel overwhelming to imagine letting go of all of the hurt that marred your memories and stole your future dreams. And if your callous spouse blamed you for their infidelity and took off with a new lover, you may wonder, "Why on earth should I forgive them?" Especially if they keep neglecting your children or trying to turn them against you.

What about the tone-deaf ex—or soon-to-be ex—who insists your kids warmly embrace their lover—the person who helped destroy your family? How do you forgive that? These feel like unforgivable betrayals no one should have to bear, let alone release.

And what do you do with the friends, relatives, or church communities who extend grace to your ex while ignoring the fact that they refused accountability, bypassed restoration, and made no effort to make amends?

It's even more painful to watch the illicit couple marry and expect everyone to pretend it's fine and move on. Add in post-settlement skirmishes that drag on for months or years, and it's no wonder you feel stuck when people tell you to "just forgive."

The fallout from a Post-Affair Divorce resembles a dirty flood that spreads wide and long. It sullies your past, stains your present, and casts a slimy shadow over your future. Given that infidelity and one-sided divorce are among the most disillusioning and painful experiences we can endure in life, you may wonder if forgiving a deceitful, rejecting spouse is wise or even possible.

If the only way to heal and find internal peace is through forgiveness, you might wonder how to do this without exposing yourself to further hurt or dishonoring your loss and pain.

Despite such wide-ranging injuries, you still have a choice—a way to reclaim your power, regain stability, and stop allowing the angst over your former spouse to drain your emotional reserves. In the next chapter, we will explore how to forgive your betrayer without betraying yourself in the process.

Chapter 24

Forgiving Your Betrayer Without Betraying Yourself

> The purpose of remembering is not to hold on but to release
> and in forgiveness to move forward lighter and freer.
> ~Dr. Jill Hubbard[1]

Psychology seems to have finally caught up with Christianity, regarding seeing the benefits and value of forgiving those who offend us. Researchers have discovered the downsides of holding onto bitterness and the upsides of forgiving.

Several academic institutions have launched forgiveness initiatives, such as the International Forgiveness Institute at the University of Wisconsin–Madison and the Stanford Forgiveness Project. Backed by foundation grants and fueled by hope, hundreds of studies in the fields of medicine, mental health, and the social sciences affirm the remarkable power of forgiveness to lower blood pressure, reduce stress and depression, boost the immune system, and increase feelings of compassion and optimism—even among the deeply traumatized.[2]

Yet even well-meaning Christians hold misconceptions about how to forgive others in a way that is both emotionally healing and spiritually grounded—without inviting further mistreatment or minimizing their own wounds.

As discussed in the previous chapter, Premature Forgiveness is a misguided way of sweeping our wounds under the rug because it shortchanges everyone from working through serious injuries authentically.

When it comes to major transgressions, Reconciling Forgiveness should be reserved for the truly penitent who demonstrate evidence of genuine heart change, not for those who justify their wrongs and refuse to make amends. A person can't reconcile with an offender who is missing in action.

So, if Premature Forgiveness is harmful and Reconciling Forgiveness is not available, what's a Betrandoned spouse to do?

Some of you may no longer feel love for your partner after enduring infidelity, mistreatment, or addiction. For you, divorce might have brought an unexpected sense of relief.

Others may ironically feel a lingering mix of love and hate toward your ex-spouse for betraying and forsaking you. In both cases, whether relieved or aggravatingly attached—it will take time and intentional effort to release the natural animosity you feel toward a life partner who walked away for another person, lifestyle, or habit.

Holding onto resentment creates distress in our bodies and occupies space in our minds that could be used more productively. Bitterness will never bring back what you lost. It won't help you resolve the unfinished business between you or empower you to live a better life. Instead, long-term resentment drains your vitality much like conscious sin steals your peace.

> Long-term resentment drains your vitality in the same way that conscious sin steals your peace.

That said, anger towards abusive or unfaithful violations has its place. Without it, we're more likely to internalize their betrayal as a reflection of our worth, believing we somehow deserved to be discarded. To prevent their rejection from defining us, we must cut ourselves loose from the rusty anchor of vitriol that keeps us "storm-tossed and not comforted" (Isaiah 54). Only then can we navigate towards still waters where we can feel safe, refuel, and be restored.

Fear of Letting Down Our Guard

Most of us know that if we nurse our grudges, they won't heal. But we sometimes fear that if we let them go, we won't have the means to protect our hearts, soothe our sores, or balance the scales. Sometimes, injured spouses get stuck in the anger stage of grief. The thought of forgiving an unfaithful, alienated spouse can feel dangerous. After all, the concern is that, without our anger, we won't have anything to shield us from further hurt. So, we cling to our resentments and use them as bricks to build bitter walls of protection, defending ourselves from the lies and attacks of our former spouse or as a bulwark against our own negative self-talk.

We draw a certain energy from anger. However, anger is only meant to alert us when our rights have been violated and our boundaries crossed. Once we see the offense, feel the pain, and experience healthy indignation over the wrong, the clouds should clear, allowing us to see a way forward. Anger was never meant to be our long-term protector. It was intended to provide us with insight and a path to avoid further harm.

> Anger was never meant to be our long-term protector. It was meant to provide us with insight and a path to avoid further harm.

In other words, anger is a phase we must walk *through*, but not dwell in. Resentment turns rancid when we stew in it too long. You've likely encountered someone bitter and spiteful and thought, *Lord, spare me! Don't let me become like them!* Yet, if we don't find a way to let go of our festering resentments, we risk becoming the very person we fear.

UNILATERAL FORGIVENESS

Intimate betrayal and rejection slice us to the core like few other experiences in life. Therefore, we must discover a way to attain peace after the storm without dishonoring ourselves. We need a path forward that doesn't compel us to pretend our partner's violations didn't occur or force us to embrace a porcupine spouse who continues to zing us with their quills.

When Premature Forgiveness only reinforces avoidance patterns, and Reconciling Forgiveness is not appropriate with an unsafe person, Betrandoned spouses are left with a third, wrenching but healthy option: **Unilateral Forgiveness.** This one-way process involves releasing our resentment over the losses and offenses tied to an affair-sparked divorce.

Our model for this type of forgiveness is Jesus Christ on the cross. Looking down at his crucifiers and those gambling for his robe, and, despite his pain, he uttered those famous words:

> "Father, forgive them, for they do not know what they are doing" (Luke 23:34).

Jesus didn't wait for them to respond or repent. He simply asked the Father to forgive his enemies for their crimes against him. They were self-absorbed and failed to grasp the severity of their actions.

Another example in the New Testament occurs during the stoning of Stephen. The religious leaders were outraged by his accurate recounting of Jewish history, leading up to the crucifixion of Christ. As they hurled stones at him, the Book of Acts records Stephen's final prayer.

> "Falling on his knees, he cried out in a loud voice, 'Lord, do not hold this sin against them.' And when he had said this, he fell asleep" (Acts 7:60).

Forgiving Your Betrayer Without Betraying Yourself

CHART ON UNILATERAL FORGIVENESS

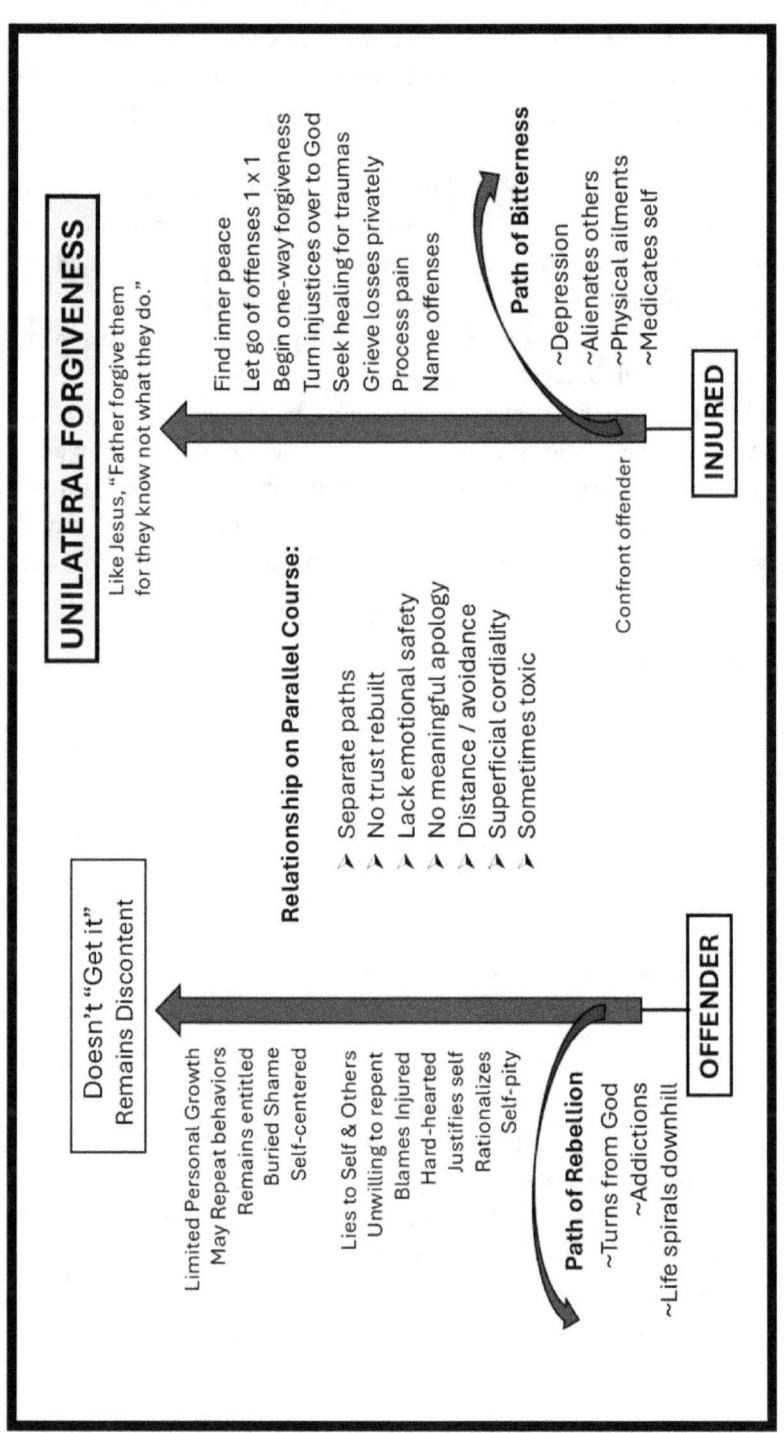

Stephen clearly named their actions as "sin." He didn't excuse them; instead, he prayed for the Lord to forgive his persecutors. Notably, Saul—who would become the Apostle Paul—was present, overseeing Stephen's execution. Years later, Paul recounted this very moment when sharing his testimony of conversion. Stephen's bold, grace-filled prayer was prophetically fulfilled in Paul's life.

Forgiving someone who is killing you sounds almost incomprehensible. While your spouse may not have tried to physically murder you—though some of you may have faced such danger—he or she destroyed much of your life: your confidence, your intact family, your fondest memories, your trust, your mental health, and your financial security. How does a person forgive such life-altering violations?

When the offending person offers no acknowledgement and makes no effort to repair the relationship, the idea of extending forgiveness to an undeserving, rejecting ex-spouse can feel insurmountable. When our sorrow feels endless, forgiveness can seem unjust—like we are minimizing their offenses or betraying our already shredded dignity. It can feel as if we are saying what happened to us doesn't matter.

Mistaken Beliefs

Mistaken beliefs about what forgiveness entails can prevent us from embracing one-way forgiveness. Most objections arise from misapplied teachings from the Bible regarding forgiving those who have wronged us. This confusion stems from equating forgiveness with reconciling with an unrepentant wrongdoer or excusing an unreformed individual for their sins. Below is a list of misconceptions about forgiveness that can hinder our willingness to forgive.

We Often Mistakenly Believe That Forgiveness:

- Must be immediate.
- Means excusing their behavior.
- Involves re-trusting our offender.
- Absolves the offender of consequences.
- Minimizes their wrongs.
- Means we'll lose the right to confront them or set boundaries.
- Means we will feel warm toward them again.
- Will leave us defenseless.
- Means the person shouldn't be held accountable.

NONE OF THE ABOVE ARE TRUE.

Instead, Healthy Forgiveness Means:

- Taking time to assess.
- Accepting forgiveness is a process.
- Not excusing the wrongs against us.
- Knowing that trust must be re-earned by the breaker.
- Recognizing that only God can absolve a person of their wrongdoing.
- Naming the offenses for what they are.
- Setting boundaries with unsafe people.
- Not expecting to *feel* forgiving before choosing to forgive.
- Not using resentment to protect our hearts. Instead, we seek godly counsel, common sense, and trust our intuition and the Lord's guidance to defend and protect us.
- Trusting God to ultimately hold the person accountable.
- Reporting criminal behavior to legal authorities.

In my case, I took time to assess how to resolve my angst. Instead of yielding to my assumed spiritual duty to quickly and superficially forgive James, as I had mistakenly done the first time, I decided to place myself on a path *toward* eventually forgiving him, but only as God enabled me. I refused to pretend that his life-altering offenses were insignificant. But I knew if I held onto my resentments, it would harm me further.

PREPARING FOR UNILATERAL FORGIVENESS

We must move through several stages on our way to Unilaterally Forgive our betrayer. Only someone who has experienced deep betrayal can truly understand your need to take time before extending forgiveness to an unfaithful spouse or a loved one who turned against you. Don't let well-meaning, Christian friends rush you into this process. First, you must take inventory of your grief, identify the debts, name the injuries, and assign proper responsibility for the wrongs committed against you.

Grieving Your Losses

As discussed in Chapter 2, our losses intensify when betrayal is followed by an unwanted divorce. God designed grief as a built-in healing mechanism—a necessary process before we can finally release our shattered expectations.

You've endured not just one, but two profound layers of grief—betrayal grief and spousal abandonment.

This cluster of losses has compounded your sorrow, leaving you with layer upon layer of grief to process. Before authentic forgiveness can even be considered, you must first grieve the specific and significant losses tied to your broken marriage.

Grieving the Debts

While we've discussed the losses faced by a Betrandoned spouse, we haven't yet considered the debts—what your partner "stole" from you or still "owes you." As referenced in the Lord's Prayer, "Forgive us our debts as we forgive our debtors" (Matthew 6:12), *debts* represent another vital category of loss that must be acknowledged and grieved.

When a spouse breaks their wedding vows or deprives you of emotional safety, financial stability, an intact family unit, faithful love, or a comforting presence, they've taken something that was rightfully yours. These unpaid relational debts leave painful gaps in your life—holes that make it hard to find a steady footing.

Name the Injuries

We must name our injuries clearly and truthfully—calling a spade a spade. That means refusing to sugarcoat or excuse our spouse's misconduct. We need to name the offenses clearly: betrayal, adultery, deception, lies, emotional or sexual abuse, desertion, and violations of the marital covenant. Referring to these actions as a "love affair" or "youthful indiscretions" only sanitizes what was, in truth, a devastating breach of trust.

Failing to acknowledge the true nature of these violations is a disservice to ourselves. We must not dismiss the weight of broken vows. For forgiveness to be meaningful, we must first understand the full impact of the wrongs committed against us. That starts by labeling each offense truthfully—then, and only then, can we take the next steps: grieving, seeking healing from the trauma, and ultimately surrendering the consequences to the Lord.

> "We must *convict* before we can forgive."
> ~ Doug Hansen

A psychology professor at Antioch University, Doug Hansen, PhD, used to say, "We must *convict* before we can forgive." In other words, we must firmly grasp how wrong something is and condemn it before we can truly let it go.

Assign Proper Responsibility

Similarly, in our minds, we must hold the betrayer accountable for their actions. Their decision to cheat was not an accident. It wasn't your fault they broke their marriage vows and disobeyed God. When we make excuses for their behavior—blaming ourselves, their upbringing, or life's hardships—we rob ourselves of a healthy, healing process.

Forgiveness becomes nearly impossible when the offense is diluted or shifted away from the person who committed it.

The truth is, your spouse chose to cope with their struggles by crossing a line into betrayal. Unless you mentally hold the one who strayed responsible for their offenses, you won't be able to forgive them. Instead, you risk agreeing with the enemy and your offender's rationalizations that their behavior was somehow justified or your fault. And that is a lie you must reject.

Consider the Context

This may seem to contradict the need to assign proper responsibility, but there's value in considering the broader context of our spouse's actions. Reflecting on their past trauma, current stressors, and family patterns can help us view their betrayal with more clarity and compassion, making it easier to release some of the personal sting we feel as we move toward forgiveness.

As I have emphasized, their fall from grace had more to do with what was happening inside them, either recently or in the past, than with you.

In James's case, his brother had suffered a heart attack, his business was struggling, he'd been significantly triggered by a past loss in his life, we were on the brink of becoming empty nesters, and I was preoccupied with a major home remodel. Factoring in his childhood trauma, I began to see his betrayal through a softened lens.

Another moment shifted my perspective. While I was wrestling with James's claim that God was loving him through another woman, I approached Sandra D. Wilson after a workshop based on her book, *Into Abba's Arms*. After hearing my story, she paused, looked at me, and said with conviction, "He has not been *gripped* with the love of God!" I'll never forget how her hand closed into a fist on that word—*gripped*.

That was not the response I expected. If James had been gripped with the love of God, what difference would that have made?

Here are my theories:

- He might not have been tempted to wander, searching for a mood-lifting experience.

- He would have been so secure in God's love for him that his deeper need for love would have been filled.
- He would have behaved more lovingly toward me.
- He wouldn't have so blatantly disobeyed the Lord.
- He would have trusted the Lord to restore his feelings of love for me.

I concluded that if James had been *gripped* by God's love for him and responded to that love by loving God in return, he would not have gone off the rails. Of all people, James needed to be immersed in that kind of love. Realizing this gave me a degree of grace for him.

Maybe you can do the same with your ex-spouse. What if you reframed his or her immoral choices as coming from a deeper void—a need to be *gripped* by God's love? It wasn't that you weren't enough. It's that they had a hole no human could fill—one that only God can satisfy.

Taking a thirty-thousand-foot view—considering the timing, context, and cumulative pressures—might help lessen the harshness you feel. It doesn't excuse their betrayal, but it may add a few drops of compassion to the bitterness still lingering in your heart.

Still, don't confuse context with justification. No matter the background or struggle, your spouse had a choice. And that choice was entirely theirs.

Identify Your Feelings

Too often, as Christians, we feel guilty for the rage or hatred we harbor toward someone we love who injures us and shatters our trust. However, unless we understand how deeply we've been hurt and express our intense anger regarding the many wounds, we may become stuck in the ditch of denial, unable to make progress on our healing journey. Deep emotions must be owned and processed, not denied or dismissed. If we are not honest with God and ourselves, we won't be able to discern which path of forgiveness—Reconciling or Unilateral—to choose. Otherwise, we may opt for the path of bitterness, undermining our opportunity for healing.

In my first career as a dental hygienist, I worked with a receptionist who verbally abused me. I tried to appease her with my "niceness," but my efforts only fueled her bullying. After three years of enduring her mistreatment, I spiraled into clinical depression and could barely function.

It wasn't until I had an honest, angry yell session with God that my façade finally crumbled. I admitted that I hated her and was furious.

That raw honesty broke through my denial and opened the door for new insights. I finally understood what it meant to forgive without condoning bad behavior. From that moment on, I stopped being insincere with God. Instead of waiting for him to change her, I began to realize that he wanted to change me. I stood up to her and spoke honestly with my boss. When he didn't want to face the truth, I quit my job. She became the tool God used to draw me into deeper intimacy with him and to nudge me into a better and more rewarding career.

I had no idea how vital that lesson of brutal transparency would be for me years later. Emotional honesty became essential in my recovery from James's affair and his retracted love. I had to admit and feel the depth of my wounds before I could process them in a self-honoring way, make wise decisions, and choose a new path forward.

It also forced me to confront a hard truth: James's affair had changed him. He would never love me the same way again. That realization was agonizing. But all the signs were there. His heart had shifted in a way that would have continued to erode my self-worth and hinder God's call on my life. The Lord had something new and better for me—even if I couldn't see it yet.

- Have you been emotionally honest about how hurt and angry you are over your spouse's disloyalty and forsaking your marriage?
- Are you trying too hard to be brave?
- Have you given full vent to your feelings without trying to censor yourself to appear cool-headed, above the fray, or super spiritual?
- Have you poured your heart out to the Lord as David did, as recorded in the Psalms? Have you selectively found a safe tribe to share these honest feelings with?
- Or have you been too afraid to be that authentic, for fear your pit will deepen and others will look down on you?

Learning to be gut-level honest with yourself and God is essential for finding your way out of the mire of a messy Post-Affair Divorce. And there is no other way to progress from bitter sorrow toward the balm of forgiveness.

CONCRETE STEPS TO ONE-WAY FORGIVENESS

Now that you've reflected on how to prepare your heart for Unilateral Forgiveness, it's time to take practical steps forward. The next section will guide you through releasing the anguish that has occupied too much space in your heart and mind.

I remember when forgiving James felt impossible—too big, too vulnerable, and too dismissive of my deep sorrow. I knew it was a worthy goal, but I couldn't imagine how to get there. So, I gave myself permission not to rush. I committed to the journey. I placed myself on a path toward unilateral forgiveness, trusting it would come in time.

My motto became: "Let go of one loss, one offense, and one angst—one step at a time. With God's help."

I learned that each release of resentment, revenge, and injustice is a step of faith, believing that what we give up, God will carry on our behalf, in his way and timing. Forgiveness isn't a matter of letting someone off the hook—it's about taking them off your shoulders and onto Christ's.

> Forgiveness is not a matter of letting someone off the hook—it's about taking them off your shoulders and onto Christ's.

The following guidelines will help you turn these giant leaps into smaller, measurable steps.

Letting Go

Let's begin by looking at the definitions of "forgive." There are two Greek words in the New Testament, and one root word in the Old Testament for the word forgive.

1. One is the Greek verb *aphiemi* (and its derivatives)—which means: "to send away, release, lose, dismiss, or let go."
2. The other Greek word is *charizomenoi* (and its derivatives)—which means: "to show favor to, show kindness, forgive, or cancel a debt." It's related to the Greek word *charis,* which means "grace gift."
3. In the Old Testament, in Hebrew, the word forgive is *śā*, which means: "to lift, carry, or take."

If forgiving your spouse's hurtful acts feels overwhelming, try thinking of it as "letting go," "sending them away," or "carrying their wrongs to the foot of the cross." This is not something you do alone—it's something you do by God's grace. One instance at a time.

The beauty of knowing Jesus is that you have someone to carry these offenses for you. He died for the sins of the world, which means he bore not only your sins but also those of your faithless spouse. So, one by one, release them into his care. Let Christ carry what was never meant for you to hold.

Forgiving an unremorseful, self-justifying, unfaithful spouse is one of the bravest and most difficult things a betrayed, forsaken spouse can do.

Currently, this may seem impossible. That's why I don't recommend forgiving the whole person all at once. Whole-person forgiveness is like throwing a bucket of soapy water at a dirty car, hoping it gets clean. It doesn't work. You must dip your sponge and scrub one grime-covered section at a time.

Instead of replaying James's offenses repeatedly in my mind, I began recording them in my journal, planning to release each one, little by little, as the Lord gave me the readiness and strength.

This took me years. Sometimes, I'd forgive an incident, and the pain would disappear. Other times, I'd let go of a specific accusation against him only to have facets of that offense return to torment me from another angle. On other occasions, I needed a spiritual truth to free me from the negative meaning I associated with a particular offense before I could let go of the angst and forgive him for the wound.

Triggers would catch me off guard—like seeing pictures of him on social media enjoying our kids without me. The stabbing ache would remind me I had another layer of grieving and forgiving to process. First, I'd express my sorrow to the Lord with "weeping and gnashing of teeth" (as some of you can relate). Then, I'd lay my specific resentment on the altar. Again.

> Forgiving an unremorseful, self-justifying, unfaithful spouse is one of the bravest, most difficult things a betrayed, forsaken spouse can do.

Over time, the wounds closed. They stopped festering and lost their grip on my thoughts and emotions. Eventually, after releasing one pain at a time, I was able to forgive James—not perfectly, but enough to stop obsessing and find peace.

Surrendering the Right to Get Even

We need God's help at every step on the journey to forgive those who've wounded us—especially when it comes to surrendering our desire for revenge.

Early in my counseling career, I worked with a young woman, "Anna," who carried deep sorrow from her parents' divorce. One particularly painful memory was when her mother forced her to ride in the car after midnight, refusing to say where they were going. The destination turned out to be her estranged father's apartment, where he was living with the woman who helped break up their marriage.

Once there, her mother handed Anna a bag of tools and instructed her to hold them and stay quiet. Anna watched in horror as her mom slashed her father's tires with violent glee. Her heart sank as the air hissed from each tire, and the car slowly settled onto the concrete.

As they drove away, Anna felt complicit in her mother's vengeful act. I still remember her rocking sobs as she recounted the moment. Though she had her own issues with her father, it was her mother's revenge that left the deeper scar—one of shame and helplessness.

Just as crime doesn't pay, neither does vengeance. While we can sympathize with Anna's mother's rage, God makes it clear: revenge isn't our role. When we try to wield the burning gavel of vindication, we end up scorched—and often wound others in the process.

A vital step on your path to forgiveness is surrendering your revenge fantasies to God. Let's be honest—we all have them, in one form or another.

The old Irish saying, "Don't get mad, get even," popularized by the Kennedys, only exacerbates the situation. Revenge might bring a fleeting sense of satisfaction, but it doesn't heal the deeper wound: the pain of being betrayed by someone you deeply loved.

That's the irony—this is someone you cared for. Seeking revenge only fuels your resentment or burdens you with added shame for violating your own values.

Revenge is often romanticized as justice, especially in movies like *The List, Unforgiven, First Wives Club, Gladiator,* and *Double Jeopardy*. While it may be satisfying to watch a hero get even, real-life vengeance stains our soul, distorts our character, and harms the people around us—just like it did in Anna's life.

Scripture is clear:

> "Do not avenge yourselves, beloved, but leave room for God's wrath. For it is written: "Vengeance is Mine; I will repay, says the Lord" (Romans 12:19).

This teaches us that taking revenge into our own hands interferes with God's role. He *promises* to repay. If we step in, he may step out. We're called to trust the Lord to discipline our offenders in the most just, thorough, and redemptive way possible.

Giving up our revenge fantasies doesn't mean we should abandon healthy boundaries or legal consequences with an abuser. But, sadly, personal crimes of the heart lack suitable legal constraints in our society. Instead, we must rely on the courts of heaven.

Ask yourself: *Do I trust God enough to deal with my ex-spouse as he sees fit?* While this sounds great in theory, living it out is far more difficult.

It helps to notice a keyword that is easy to miss in Romans 12:19: "*Beloved.*" You are greatly loved by God, which means you are cherished and treasured by him. When we understand the Lord's love for us, we can trust him and surrender to his will more easily, believing he will accomplish what is right and best for everyone involved, in the long run.

Such trust requires us to exercise another step of faith—that God is big enough to handle it. You may question this when your former spouse seems to move on without consequences, enjoying a carefree life while you are still reeling.

But this is where faith steps in. God sees everything—the present, the future, and unseen spiritual realities we can't comprehend. No act of evil escapes his notice, and no wound inflicted on a believer goes without his concern or eventual redemption—whether in this life or the next.

In the meantime, God uses our sorrow to shape our character and deepen our dependence on him.

Here are a few verses I find comfort in:

> "Are not two sparrows sold for a penny? Yet not one of them will fall to the ground outside your Father's care. And even the very hairs of your head are all numbered. So don't be afraid; you are worth more than many sparrows" (Matthew 10:2931).

In other words, God sees and values you. Nothing escapes his notice. That is why Jesus says, "Do not be afraid." We are in his care. Every detail of your life matters to him.

> "I consider that our present sufferings are not comparable to the glory that will be revealed in us" (Romans 8:18).

This verse reminds us that our present sufferings are nothing compared to the glory God is cultivating within us. What we perceive as unfair or devastating, he sees as an opportunity to refine our souls—producing a lasting beauty shaped by the Spirit. When we choose to trust him through our pain, we can be confident that a great reward awaits.

St. Peter reinforces the above truth in his letter to the dispersed believers, who were suffering unjust persecution under Roman rule.

> "In this [our imperishable inheritance], you greatly rejoice, though now for a little while you may have had to suffer grief in various trials so that the proven character of your faith—more precious than gold, which perishes even though refined by fire—may result in praise, glory, and honor at the revelation of Jesus Christ" (1 Peter 1:6–7).

When you remain faithful to the Lord amid the grief of unfair "fiery trials," he will not waste your sorrows. Scripture says your tested faith is more precious than gold. So, hang on. Even if you can't yet see the fruit, trust that God is making things right.

The invisible work he is doing within you carries immense value and weight in God's economy. Your character, your spiritual maturity, and your increased faith in the face of crushing heartbreak stand as remarkable testimonies of God's work in your life, serving as lasting qualities you will take with you to heaven.

Entrusting the Injustices to God

As I study God's Word, I'm surprised to notice how many verses reveal God's sentiments. He loves justice and hates injustice—even more than we do.

> "For I, the LORD, love justice; I hate robbery and iniquity" (Isaiah 61:8).

> "What then shall we say? Is God unjust? Not at all!" (Romans 9:14, NIV)

> "'No weapon formed against you shall prosper, and you will refute every tongue that accuses you. This is the heritage of the servants of the LORD, and their vindication is from Me,' declares the LORD" (Isaiah 54:17).

Only God can truly vindicate us. He alone can wield the gavel of justice without being scorched by it. When we try to take that gavel for ourselves, our hands get burned.

It's one thing to witness an injustice and take action to remedy it, such as when your ex-spouse refuses to pay child support. But it's another to take personal matters into your own hands and try to balance the scales. The truth is, we can never pile enough personal revenge on the scales to make up for our pain. That's why Jesus came. Only he could bear the full weight of injustice, rise again, and offer us healing and hope.

A Visual Tool

Imagine you're a judge with a large metal file cabinet in your chambers, each drawer holding cases yet to be tried. One drawer contains a bulging manila folder—your ex-spouse's case. It's filled with detailed records of their marital offenses: documented infractions, sketches of the emotional weapons used, and witness testimonies of betrayal and pain. You've reviewed it countless times, building your argument, reaffirming the evidence.

But there's one problem—you lack the authority to prosecute. You're not qualified to serve as judge, jury, or executioner in this case. With a heavy sigh, you realize it's time to recuse yourself.

Still, the case must be heard. So you look to the larger, more majestic courtroom next door. God presides there as the true and righteous Judge. His authority is higher than yours, and his justice is perfect. You take the folder from your drawer, walk into his courtroom, and hand over the case. You're no longer responsible for its outcome.

As you exit and close the door behind you, a surprising sense of freedom washes over you. The burden is no longer yours to carry. The judgment, consequences, and final sentence now rest with the One who sees all, knows all, and judges rightly.

This is the essence of forgiveness—entrusting your adversary's case to the only Judge worthy of ruling on it. No need for revenge. It's not your job anymore.

Example of Cheryl

I recently reconnected with a former client of mine, someone I hadn't seen in 17 years, who had been betrayed and abandoned. She shared that it took her about eight years to recover from her Post-Affair Divorce. "Cheryl" was very intentional about her healing process. She attended a Divorce Care class at her church for two years and then went on to lead these same classes for another two years. I will never forget the day she walked through the doors of my church, bringing along fifteen of her attendees—a fifty-minute drive for them—while I facilitated a three-hour divorce recovery class called "Landing on Your Feet." She became a beacon of encouragement for others who had experienced similar losses, actively helping them find resources for healing.

During our recent conversation, I asked her how she managed to forgive her ex-husband and his lover. She said she asked God to help her arrive at a place where she could sincerely forgive them. "I needed the Lord to show me how I was meant to forgive."

One day, the Lord said, "Okay, you are far enough in your healing—it's time we look at you." Puzzled, she didn't understand what he meant by that, so she tucked the impression away for future reference.

Soon after, while driving home from work, an old, shameful memory surfaced—something she had done that deeply hurt another person. "It was an ugly thing," she admitted. Confused initially, she asked herself, *Why am I thinking about this?* But instead of brushing it aside, she let the Lord sit with her in that moment. She acknowledged her sin, poured out her regret, and asked for his forgiveness.

The next day, the same thing happened. While driving home from work, another sinful thing she'd done in the past came to her mind. Once more, she confessed her wrongdoing and asked the Lord to forgive her. She told me, "I felt like weeping that I had ever been so shallow in my faith and love for my Savior."

The following weekend, she met two girlfriends for dinner at a popular restaurant. For some reason, one of the gals didn't like their assigned table, so they asked the waitress to find a different table. After they were re-seated, her friends noticed that Cheryl's ex-husband and his lover-turned-wife were sitting in the booth behind Cheryl. Unnerved, they asked the waitress to move them again. Though awkward, the encounter felt too coincidental to ignore.

Later that evening, back at home, the pieces clicked into place. She recalled the memories God had stirred in her heart the previous two nights.

> So *that* is why God wanted me to remember how capable I was of evil. He wanted me to have a picture of my own sin and the Lord's forgiveness before I walked into this situation in the restaurant. Without the Lord, *I* could have done the same thing as my husband and his lover. The only reason I haven't succumbed to a similar sin is because of Jesus. If it wasn't for my faith and the grace of God, I could be that ugly, too.[3]

In humility, she felt the last vestiges of rancor drain from her heart.

Today, Cheryl leads a deeply fulfilling life. Her early loneliness has subsided. She's retired, reads avidly, travels freely with her girlfriends, and often visits her adult children and grandchildren who live out of state.

Her decision to seek healing, forgive, and pursue fresh purposes has borne fruit in ways she never could have imagined twenty years ago.

Forgiveness is Not a Feeling: It's a Decision

Forgiving an unrepentant spouse is a process. It starts with grieving our losses. First, we must identify our hurts, grieve them, and exhaust our anger with the help of God and others. Then we choose, by an act of the will, to release each resentment, one at a time. When we make the choice to forgive, we also relinquish our right to retaliate and, instead, entrust the injustices to God.

The relief and peace we crave usually arrive *after* forgiving, not before. If we wait for warm feelings toward our offenders to arrive first, whether towards our spouse or the affair partner, we'll stay trapped in tension and bitterness.

Reality also tells us we can't force forgiveness until we're ready. God often ministers first through Scripture, a moment of divine insight, or the care of others—preparing our hearts to let go of our resentments, relinquish revenge fantasies, and hand over each injustice.

Forgiving in this way is an act of faith:

- Faith that God will take over from here.
- Faith to obey his call.
- Faith he will redeem our sorrows for lasting good in our lives.
- Faith that he can fill the void left by our resentments with peace.

Besides your partner's offenses, you likely have other matters to release as well—specifically, the lingering regrets that you continue to punish yourself for. Instead of dwelling on these regrets, there are more constructive ways to channel your mental and emotional energy. In the next chapter, we'll explore how to do just that.

Chapter 25

Letting Go of Regrets

To him who is able to keep you from stumbling and to present you before his glorious presence without fault and with great joy.
~Jude 1:14 (NIV)

One of the most painful moments during our crisis happened in a couples' session with our first counselor, Dr. Tim. Near the end, James looked at me with accusatory eyes and said, "I don't even like you!" My heart dropped to my stomach. Since we'd driven separately, I sobbed the entire hour-long drive home. When I told my friend Elizabeth what James said to me, she said, "Nuh uh. James doesn't like *James*."

That thought never crossed my mind. Outwardly, James appeared confident. He'd been a star athlete and had a near-photographic memory. But as I reflected, I realized he was also quick with snide remarks, often disguised as teasing. Maybe those were cover-ups for deeper insecurity. Why else would he need to one-up others?

Perhaps his cruel words to me were projections of his own self-disdain. I was a mirror to him, reflecting his shortcomings as a husband. Rather than repent and work on himself, it was easier for him to resent me as the obstacle to an imagined happy life with the other woman—someone who fed his ego and hadn't lived with his flaws yet.

Regardless of his reasons for claiming he didn't like me, after years of professing his love, it took me a long time to begin liking myself again.

Deep down, I worried that I somehow deserved James's scathing rejection. My insecurities haunted me. What were my failings in the marriage? Could I have done anything different to draw him back? Will I always be discarded by any man who shows initial interest in me?

These self-doubts didn't start with my marriage, although our breakup magnified them. They were rooted in my childhood, when my father chose alcohol over me, my safety, and our family's well-being. James's betrayal only reinforced a painful belief I had carried for years: *I am not worth it.*

Perhaps you can relate. Maybe your partner gambled away your security with an affair, or a string of them—and you've been left holding questions that dig at your identity. *Why wasn't I enough? Could I have prevented this? Am I somehow to blame for the collapse of our marriage?*

In the previous chapter, we explored how to gradually forgive those who have betrayed us. But here's the hard truth: Sometimes the more difficult person to forgive is ourselves.

WHY WE BEAT OURSELVES UP

The "If Onlys"

According to Elizabeth Kubler-Ross, one of the stages of grief after death is the "Bargaining Stage."[1] When we are bereaved, we may find ourselves trapped in the "If Only" phase, tormenting ourselves with thoughts like "If only I had done this" or "If only I hadn't done that, this tragedy could have been avoided."

Then come the regrets: "What if I'd taken their complaints more seriously? Kept the house neater? Prioritized more time together?"

Maybe you wonder if insisting on counseling earlier or not giving up when they refused could have changed things. Or perhaps you ask yourself if more frequent sex might have made a difference.

If only. If only. If only.

Most betrayed spouses internalize their partner's affair as a reflection of their own inadequacy. You may find yourself wondering: *What was missing in me? Am I unlovable? Was it my body, my personality, my appearance? Why was someone else more appealing than me?*

So, the "If Onlys" keep cycling through your mind, convincing you that *maybe* you could have done something differently. But losing the loyalty and love of a spouse is a profound loss—one you couldn't control. It often takes years to fully grasp how powerless we are over another person's choices and the death of a marriage.

If you're stuck in the Bargaining Stage of grief, flogging yourself with regret, you are not alone. But you may need a gentle nudge—from a friend, counselor, or a support group—to stop spinning your wheels, take your foot off the brake, and begin moving forward again.

We can torment ourselves by endlessly spinning in the tumbler of "If Onlys," as if replaying events or wishing hard enough might rewrite the ending. In doing so, we deceive ourselves into believing we had more control over our spouse's choices than we actually had.

Please hear this clearly: you did not *make* your spouse stray. You didn't force them to abandon the marriage. Even if you unknowingly contributed to their vulnerability during a season of crisis, your partner alone was responsible for how they chose to cope.

You didn't push them into someone else's arms. Still, like every human being, you likely have areas to grow. Be thankful if this crisis has helped reveal places in your life you'd like to strengthen.

But here's the danger: After a Post-Affair Divorce, you may be tempted to overemphasize your flaws while minimizing your strengths. Some of the traits you're blaming yourself for may be unchangeable, inborn parts of who you are. Others may be growth areas you can humbly work on.

Rather than spiral into despair, the path forward is to distinguish between your "Unchangeables" and your "Changeables," see your growth areas as opportunities, not as failures, and, most importantly, forgive yourself. Let's begin with how to approach what you can't change.

ACCEPT YOUR "UNCHANGEABLES"

Your Personality is God's Gift to You

One misguided self-criticism we impose on ourselves is the belief that there must be something horribly wrong with us; otherwise, our spouse wouldn't have betrayed and left us. Really? Did your spouse marry you after only a couple of days, on a whim in Las Vegas? Were you pressured into marriage as a teenager before either of you had matured or truly gotten to know each other? If not, it's safe to assume your spouse chose you intentionally. Most people marry someone they like and enjoy being around.

President George W. Bush and Laura only dated for three months before they married, and, as of the writing of this book, their marriage has lasted 48 years. Of course, it helped that they married at age 31. However, do not fall for the "he/she didn't know me very well, and once they did get to know me, they didn't like me" excuse for your spouse's change of heart. Laura hung in there and stood by George W. as he faced and overcame a drinking problem. And they are still together today.

Your spouse fell in love with you the way you are. They generally enjoyed your personality and found you attractive. You were you, and they liked and loved you for that.

Ask yourself: Am I still the same essential person my partner fell in love with? Or have I changed in some drastic manner? I assume most of you haven't changed very much. And even if you have changed, that's still not an excuse for an affair.

More often, the strayer is the one who has changed. While other factors may have contributed, their secret sexual or romantic life was probably the primary factor that eroded their warm feelings toward you.

So, if your spouse, like mine, used the excuse of not liking you or your personality anymore, what are you supposed to do with that? How can you forgive yourself for simply being *you*?

Answer: You shouldn't have to.

Your Personality is Inborn

God created your core personality and temperament with intention and care. While past relationships may have shaped some of your behaviors or beliefs, your true self—your soul, will, and temperament—remains uniquely and consistently yours. You are not just a product of genetics or environment; you are a masterpiece with divine fingerprints.

As the psalmist says,

> "I praise you, for I am fearfully and wonderfully made. Wonderful are your works; my soul knows it very well" (Psalm 139:14).

But does *your* soul know it? Do you believe it?

After being battered by betrayal and rejection, your self-esteem may be in shambles. You might wonder how to reclaim the person you were before your spouse's hurtful words and actions shook your identity. The answer starts here:

Disown the lies. Release the shame. Reject the false narratives your ex-spouse may have spoken over you.

Then, with courage and intention, reclaim the person God created and cherishes.

Renewed acceptance begins by resting in God's unwavering acceptance of you. Christ gave everything to rescue you from the enemy's grip—the same enemy who now tries to use your ex's betrayal to diminish your worth and shake your faith.

Don't let him succeed. Instead, anchor yourself in the truth of who God says you are and how deeply you matter to him.

Accept God's Love

God both loves and likes you. Since he is the wisest, best, and most powerful Being in the universe, his "vote" should carry the most weight with you. Begin by meditating on Scriptures that affirm your worth to God. When you reflect on verses in the Bible that express God's love for you, your confidence can re-blossom. For example,

> "For Your loving devotion extends beyond the heavens, and Your faithfulness reaches to the clouds" (Psalm 108:4).

That is how immense God's love for you is—miles above the earth, beyond the clouds, and above the heavens. The Psalmist wants you to know that there is no limit to God's loving devotion to you.

> "Oh give thanks to the LORD, for he is good, for his steadfast love endures forever!" (Psalm 107:1, ESV)

One of the qualities that makes God so good is that his tremendous love for you remains constant and eternal. We need to continually thank him because his love is unchanging, reliable, and everlasting.

> "*Who* shall separate us from the love of Christ? Shall trouble or distress or persecution or famine or nakedness or danger or sword?" (Romans 8:35, emphasis added)

Notice how this passage begins with "Who," before listing the situations that make us question God's love. The point is clear: No person—including a straying spouse—and no circumstance—including a Post-Affair Divorce—can separate you from the love of God.

None of these hardships can drive a wedge between you and the Lord's unwavering affection. Above all other loves, God's love is the most faithful and pure. He loves you "with an everlasting love" (Jeremiah 31:3). You never have to fear abandonment with him. He will remain faithful to you—always.

Remove Your Ex-Spouse from Their Pedestal

Remember when we talked about the excruciating pain we feel when our spouse abandons us and how it can cause us to exaggerate our betrayer's importance to us? As Susan Anderson says, "You elevate their status and power as a way of justifying why you feel so devastated."[2]

In our pain, we often amplify their worth, opinions, and emotions far beyond what they deserve. Without realizing it, we may even elevate them to idol status—someone we obsessively honor, long to appease, and bend over backwards to win back. We twist ourselves into emotional pretzels, hoping our efforts will somehow reverse the damage caused by their betrayal.

But these feelings, while deeply human, are not unique to you. It's normal for your attachment to intensify when rejection threatens your sense of identity and emotional security.

You Must De-Throne Your Former Spouse

Remove your former spouse from the altar of your heart. They are not your god. Only God is. He alone is your Savior. The sooner you stop centering your thoughts, purpose, and identity around your ex, the better.

Yes, you'll still have occasional triggers and waves of grief—but thoughts about your former spouse will no longer be at the center of your life. Fix your eyes on Jesus, "the author and perfecter of your faith" (Hebrews 12:2). He is the only One worthy of your unwavering trust and allegiance.

I know—it's easier said than done, especially in the thick of pain. But hear this: Your ex is not the only, or even most important, person in your world. They are not the measure of your worth. In most affair-driven divorces, the one who walked away is no longer a reliable voice in your life.

Instead of trying to prove your value to someone who broke your trust, invest your heart in God, your healing, your children, and the people who truly love you. That's where your restoration will take root.

I remember walking into a Hall of Mirrors at an amusement park for the first time. I was amazed at how the shape of the mirror influenced my reflection. When a mirror was curved or "bent" in a certain way, I looked short and fat. In another distorted mirror, I appeared overly tall and thin. And in yet another oddly shaped mirror, my head looked like it would explode. The more warped or wobbly the mirror, the less I liked how I looked in its reflection. I only saw my true likeness when I looked into a straight mirror.

The same applies to how we perceive ourselves, as reflected by those close to us. If your spouse is emotionally "bent" by an affair, addiction, or unresolved trauma, you won't receive an accurate reflection of yourself from them. Their distorted lens—clouded by inflated hormones, bitterness, narcissism, pride, or pain—can warp how they see you.

Instead, seek straight mirrors: God's Word, safe friends, trusted family, wise mentors, and a Christ-centered community. God delights in you. Your faithful friends value you. Now it's your turn to begin liking and affirming your true self again.

As I mentioned in an earlier chapter, my friends noted that after my divorce, I stopped over-apologizing, a habit I had developed while living with

James's periodic anger and disapproval, which increased when he thought he was in love with the other woman.

Later, when I began dating Dan, I braced for him to correct me or criticize my behavior. When the insults didn't come, I'd ask, "Did I embarrass you in front of your parents?" Dan would laugh. He felt just the opposite. He liked my personality and was proud to see how much his parents enjoyed my company. After we married, it took me several years to accept his acceptance of me and to stop asking him if I had embarrassed him after a family event.

You don't need to find a new spouse before embracing your true personality. You just need to surround yourself with healthy, affirming people—reasonably straight mirrors—who genuinely enjoy being with you.

Superficial Unchangeables

In addition to criticizing your own personality, you may also find yourself blaming your physical appearance or health for your partner's betrayal. It's a common trap for betrayed spouses—to believe that if only they had looked different, stayed fitter, or aged more gracefully, the affair wouldn't have happened. Yes, your body has changed—perhaps from childbirth, injury, illness, or simply the passage of time. Maybe you're not as toned or don't have as much hair as you once did. But your spouse vowed to love you "in sickness and in health." Their betrayal was not caused by your imperfections—it violated those vows.

Loving spouses adjust their expectations as bodies age and circumstances change. That kind of faithful commitment is essential for families to thrive—and it reflects God's original design for marriage.

I admire my sister-in-law, Debbie, for adjusting her expectations over 50 years of marriage. When she married Marc, he was a striking, athletic football player and expert skier. Their attractive wedding photo looked like it belonged on the cover of *Brides* magazine. What she couldn't have known back then was that Marc would soon develop juvenile diabetes, eventually requiring a kidney/pancreas transplant and losing the lower half of both legs. Through countless hospital stays, surgeries, medications, and prosthetics, Debbie has remained faithfully and lovingly by his side—committed not to a perfect body, but to the man she vowed to love.

On the other end of the scale is the story of a girlfriend of mine, "Nancy," whom I met while finishing my undergraduate degree. I enjoyed our lengthy discussions about how our Christian beliefs were challenged by some of our atheistic, Marxist, or New Age professors and fellow students. As we talked about our faith, she also confided how self-conscious she felt about her weight. Her father often prodded her over the extra fifteen pounds she seemed to carry.

I was surprised; in my view, she was rather beautiful, and her weight fit her frame.

Then she met "Philip," a non-believer who seemed enamored with her. Instead of waiting for a Christian man with shared values, she chose to live with him and later married him. Years later, when we met up again, her mood was heavy. Philip, like her father, had begun criticizing her weight, only worse. She felt constantly hounded and belittled.

Eventually, Nancy was diagnosed with ovarian cancer. When I received her Christmas photo that year, she looked frail and gaunt from the treatments. I couldn't help but think, "Well, Philip got the skinny girl he wanted. I hope he's satisfied."

When I called a year later, unaware she had only weeks to live, she wept on the phone. Philip had started seeing other women and ultimately left her. He said he couldn't "handle" her illness. Nancy had to move back in with her parents, who became her caretakers.

There was one redemptive thread: Her father, deeply remorseful for his past criticism, lovingly remortgaged their home to pay for experimental treatments that extended her life, though they could not save her.

I still think about Nancy when I hear of people who are criticized for their unchangeable traits or health challenges. When we begin to criticize ourselves for those very things, it grieves not only our Creator but also those who truly love us.

This isn't to excuse neglecting reasonable self-care. But many traits we've been shamed for are biologically fixed. It reminds me of the moment in Genesis when Adam and Eve hid in shame, and God asked, "Who *told you* that you were naked?"

Sin does that. It causes shame, self-rejection, and judgment toward ourselves and others when we should be offering grace. So I'll ask you the same question: *Who told you that you should be ashamed of your personality or appearance?* Certainly not the Lord.

Now is the time to stop agreeing with the enemy, your unloving ex-spouse, or anyone else who has belittled you for your "Unchangeables." Instead, this is your invitation to start celebrating how God created your essential self—inside and out.

ACKNOWLEDGE YOUR "CHANGEABLES"

Just because the Lord loves and accepts you as you are doesn't mean you have no room to grow. We are all sinners saved by grace and, hopefully, on a journey of what the Bible calls "regeneration"—Spirit-inspired growth that leads us to become more like Christ. In our walk with the Lord, he continues to refine us, developing our character and seeking to reveal his glory through us more clearly than before.

Teachable Yet Discerning

One of the most essential qualities anyone can develop, besides being a loving person, is having a teachable heart. This means being open to correction from God and others. He often uses loved ones, bosses, and spouses as tools to refine our rough edges. A teachable heart chooses growth over defensiveness. For trauma survivors, the challenge lies in learning to discern between legitimate correction and distorted criticism.

When your spouse or friends point out habits that bother them, take time to evaluate their feedback. Ask yourself, "Is this a genuine growth area or a reflection of their personal issues?" Discern between constructive insight and unfair recrimination, especially when dealing with someone "bent" by unresolved pain or skewed emotions.

It's important to distinguish deal-breakers from petty preferences and to grow where needed without losing your core identity. Your personality may be set in stone, but your habits are not.

This discernment is especially vital when criticisms come from an unfaithful spouse. Their negative feedback is often an attempt to deflect from their own guilt and is usually distorted by emotional fog. When this happens, don't take it to heart. Reject those twisted judgments and focus instead on what God says is true about you.

Sometimes, I encounter situations where a passive, unfaithful spouse has a history of secretly harboring resentments that they failed to address with their partner. Yet, once embroiled in an outside romance, these formerly silent sufferers suddenly find the courage (and heartlessness) to vent a host of grievances they held inside for years. These complaints tend to be disproportionate and blindside a trusting, shell-shocked, betrayed spouse.

If this has happened to you, don't be fooled. Infidelity is a passive-aggressive way to protest and painfully exit a marriage. If your spouse waited until they were emotionally or physically involved with someone else to finally express their "truth," the deeper issue is their avoidance of honest communication.

By withholding their frustrations, they robbed you of the chance to address and change any bothersome behaviors—assuming the complaints were even legitimate and not simply justifications for their affair. And by timing their criticisms to coincide with a new romantic attachment, they betrayed you in more ways than one. Their unwillingness to express themselves earlier speaks more to their own conflict-avoidance and emotional immaturity than it does to your worth or your role in the marriage. Their grievances, no matter how passionately delivered, are often rooted in their own unresolved insecurities or inability to accept differences in a healthy relationship.

Yes, like most marriages, yours likely had challenges—issues that may have needed adjustments on both sides. But once the tsunami of infidelity hit, the relationship lost its footing. It would have required a significant recovery effort before you could even begin to address the dynamics that existed before the affair.

Address Your Blind Spots

Everyone has blind spots. After walking through the pain of a Post-Affair Divorce, you may see some of yours more clearly. This is your opportunity to acknowledge what Celebrate Recovery calls your "hurts, habits, and hang-ups" and begin making healthy changes.

Maybe you let your parents interfere too much, spent beyond your means, or clung to perfectionism that made others walk on eggshells around you. Perhaps you were overly critical, dependent, domineering, or came from a dysfunctional family without realizing how it affected your marriage.

Perhaps one of your flaws is unchecked anger, untreated depression, or withholding affection. Maybe you ignored a mental health issue—yours or your spouse's—or failed to get help for an addiction. These are valid growth areas, and now is the time to address them.

While these challenges would've been easier to tackle before infidelity entered the picture, it's not too late to learn, grow, and become healthier moving forward.

The More Common Problem

However, based on my observation, most betrayed spouses were not so much offensive as they were overly kind. Yes, it is possible to be too nice, too adaptable, and too tolerant of inappropriate behavior. Inconsiderate people often seek out pleasers to pair up with. If you are inclined to be a pleaser, examine your romantic history. Do you tend to attract self-centered or abusive people into your life?

If being nice has been your modus operandi for gaining others' affection or for appearing as a "good Christian," reconsider your approach. A person who projects excessive geniality invites disrespect due to their lack of honesty, weak boundaries, and tendency to be a pushover.

> Based on my observation, most betrayed spouses weren't so much offensive as they were overly kind.

People-pleasers are often misjudged as weak, which unfortunately attracts controlling or self-absorbed individuals who sense they can violate boundaries without resistance. If this resonates with you, it may be time to explore how to identify your true feelings and express them with clarity and courage.

The goal isn't to become aggressive—but to be authentic. Seek counseling, read helpful books, and practice assertiveness. Books like *The Givers and the Takers* by Evatt and Feld, or *Boundaries* by Cloud and Townsend, are excellent places to start.

And hear this clearly: Your willingness to accommodate others never justified your spouse's betrayal. If they were truly troubled by something in your relationship, they owed you truthfulness—long before their heart strayed. Chances are, the real issue wasn't your "flaws" but their lack of honesty, lovingness, or moral resolve.

Rather than beat yourself up, now is the time to take a personal inventory of your growth areas and determine which ones to improve and which to accept as "you being you." What can you embrace as your God-given design, and what needs improving? Don't just sit there marinating in the Pool of Regret. *Do* something. Healing begins with movement.

WHAT TO DO

Accept Your "Unchangeables"

No matter how hard you try, you cannot change your temperament, personality, genetically determined looks, or overall body type, including your height, facial features, or bone structure. Stop comparing your physical features to those of movie stars, social media influencers, or anyone younger than yourself.

> "Which of you by worrying can add one cubit to his stature?" (Matthew 6:27, NKJV)

Instead, thank God for how he uniquely fashioned you. Don't forget—it is useless to compare yourself with the superficial qualities of an idealized lover. They are just as imperfectly human as you are. The only difference is that this person began cavorting with your spouse in an artificially-charged, forbidden, baggage-free relationship with someone who didn't belong to them. They have serious character flaws that will become evident to your ex once the glow of their rose-colored glasses wears off.

Now is the time to agree with God that his design of you was good. Stop resisting how the Lord has made you; instead, thank him for it. This will free your mind and heart to appreciate your strengths and value your more essential qualities, such as godly character, wisdom, and compassion.

Re-center Your Life on God

Instead of revolving your life around what your ex-spouse or others think of you, spend time alone with God. Look to him as your source of peace, love, and truth. Express your most intimate feelings to him and immerse yourself in Scripture. The Bible reveals God's heart for you and serves as the most accurate reflection of your value to him and the goodness of God's design and purpose for your life.

> Stop resisting how the Lord has made you; instead, thank him for it.

Many forsaken Christian spouses find solace through music. Listening to the lyrics, singing along, and worshiping the Lord can fill us with wonder and draw us closer to him. So can spending time in nature. My husband, Dan, feels closest to God when he is hiking on Mount Rainier, soaking in the wonder of our Creator's artistry.

Of course, writing your honest feelings to God in your journal is very therapeutic and helps expand your sense of intimacy with him. Pastor John Wimber used to say, "The key to intimacy with God is self-disclosure." I have found this to be true in my own life.

Reframe Your "Changeables" as "Growth Areas"

Instead of berating yourself for your weaknesses, view your changeable flaws as opportunities for improvement. Roll up your sleeves like a farmer tending a neglected garden. Pull out the weeds of bad habits, clip off your dead-head attitudes, and water the soil of your heart with what is true and good. If the task seems too large, be humble enough to seek help. Find a life coach, counselor, podcast, or support group, and research what you need to learn. These efforts will yield great rewards and allow the beauty and usefulness God intended for your life to thrive and bless others.

Create an ACTION PLAN to Address Your "Growth Areas"

Everyone has areas in their lives that need sanding, polishing, or refining. Instead of endlessly recriminating yourself for your faults and imperfections, mistakenly believing this will atone for your missteps or help you "win" your partner back, your efforts would be better spent stripping the layers of chipped paint off and applying a fresh coat of stain to bring out your underlying beauty. You likely don't need a complete overhaul. Just a little refinishing will do.

If you realize one or two of your shortcomings are troublesome defects, confess these to the Lord and find an accountability partner to support you as you repent and seek to change. For example, if you struggle with a compulsion or addiction, rather than engage in an endless cycle of thinking, "I'm such a louse, no wonder my spouse fell in love with someone else," reach for outside help such as specialized counseling, a support group, or a treatment center. There is no shame in seeking assistance to overcome a bad habit or shore up a weakness.

If you have identified a fault, such as "I refused to listen to my spouse's complaints about my spending habits," create a plan to correct this tendency. This may involve taking a class on realistic budgeting or reading an inspiring book, like *Heal Your Relationship with Money* by Kara Stevens. Another option is to discuss this issue frankly with a financial advisor or counselor you respect. People who mismanage money usually have emotional reasons for doing so or grew up in a family that lacked financial discipline.

If you are like me, you struggle with human frailties such as anxiety or idiosyncrasies that might irritate an impatient spouse but would be endearing or at least not bothersome to another. If you have a trait you consider worthy of change, then own it and make steps to improve.

Whatever your unique issues, don't mistake these for allowable reasons your partner left you. The lack of tolerance within your ex-spouse was likely exaggerated by their temporary euphoria and magnified by their guilt.

Let Go of Your Regrets

Most of a Betrandoned person's regrets aren't about outright sins or character flaws. Many of our regrets are situational, such as how we responded to the trauma of betrayal or the fear of being abandoned. Some regrets stem from typical human weaknesses that became more evident during a marital crisis. Extreme stress can bring out the worst in anyone.

Common regrets I hear from betrayed spouses concern their past feelings of desperation. Those who pleaded with their spouses to stay when they threatened to leave usually look back and feel chagrined by their lack of self-respect. They feel awful over memories of playing the "Pick-me Dance" that Tracy Shorn refers to in her book and blogs.[3] Or they look back with regret for wanting to salvage a marriage that became life-taking rather than life-giving to them.

Now that you understand the science and power of relationship attachment, as we touched on in previous chapters, you recognize there are logical reasons why the loss of your spouse felt life-threatening and caused you to react in unflattering ways. Forgive yourself for not realizing you overvalued your spouse and undervalued yourself. You thought you couldn't live without them. But you can, you did, and you will.

I suspect that many of your regrets are over the illusion that you had more control over your marital tragedy than you actually did. You may have bemoaned the "If Onlys" I discussed earlier, thinking that if you'd done something different, your marriage would have survived. I like what my friend Meredith says, "I couldn't stop that train from derailing. I'm not that powerful."

Still, others of you may regret marrying your spouse in the first place. Perhaps you overlooked the warning signs of trouble ahead or dismissed the concerns of close family and friends about your future marriage.

Rehearsing regrets bears no fruit and serves no good purpose. Let the "If Onlys" die a speedy death. You don't need them to make sense of your insensible loss or to find enough footing to move forward in your life. While there is some value in self-reflection, I like the saying,

> "The reason your front windshield is bigger than your rearview mirror is that where you're going is bigger than where you've been."[4]

If you experienced a later-in-life "grey divorce," *bigger* may not refer to the number of years ahead; it may mean greater in significance. Seek to finish strong by having a positive impact on your kids, grandkids, and other onlookers. Yet, remember that the ultimate "bigger" is your eternal future in heaven.

When you commit your ways to the Lord, he can transform your trials into precious qualities that will enhance your future beyond the horribleness of the past. Who can put a price on a greater love for truth, a closer walk with Christ, deeper faith and reliance on God, an expanded ability to empathize with others, and a bigger heart to love the wounded?

Drop the heavy load of regrets at the foot of the Cross. You can't change the past—or control your spouse's descent into deception. Once they bought into the Big Lie of Emotional Distortion and landed on the wrong side of the fence after wrestling with Cognitive Dissonance, they became deluded, excusing their wayward choices. That wasn't something you could fix.

What you *can* do is shift your focus. Instead of replaying the pain or insults, redirect your thoughts toward what Scripture encourages:

> "...whatever is true, whatever is noble, whatever is right, whatever is pure, whatever is lovely, whatever is admirable—if anything is excellent or praiseworthy—think about such things" (Philippians 4:8, NIV).

Ask yourself:

- Am I thinking about the lies I was told, or focusing on what is *true*?
- Am I concentrating on the ignoble wounds I have endured or the *noble* actions I have taken?
- Am I fixated on what was wrong, or choosing to dwell on what is *right*?
- Am I replaying the impure and unlovely acts of my former spouse, or noticing the *pure and lovely* blessings in my life?

It's time to turn off the mental screen replaying their ungodly choices—and tune into the blessings God has placed in your life. A powerful way to do this is by keeping a *Gratitude Journal*. Here are a few things you might include:

- I am still alive.
- My compassion and wisdom have grown by leaps and bounds.
- I'm emerging from betrayal with a deeper trust in my Beloved Lord.
- Scripture has become precious to me in fresh and life-giving ways.
- I've gained new and genuine friendships.
- I've learned to trust my intuition and respond with greater wisdom.
- I've become a better, more compassionate listener.
- I have a roof over my head.
- I don't carry the same guilt my ex-spouse does.
- I've recalibrated my values and no longer sweat the small stuff.

It takes extraordinary courage to emerge from the rubble of a Post-Affair Divorce with your sanity, character, and faith not only intact—but strengthened.

Accept Christ's Forgiveness

It can be challenging to tell the difference between legitimate guilt and unhealthy shame. But if you've identified real wrongs you've done, bring them to the Lord. Confess them to God and ask for his forgiveness. He promises that "if we confess our sins, he is faithful and just to forgive us and cleanse us from *all* unrighteousness" (1 John 1:9, emphasis added).

If God doesn't hold your sins against you, why should you keep holding them against yourself?

There's a wise saying: "It is wrong to sin, but it is *more* wrong not to accept forgiveness and to get up." Don't lie in the mud or keep punishing yourself secretly like Pastor Dimmesdale in *The Scarlet Letter*.

Instead, rest in one of the most beautiful truths of the Christian faith: Jesus did for you what you could never do for yourself—atone for your sins. He paid for *all* of them. You can't punish yourself enough to wipe them away.

But you can confess them, receive his forgiveness, and thank him for wiping the slate clean.

Then, get up—and move forward into the brighter, redeemed future waiting for you.

Forgive Yourself

Another important aspect of freeing yourself from self-condemnation is forgiving yourself for your shortcomings. For example, forgive yourself for your past denial. You are human. You wanted to believe the best. You've grown and learned so much since then. Let go of the shame that says, "I was such a fool." You're no longer naïve—you're wiser now. Rather than an "X," you deserve a "star" on your recovery chart.

Many Betrandoned spouses endure mistreatment no one should have to bear—repeated affairs, verbal or emotional abuse, threats, and more. If you experienced abuse growing up, you may have clung even harder to a destructive relationship, craving reassurance that you were lovable. But now is the time to face reality and stop seeking validation from someone who is no longer capable of loving you well.

> "Forgive yourself for the blindness that put you in the path of those who betray you. Sometimes, a good heart doesn't see the bad."
> ~Anonymous Facebook Meme

Turn off the *Regret Loop* in your mind and flip the switch to *Lessons Learned*. Build on those lessons. Focus forward. Give your energy to loving your children and engaging in meaningful, life-giving pursuits.

When you accept the Lord's design and love for you, you can realign with truth, grow in areas that need work, release your regrets, and extend grace to yourself. As the lies fall away and the weight of perfectionism lifts, you can move ahead with greater peace and confidence—no matter what challenges still lie ahead.

Now that we've walked through the many facets of healing from Betrandonment, let's close this book with stories meant to breathe hope and inspiration into your future.

SECTION VII

Recovering With Grace

"Your people will rebuild the ancient ruins; you will restore the age-old foundations; you will be called Repairer of the Breach, Restorer of the Streets of Dwelling."
~Isaiah 58:12

By now, you've seen just how much of your former life has been torn down—some of it dear to you, some best left behind. With God's help, you've set aside the lies and the false shame and cleared a new path for your feet. The way forward may not resemble the one you envisioned. It might feel rugged or unfamiliar. But you won't walk it alone. And it's not just for you—it's for your children and anyone who draws strength from your journey.

You've faced the wreckage. You've done the hard work. Now it's time to build on the solid truths you've discovered—blending the wisdom you've gained with the gold you've salvaged from your past.

This is redemption in motion. God is still writing your story. What was meant to harm you, he is using for good—not as the world defines good, but in the lasting, life-giving way as only he can.

You're no longer just surviving. You're rising—stronger, wiser, and full of grace.

Chapter 26

Your Story is Not Over

*Let us not abate our courage in doing what is right; for in due time
we shall reap a reward, if we do not faint.*
~Galatians 6:9

I'll never forget the moment I saw Joni Eareckson Tada paint with her mouth. She was on stage at a leadership conference I attended, holding a large paintbrush between her teeth. As she spoke, she described her carefree teenage years—riding horses, laughing with friends, full of dreams and unshakable confidence. All the while, she steadily worked on a painting: a stunning landscape of blue skies, towering mountains, and a sunlit beach.

The audience sat in quiet awe—not just of her artistry, but of the talent she possessed to create beauty without the use of her hands. Then, just as the scene neared completion, she dipped her brush once more and, without warning, slashed a thick, black stroke across the middle of the canvas.

The room gasped.

The beautiful picture was ruined—or so it seemed. That's when Joni began to tell the story behind the streak. At age seventeen, she dove off a dock into shallow water, not knowing it would change everything. The impact fractured her neck and left her paralyzed from the shoulders down. Had her sister not noticed she hadn't resurfaced, she would have drowned. In an instant, her vibrant, physical life vanished. What followed were months of depression, suicidal thoughts, and the deep grief of a young woman losing not just her independence, but the future she'd once imagined.

As she shared her pain, she began to rework the painting. With slow, deliberate strokes, she transformed the black gash. She added sweeping fronds above it, roots and blades of grass below. Before our eyes, the dark streak became the trunk of a palm tree—strong, grounded, and central to the scene.

The very mark of suffering had become a centerpiece of beauty in God's painting of her life.

She recounted meeting a bitter war veteran at one of her art exhibits, a man who mocked her belief in a God who would allow such suffering. Her response was both humble and powerful:

> "I'd rather be sitting in this wheelchair, knowing God, than standing like yourself, without Him."

If you know her story, you know how deeply Joni has impacted lives across the globe—especially those living with disabilities, through her organization, "Joni and Friends." She didn't deny the devastation of her accident. She grieved it. She wrestled with God. And in time, she discovered that even this could become a part of something greater.

Her life is a living testimony that suffering does not have to be the end of the story. The same can be true for you.

What follows are stories of some remarkable Betrandoned individuals I've met since my own journey began many years ago. Some have found joy in remarriage, while others have remained single, surrounded by a vibrant community of friends and family.

I wish I had the space to tell others' amazing stories of survival. Many, who, amidst hardship, went back to college and got an education to better their earning capacity. Single moms who took on two or three jobs just to make ends meet. People who had to battle illness or accidents while suffering unspeakable loss, or even homelessness. Yet those who pressed into their relationship with Christ and reached out for support grew in ways they are thankful for years later and are testimonies of the sustaining power and healing grace of God.

Elizabeth's Story

I'll start with my friend, Elizabeth, whom I've mentioned before. We found out about our spouses' betrayals around the same time. I don't know what I would have done without her. In my opinion, her experience was even more shocking and devastating than mine.

She and her husband of 33 years were well respected in the community and deeply involved in their children's lives—attending countless games and supporting their athletic pursuits through high school and college. They served faithfully at their church and supported an area youth ministry.

When she discovered her husband's secret post-office box, she uncovered decades of his involvement with prostitutes locally and out of state. I'll never forget visiting her after these discoveries—wide-eyed, traumatized, and sobbing uncontrollably.

I admired her willingness to even consider reconciliation during their two-year separation, including joint and separate counseling sessions. At one point, their therapist advised that her husband should come home and confess—not just to his wife, but also to their children—acknowledging the betrayal and emotional damage he'd caused. While he witnessed his wife's pain, he seemed unaware of its depth and offered their children only a sanitized version of the truth. Sadly, the kids thought she was overreacting.

Though he initially appeared willing to make an effort to save their marriage, she saw no lasting fruit—nothing she could trust. He remained emotionally remote and secretive. The long-term effects of his sex addiction, combined with deeply rooted rationalizations, had impaired both his ability and willingness to change. In the end, she found him too emotionally unsafe to trust.

Two addiction counselors assessed his condition and concluded that meaningful recovery was unlikely for him. After multiple meetings with her husband, even their pastor gently encouraged her to pursue divorce.

The costs of therapy, attorney fees, and their settlement caused her to lose nearly everything: their beautiful custom farmhouse on acreage, her lovely gardens, the freedom to work only part-time to stay on top of their property, kids' activities, and volunteer work, not to mention the many thousands of dollars he had drained from their family to maintain his addiction. She lost their secure retirement, her future dreams, and her intact family.

Because she didn't want to further diminish their father in their eyes, Elizabeth chose not to speak ill of him. Unfortunately, the children resented her for the divorce, which she found excruciating after pouring so much of herself into them. But over time, as young adults with families of their own, their hearts began to soften.

Elizabeth bought herself a small bungalow with her remaining money and held several responsible jobs; her experience working for a reputable catering company had opened the door for her to become a manager and earn an income.

Still, the stress from all she had endured took a toll on her health. Despite having no family history of cancer, she experienced recurring bouts of kidney cancer over eight years, which eventually spread to her liver.

Thankfully, Elizabeth had cultivated one of the most extensive networks of personal friends I've ever seen. When she needed rides to distant hospitals for her many surgeries and treatments, her friends rallied without hesitation.

She credits the Lord's guidance for helping her find a therapeutic protocol to use alongside her other treatments, with her oncologist's full support. Based on numerous PET scans over the past two and a half years, the protocol has eliminated all evidence of cancer in her body (as of the writing of my book).

What astounds me about Elizabeth is her steadfast love for Christ and her large group of devoted friends. And while the reverberations of her husband's sin have left their mark on them, two of her three adult children have come around and include her often with their families. She is one of the bravest, most honest, and most solid women of faith I know.

If you asked her today—twenty-five years later—whether her sorrows were worth her losses, she would say, "Yes, in many ways. Most of all, because I'm closer to Jesus than ever. He comforted me and brought more surprises and blessings than I could have imagined—especially the healing of my broken heart."

Terilyn's Story

While Terilyn (page 165, 212) and her husband, "Jack," were in the middle of buying a home, she sensed something was off. She asked him, "You're having an affair, aren't you?" He denied it. Within a week, he threatened her with divorce, and she asked him to join her in marriage counseling.

After storming out of their second counseling session, he finally admitted, "I'm polyamorous, and I'm seeing someone." Terilyn turned to him and said firmly, "Either end the affair, or you're not moving into our new house with us."

Jack's response was chilling. With steely eyes, he stormed to his car, peeled out of the parking lot, and drove off in a fury—violently tossing objects around as he went. When Terilyn got home that evening, the chaos continued. Items had been thrown around the house, evidence of his ongoing rage. That night, they had a tense and disturbing exchange in which Jack accused her of trying to take the children from him—completely ignoring the affair and his own destructive behavior.

Though he claimed to break off the relationship, Terilyn could tell his heart wasn't back. She no longer felt emotionally safe. Still hoping to salvage their family, she moved into the new home with Jack and their three children.

Three years later, she discovered Jack had secretly reconnected with his former lover. "I can't do this anymore," Terilyn told him. "I don't want a divorce, but you need to decide if you don't either." She eventually told him, "Here's your freedom to leave, if that's what you want."

During the separation, Jack quickly moved in with a new girlfriend and married her shortly after the divorce was final.

When I asked Terilyn how God redeemed her heartbreak, she said, "I knew I had to be intentional about four things: press into God, keep my job, keep my friends, and keep my kids."

No matter how low she felt, she showed up daily as a school psychologist, studied God's Word, made time for close friends who made her laugh, and prioritized meaningful moments with her children. She planned family dinners, one-on-one outings, and regular game nights. She checked in emotionally with each child and made up for lost time with fun family vacations—something they hadn't experienced when she was married.

> "I knew I had to be intentional about four things: press into God, keep my job, keep my friends, and keep my kids."

Over time, Terilyn prayerfully swallowed her pride and stayed cordial with her ex and his new wife—for the kids' sake. It paid off.

Today, Terilyn says God has healed her from the inside out. "I used to shrink or second-guess myself. Now, I can acknowledge someone's point of view and still stand firm. I'm learning to walk in the fullness of who God created me to be—not in a secular-feminist way, but with calm confidence."

She adds, "I used to think I was too much—too intense for people. Now I don't carry that shame or doubt anymore. I know who I am in Christ."

Terilyn continues to thrive in her career, organizes Christian women's retreats, trains leaders who help her mentor Muslim girls in Morocco, and has led a Betrandoned support group—allowing God to redeem her pain for a greater purpose.

Sandy's Story

Sandy[1] is another woman I deeply admire. After more than two decades of marriage, her husband had an affair with a much younger woman, got her pregnant, forced Sandy to be the one to file for divorce, lived with and later married his affair partner. When I asked Sandy how the Lord has redeemed her story, she had much to share.

"I had avoided healing from my early sexual abuse," she admitted. "But the trauma of my husband's betrayal and rejection forced me to seek healing for *all* of it."

Her words reflect a truth I often share with clients: *God uses current circumstances to access unhealed parts of ourselves.* That was certainly true for Sandy.

She went on to say, "It deepened my relationship with Jesus. I've never known the Lord like I do now. He's not just my God—He's my Comforter, Defender, and closest Friend."

Her suffering also awakened something new in her. "He's given me empathy I never had before. I can sit with others in their pain—not with answers, but with compassion. My heart breaks differently now. Softer. More like His."

Today, Sandy is emotionally grounded and more in tune with her own needs. She has become bolder in expressing herself and practices a healthy balance of self-compassion and care for others.

After her experience, Sandy founded a ministry called *Glory from Your Story* to comfort and empower betrayed and forsaken women. She has also led several Betrandoned support groups using the Workbook. She affectionately calls their private Facebook community "Betrandoned Warrior Sisters," a space where women uplift and encourage one another through shared pain and growing faith.

She is the Executive Director of *LifeTalk*, a faith-based pregnancy resource center. And in October 2023, Sandy married Dan—a faithful, loving man with two sons. Together, they enjoy a blended family, with some children still at home and others grown.

Sandy's life is a living picture of God's redemptive power: not just in restoring what was lost, but in rebuilding something even stronger—with beauty and meaningful purpose.

Gary's Story

> Gary poured himself into his relationship with Christ. He told me, "My unwanted divorce changed me for the better. I prayed, 'God, you're my only help.'"

In the aftermath of his soon-to-be-affair-sparked divorce, Gary (from Chapter 18) attended a divorce-recovery program at a nearby church. As it happened, my future husband, Dan MacDonald, was in the same small group, along with a lovely woman named "Sara" (page 154). One evening, as Gary shared his story with the group about losing his wife to another man, he pictured his broken heart lying on the floor for all to see.

When Sara's turn came, she wept as she described her husband's rejection and how he had left her for a younger woman. As she spoke, Gary envisioned her heart being placed on the floor right beside his. He couldn't help but wonder—was this a sign from God?

Gary gently suggested that he'd like to get to know her better as a friend and take plenty of time to do so. She was impressed that he wanted to take things slow. As they became acquainted, Gary learned that Sara was "floored" that a man could go through such a similar experience as her own. She had assumed only men left their wives and families to be with an outside lover.

In the meantime, Gary poured himself into his relationship with Christ. He told me, "My unwanted divorce changed me for the better. I prayed, 'God, you're my only help.'"

In the meantime, he did his best to be the father his four children needed and fill in the gaps caused by their mother's forsakenness. His Christian buddies came around him for support.

One of his friends was a mutual friend of Sara's, who commented to Gary, "She'd be *perfect* for you." With the memory of two hearts on the floor next to each other fresh in his mind, Gary privately agreed.

Over time, Gary and Sara fell in love and scheduled a date to get married. They asked my husband, Dan, to officiate the ceremony, which I was also privileged to attend.

Twenty years later, Gary and Sara are still together. He appreciates how she took his kids and grandchildren into her heart, which he also sought to do with her disillusioned daughters.

He told me, "Sara's stability and kindness were gifts to me from God." He likes that she is "gorgeous and sassy," able to speak up, unlike his former wife, who tended to cry and then shut down when she was upset, not allowing matters to be resolved.

But most of all, he credits the Lord with healing his broken heart and giving him a new and satisfying life. All six of their adult children follow the Lord in their own ways, which doesn't always happen after such a tragic family breakup, especially when the other parent forsakes their former faith.

Considerations Regarding Remarriage

When we're young, our ideals are often shaped by the culture around us—including the Christian subculture we may have grown up in. Too often, we're guided by chemistry, feelings, or unrealistic expectations in our first serious relationship. We may prioritize surface qualities over taking the time to truly know someone's character. And in the glow of new romance, it's easy to ignore the quiet warnings from our gut or pay heed to the concerns of others.

It's usually not until we've walked through deep pain and gained life experience that we develop the discernment and maturity needed for healthier relationships. After enduring trauma or grief, we often come to know ourselves better and ideally begin to heal from the wounds and dysfunctions of our past.

The hard-won lessons from your broken marriage will serve you well going forward. Hopefully, you've learned to trust your deeper instincts and take them seriously. Self-doubt won't trip you up the way it once did. When concerns crop up, you'll examine them carefully and speak up rather than gloss over them. If you still suspect a warning bell is your trauma talking and not your deeper gut, seek a trauma therapist for extra help.

Now that you've faced the unthinkable and survived, the little things won't shake you as easily. You know what truly matters. You'll find it easier to offer grace and make space for harmless differences—because your sense of worth no longer hinges on someone else. You've learned to rest in Christ's love first.

From what I've observed, disappointing remarriages often happen when someone rushes into a new romance or physical intimacy too quickly after divorce. Having been previously married, it's easy to fall into familiar patterns—especially sexual compromise—which can cloud your judgment when red flags appear.

When considering a potential partner, the older we get, the slimmer the pickings. So please be careful. I've heard horror stories of freshly separated or divorced people who, in their vulnerable state, met someone who "love bombed" them and were fooled into living with or marrying someone who turned out to be a flattering narcissist.

Still others report meeting a supposedly Christian man or woman on a Christian dating site who expected sex on the first or second date. You've already suffered from living with a person who threw their morals to the wind. Don't gamble on someone who rationalizes sin.

On the other hand, as imperfect people, everyone possesses some form of brokenness in their past. No one arrives at midlife without baggage of some sort. Some questions to consider when dating:

- "Did this person cheat in prior serious relationships?"
- "If they have a history of serious mistakes, did they learn from their past wrongs?"
- "Have they shored up their character by living differently for a considerable length of time (years, not months)?"
- "Are they willing to apologize when wrong?"
- "Do they have a tender, responsive heart toward God?"
- "Do they have a good relationship with their kids?"
- "Do they have meaningful friendships?"
- "Do you like yourself when you are with them?" (the *Straight-Mirror* vs. *Bent-Mirror* test).

When it comes to a future remarriage, remember: You will love differently the second time around. My love for Dan is deeper and more grounding than what I had with James. I don't place him on a pedestal—and that's a good thing. My identity is now rooted in Christ, not in my husband. That shift has given me the freedom to be my authentic self and less on edge with Dan than I was in my prior marriage.

That said, second and third marriages come with added complexities. While first marriages typically end because of problems between the couple, later marriages often dissolve due to conflicts surrounding the children. Stepfamilies are born out of grief and loss and often carry more loyalty struggles and relational landmines than first-time families.

I wish I had the space here to fully unpack the challenges of parenting, co-parenting, and navigating stepfamily dynamics after a Post-Affair Divorce. For many betrayed spouses, their deepest grief goes beyond the betrayal and divorce—it's the lasting impact on their children and the emotional toll of custody battles and uncooperative ex-spouses.

If you do marry again and form a blended family, recognize that your new partner comes as a "package deal." Their children and extended family may not feel as natural to you as your first family did—especially in the beginning. But if you choose to invest in them and love them as your own, you can make a positive, indelible impact on kids who've experienced the upheaval of a broken home. In time, the bonds you build will become part of your legacy.[2]

And when grandkids arrive—whether from your side or theirs—they won't know the difference. To them, you'll simply be the Nanna or Grandpa they adore.

Take your time. As the saying goes, get to know a potential partner through all four seasons, so you can see how they respond to different situations and relationships.

What if You Don't Remarry?

And, if remarriage isn't part of your story, your life can still be full and meaningful. You can nurture lifelong friendships, embrace new callings, and pursue repurposed goals, just like Elizabeth, Terilyn, and Cheryl (Chapter 24).

If you don't meet someone who truly enriches your life—emotionally, spiritually, and relationally—it's better to remain unmarried than to tie yourself to someone who doesn't share your values or is unloving, neglectful, or emotionally draining.

> It's better to remain unmarried than to tie yourself to someone who doesn't share your values or is unloving, neglectful, or emotionally draining.

Whether your path leads to remarriage or to renewed singleness, may your aim be the same: to become the most loving, grounded, and authentic version of yourself. Keep deepening your walk with the Lord, nurturing meaningful friendships, investing in your children and grandchildren, pursuing satisfying ways to serve God, and living in a way that glorifies him.

My Story

You've already read parts of my journey through my Post-Affair Divorce—specifically the moments that led to hard-won lessons, recovery, and healing. And, by "recovery," I don't mean a life free of sorrow. I still face trials and occasional echoes of loss. But compared to the despair of those early days, I am grateful to be alive, grounded, and thriving.

Here are a few things I would never trade:

- **A deeper walk with the Lord.** I had nowhere else to turn, which was a blessing. He showed up through Scripture, prayer, wise friends, and a trauma-informed therapist.
- **A purified faith**. Real faith is forged in fire. Mine is now more grounded, less superficial, and more willing to let God be God.
- **An increased love for Scripture.** God's Word became my anchor when everything else spun out of control. The truth of Scripture transcended my emotions, my ex-husband's choices, and the instability around me.
- **Renewed confidence**. Though rejection amplified old insecurities initially, God helped me shed the lies of unworthiness and rebuild my self-esteem in him.
- **A kinder, more compassionate self**. Pain softened my edges. I listen better now. I judge less. I like the woman I've become.

Seismic loss has a way of clarifying what really matters. It changed how I chose friends, and it reshaped what I looked for in a future partner. Gone was the idealistic young woman hoping for a strong, impressive Christian leader to validate and complete her. I began to see how much I had projected an idealistic image onto my former husband—one that didn't reflect his full, broken humanity.

This time, I wanted something different: someone kind, strong without being domineering, emotionally safe, and spiritually genuine. Neil Clark Warren's book *Date or Soul Mate?*[3] helped me define my new "Ten Must-Haves" and "Ten Can't-Stands." I traded my former goal of finding an "impressive Christian man" for someone "strong in character, loving, empathetic, and faithful." Sarcasm, which had always felt like subtle criticism, joined my deal-breaker list.

After a few low-key dating experiences, some friends introduced me to Dan MacDonald. Our initial conversation left me thinking, *He's led such an exciting life, I'd never get tired of this man!*

On our first date, walking along the waterfront, I fondly noted, *he shares his faith naturally and talks to God like I do.* We also discovered we had a number of mutual friends whom I respected from past seasons of life.

On our second date, a challenging hike to Panorama Point on Mount Rainier, I saw how much he loved nature and possessed spiritual depth. On our way to the mountain, he even preached at a small country church on Romans 8:28 with a clarity and humility I found refreshing.

As we became more acquainted, I saw in Dan *every one* of my Must-Haves—and *none* of my Can't-Stands. That summer was filled with hikes, outdoor concerts, meaningful conversations, and the joy of meeting each other's families. I thought his young adult daughters were adorable. And, when I met his parents, Harry and Hope, I instantly felt welcomed. Their warmth, hospitality, and ministry stories moved me. I saw firsthand the kind of home that shaped Dan into such a loving, kind-hearted person.

Dan proposed on December 7 (Pearl Harbor Day), and we were married on May 1, 2004—May Day. Our wedding theme was "Redemption." Dan set a poem I'd written to music and sang it to me at our wedding. When our guests stood to sing "Great Is Thy Faithfulness," I had goosebumps. It was, truly, a new and more mature "happiest day of my life."

While my personal life was being restored, so was my professional calling. Though I stepped back temporarily due to PTSD, my counseling practice didn't just recover—it expanded. I became more passionate about helping couples heal when possible, so others wouldn't face the compounded devastation I had.

The article I'd once written for unfaithful spouses eventually became *How to Help Your Spouse Heal from Your Affair*—a book I thought would be a minor resource—ended up helping thousands. Letters from readers still remind me that God uses our broken places for good.

I've since led groups, spoken at conferences, and walked alongside many betrayed men and women. Every time I do, I remember how far God has brought me—and how much he can do for others.

What I thought was the end of my life turned out to be a temporary rough patch leading to new and deeper purposes for me.

I hope you caught the primary Source of healing from the aforementioned stories: Jesus Christ and his revitalizing love and purpose. No human person can restore what the enemy has stolen from you. Only God can make up for a pummeled self-esteem, broken family, and the feelings of inadequacy that we've battled off and on our entire lives. Sometimes it takes losing everything to realize how much we need the Lord.

I love how author Allie Beth Stuckey puts it:

> There's a reason Jesus describes himself as Living Water and Bread of Life: he satisfies. The searching for peace and for purpose stops in him alone. He created us; therefore only he can tell us who we are and why we're here.[4]

I would add that only God can redeem the hardships in our lives, especially when we entrust all the messiness to him. If he can rebuild my life and the lives of other Betrandoned people, he can rebuild yours, too.

I hope this book has provided stepping stones to help free you from the trauma, grief, abuse, shame, lies, discouraged faith, and emotional injuries of intimate betrayal—and to discover the many ways God desires to redeem your Post-Affair Divorce into a renewed, replenished, and meaningful life.

May the following promise and prayer be an encouragement to you:

> "The LORD *will* fulfill His purpose for me. O LORD, Your loving devotion endures forever—do not abandon the works of Your hands" (Psalm 138:8, emphasis added).

Endnotes

Introduction: My Story

1. https://www.nydailynews.com/life-style/facebook-ruining-marriage-social-network-named-divorce-filings-2011-article-1.1083913

2. https://onlinelibrary.wiley.com/doi/epdf/10.1111/j.0038-4941.2004.08501006.x?r3_referer=wol

3. Glass, S., & Staehli, J. (2003). *NOT "Just Friends:" Protect Your Relationship from Infidelity and Heal the Trauma of Betrayal.* New York: The Free Press. 8.

4. Personal interview with CSAT, CSAT-S, therapist Rob Baker, July 1, 2022.

5. I include polyamory, which means "many loves," as affair behavior, despite polyamorist apologists' efforts to whitewash their adulteries because they supposedly do so with their spouses' "consent" (often with one partner pressured or manipulated into agreeing). This dressed-up version of wife-swapping or "open marriage" from the 1960s still qualifies as extra-marital sex. Their "rules" of engagement, used to legitimize their liaisons, are difficult to enforce, wreak havoc on families, and often lead to the eventual breakup of their marriages. I expect objective, longitudinal studies will bear this out.

6. Scott S.B, & Rhoades G.K, & Stanley S.M, & Allen E.S, & Markman H.J. (2013). Reasons for Divorce and Recollections of Premarital Intervention: Implications for Improving Relationship Education. Couple & Family Psychol. 2013 Jun;2(2):131-145. doi: 10.1037/a0032025. PMID: 24818068; PMCID: PMC4012696.

   Note 1: Table 1 shows that the second most common reason for divorce cited by couples was "infidelity," endorsed by 59.6% (rounded up to 60%) of the participants. Yet, when the results of the couples were separated out, at least one partner reported infidelity as a major contributing factor 88.8% of the time (underlining, mine). I give more credence to the latter statistic (88.8%), as it likely points to reports by betrayed spouses. I've learned that the unfaithful tend to downplay the role infidelity played in the breakdown of their marriages.

   Note 2: Another larger survey in Oklahoma found 62% of female respondents reported infidelity and extramarital affairs as contributing to their divorce. Johnson, Christine & Stanley, Scott & Glenn, N. & Amato, P. & Nock, S. & Markman, Howard. (2002). Marriage in Oklahoma: 2001 Baseline Statewide Survey on Marriage and Divorce. Oklahoma State University Bureau for Social Research. 16.

7. https://www.cdc.gov/nchs/fastats/marriage-divorce.htm. According to the National Center for Health Statistics, there were 746,971 divorces in 2018 (based on 45 reporting states and D.C.; I used the results from 2018 since COVID-19 skewed some statistics in 2020-2021). When this number (746,971) is multiplied by 88% and divided by 365 days, it suggests there are an average of 1800 affair-impacted divorces per day (not including the other five states that no longer report divorce statistics). If the more conservative number of affair-sparked divorces (60%) is considered, that means a minimum average of 1200 infidelity-inspired divorces occur each day in the United States. This is how I postulate the average range of infidelity-influenced divorces as between an astounding 1200 and 1800 per day.

8. Marin, R. A. & Christiansen, A. & Atkins, D. A., (2014) Couple and Family Psychology: Research and Practice. American Psychological Association. Vol. 3, No. 1, 1–12 2160-4096/14/DOI: 10.1037/cfp0000012

9. https://www.pewresearch.org/fact-tank/2017/03/09/led-by-baby-boomers-divorce-rates-climb-for-americas-50-population/

10. Wolfinger, N. "America's Generation Gap in Extramarital Sex." Institute for Family Studies. July 5, 2017. https://ifstudies.org/blog/americas-generation-gap-in-extramarital-sex

11. Parejko, J. (2002). *Stolen Vows: The Illusion of No-Fault Divorce and the Rise of the American Divorce Industry*. 26, 72–73

12. Former client's story, used by permission.

13. Becky, at https://riseuprestored.com/my-story-1, used by permission.

14 Notes from a professional workshop, "Crises in Fidelity and Infidelity." Frank Pittman III, M.D. April 24-25, 1987.

CHAPTER 1: My Battle

1. Rudd, M. David. "The Risk of Suicide in Clinical Practice: Recognizing the Links Between PTSD and Suicidality." Journal of Clinical Psychology, vol. 62, no. 12, 2006, pp. 1545–1550.

CHAPTER 2: Betrandonment Grief

1. The term, "ambiguous loss" was introduced by Pauline Boss, a professor at Harvard University and author of the book, *Ambiguous Loss: Learning to Live with Unresolved Grief*, (1999). A more recent book on ambiguous loss as applied to marital rejection is *SoulBroken: A Guidebook for Your Journey Through Ambiguous Grief* (2022) by Stephanie Sarazin.

2. http://widowconnection.com/resources/7-tips-to-help-a-widow/

3. Personal communication with a Zoom group member. April 23, 2025

4. Dobson, J. (1983). *Love Must Be Tough: New Hope for Families in Crisis*. Waco: Word Books. 82.

5. Personal communication with a Zoom group member. December 1, 2022.
6. Written communication with a former client. Used by permission.
7. Middleton-Moz, J., Dwinell, L. (1986). *After the Tears: Helping Adult Children of Alcoholics Heal Their Childhood Trauma*. Health Communications. The exact quote is by Lorie Dwinell, whom I heard at an Adult Children of Alcoholics seminar in 1984.
8. Email exchange with an anonymous woman in a private Facebook group, July 9, 2023.
9. Erickson, Ruth. (2022). *(UN)Faithful: Finding Healing After Your Husband's Affair (Whether Your Marriage Survives Or Not)*. Wellington, New Zealand: Torn Curtain Publishing. 188, 189.

CHAPTER 3: The Trauma from the Drama

1. Glass, S., & Staeheli, J. (1998). *NOT "Just Friends": Protect Your Relationship from Infidelity and Heal the Trauma of Betrayal*. New York: The Free Press. 96.
2. http://traumadissociation.com/ptsd/history-of-post-traumatic-stress-disorder.html
3. https://drjillmanning.com/betrayal-trauma/
4. Risner, Vaneetha R. (2021). *Walking Through Fire: A Memoir of Loss and Redemption*. Nashville: Nelson Books. 123.
5. Glass, S. Infidelity. (2002). AAMFT brochure, Item #1053.
6. Carnes, P. (2019). *The Betrayal Bond: Breaking Free of Exploitive Relationships*. Deerfield Beach, Florida: Health Communications. 67.
7. Rosse, R., M.D. (1999). *The Love Trauma Syndrome: Free Yourself from the Pain of a Broken Heart*. New York: Plenum Publishing Corp. 12.
8. Rosse, R. 14–15.
9. Anderson, S. (2000). *The Journey from Abandonment to Healing*. New York: Berkley Books. 39, 44–49.
10. Three books I recommend on the subject of trauma: *The Body Keeps the Score* by Bessel Van der Kolk, *Your Sexually Addicted Spouse* by Barbara Steffens and Marsha Means, and *Intimate Deception* by Dr. Sheri Keffer.

CHAPTER 4: Healing the Trauma

1. Smith, J. E. (2015). Infidelity and posttraumatic stress disorder (PTSD): What it's all about and what you can do about it [PDF]. https://www.emotionalaffair.org/wp-content/uploads/2015/08/Infidelity-and-Posttraumatic-Stress-Disorder_Smith.pdf.
2. Glass, S., Staeheli, J. (1998). *NOT "Just Friends": Protect Your Relationship from Infidelity and Heal the Trauma of Betrayal*. New York: The Free Press.

96. She also says this in her seminars

3. Schiraldi, Glenn, Ph.D., (2000). *The Post-Traumatic Stress Disorder Sourcebook*, New York: McGraw-Hill. 7.

4. Frank, J. (1995). *Door of Hope: Recognizing and Resolving the Pains of Your Past*. Nashville: Thomas Nelson. 75. [Therapist and author Jan Frank credits Robert Schuller for the phrase, "face them, trace them, and erase them," regarding problems in our lives. When I attended her workshop for therapists, I noted she added the word "replace" to the end of the sequence in her work with victims of sexual abuse. I liked this series of words so much that I adopted it in my work with traumatized clients and in this book, only changing the order to Face, Trace, Replace, Erase.]

5. Quote from Dr. Nickerson's Instagram page, posted 6/16/25, used by permission.

6. van der Kolk, B. (2002). In Terror's Grip: Healing the Ravages of Trauma. Cerebrum. 4.

7. Williams, F., Ph.D. (2022). *Heartbreak: A Personal and Scientific Journey*, New York: W. W. Norton & Company, Inc., 116.

8. Theophostic Prayer (Theo = "God," Phostic = "Light") came under a degree of criticism for certain aspects that Ed Smith no longer promotes (particularly his prayer against demonic forces at the start of a session). The ministry has been renamed Transformation Prayer Ministry, and in the right hands, I believe it is still a powerful tool. For an objective evaluation of Dr. Smith's approach, see Christian Research Institute's article by Elliot Miller: https://www.equip.org/article/theophostic-prayer-ministry-part-one/

CHAPTER 5: Betrayal as Abuse

1. Former client. Permission given to use her story, September 3, 2023.

2. https://www.psychologytoday.com/us/blog/anger-in-the-age-entitlement/201311/why-frame-abuse-betrayal

3. Ibid.

4. Ibid.

5. Personal communication with a private Facebook member. 2023.

6. https://www.betrayalviolenceinstitute.com/

7. To further understand this tactic, read up on "Spiritual Bypassing," where individuals use spiritual-sounding language as a defense mechanism.

8. S. Rachman (2010). Betrayal: A psychological analysis, Behaviour Research and Therapy, Volume 48, Issue 4, 2010, Pages 304-311.

9. Seyed Aghamiri, Fakri & Luetz, Johannes & Hills, Karenne. (2024). The Lived Experiences and Well-Being of Female Partners Following Discovery or Disclosure of Their Male Partner's Compulsive Sexual Behaviours: An Australian Phenomenological Study. Sexuality Research and Social Policy. 1-28.

10. Mayer E. A. (2011). Gut feelings: the emerging biology of gut-brain communication. Nature Reviews Neuroscience, 12 (8), 453–466. https://doi.org/10.1038/nrn3071Mayer; and, https://www.scientificamerican.com/article/gut-second-brain/ and, https://www.brainfacts.org/brain-anatomy-and-function/body-systems/2021/trust-your-gut-how-the-brain-gut-connection-helps-us-decide-intuitively-100121

11. de Becker, G. (2021). *The Gift of Fear: Survival Instincts that Protect Us from Violence*. New York: Back Bay Books.

12. https://www.hoperay.com/podcast

CHAPTER 6: Double Humiliation

1. *Ghost Town* (movie, 2008). Permission to quote Gwen's three questions, granted by screenwriters: David Koepp and John Kamps.

2. Risner, Vaneetha R. (2021). *Walking Through Fire: A Memoir of Loss and Redemption*. Nelson Books: Nashville. 139.

3. https://julietjeskeblog.com/2012/05/on-being-a-straight-spouse-broken-memories/

4. https://www.out.com/news-opinion/2015/8/13/meet-women-who-pick-pieces-after-their-husbands-come-out

5. https://www.out.com/news-opinion/2015/8/13/meet-women-who-pick-.pieces-after-their-husbands-come-out

6. https://www.blogtalkradio.com/bonnielkaye

7. https://ourpath.org/ and, https://www.healingbeyonddiscovery.org/resources

8. Krieg, L. & Krieg, M. (2020), *An Impossible Marriage: What Our Mixed-Orientation Marriage Has Taught Us About Love and the Gospel*. Downers Grove: Intervarsity Press.

CHAPTER 7: The Shame of Divorce

1. Personal communication with a private Facebook group member, 2023.

2. Our culture and even some in the Christian community have radically shifted in their views on gender and same-sex relationships in the past 20 years. I have dear friends and relatives who align with our culture on this topic. I seek no animus with them. However, Jesus quoted these Old Testament passages in his discussion with Jewish leaders to explain God's original intent for marriage, which we ought not to easily dismiss

3. For further reading, consider Beyer, E., editor (2017). *Mutual by Design: A Better Model of Christian Marriage*. Minneapolis: Christians for Biblical Equality; and Instone-Brewer, D. (2006) *Divorce and Remarriage in the Church: Biblical Solutions for Pastoral Realities*. Westmont, Ill: Intervarsity Press.

4. While Jay attributes their reconciliation to him realizing his wife's love for him, if you read between the lines, I believe you'll see that Julie's stance of finally setting boundaries and showing more self-respect played a key role in influencing his change of heart back toward her.

CHAPTER 8: The Shame of Rejection

1. Bennett, M. (1991). *Sudden Endings: Wife Rejection in Happy Marriages.* New York: William Morrow and Company, Inc., back cover of the book.
2. Stark, V. (2010). *Runaway Husbands: The Abandoned Wife's Guide to Recovery and Renewal.* Montreal, Canada: Green Light Press.

CHAPTER 9: Shame for Leaving

1. Personal communication with a private Facebook group member, June 2025.
2. https://www.merriam-webster.com/dictionary/rail
3. https://leslievernick.com/
4. https://www.amazon.com/Leave-Cheater-Gain-Life-Survival/dp/0762458968/

CHAPTER 10: Missing the Red Flags

1. Minwalla, O., PhD (2021). White paper, PDF. "The Secret Sexual Basement: The Traumatic Impacts of Deceptive Sexuality on the Intimate Partner and Relationship." https://minwallamodel.com/wp-content/uploads/2023/03/The_Secret_Sexual_Basement_Nov_2021.pdf
2. Freyd, J., PhD, Birrell, P., PhD. (2013). *Blind to Betrayal: Why We Fool Ourselves We Aren't Being Fooled*, Hoboken, New Jersey: John Wiley & Sons, Inc., 68.
3. Ibid. ix.
4. Ibid. x.
5. Ibid. 85.
6. Stack, S., Wasserman, I., & Kern, R. "Adult Social Bonds and Use of Internet Pornography," Social Science Quarterly, 85 (2004): 75-88.

CHAPTER 11: Shame for the Rage

1. Stosny, S. PhD (2013). *Living & Loving After Betrayal: How to Heal from Emotional Abuse, Deceit, Infidelity, and Chronic Resentment.* Oakland: New Harbinger Publications, Inc., 79.
2. Hollenbeck, Ed.D., LMHC, C. M., & Steffens, Ph.D., B. (2024). Betrayal Trauma Anger: Clinical Implications for Therapeutic Treatment based on the Sexually Betrayed Partner's Experience Related to Anger after Intimate Betrayal. Journal of Sex & Marital Therapy, 50(4), 456–467.https://doi.org/1

0.1080/0092623X.2024.2306940

3. https://instagram.com/hopeafterbetrayal
4. Personal communication with a support group member, October 19, 2023.

CHAPTER 12: The Iceberg Below

1. https://www.youtube.com/watch?v=SHWEpO6r0S4, by Academic TV.
2. Weil, B. (2003, second edition). *Adultery: The Forgivable Sin*. Poughkeepsie, NY: Hudson House. xxiv.
3. Ibid. 41.
4. https://www.dailymail.co.uk/news/article-13946693/ethel-kennedy-stood-husband-robert-affairs-death.html
5. I could not find the original article from The Boston Globe as referred to by blog writer, Stanton Peele, Ph.D., J.D. Here is his blog post that quotes The Boston Globe. https://www.psychologytoday.com/us/blog/addiction-in-society/200805/the-top-seven-kennedy-sex-scandals
6. True story by a group support member. Used by permission.
7. https://drkathynickerson.com/blogs/relationship/why-infidelity-isn-t-about-morality-what-pain-fear-and-psychology-teach-us-about-betrayal
8. Girous, C. (2021). Early Exposure to Pornography: A Form of Sexual Trauma. Journal of Psychiatry Reform, Vol. 10, No. #15. https://journalofpsychiatryreform.com/2021/12/07/early-exposure-to-pornography-a-form-of-sexual-trauma/ ISSN 2371-4301
9. Jespersen AF, Lalumière ML, Seto MC. (2009). Sexual abuse history among adult sex offenders and non-sex offenders: a meta-analysis. Child Abuse & Neglect. Mar;33(3):179-92.
10. True story by a former client. Used by permission.
11. Thoburn, J.W., Balswick, J.O. An evaluation of infidelity among male protestant clergy. Pastoral Psychology, 42, 285–294 (1994). https://doi.org/10.1007/BF01789516
12. Former client. Story used by permission. January 18, 2025.
13. Personal communication with a Zoom group member. Jan 11, 2024.

CHAPTER 13: Underlying Disorders

1. True story by a former client. Used by permission.
2. https://www.onlyyouforever.com/why-church-leaders-are-vulnerable-to-infidelity-pornography/
3. Altınok A, Kılıç N. (2020). Exploring the associations between narcissism, intentions towards infidelity, and relationship satisfaction: Attachment styles as a moderator. PLoS ONE 15(11): e0242277.

4. Ibid.

5. Gillette, H. https://psychcentral.com/relationships/signs-youre-dating-a-cheating-narcissist

6. Russ, E., Shedler, J., Bradley, R., Westen, D. (2008). Refining the construct of narcissistic personality disorder: diagnostic criteria and subtypes. Am J Psychiatry. Nov;165(11):1473-81.

7. Stinson, F. S., Dawson, D. A., Goldstein, R. B., Chou, S. P., Huang, B., Smith, S. M., Ruan, W. J., Pulay, A. J., Saha, T. D., Pickering, R. P., & Grant, B. F. (2008). Prevalence, correlates, disability, and comorbidity of DSM-IV narcissistic personality disorder: results from the wave 2 national epidemiologic survey on alcohol and related conditions. The Journal of Clinical Psychiatry, 69(7), 1033–1045. https://doi.org/10.4088/jcp.v69n0701

8. Mitra, P., Fluyau, D. Narcissistic Personality Disorder. [Updated 2023 Mar 13]. In: StatPearls [Internet]. Treasure Island (FL): StatPearls Publishing; 2024 Jan. Available from: https://www.ncbi.nlm.nih.gov/books/NBK556001/

9. Freyd, J., Ph.D., Birrell, P., Ph.D. (2013). *Blind to Betrayal: Why We Fool Ourselves We Aren't Being Fooled.* New Jersey: John Wiley & Sons, Inc. 119.

10. True story by a woman in our Zoom group. Used by permission.

11. Written communication with a woman in my Zoom support group. Used by permission.

12. https://www.caregiver.org/resource/coping-behavior-problems-after-brain-injury/

CHAPTER 14: Footholds

1. Stack, S., Wasserman, I., and Kern, R. "Adult Social Bonds and Use of Internet Pornography," (2004). Social Science Quarterly, 85. 75-88.

2. McQuivey, J.L, Ph.D. (2019). "The Road to Infidelity Passes Through Multiple Sex Partners." Institute for Family Studies. https://ifstudies.org/blog/the-road-to-infidelity-passes-through-multiple-sexual-partners

3. If your spouse struggled with a sex addiction of any kind, they needed professional counseling by a Certified Sex Addictions Therapist (CSAT), found on the https://www.iitap.org website. At the same time, ministries such as Pure Desire, Be Broken, Pure Life Ministries, and Prodigals International can serve as valuable spiritual adjuncts to recovery.

4. Based on a conversation with a Zoom group friend, February 2024. Used by permission.

5. Strawberry, D. (2010). *Straw: Finding My Way.* New York: ECCO, an imprint of HarperCollins.

CHAPTER 15: Emotional Distortion

1. https://www.nytimes.com/2000/07/07/nyregion/safety-board-blames-pilot-error-in-crash-of-kennedy-plane.html
2. Fisher, H., Ph.D. (2004). *Why We Love: The Nature and Chemistry of Romantic Love*. New York: St. Martin's Press. 71.
3. Hein, H. (2000). *Sexual Detours*. New York: St. Martin's Griffin, 42.
4. Dr. Pat Love is the author of many books on sex and marriage; she refers to the concept of "barriers" heightening the intensity of sexual attraction, based on the research of Helen Fischer and others, in one of her workshops at a Smart Marriages conference.
5. Fisher, H., Ph.D. (1992) *Anatomy of Love*. New York: Random House.163.
6. Fisher, H., Ph.D. (2004). *Why We Love: The Nature and Chemistry of Romantic Love*. New York: St. Martin's Griffin, 16-17
7. Fugère, M. Ph.D. (July 17, 2017). The Allure of Forbidden Relationships: And why it isn't helpful to try to prevent them. Psychology Today Online. https://www.psychologytoday.com/us/blog/dating-and-mating/201707/the-allure-forbidden-relationships#:~:text=Althought%20forbidden%20%relationships%20%may%20%be%20streanthened%20by%20the.more%20likely%20to%20endure%20%28%Sinclair%20et%20al.%2C%202014%29.
8. FAA's Pilot's Handbook of Aeronautical Knowledge, (2023) 17-10; Pages 17-6 through 17-29 offer more detail on how the body's non-visual senses can lead to dangerous "convincing sensory illusions." https://www.faa.gov/regulations_policies/handbooks_manuals/aviation/faa-h-8083-25c.pdf
9. Several of these factors correlate with FAA's "five hazardous attitudes" listed on page 2-5 in the Pilot's Handbook of Aeronautical Knowledge, including: anti-authority, impulsivity, invulnerability, macho, and resignation.
10. https://www.forbes.com/sites/kimelsesser/2019/02/14/these-6-surprising-office-romance-stats-should-be-a-wake-up-call-to-organizations/?sh=-5467922c23a2
11. https://www.timeshighereducation.com/news/risk-takers-more-prone-to-infidelity/177569.article
12. https://www.timeshighereducation.com/news/risk-takers-more-prone-to-infidelity/177569.article
13. Breines, J. PhD. points out how a person's "need for novelty" can contribute to a desire for outside trysts in this article: https://www.psychologytoday.com/us/blog/in-love-and-war/201403/how-likely-is-your-partner-cheat
14. Fitzgerald, V. LCSW. (2019). The Affair "Bubble" Is a Place of Deception and Delusion. https://healingprose.com/?p=710
15. Farrar, S. (1995). *Finishing Strong: Finding the Power to Go the Distance*. Sisters, Oregon: Multnomah Books. 217.

16. Finlayson, A. (1892). Life's Clothing: The Righteousness of Christ. The Quiver: An Illustrated Magazine for Sunday and General Reading. London: Cassell & Company, Ltd. 661.

CHAPTER 16: Cognitive Dissonance

1. Pseudonym.
2. Festinger, L. (1957). *A Theory of Cognitive Dissonance.* Stanford, CA: Stanford University Press.
3. Tavris, C. & Aronson, E., *Mistakes Were Made (but not by me): Why We Justify Foolish Beliefs, Bad Decisions, and Hurtful Acts.* Orlando: Harcourt, Inc. 37.
4. Ibid. 30–31.
5. Ibid. 70.
6. Personal communication with a Zoom group member. April 11, 2023.

CHAPTER 17: Rewriting the Marital History

1. Gottman, J. & Silver, N. (2012). *What Makes Love Last? How to Build Trust and Avoid Betrayal.* New York: Simon & Schuster, 35.
2. https://www.gottman.com/blog/the-magic-relationship-ratio-according-science/
3. Permission to quote *The Story of Us* movie, granted by script writers Alan Zweibel and Jessie Nelson.
4. Tavris, C. & Aronson, E. (2007). *Mistakes Were Made (but not by me): Why We Justify Foolish Beliefs, Bad Decisions, and Hurtful Acts.* Orlando: Harcourt, Inc. 172.
5. Interview with a member of our Zoom support group. Used by permission
6. Interview with a member of our Zoom support group. Used by permission
7. Interview with a member of our Zoom support group. Used by permission
8. Tavris, C. & Aronson, E. (2007). *Mistakes Were Made (but not by me): Why We Justify Foolish Beliefs, Bad Decisions, and Hurtful Acts.* Orlando: Harcourt, Inc. 6.
9. Ibid. 173.
10. Glass, S. & Staehli, J. (2003). NOT "Just Friends:" Protect Your Relationship from Infidelity and Heal the Trauma of Betrayal. New York: The Free Press. 126.
11. Ibid. 218.
12. Ibid. 358.
13. Interview with a member of our Zoom support group. Used by permission.

CHAPTER 18: The Alien Syndrome

1. Personal communication with a friend, July 9, 2025. Used by permission.
2. Personal conversation with a betrayed and abandoned therapist at a professional workshop, February 5, 2005.
3. True story by a former client. Used by permission.
4. Personal communication with a Zoom support group member, 2024
5. Personal communication with a Zoom support group member, 2023.
6. Riley, L. (2006, September). Affairs: What is true about affairs and what is not? Lifeworks Group. https://lifeworksgroup.blogspot.com/2006/09/affairs-what-is-true-about-affairs-and.html
7. Personal communication with a Zoom group member, 2023.
8. Personal interview with CSAT, CSAT-S therapist Rob Baker, July 1, 2022.
9. Personal communication with a Zoom group member, 2024
10. Benvenuto, C. (2012). *Sex Changes: A Memoir of Marriage, Gender and Moving On*. New York: St. Martin's Press. 3.
11. Ibid. 4.
12. Ibid. 84.
13. For more reading on the different types of transgenderism, I recommend the research of Dr. Raymond Blanchard. https://4thwavenow.com/2017/12/07/gender-dysphoria-is-not-one-thing/comment-page-3/#comment-36997
14. Written communication with a Zoom group member, 2023.

CHAPTER 19: Religious Excuses

1. Dobson, J. (1983). *Love Must be Tough: New Hope for Families in Crisis*. Waco: Word Books. 85.
2. Crabb, L. *Shattered Dreams*. (2001). Colorado Springs: Waterbrook Press. 191.
3. Ibid. 191.
4. As worded in Clarence Jordan's loosely translated *Cotton Patch Version of Paul's Epistles*. (1968). New York: Association Press. 25.
5. Crabb, L. *Shattered Dreams*. (2001). Colorado Springs: Waterbrook Press. 218.
6. Gaither, M.W. (2008). *Redemptive Divorce: A Biblical Process That Offers Guidance for the Suffering Partner, Healing for the Offending Spouse, and the Best Catalyst for Restoration*. Nashville: Thomas Nelson. 134.
7. Yancey, P. (1997). *What's So Amazing About Grace?* Grand Rapids: Zondervan. 180. (Referenced before Yancy's sad admission on January 6, 2026.)

8. Based on the King James Version of the Bible, listed at https://stillfaith.com/topics/obedience/
9. Based on the KJV, listed at https://stillfaith.com/topics/repentance/
10. Based on the KJF, listed at https://stillfaith.com/topics/adultery/
11. I hand-counted the rest of these references in the New American Standard Exhaustive Concordance of the Bible.
12. https://theancientbridge.com/2015/11/torah-portion-toldot-did-jacob-have-four-wives-or-only-two/
13. Gilson, R. (2020). *Born Again This Way: Coming Out, Coming to Faith, and What Comes Next*. UK: The Good Book Company. 52.
14. Personal communication with a friend. Used by permission with the names changed. August 22, 2022.
15. Story recounted by a Zoom group member. Used by permission.
16. Besides Scripture, one resource I've enjoyed for helping me recognize God's heart and voice is the devotional, *Jesus Calling: Enjoying Peace in His Presence*, by Sarah Young. Alongside her impressive educational credentials, she has captured the emotional tone and loveliness of Jesus' voice in her writings. Another resource is the movie series *The Chosen*, created by Dallas Jenkins. While the writers take some liberties to consolidate and contemporize biblical events, they've done a beautiful job depicting Christ's relatability, love, and compassion against the backdrop of Jewish history.

CHAPTER 20: Shattered Beliefs

1. Pseudonym, permission obtained to use her story.
2. Keener, M. K. (2025). *Comfort in the Ashes: Explorations in the Book of Job to Support Trauma Survivors*. Downers Grove: Intervarsity Press. 16.
3. An analogy I've also taken from Keener. If you wish to read a fascinating look at the theological implications of trauma on a person's worldview, I highly recommend her book. It expands upon what I discovered from the Book of Job early in my own recovery, in more eloquent terms.
4. "The Weaver," or also sometimes referred to as the "Tapestry Poem," was penned by Grant Colfax Tullar (1869-1950). https://www.webtruth.org/christian-poems-poetry/the-weaver-poem-by-grant-colfax-tullar/
5. "The Hound of Heaven," a well-known poem by Frances Thompson, 1890. https://www.umilta.net/hound.html

CHAPTER 21: When Helpers Harm

1. Pittman, F. (1997). Just in Love. Journal of Marital and Family Therapy, 23(3), 309-312.

2. Glass, S., Staeli, J. (2003). *NOT "Just Friends:" Protect Your Relationship from Infidelity and Heal the Trauma of Betrayal*. New York: The Free Press, 7.
3. Ibid. 40.
4. Pittman, F. (1997). Just in Love. Journal of Marital and Family Therapy, 23(3), 309-312.
5. Pseudonym, permission given to use her story.

CHAPTER 22: Is it Charm or Contrition?

1. Story used by permission.
2. Presentation by therapist and workshop leader, Rob Jackson, October 2000.
3. Personal conversation with therapist Rob Jackson, 2002.
4. My favorite book for churches seeking a model on how to support Christian couples in distress is *Restoring the Fallen* by Earl and Sandy Wilson.

CHAPTER 23: Misconceptions About Forgiving

1. Flanigan, B. (1992). *Forgiving the Unforgivable: Overcoming the Bitter Legacy of Intimate Wounds*. New York: Wiley. 29.
2. Ibid. 28.
3. Ibid. 29.
4. For more steps on what it takes for a straying spouse to earn back much-needed trust, I recommend my book, *How to Help Your Spouse Heal from Your Affair*. For more specific repair from the impact of sex addiction, *Worthy of Her Trust* by Arterburn and Martinkus, or *Help Her HEAL* by Carol Sheets, the latter of which is best done in conjunction with a Certified Sex Addiction Therapist. For spouses who struggle with a lack of dignity, I recommend *Love Must be Tough* by James Dobson and *The Emotionally Destructive Relationship* by Leslie Vernick.

CHAPTER 24: Forgiving Your Betrayer Without Betraying Yourself

1. Fields, L., Hubbard, J. (2014). *Forgiving our Fathers and Mothers: Finding Freedom from Hurt and Hate*. Nashville: W Publishing Group. 173.
2. Fields, Leslie Leyland. "Forgiving the Sins of My Father: How he taught me the deeper meaning of mercy." Christianity Today, vol. 58. May 5, 2014.
3. Personal conversation and email exchange with a former client, Oct. 2024. Used by permission.

CHAPTER 25: Letting Go of Regrets

1. Kubler-Ross, E. (1970). *On Death and Dying*. New York: Simon & Schuster.
2. Anderson, S. (2000). *The Journey from Abandonment to Healing*. New York: Berkley Books. 131.
3. Shorn, T. (2016). *Leave a Cheater, Gain a Life: The Chump Lady's Survival Guide*. Running Press Adult. Blog: https://www.chumplady.com/the-pick-me-dance/
4. While this quote has been attributed to people such as Joel Osteen and Jelly Roll, I found an earlier version by Kirk Franklin on Facebook, March 5, 2014.

CHAPTER 26: Your Story is Not Over

1. Permission given to use her real name, July 22, 2025.
2. Three good resources for stepfamily living: *Strengthening Your Stepfamily* by Einstein, E., and Albert, L. (2005), *Restored and Remarried* by Gil & Brenda Stuart (2009), and any book by Christian stepfamily specialist, Ron Deal.
3. Warren, N.C. (1999, 2005). *Date? Or Soul Mate? How to Tell if Someone is Worth Pursuing in Two Dates or Less*. Nashville: Thomas Nelson.
4. Stuckey, A.B. (2020). *You're Not Enough (And That's Okay): Escaping the Toxic Culture of Self-Love*. New York: Sentinel. 26.

Appendix A
Symptoms Of Betrayal Trauma / PTSD

Past	Recent	**INTRUSIVE SYMPTOMS**
☐	☐	Reliving the events surrounding the shock of betrayal, over and over again
☐	☐	Uninvited flashbacks, intrusive and distressing memories, and recurrent images
☐	☐	Frequent nightmares, frightening dreams
☐	☐	Emotional and physical duress when traumatic memories are triggered
☐	☐	Haunting grief, shame, or guilt over how you reacted to the trauma
☐	☐	Guilt for surviving what others did not
☐	☐	Obsessing about the trauma and being plagued by fears of further danger
☐	☐	Intrusive, uninvited thoughts that seem to come out of nowhere

Past	Recent	**AROUSAL SYMPTOMS**
☐	☐	Hypervigilance (feeling on edge, "on guard" even when in safe situations)
☐	☐	Easily startled or jumpy
☐	☐	Shaky, jittery inside, or trembling hands
☐	☐	Difficulty concentrating
☐	☐	Outbursts of anger and/or extreme irritability or aggression
☐	☐	Sleep disturbances: unable to get to sleep or stay asleep, lack of restorative sleep
☐	☐	Intense fear of the event happening again; terrified of repeat traumas (physical, relational, or emotional)
☐	☐	Reckless, risky, self-destructive behavior (including misuse of drugs or alcohol, risky sexual encounters, cutting, suicidal thoughts/attempts)

Past	Recent	**AVOIDANCE SYMPTOMS**
☐	☐	Avoiding people, places, conversations, or situations that remind you of the betrayal-trauma(s)
☐	☐	Going out of your way to not see or hear any reminder of the event(s)
☐	☐	Avoiding thinking about the trauma or feelings associated with it

Past	Recent	**NEGATIVE CHANGES IN THOUGHTS OR MOOD**
☐	☐	Some loss of memory about the event
☐	☐	Easily lose track of what you're doing; frequently lose items like keys
☐	☐	Feeling hopeless or helpless about the future
☐	☐	Decreased interest in enjoyable activities
☐	☐	Persistent and exaggerated negative feelings and beliefs about self, others, or the world/life/God
☐	☐	Exaggerated tendency to blame oneself or others for the adverse event
☐	☐	Distorted, negative beliefs about the cause or impact of the traumatic event(s); ascribing self-deprecating meaning or significance to the trauma

Past	Recent	**OBSESSIVE SYMPTOMS**
☐	☐	Obsessing over what happened, trying to put the pieces together–esp. if the betrayer's stories didn't add up or seemed incomplete
☐	☐	Reviewing past events and conversations, trying to identify Red Flags missed, to avoid being "fooled" again
☐	☐	Preoccupied with reading tabloids or stories of others' experiences of partner betrayal
☐	☐	Battling self-recrimination over being replaced and rejected by one's partner

Past	Recent	**DISSOCIATIVE SYMPTOMS**
☐	☐	Feeling like you are outside your body, watching what is going on
☐	☐	Feeling detached or estranged from others
☐	☐	Feeling like you are walking around in a daze, or a dream
☐	☐	"Spacing out" or "zoning out" while at home, work, or social events
☐	☐	Feeling emotionally "numb," things seem surreal; feeling as if you are not living in reality
☐	☐	Creating a fantasy life, pretending it really didn't happen

Past Total: _____ Recent Total: _____ [The higher the number of boxes checked, the greater the chance your symptoms indicate some form of Betrayal Trauma / PTSD]

This is not a substitute for a personal diagnosis. Take it with you to your therapist for further evaluation.

Appendix B

Chart on Types of Trauma, Indicating Increasing Chances for Developing PTSD

The further to the right and the further down the chart, the more intense and potentially damaging the trauma. Remember, it is the *meaning* of the trauma that does the worst injury.

TYPES OF TRAUMA	Increased Intensity →		
Source	**Type I -** Sudden or Brief	**Type II -** Repeated or Prolonged	Increased Intensity ↓
Acts of Nature/Natural Disasters	Tornados, floods, accidental death (falling off a cliff, avalanche); Sudden accidental death of a loved one (heart attack or stroke)	Gruesome, terrible death of a spouse or child, such as by a disfiguring disease.	↓
Unintentional Human (Stranger)	Car accident, human-caused accidental death or near-death of a child or spouse; self, child, or spouse handicapped by a human accident, stray bullet, or medical mistake.	Chemical spills, technological disasters (like Chernobyl).	↓
Intentional Human (Stranger)	Assault, rape, murder, sniper, threatening robbery, loved one killed or maimed by a drunk driver, or arsonist.	Holocaust victim, torture, combat/war, witnessing the murder of a family member or close friend.	↓
Intentional Human (Intimate)	Assault, date-rape, sexual abuse, spousal infidelity, suicide by a loved one, parental or spousal abandonment, murder, or torture of a loved one.	Domestic violence, childhood sex or physical abuse, incest, alcoholic home, spousal sex addiction, or prolonged affair(s).	↓

Chart inspired by the work of Dr. Glenn Schiraldi, author of *The Post-Traumatic Stress Disorder Sourcebook*, 2000. Adapted by Linda J. MacDonald. Used by permission.

Appendix C
Partial List of Therapies for Trauma
Collected by Linda J. MacDonald, M.S.

Here is a partial list of the kinds of therapies that can relieve PTSD symptoms and the self-esteem injuries associated with them. This is not an exhaustive list, as new trauma-focused therapies are being developed all the time. Effective trauma therapy needs to access the parts of the brain where fragmented memories are stored, recalibrate the meaning, take them out of isolation, and connect them with the logical, sequential parts of our brains.

This can be achieved by utilizing what therapist Shelley Bartels calls our "sanctified imagination" or, as therapist Helen Hofman calls it, our "Redeemed Imaginative Tools" to revisit and reframe painful memories in ways that mere talk therapy can't reach alone.

The Bible is filled with metaphors, symbols, parables, dreams, visions, and illustrations, which the Lord uses to teach us godly truths. In the same way, a skilled Christian trauma therapist can guide you back to former abusive experiences and allow the Lord to inject himself into the memory with truth-filled, nurturing messages and corrective visuals to counter the negative beliefs we associate with each distressing event.

If you are experiencing the kinds of symptoms I discussed in Chapters 3 and 4, consider finding an experienced trauma-informed therapist who uses at least one of these modalities.

- **Transformational Prayer Ministry,** developed by Ed Smith. (Formerly known as Theophostic Prayer.) https://www.transformationprayer.org/
- **Lifespan Integration,** developed by Peggy Pace, M.A. The Trauma Protocol is especially useful to help victims of trauma. https://lifespanintegration.com/
- **The Healing Timeline**, by Cathy Thorpe, M.A. Cathy incorporates a simpler method for healing memories. It can also be used by coaches and Lay Counselors. https://healingtimeline.org/
- **Prolonged Exposure Therapy** Prolonged exposure to the activating event, actual or imagined. https://www.choosingtherapy.com/post-traumatic-stress-disorder/

https://www.usmedicine.com/current-issue/prolonged-exposure-therapy-showed-some-advantages-in-treating-ptsd/

- **Eye Movement Desensitization and Reprocessing (EMDR),** developed by Francine Shapiro, Ph.D. One of the most researched and clinically validated treatments for trauma. https://www.emdria.org/
- **Attachment-Focused EMDR,** adapted by Laurel Parnell, Ph.D. https://drlaurelparnell.com/
- **Accelerated Resolution Therapy (ART),** founded by Laney Rosenzweig.
  ART is a brief therapy modality that uses eye movements to help clients resolve their issues. guides the client to replace the negative images in the mind that cause the symptoms of Post-Traumatic Stress with positive images. https://acceleratedresolutiontherapy.com/
- **Internal Family Systems,** developed by Richard Schwartz, Ph.D. https://internalfamilysystems.pt/index.php/intervenientes/richard-schwartz.
  I especially appreciate how Jenna Riemersma frames Internal Family Systems from a Christian perspective.
  https://www.amazon.com/Altogether-You-Experiencing-spiritual-transformation/
- **Cognitive Restructuring** for Betrayal Trauma, as taught by Doug Weiss and Robert Weiss.
  https://www.drdougweiss.com/ (Dr. Doug Weiss' site)
  https://sexandrelationshiphealing.com/ (Dr. Robert Weiss' site)
- **APSATS Three-Dimensional Model.**
  Specialized training for therapists who treat partners/former partners of sex addicts.
  https://www.apsats.org/specialists#!directory/map
- **Complex Trauma Treatment.** Training by Janina Fisher, Ph.D. https://janinafisher.com/
- **The Institute for Sexual Health.** Developed by Dr. Omar Minwalla. He has extensive experience working with both offenders and partners. Any therapist trained by him will be very effective.
  https://www.minwallamodel.com/
- **Somatic Experiencing and Sensorimotor Body Therapies.**
  Dr. Peter Levine, Dr. Pat Ogden, & others. Somatic therapies focus

on helping the body release the pent-up energy and traumatic shock still trapped in the body.
https://traumahealing.org/se-101/

- **Brainspotting (BSP).** Developed by Dr. David Grand. Brainspotting (BSP) is a relatively new method for processing trauma that focuses on locations in the visual field and the corresponding 'spots' in the subcortical brain.
https://brainspotting.com/

- **The Safe and Sound Protocol (SSP),** auditory-based therapy. Developed by Dr. Stephen Porges.
https://www.whatisthessp.com/,
https://integratedlistening.com/polyvagal-theory/porges/
https://integratedlistening.com/polyvagal-theory/porges/

- **Emotional Transformation Therapy (ETT).** A therapeutic method that incorporates light, color wavelengths, and eye movements. Developed by Dr. Stephen R. Vasquez.
https://www.etttraining.com/

- **Kali Connection Therapy (KCT),** developed by Mara Giovanni. KCT blends bilateral stimulation, cooperative movement, and attunement to create a safe and engaging way to promote healing.
https://www.kaliconnectiontherapy.com/

- **Art Therapy or Dance Therapy for PTSD Victims.**
https://www.healthline.com/health/art-therapy-for-ptsd

Appendix D

Results of the Rationalizations Survey

I collected anonymous surveys from 81 betrayed spouses from my workshops and website. Consider ✓ excuses you heard during your crisis.

Out of 193 Total Answers	You ✓	BLAME RATIONALIZATIONS: (Top 10 answers in this category)
29		"It's *your* fault." (the "you made me do it" excuse.)
27		"If you weren't so _____, I wouldn't have gotten involved with _____ (the other person/habit).
19		"It's *not* about about ____ (the other person), it's about our *marriage* (i.e. you)."
18		"You're too serious (or not playful enough)."
13		"He/she understands (or 'gets') me."
13		"We've been roommates for years."
13		"You weren't meeting my needs anymore."
9		"You are boring."
8		"You will never forgive me (so I need to leave)."
7		"I could be myself around him/her" (implying, "but not around you").

92 Total	You ✓	ENTITLED RATIONALIZATIONS: (Top 6)
27		"It's not about you" (despite the fact it feels very *personal* to you).
24		"I was unhappy" (and therefore I was entitled to act out).
13		"I've lived for everyone else. Now it's *my* turn!"
10		"I need passion in my life."
7		"I was lonely" (as if this had nothing to do with their own lack of investment in the marriage).
5		"I'm having a midlife crisis" (as if this justifies the affair).

76 Total	You ✓	**MINIMIZING RATIONALIZATIONS: (Top 5)**
23		"It just happened" (no ownership of choices made).
20		"It's not an affair because we didn't have sex (i.e. vaginal intercourse)" (often, still a lie, or minimizes kissing, fondling, oral sex, "everything, but…")
12		"He/she didn't mean anything to me."
10		"It was *only* sex."
4		"We *only* kissed."

69 Total	You ✓	**REWRITING MARITAL HISTORY RATIONALIZATIONS (Top 7)**
17		"I love you, but I'm not *in* love with you."
9		"I just don't love you anymore."
9		"He/she's my Soul-mate" (implying, "and you're not").
8		"I never loved you" (some reported hearing this, despite 30–40 years of marriage and several children together).
8		"I need to be free of performance pressure" (i.e., "You've always put too much pressure on me to do the right thing. I need to stop worrying about what others think, including you.")
7		"I married you when I was too young."
5		"I married you too soon (or too quickly)."

43 Total	You ✓	**RELIGIOUS RATIONALIZATIONS (Top 5)**
22		"God will forgive me."
7		"God has forgiven me. How come you can't?"
7		"You are so judgmental" (i.e., you are too religious).
5		"People in the Old Testament had concubines."
4		"King David did it."
3		"God told me I could choose" (between you and the lover).

10 Total	You √	**HERO SYNDROME RATIONALIZATIONS** (Main answer in this category)
10		"He/she has had a hard life. I felt sorry for him/her. He/she needed me" (as if the spouse didn't).

The respondents were allowed to check all of the excuses they heard from their unfaithful spouses. Sometimes betrayed spouses heard contradictory things (such as, "It wasn't an affair because we didn't have sex" only to hear "It was only sex" at a later time.)

You are welcome to put a √ in the boxes of the rationalizations you heard from your unfaithful spouse. I hope this brief survey helps you see there is "nothing new under the sun" (Ecclesiastes 1:9). People who stray come up with all kinds of excuses to justify bad behavior. This is not an exhaustive list of the rationalizations that respondents heard, but these were the most common ones.

Acknowledgments

I am deeply grateful to the many people who supported me in this project. Foremost is my beloved husband of twenty-one years, Dan MacDonald. After retiring from pastoral ministry, he gave me the gift of time and space to write. He listened patiently on long walks and over dinners, read my chapters, and offered wise suggestions. Besides Jesus, he's been my greatest support!

Special thanks go to Stephanie Miller, with Butterfly Beginnings, who served as both developmental and line editor for three years. Her expertise shaped the book's structure, sharpened my stories, and inspired me to create the companion workbook—a decision that has already blessed many readers.

I also appreciate Sheri Carlson poring over my early manuscript, offering invaluable suggestions with the eyes of an experienced English teacher. And Lisa Eberle's input as well. Thanks to Marcy Pusey for her last-minute feedback. I don't know what I would have done without Kim Mosiman of Writer-2-Writer for guiding me through the book-launch process with kindness and skill.

I'm indebted to my Betrandoned Zoom support group—you know who you are—for reading drafts, offering feedback, and sharing your stories to use under pseudonyms. You've become dear friends. Additional thanks to the women who participated in my early "Grippers" support groups, learning to open your hearts and grip the Lord's hand in your recoveries. Your stories made me cry, some of which are shared or hinted at in these pages.

Others who contributed along the way include Stephanie Boersma, who welcomed me into her *Reclaimed* community to both give and receive; Ruth Erickson, who generously read my entire manuscript and wrote the Foreword during a busy summer; and Sandy Wilson and Karen Crawford, who invited me to present at conferences they hosted for betrayed women—events that helped shape this material.

It took me a while, but I can honestly say that I am grateful for my years with "James." Despite our painful ending, I value the ministry we shared, the travels and friendships we enjoyed, and, most of all, our two sons and their families. For them and the lessons I learned, it was all worth it.

Above all, I thank God for lifting me out of sorrow, guiding me through Scripture, and filling my life with new joy and relationships.

About the Author

Linda J. MacDonald, M.S., is a licensed marriage and family therapist and author specializing in infidelity recovery. With over 33 years of clinical experience—and a personal story marked by betrayal—she understands the devastation of infidelity from both sides of the counseling room.

Her first book, *How to Help Your Spouse Heal from Your Affair,* has sold over 137,000 copies and earned over 2,500 positive reviews.

Partway through her career, Linda lost her first marriage to an affair—a crisis that nearly unraveled her faith and sense of purpose. But by God's grace, she rebuilt her life and discovered a deeper calling: to help others recover from the grief, shame, and trauma of an affair-sparked divorce.

In *Redeeming the Post-Affair Divorce,* she blends clinical insight with spiritual wisdom to guide readers toward healing—restoring the heart, mind, and soul.

Linda co-founded three Christian counseling centers and recently retired to focus on writing, teaching workshops, and speaking on podcasts about infidelity recovery. Remarried for 21 years and a joyful grandmother of eight, she enjoys hiking, camping, crafting, and spending time with her friends and loved ones.

OTHER BOOKS by Linda J. MacDonald

Learn how to order:
https://www.lindajmacdonald.com/books

Want to go deeper? Here is the accompanying Workbook that Linda mentioned throughout this book. It contains many valuable tools for healing from your Post-Affair Divorce:
- Relevant Bible studies
- Charts
- Exercises
- Room to journal

Perfect for personal reflection and small group sharing.

Discover the difference between those who blow up their marriages after their affair and those who manage to repair and rebuild their marriages into thriving relationships!

The first book written specifically to help the unfaithful have the best chance to save their marriages post-affair!

Concise, easy to read, and apply—even for the self-help phobic.

www.ingramcontent.com/pod-product-compliance
Lightning Source LLC
Chambersburg PA
CBHW071403130526
44581CB00014B/120/J

Betrandonment Grief

outside your grief cocoon. Hurting spouses need to connect—with those who know their history as well as with new individuals who understand personal loss or have faced similar experiences. Without these connections, it's easy to feel stuck, marinating in sorrow to our own detriment.

I will never forget one woman who attended one of my all-day workshops on "Recovering from the Post-Affair Divorce." After the event, "Elaina" wrote me an email, telling me that despite having attended several partner groups for spouses of sex addicts, this was the first time she had participated in a meeting where she felt so understood. From the moment she walked in, she sensed a deep connection with the other women who had been both betrayed *and* abandoned. She didn't need to explain herself, nor did she feel out of place. Elaina raved about what a wonderful experience it was to be with other women who "got" her.

Do you have friends, family, or a therapist who "gets" your pain? Who can relate to your grief with no compulsion to make it all go away? Have you found people who will sit with you and allow you to cry? There is something profoundly healing about grieving in the presence of those who truly care and understand your experience.

In addition to support from those who understand, it's comforting to know that our Lord comprehends Betrandonment grief like no one else. I have found great solace in spending time with the Lord, knowing he can relate to my pain. Accept his invitation, "Come to Me, all you who are weary and burdened, and I will give you rest" (Matthew 11:28).

All three persons of the Trinity, God the Father, God the Son, and God the Holy Spirit, understand what it's like to suffer betrayal and rejection. Why? God has experienced profound grief over the betrayal and rejection by his people and the ones he came to save. In the billions, Who is more qualified to understand the depths of our traumatic grief than God himself?

God Comforts Us in Our Afflictions.

After Jesus rose from the dead, he promised to send us a "Comforter," referring to the Holy Spirit. While on earth, Jesus was confined to his human body, but once he paid for our sins and the temple veil was torn in two, the personal presence of the Lord was no longer limited to the Holy of Holies. After he ascended to heaven, he sent the Comforter to dwell in our hearts. The Holy Spirit has become God's representative to the world.

> Who is more qualified to understand the depths of our traumatic grief than God himself?

31

"Blessed be the God and Father of our Lord Jesus Christ, the Father of mercies and God of all comfort, who comforts us in all our affliction so that we will be able to comfort those who are in any affliction with the comfort with which we ourselves are comforted by God" (2 Corinthians 1:3–4).

The Holy Spirit comforts us and uses our experience of God's solace to, in turn, comfort others and give them hope. In other words, as the Lord meets us in our sorrow, he equips us to be there for others with heartfelt compassion.

Lifeline Verses

"Pamela," a woman in a private Facebook group I belong to, adopted what she called her Lifeline Verse to bring her comfort during her greatest moments of grief.

I have this verse (2 Kings 20:5, NLT) hanging in several places: I keep speaking it over my mind, soul, and body. "This is what the Lord, the God of your ancestor David, says: I have heard your prayer and seen your tears. I will heal you." This verse isn't a Bible Band-Aid but a lifeline ... What I breathe when I can't.[8]

She pasted it all over her house to remind her that God had heard her prayers, seen her tears, and would heal her life. Be assured, like Pamela, that God has heard your prayers, seen your tears, and plans to heal you.

My personal Lifeline Verse became Isaiah 41:9 (NLT):

"'I have called you back from the ends of the earth, saying, 'You are my servant.' For I have chosen you and will not throw you away.'"

I felt torn from the life I'd known, so the idea of being "called back from the ends of the earth" felt very relevant. And the line, "For I have chosen you and will not throw you away," came to mean the world to me. I needed assurance that, despite feeling discarded by my husband, God would not similarly abandon me.

Do you have a Lifeline Verse such as this? Perhaps, like Pamela or me, you have found a meaningful Scripture to post around your house. You need reminders that God will hear your prayers, heal your broken life, and keep you safely in his hands.

It Takes Time

As maimed spouses, we have lingering doubts about our worth, our identity, and lovability. It is difficult to fathom that the one we thought would